PENGUIN BOOKS

ROAD TO THE DALES

Praise for Gervase Phinn:

'A hero in school staff-rooms' *Daily Telegraph*

'Gervase Phinn is a natural storyteller . . . He has a marvellous
ear for one-liners and a constant flow of anecdotes about the
things children say' *Yorkshire Post*

'Funny, touching and entertaining' *Daily Express*

'Dubbed the James Herriot of schools, he writes with enormous
warmth and wit about his romantic adventures, career struggles, and –
above all – the children in the schools he visits, with uncanny ability to
charm and embarrass him in equal measure . . . Uproarious and
touching by turns' *Daily Mail*

'Colourful, funny and honest' *Sunday Express*

'A natural storyteller, he combines the timing of a professional
comedian with palpable warmth and the ability to deliver a message
that is much more than just a series of jokes'
The Times Educational Supplement

Gervase Phinn is a teacher, freelance lecturer, author, poet, school inspector, educational consultant and visiting professor of education – but none of these is more important than his family.

For fourteen years he taught in a range of schools, then acted as General Adviser for Language Development in Rotherham before moving on to North Yorkshire, where he spent ten years as a school inspector – time that has provided so much source material for his books. He holds five fellowships, honorary doctorates from Hull, Leicester and Sheffield Hallam universities, and is patron of a number of children's charities and educational organizations.

Gervase lives with his family in Doncaster.

Road to the Dales

The Story of a Yorkshire Lad

GERVASE PHINN

PENGUIN BOOKS

PENGUIN BOOKS

Published by the Penguin Group
Penguin Books Ltd, 80 Strand, London WC2R ORL, England
Penguin Group (USA), Inc., 375 Hudson Street, New York, New York 10014, USA
Penguin Group (Canada), 90 Eglinton Avenue East, Suite 700, Toronto, Ontario, Canada M4P 2Y3
(a division of Pearson Penguin Canada Inc.)
Penguin Ireland, 25 St Stephen's Green, Dublin 2, Ireland (a division of Penguin Books Ltd)
Penguin Group (Australia), 250 Camberwell Road, Camberwell, Victoria 3124, Australia
(a division of Pearson Australia Group Pty Ltd)
Penguin Books India Pvt Ltd, 11 Community Centre, Panchsheel Park, New Delhi – 110 017, India
Penguin Group (NZ), 67 Apollo Drive, Rosedale, Auckland 0632, New Zealand
(a division of Pearson New Zealand Ltd)
Penguin Books (South Africa) (Pty) Ltd, 24 Sturdee Avenue, Rosebank,
Johannesburg 2196, South Africa

Penguin Books Ltd, Registered Offices: 80 Strand, London WC2R ORL, England

www.penguin.com

First published by Michael Joseph 2010
Published in Penguin Books 2011

006

Copyright © Gervase Phinn, 2010

The moral right of the author has been asserted

'Burnt Norton' from *Four Quartets* by T. S. Eliot, reproduced by permission of Faber and Faber Ltd
and in the USA copyright 1936 by Harcourt, Inc. and renewed 1984 by T. S. Eliot, reproduced by
permission of the publisher Houghton Mifflin Harcourt Publishing Company
'Dreamboat' lyric reprinted by permission of Winston Music Publishers © ® 1982 ASCAP

Every effort has been made to trace copyright holders and to obtain permission for the use of
copyright material. The publisher apologizes for any errors or omissions and would be grateful to be
notified of any corrections that should be incorporated into future editons of this book

Printed in Great Britain by Clays Ltd, St Ives plc

A CIP catalogue record for this book is available from the British Library

ISBN: 978-0-141-02672-5

www.greenpenguin.co.uk

Penguin Books is committed to a sustainable
future for our business, our readers and our planet.
This book is made from Forest Stewardship
Council™ certified paper.

For my parents, Pat and Jimmy Phinn,
who allowed me to dream

Acknowledgements

I am grateful to my wife and family for their continued support, and to my editor, Lindsey Evans, who has been exceptionally wise and patient throughout.

When I was a Boy

When I was a boy:

My bunk bed was a pirate ship
That sailed the seven seas,
My sheets they were the silvery sails
That fluttered in the breeze.

I'd dream of clashing cutlasses
And the crack, crack, crack of the gun
And the boom, boom, boom of the cannons
And the heat of the tropical sun.

I'd dream of far-off oceans
And treasure by the ton,
And mountainous waves
And watery graves
And islands in the sun.

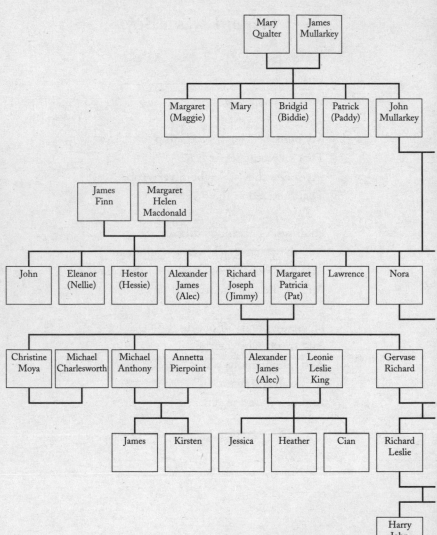

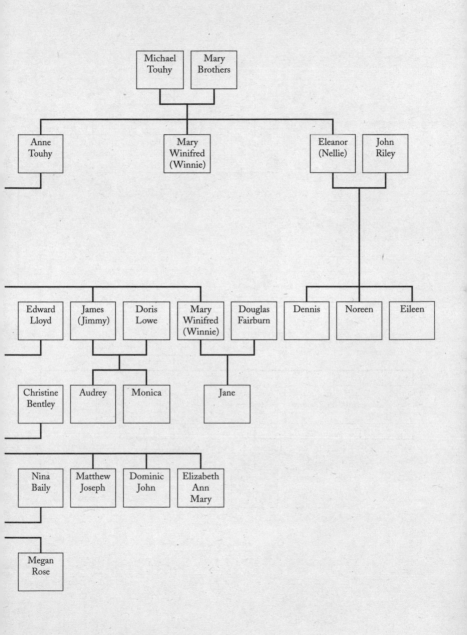

Foreword

Footfalls echo in the memory
Down the passage which we did not take
Towards the door we never opened
Into the rose-garden. My words echo
Thus, in your mind.

           − T. S. Eliot, *Four Quartets*

T. H. ('Taffy') Williams, headmaster of South Grove Secondary Modern School, stood on the stage in the school hall. He was a striking-looking figure: tall, lean, straight-backed, with short silver-white hair neatly parted, dark Celtic complexion and those pale blue all-seeing eyes. It was the leavers' assembly.

'Today, you will be leaving,' he said in that deep, resonant Welsh valley voice of his. 'Today, you will walk down the top corridor of the school for the last time, past the row of classroom doors through which you have entered many, many times over the last four or five years, and you will go out into the wide world beyond. Some of you will start work and leave behind the complexities of English grammar and the frustrations of algebra and trigonometry, the dates in British history and the maps of far-off countries, and you may well be heartily glad of that. Some of you have chosen to continue your studies and move on to A levels and maybe college or university. But whoever you are and whatever you do, as you walk down that corridor for the last time, I want you to pause for a moment and remember one thing: life is like that corridor, lined with many different doors. Some will be bolted and barred and however hard you push and pull, strike and shout they will remain forever closed to you. Some will be wide open and you will walk through with little effort and no hindrance. Some will be ajar, and with a little exertion and curiosity, you will be able to see what lies behind. Most doors, however, will be closed – but they will seldom be locked. These are the doors of opportunity, boys. The doors of opportunity. It is up to you which of these closed doors you choose to try, and to discover what is behind, waiting for you –' he paused for effect – 'and which to pass on by.'

I guess for many of the pupils in the school hall that heady July morning the headmaster's metaphor was lost upon them, but for me, an ambitious, rather studious, idealistic sixteen-year-old, those words have remained a vivid memory. The closed doors in my own life have been rarely, if ever, locked and I have been immensely fortunate that I have had caring, supportive, encouraging people all along the way who have helped me through them.

I should say from the start that this account of my early life is no misery memoir. It will not stand on the bookshop shelf under the heading 'Tragic Life Stories' along with the heart-rending autobiographies of unbelievably unhappy childhoods – nightmare families, loveless homes, brutal parents – all described in vivid detail; of children beaten and starved, rejected and abused, bullied and tortured. Such accounts, where the authors describe how they have overcome the huge disadvantages of miserable upbringings, have become instant best-sellers and the reading public appears to love them. Perhaps in doing so the readers' own lives seem less wretched and more bearable. Perhaps they are heartened by these sad stories of children who have a shining spirit to survive, cope and forgive. For me, such memoirs are painful to read, for mine was a very happy childhood. I did not suffer from great poverty as a child, nor was I born into an affluent and privileged home. I was not smacked or told I was unwanted. I was not bullied by my brothers or told by my parents I was a disappointment to them. I felt loved and cherished.

My journey through childhood was neither a painful nor a shameful one. It was blessedly free of poverty, neglect, cruelty and exploitation and I have many fond memories. I have never subscribed to the prevalent view that childhood is simply a stage on a road to adulthood, something to be got through on the way to something better, and, unlike some writers of the many memoirs and autobiographies I have read, I have never sought to distance myself from it or to negate it. Indeed my childhood has acted as an inspiration for the present and the future, a place to which I sometimes escape, where I can, in a sense, avoid growing up.

There are some, of course, who believe that those of us who have had a pretty ordinary, uneventful and happy childhood really have nothing much to write about. 'When I look back on my childhood,' writes Frank McCourt in *Angela's Ashes: A Memoir of Childhood*, 'I wonder how I managed to survive it at all. It was, of course, a miserable childhood: the happy childhood is hardly worthwhile.'

Well, my childhood was very happy and extremely worthwhile. I thank God that it was so very different from Frank McCourt's. Mine was a joyous upbringing. Growing up, I imagined that all children had loving and amusing parents like mine, who wanted the very best for their children, who read not at them or to them every night but with them; parents who talked with them, sang to them, laughed with them. I thought all pupils had committed, enthusiastic and good-humoured teachers who enjoyed the company of the young and did their very best for them. My life was full of happiness and conversation, music and books.

To recall childhood is without doubt the most vivid and

convincing part of any autobiography, for our early memories are preserved in a bright, new and exciting world of first experience. What is so striking and extraordinary is that these recollections of a time, which will never come again, change, disappear, and then suddenly return to us after many years. The smell of seaweed, the sight of screeching gulls circling over a wind-roughened sea, the sound of crashing waves, the taste of candy floss, the feel of the wind blowing wet sand in my face, the tang of brine so sharp it stings my lungs . . . All these things take me back to the seaside and the memory of walking down the promenade at Blackpool clutching my bucket and spade in one small hand, the other held tightly by my father. The sight of the steam train on its journey from Settle to Carlisle, clickety-clacking down the line, puthering sulphurous smoke and smut and sounding its shrieking whistle, reminds me of the heady childhood days when, as a boy, I stood on the bridge over the railway line waiting for the engine to thunder beneath and envelop me in a cloud of acrid smoke.

So this is my story, a memoir of an ordinary boy who met some extraordinary people, and the journey he was able to embark on as a result of the many doors opened for him in his early life. From my earliest memories of infancy and growing up, my story shows the powerful influence of my family and friends, schooldays and holidays, leading on to my first tentative steps into the adult world, those formative years that shaped who I am and what I became.

Some autobiographies seem to me to owe more to the imagination than many novels, and perhaps what follows may seem to the reader to be in that category – after all, I am a storyteller. As Dr Johnson once observed, 'No good story was ever wholly true.' So, in recalling my past, I have inevitably embroidered, made and dropped stitches, and some recollections, I guess, are not entirely reliable because they have been viewed in the surreal light of early experience. I am also sure that some of my memories are rose-tinted, as memories often are, and that the passing of the years has allowed my memories to be recast in a better light. But, above all, I have tried to be honest, open, and entertaining as well. Out of respect for their privacy, I have changed the names of some of the people who appear in these pages.

I was born Gervase Richard Phinn on 27 December 1946, the same year as George Best, Noddy Holder of Slade, Paul McCartney, Edwina Currie, Janet Street-Porter and the infamous Harold Shipman and Peter Sutcliffe. This was the year Winston Churchill warned of the Iron Curtain descending over Soviet-dominated Eastern Europe, the year the Nuremberg war trials returned death sentences on leading Nazis, including Ribbentrop and Goering. Lord Haw-Haw was hanged for treason and the United States Navy tested the atomic bomb at Bikini Atoll in the South Pacific. The Bank of England, coal and other industries were nationalized and Heathrow airport opened. Strapless bras became popular and Tide, the revolutionary detergent designed for automatic washing machines, landed on the shelves in the corner shops.

I was one of the 'baby bulge' children, growing up in the Welfare State, at a time when Stalin finally died, Sir Edmund Hillary scaled the highest mountain in the world, the recent 1944 Education Act had firmly established grammar schools, technical high schools and secondary moderns, and the country celebrated in grand fashion the accession of a new young Queen. It was an age when *Muffin the Mule* and *The Flowerpot Men* made their first appearances on television, when Alma Cogan, 'the girl with the giggle in her voice', sang 'Hernando's Hideaway', and the comedian Al Read entertained us on the wireless with his inoffensive anecdotes. It was a period when the great Stanley Matthews played in the Cup Final, there was little unemployment, the National Health Service was in its fledgling years, and sweet rationing ended. This was a new age, full of optimism and good humour, free from the privations of the war years; it was a time when young people started to assert their individuality and independence. The blue and brown serge suits of the 'demob style' gave way to bold, colourful designs in clothes. Teddy Boys outraged the older generation as they strutted around the streets like latter-day Edwardian dandies, dressed in their pale blue frock-coats with velvet collars and their 'brothel-creeper' shoes, when Lonnie Donegan sang 'Does Your Chewing Gum Lose Its Flavour on the Bedpost Overnight?', when skiffle groups flourished, milk bars opened and fish fingers made their appearance.

I came into the world weighing eight pounds and one ounce at Number 1, Richard Road, Rotherham, delivered by the midwife, Nurse Mabel Knowles. I know this to be true because Miss Knowles, then in her eighties, came to see me when I was performing my one-man show, *An Evening with Gervase Phinn*, on stage in Barnsley many years later. 'I've seen you with no clothes on,' she said mischievously after the performance. 'It was me who brought you into the world.' Then she added, 'You were a big baby and had a lot to say for yourself and you've not changed much, have you?'

I was the fourth and last child of Richard James (Jimmy) Phinn and Margaret Patricia (Pat) Phinn. The eldest of the children was Christine Moya, then came Michael Anthony (Mike) and Alexander James (Alec). I was the last, the least able and probably the most indulged.

My mother, certain I was to be a little girl, decided on the name Elizabeth Ann Mary and bought a pink, frilly cot in readiness and matching pink, frilly clothes. Christine had hoped for a little sister to look after and play with, so when she saw me – a round, red and very vociferous baby boy – she was said to have scowled and sulked. It took a few days before she would hold me, but then she spent much of her time around the cot and the pram. Later when I grew a little bigger she would sit me amidst her dolls and practise being a teacher.

Just after I was born my parents moved up the hill to Number 19, a pre-war, shiny redbrick, semi-detached house, three up, three down, with an inside toilet, a small front garden and long back garden. The house was larger than Number 1 and had the advantage of being up the hill, well away from the busy Broom Valley Road, with a spacious detached garage, a garden shed and a greenhouse. Unlike other houses on the street, it also had French windows in the living room and a gate at the end of the garden, which led to a large allotment. We had a small back yard, a tussocky lawn, a rockery and flower borders all dominated by a large blossoming cherry tree. Mum and Dad had the double bedroom at the front of the house, Christine the small boxroom at the rear, and I shared a room with my brothers. Michael had a single bed, Alec and I shared a double.

Downstairs there was a small kitchen, a narrow hall and an all-purpose living-cum-dining room, where we spent most of our lives. The living room had an open fire and each morning one of the boys would go through the ritual of clearing out the ashes and putting them into a bucket by the back door for Dad to later put on the garden. Then the coal-scuttle was replenished and screwed-up balls of newspaper were arranged in the grate, with bits of chopped wood and lumps of coal placed on top. I loved the open fire and would toast pikelets (thin crumpets) before covering them liberally with butter. In winter, I would roast chestnuts in the embers. They would pop, spit, and come out of the fire with blackened shells and soft, sweet interiors.

I remember setting off for school each morning past houses with every chimney belching out smoke from fires like our own. I would arrive at the top of Alma Road, where a cocktail of pollutants from the Don Valley mixed with the coal smoke from the houses to produce a cloak of thick, evil-smelling smog.

It had a corporeal presence; it felt like something you could reach out and touch. Sometimes, when the steelworks were in full production, the carbon and the sulphur would burn your windpipe if you didn't wear a scarf around your mouth, and you could taste and feel its damp greasy fingers on your skin. It was like the backdrop of a novel by Conan Doyle.

The front room of the house at Richard Road was sacrosanct and 'kept for best'. It was, I imagine, regarded as the working-class equivalent of the upper-class drawing room, always neat and tidy and where visitors were received. The only time it was used (and the electric fire turned on) was when an important visitor such as the priest or the doctor called, or my mother retired there to play the piano. It was kept scrupulously clean and tidy and smelt musty and unused. I was allowed to go in there to read quietly, but toys, drinks and food were taboo. A heavy green brocade three-piece suite dominated the room and the remaining space was occupied by the polished mahogany piano (my mother called it her 'upright grand'), a small occasional table, a radiogram and a veneered glass-fronted china cabinet in which were kept all my mother's bits of cut glass and china.

On the wall there were two large reproduction prints of Pre-Raphaelite paintings, given to my mother by a grateful patient as a thank-you present when she was a nurse. One was of Dante on a bridge. The other depicted a group of beautiful young women with long auburn hair and faraway looks and five noble, handsome knights in shining armour looking on. The melting colours, the combination of mystery and sensuality, the classical perfection and balance, fascinated me. I discovered later (when my second son, Matthew, was studying for a degree in fine art) that the latter painting is *Laus Veneris* by Sir Edward Coley Burne-Jones. As a youngster I would sometimes sit on the settee and stare at the picture of the Pre-Raphaelite beauties, illuminated by a pallid light shining through the net curtains, which were always drawn, and imagine the world in which the characters lived: a distant, exotic, colourful world very different from my own. More often, I would take my book into the front room – *White Fang* or *Kidnapped*, a Biggles adventure or *King Solomon's Mines* – and become lost in the stories, entering other exciting places, reading about fascinating characters and losing all sense of time. In that front room, curled up on that heavy settee, I vanished from the known world into the imaginary.

Richard Road was a monocultural world, a friendly and supportive community of largely like-minded people. It was a safe, warm environment for children to grow up in and we had the freedom to play out all day on the street or at the park, something which is sadly denied to many children today. We were pushed out of the door on Saturday morning and expected not to appear back home until it started to get dark. It was an unashamedly unregulated and unsupervised world, and parents didn't worry about their children falling under a bus or being abducted or set upon. These days so many parents seem obsessively concerned with giving their children long and happy childhoods, with keeping them safe from harm and injury, in need of constant protection, away from potential risks, that they underestimate their offspring's abilities and resilience and deny them the great sense of freedom those of my generation had when we were young. As happy as crickets, we were unhindered by adult restraint.

The inhabitants of Richard Road, who ranged from teachers to coal merchants, butchers to steelworkers, nurses to office managers, were solid, hard-working, ordinary, respectable folk and certainly didn't include any of the prosperous manufacturing families and professionals, who lived in the large detached houses and villas in the 'posh' part of town up on Moorgate. There was a real human warmth and neighbourliness in the street where I lived; there was a sense of togetherness and belonging seldom found in communities today. It was an egalitarian world where people didn't consider themselves superior to others and did not attempt to be so. Life for most people seemed distinctly better than it is now.

The war had ended and there was a great sense of relief that the deprivation, disruption and destruction of those violent years were now over. People wanted to settle down to a quiet, peaceful life again, visit the shops, go to the pictures, to dances and football matches, to enjoy themselves and raise families. There was a great sense of national pride in the air. The images and memories of the war were still very much in people's minds and the next generation was made acutely aware of this, on the wireless, at the cinema, at school and in conversation. We walked tall, knowing that Great Britain had stood alone against the might of a ruthless, determined and better equipped enemy and had thoroughly thrashed it, the only country to have fought the war from the very first day to the very last. We were proud to be British.

The books, comics and magazines we read, the films we saw, the toy soldiers, cigarette cards and merchandise emblazoned with patriotic motifs, firmly established in our young minds just how lucky we were to be British and part of a great empire. Rider Haggard and G. A. Henty had written imperial adventures at the turn of the century, describing the glorious deeds and daring adventures of the British; now a new crop of literature appeared and we identified with the bravado of the fictional heroes.

There was a great sense of renewal in the air too. England was becoming economically healthier, more productive, expansive and optimistic. There were higher living standards, guaranteed employment, greater educational opportunities and more varied recreational facilities. The Labour Government of 1945–51 launched a new kind of consensus based on a mixed economy and the welfare state. Major industries and institutions like coal, railways, road transport, civil aviation, electricity, gas, cable and wireless and even the Bank of England were brought into public ownership. Child allowances were introduced, old age pensions increased and the school-leaving age was raised. England was fast becoming a property-owning country. When Harold Macmillan (dubbed 'Supermac') and the Conservatives came to power in 1951 people really did think, as the Prime Minister was soon to tell them, that they had 'never had it so good'.

Many, like my parents, bought homes on cheap mortgages and felt proud to own a house, which they kept neat and tidy. All along Richard Road, inside and out, the houses were decorated, gardens were carefully tended, pavements were kept litter-free and walls were absent of graffiti. It was a road typical of so many streets throughout the country, streets lined with ordinary, utilitarian, three-up, three-down redbrick semis with bathrooms and inside toilets and small front gardens.

Although there was a genuine feeling of community in Richard Road, I felt different from the other children my age when I was growing up. This stemmed from a number of things. First, I was from a staunchly Roman Catholic family (which was large by the standards of the time) and no one else on the street shared my religion. Then there was the fact that I had a mother somewhat older than those of my friends (she was thirty-eight when she gave birth to me) and, unlike most other mothers on the street, she had a full-time job. My life was significantly different too in other respects.

It is a fact that many children of the post-war working-class generation were brought up not to have what was considered unrealistic expectations in life because that would inevitably lead to disappointment. Youngsters, unless they were at the local grammar school or high school, on the whole did not aspire to do anything else beyond going down the pit or working in the steelworks, or perhaps enlisting in the army. If they were lucky, they might secure an apprenticeship. Few aspired to do anything different. Many followed in their fathers' footsteps and started a job that they would do for the rest of their lives. Children were sent out to work as soon as possible in many cases, and there was little chance of being supported through higher education. Within a marriage the man usually made all the important decisions, including sometimes how his wife voted.

As the subsequent pages of this memoir will reveal, this was not a world I recognize. I was certainly 'enjoyed' by my parents when I was young and they spent many hours with me. I was, like my brothers and sister, supported through higher education and was encouraged to have hopes and ambitions. Interestingly too, the important decisions in my family were taken by my mother.

Of course, I was different in another way. My unusual name stressed my difference. 'Gervase' wasn't just an out-of-the-ordinary name – it was unusually different, particularly in the 1950s when everyone around me seemed to be called Terry or Tony or Trevor or Tom. As a child you want to be one of the crowd, like everyone else; just ordinary. Being called Gervase in post-war Rotherham certainly set me apart.

As a child I never really liked the name and insisted on it being pronounced 'Jervis'. It sounded more masculine. My brothers and sister still pronounce it 'Jervis' to this day, as does my wife Christine.

I will digress a little here, if I may, to give a brief history of the name, for throughout my life I have frequently been asked where it originates.

2

'Gervase' comes from a Norman French form of the Old Germanic name Gervas, said to mean 'spear servant' from 'ger' (spear) and 'vass' (servant). The name was introduced into England by the Normans and was relatively common for a few centuries. The blacksmith in *The Miller's Tale*, the rudest and funniest story of Chaucer's epic poem *The Canterbury Tales*, is a Gervase, and famous bearers of the name include the twelfth-century English author Gervase of Tilbury, the thirteenth-century English chronicler Gervase of Canterbury, and the sixteenth-century military commander and equestrian Gervase Markham. I guess I am unique, as the only Gervase of Rotherham.

It is a fact that wherever I go I have to either repeat or explain this unusual name of mine. I have got quite accustomed to this by now and have come to expect that it will inevitably be misspelt or mispronounced. The spell-checker on my computer changes my name regularly to 'Greasy Pin'. Over the years I have collected a delightful range of inventive spellings that have appeared on my letters. They range from 'Grievous Pain' to 'Gracious Dhin'. I have been called 'Germane', 'Germain', 'Germinal', 'Gercase', 'Jarface', 'Gerund', 'Garfase' and even 'Geraffe'. One letter arrived addressed to 'Sharparse Thinn'. It sounded like the character Grytpype Thynn from *The Goon Show*. I did enquire of the sender, when I met him, 'Do you think any parents would call their child Sharparse?' 'Well, I thought you might be from the ethnic minorities,' came the reply, 'and it was pronounced Shaparsi.'

The late Miles Kington, a fan of the crime writer Edmund Crispin (whose main protagonist is the sleuth Professor Gervase

Fen), doubted that I actually existed. In his amusing piece in the *Independent* – 'Now where have I heard that name before?' – he discounted coincidence. 'The similarity between Professor Gervase Phinn and Professor Gervase Fen,' he observes, 'is really so boring that we shall have to discard it.' Gervase Phinn, he concludes, 'is really called Felix Proctor or something banal, but because of his work as a schools inspector he had to use a pseudonym and decided to adopt (and adapt) the name of a fictional detective'. The journalist does, however, posit another theory: 'that Mr Phinn's parents loved the detective novels of Edmund Crispin so much that they decided to call their little baby Gervase Phinn, and it is an entirely genuine name'. Ah, Miles, how wrong you were.

My name is indeed entirely genuine but I was not named after a character in a detective novel. My mother, a devout Roman Catholic, after two difficult pregnancies, was advised not to have any more children. With my eldest brother Michael she very nearly died, and doctors were strongly in favour of her calling it a day. But they had not reckoned with my mother. She was a woman of very strong views, great courage and with a stubborn streak, and being an obedient R.C. would have no truck with artificial forms of 'family planning'. She went on to have two more children. I was the last – perhaps a happy little accident. Heavily pregnant with me, she commissioned a special mass at St Bede's Church to pray for my safe delivery. I imagine that she sat on the front pew wondering what to call the new baby and listening as the priest intoned the long litany of saints:

All you holy Patriarchs and Prophets pray for us: St Peter, St Paul, St Andrew, St James, St John, St Thomas, St Philip, St Bartholomew, St Matthew, St Simon, St Thaddeus, St Matthias, St Barnabas, St Luke, St Mark.

At the very end, almost like afterthoughts, were the two appendices saints: St Gervase and St Protase. Poor St Gervase suffered a dreadful end (beaten to death with a lead-tipped whip) before the megalomaniacal Emperor Nero, and for some odd reason became the patron saint of haymakers. I guess my mother felt a little sorry that he came last in the litany of saints, or maybe she just liked the sound of the name, or perhaps she offered up a special prayer to a neglected member of the great and the good with the promise to name her baby after him if I arrived safely. My mother never would tell me. She was at great pains, however, to assure me that I was not 'a little accident'.

Just after my first Dales book was published, I was in Oxford, to speak at the Literary Festival. Having forgotten a copy of my book *The Other Side of the Dale*, from which I intended to read, I called in at a large bookshop in the centre of the city to buy my own book.

'Have you any books by Gervase Phinn?' I enquired of a rather snooty-looking assistant.

She gave a small, rather patronizing smile. 'I think you will find the name is pronounced Shervay Fine – and you'll find *her* books in the travel section.'

'Gervase is a perfect name for a character out of romantic fiction,' I was told by a fellow writer at another literary festival. 'In my next historical novel I shall have a character called Gervase. I can picture him now.' In due course the novel was published and, sure enough, a character with my name appeared. I thought I might be the Regency buck, with coal-black curls, swarthy skin, dark smouldering eyes and tight-fitting breeches. As it turned out I appeared as Lord Gervase de Morton, a bloated, raddled old roué with quivering jowls, a wet handshake and extremely questionable habits.

The name Gervase in literature is usually given to aberrant aristocrats, narcissistic, dandified poseurs and devious, upper-crust, well-connected villains. In *Slightly Tempted* (a story of 'sparkling courtship, scandalous passion and all-consuming love') by Mary Balogh, Lord Gervase Ashford is the notorious rake intent on ravishing the beautiful Lady Morgan Bedwyn. In *The Faun's Folly* by Sandra Heath, Lord Gervase Mowbray, Duke of Wroxham, is only marginally better. Georgette Heyer, in *The Quiet Gentleman*, had a central character called Gervase, Earl of St Erith, and in *The Queen's Man* by Sharon Kay, Gervase Fitz Randolph is no better than he should be. In *Mistress Wilding* by Rafael Sabatini, portly Sir Gervase Scoresby is someone not to be trifled with, and in *Mr Castonel*, the eponymous hero is Mr Gervase Castonel: 'It was a prepossessing face; it was silent, pale and unfathomable with grey impenetrable eyes that disliked the look of you; and dark hair.'

So I think I have made my point: the Gervases in literature are well-connected but not very nice. When I met the novelist Margaret Dickinson at another literary event, I suggested rather facetiously that she might like to name the hero of her next novel, *Suffragette Girl*, Gervase and use my second name, Richard, as his surname. To my surprise and delight, she agreed. True to her word the novel features a young, dashing military hero called Gervase Richards.

When I started school my name was placed on the register alongside Marjorie and Margaret, Judith and Jennifer. The teachers thought it was a girl's name. This has been another cross to bear – being mistaken for a woman. I spoke at a conference in Tamworth a few years ago and the evening before, sitting quietly in the bar, I eavesdropped on a couple of teachers in animated conversation.

'Have you heard this Gervase Phinn speak before?' asked one.

'No,' replied her colleague, 'but my head of department came on this course last year and said she was quite a good speaker.'

One of the first schools I visited when I became a school inspector was a large comprehensive. After observing a number of lessons, I was sitting with the Head of the English Department in the staffroom to share my deliberations, when my unusual name entered the conversation.

'Is it Welsh?' enquired the Head of English.

'No,' I replied.

'It sounds very Welsh. I have a cousin in Cardiff called Geraint and another called Gwillam. I thought it might have been of Celtic origin.'

'It's not Welsh,' I told her.

'Is it Irish then?'

'No, my name's not Welsh or Irish,' I replied. 'In fact, the name Gervase –'

'It ees a French name.' The French assistant, Michelle, who was sitting behind us, interrupted the conversation. She was a strikingly good-looking young woman with dark, long-lashed eyes and a mass of raven-coloured hair. 'Gervais ees pronounced "Gervez" with a soft sounding "g", as in zer word "genre". It ees a French–Norman name and ees very common in France.'

'Really?' I said, disappearing into the dark eyes of the speaker.

'It ees a most beautiful name,' she sighed, and fluttered the incredible eyelashes.

'Would you mind pronouncing it again?' I said. 'I rather like the way you say it.'

'Ggggervez,' she repeated in the most seductive of voices. 'Ggggervez ees an 'ouse'old name in France. Everywhere you go you will 'ear the name Ggggervez.' She smiled widely and then added, 'It ees the name of a yoghurt.'

'Your name? Is it a Welsh name?' asked the headmaster when I was about to leave the school.

'I've had this conversation before, with your Head of English,' I replied, shaking my head. 'No, it's French actually. French–Norman. St Gervase was a second-century Roman martyr put to death under the Emperor Nero.'

'You don't say,' said the headmaster, trying to look interested.

'It was a popular name in medieval times,' I continued. 'I believe William the Conqueror had several knights of that name with him when he invaded. The name literally means "spear-carrier".'

'There's a thing,' said the headmaster, smiling. 'Your predecessor as the Senior Inspector for English in North Yorkshire was a David Spearman.'

'That's right,' I told him. 'Quite a coincidence.'

The headmaster leaned back in his chair and gave a wry smile. '"Spear-carrier", eh?' he repeated. 'Well, I should think that that's a very appropriate handle for a school inspector.'

'Yes, I suppose it is,' I replied. 'I always seem to be on the sharp end of things in this line of work.'

'I wasn't meaning that,' said the headmaster. 'I have always been of the opinion that school inspectors are like cross-eyed javelin throwers. They hurl a lot of spears in the direction of schools, missing the point most of the time, but occasionally, and by sheer accident, they happen to hit the right target. Good afternoon to you, Mr Phinn.'

Now I delight in my unusual name. It is unique. Go on the internet and type in a name like John Smith and there will be millions and millions of hits, but there is only one Gervase Phinn. Any success I have had with my books is due, in no small part, to my name. Following my reading of the Dales books on Radio Four's *Book of the Week*, people would go into bookshops and ask for 'the book by the school inspector with the funny name' and booksellers would know immediately what the customer was looking for. Shakespeare's Juliet got it tragically wrong. 'What's in a name?' she asks Romeo. 'That which we call a rose by any other name would smell as sweet.' Actually there is quite a lot in a name.

Recently I received a delighted letter from a new and very proud father. He informed me that his wife had been taken to hospital to have their overdue baby induced. Neither of them was keen for the baby to be brought into the world artificially. Then, as his wife lay in bed listening to my Dales books on tape, she began to giggle and then chuckle and soon she was convulsed with uncontrollable laughter. It brought the baby on.

'We are so grateful to you,' he wrote, 'that you hastened the arrival of our little baby son.'

I wrote back congratulating the new parents. 'Perhaps you might like to call your son Gervase, after me,' I suggested mischievously.

'We are not that grateful,' came back the reply.

3

I cannot recount the number of times I have had to spell the name Phinn. It has appeared as 'Flynn', 'Finn', 'Thin', 'Tinn', 'Pinn', 'Sinn' and 'Chinn'. My favourite appeared when I was in my first year of teaching. A letter arrived addressed to 'Mr Phunn, Master-in-Charge-of-Games'.

'All Phunn and games, eh, Gervase?' Mr Morgan, headteacher, remarked dryly as he passed me the letter.

In that first year of teaching, a distressed mother on parents' evening confided in me: 'I'm really very worried about my son's spelling, Mr Perhinn.'

'I wouldn't worry, Mrs Atkinson,' I reassured her, 'your Perhillip is doing very well.'

The surname Phinn, I was to learn, has a long and distinguished provenance. Those who investigate their past, searching through records, visiting churches to pore over the registers of births and deaths, scanning the census returns, surfing the internet, are ever hopeful that they will discover a famous (or indeed infamous) forebear. I have visions that one day, when I find the time, I will investigate my family history to discover that I am a direct descendant of dashing Sir Rupert Phinn, Cavalier commander at the Battle of Barnsley, Admiral Lord Horatio Phinn, hero of a great naval battle in Bridlington Bay, Lady Georgiana Phinn, mistress of George IV, Oscar Fingal O'Flahertie Wills Phinn, the famous Irish playwright and shining wit. Of course, I have an idea that to my chagrin I will discover I come from a long line of builders, farm labourers, domestic servants and factory workers.

The family name, until relatively recently, was the common

enough Irish name Finn. My forebears, on my father's side, are said to have fled Ireland during the Great Famine of 1846 and settled in Scotland. Dad always maintained that we were descendants of the great Irish king Fionn McCool (the fair-headed one), of folklore fame, who lived two and a half thousand years ago, and that one day we would move to the great castle in Ireland when he claimed his birthright. He was a great storyteller was my father.

Grandfather James Finn married a Scot, Margaret Helen Macdonald. She was something of a snob by all accounts and exceedingly proud of her Scottish ancestry and her Scottish Catholicism, asserting that she was descended from the ancient clan of Macdonald of South Uist, that bleak island of great melancholy stretches of heather-covered moors and bogland in the Outer Hebrides. It is not generally known that a large number of the inhabitants of these islands are Roman Catholic. They trace back their ancestry in those remote outposts many centuries, undisturbed by the turmoil of the Reformation, and have kept a faith that dates back to the ancient Celtic Church.

At the time of my grandparents' marriage there was much anti-Irish racism in Scotland, so she styled herself Mrs Macdonald-Phinn, to disguise any Irish connections and place her 'a cut above' the hoi polloi. All the children of the marriage – John, Hessie, Nellie, Alexander and my father, Richard Joseph – were burdened with the double-barrelled surname. Joining the Royal Air Force my Uncle Alec, upon informing the commanding officer that his name was Alexander James Macdonald-Phinn, was told: 'Well, at ease, all four of you.'

My father told me that it was well known in the family that 'Grannie Mac' would never shop at Campbell's Butchers in the High Street, not after 'what that treacherous, deceitful band of scoundrels and poltroons did at Glencoe'. It was on 13 February 1692 that 'the abominable, false, cunning and perfidious' Campbells, 'the best of them to be pitied but never to be trusted', massacred the Macdonalds in the cold and lonely valley where, to this day, no birds are said to sing. She evidently had a very good memory, my grandmother.

On the anniversary of the massacre she would read the 'Lament of Glencoe' to her five children.

> Chill was the air and deep was the snow,
> And the cold moon gave scant light,
> When the treacherous Campbells fell on Glencoe
> Like a wolf pack in the night.
>
> With sword and knife, they spared no life,
> With blood they bathed the ground.
> Man and boy, woman and bairn,
> They murdered all they found.

In January 1979 I was appointed Head of the English Department at St John Fisher Roman Catholic High School in Sheffield. The headmaster was a Mr Campbell. On the anniversary of the massacre I wore a black tie and Sister Brendan, a teaching colleague, enquired why I was wearing it. It took her a time, innocent as she was, to fully appreciate my unusual sense of humour. In graphic detail, I explained to the nun that the defenceless Macdonalds had been put to 'fire and sword' by the very people who had offered them hospitality. Without warning, I told her, Captain Campbell of Glenlyon and his troops fell upon the community, burning all the houses and massacring the people. Some thirty-eight out of 200 inhabitants, including MacIain himself, the clan chief, were cut down that day by the vulpine Campbells. Others, who had fled into the mountains, died in the next week from cold and starvation.

'But what has this to do with you?' asked the baffled nun. 'You are called Phinn, not Macdonald.'

'My grandmother was a Macdonald,' I told her.

'And whenever did this terrible thing happen?' she continued, imagining that it was something which had occurred but a few years before.

'1692,' I told her, keeping a deadly serious face.

'1692!' she exclaimed.

'And when, on this day of all days, sister,' I continued, shaking my head sadly and keeping a deadly solemn face, 'Mr Campbell sees the black tie, he will know the significance and feel suitably ashamed.'

'I think it's about time to bury the hatchet, Mr Phinn,' said the nun, clearly believing me to be serious. 'All the troubles of the world are caused by people harbouring resentments and remembering past wrongs. I think it's about time you learnt to forgive and forget.'

'Easier said than done, sister,' I replied ponderously. 'Easier said than done.'

After assembly, the headmaster approached me to discuss a timetable change. Sister Brendan watched like a hungry blackbird as he left the stage and walked with a determined step in my direction. I touched my tie and looked knowingly at her and nodded.

'What did Mr Campbell say to you after assembly?' asked the nun at morning break.

'He apologized, of course,' I told her before going on yard duty.

Following my grandfather's death (he was an engineer and died of enteric fever in Peru), my grandmother remarried a Mr Craig. One wonders if she continued in life with a triple-barrelled name. On her death, when my father was fourteen, the five Phinn children were dispersed. John left for America, Hessie and Nellie moved south, Alec joined the Royal Air Force and my father went to live on an uncle's farm in Kirkintulloch before joining the army on his seventeenth birthday.

A photograph of 'Grannie Mac' shows a tall, elegant and

superior-looking woman in black, her dark hair scraped back savagely on her scalp and her long white hands clasped before her. She had never experienced illness all her life and died as she would have wished – on her knees. At the conclusion of a Celebration Mass at the Scottish Convention of the Union of Catholic Mothers, my grandmother stood as the priest left the altar, made the Sign of the Cross, knelt down and promptly expired.

The only possessions that her children inherited were her rosary beads, a few photographs and a faded sampler in a plain wooden frame, reputedly embroidered by an ancestor.

> Do, by your fair endeavours profess,
> An elegance of mind, as well as dress.
> Be this your ornament and know to please
> By graceful nature's unaffected ease.
> And do not think that by another's shame
> You can raise your merit or adorn your fame.
> – Mary Margaret Macdonald, 1801

I should like to think that Margaret Helen Macdonald-Phinn remained true to these words.

My brother Alec, who lives on the shores of Galway Bay, was so heartily tired of the misspelling of his surname and, I guess, wanting to stress his Irish ancestry, that he changed the name back to the original. When he was touring America with his Irish folk group, De Dannan, he undertook a bit of family history research and discovered a John Phinn in the telephone book in the town in Maine where my uncle was said to have settled. My brother telephoned, said he thought he might be a nephew, made an appointment and arrived at an extremely elegant house. The door was answered by a large friendly man. 'I'm John Phinn,' he said, smiling widely, 'and I've been expecting you.' Then they both burst into fits of laughter. John Phinn was black.

Having passed the training as an OFSTED Registered Inspector, I received my certificate officially authorizing Mr G. Phinn to lead inspections in schools. A week later I received a second certificate officially authorizing a Mr G. Dhin to do the same. Then all the official materials, guidelines, policies, code of conduct and updates arrived from London – in duplicate. One wet Monday morning Brian, the good-humoured and hard-pressed postman, stood panting at the door, weighed down by large brown paper packages.

'Are you living with a Sikh?' he asked, unburdening himself.

Each week Brian would knock on the door with yet another consignment of parcels and letters. He would then watch me bemused as I headed for the garage, where I kept the inspection documents in two heavy metal lockable cupboards. It must have appeared highly suspicious. One morning he waited at the gate as I unlocked the garage, crept into the darkness, clicked on the flickering light and unlocked the metal cupboard where I stashed away the brown paper parcels. After observing me for a moment, he asked, 'Are you into pornography, then?' I explained that nothing could be further from the truth.

Despite contacting OFSTED head office in London, the duplicated materials continued to arrive and also letters addressed to the fictitious Mr G. Dhin. One was an invitation to join an inspection team preparing to visit a multiracial, multicultural inner city school. 'We feel it would be appropriate, Mr Dhin,' wrote the lead inspector, 'to have on our team of inspectors a member of the ethnic minority.' I imagine that they thought I was Gunga Din.

4

There is a whole lot of truth in the old Irish proverb: 'One good mother is worth a hundred schoolmasters.' In my view, the relationship between the child and the parent is the most critical influence on that child's life, and it is the mother in particular who has the most significant effect. She can make a child's life joyous or miserable, she can encourage or disparage, she can build up a child's feeling of self-worth or stress his limitations, she can hurt or heal. She can promote respect, give security and support self-fulfilment for her child or she can be critical, neglectful and disregard his suffering. How a child views the world and how he fits into it is largely down to his mother.

My mother was a remarkable person and my greatest teacher. When I was young I thought that all children had mothers like mine: loving, funny, generous, ever-supportive, who took out their false teeth and pretended to be witches, who baked them gingerbread men, discussed things with them, sang songs and wrote them little stories. I thought that all children had mothers who told wild and wonderful tales, cracked jokes, played tricks, teased them gently. For as long as I could remember, since I was a small boy, I always felt valued and loved and perceived myself to be her favourite. 'A man who has been the indisputable favourite of his mother,' wrote Sigmund Freud, 'keeps for life the feeling of a conqueror, that confidence of success which often induces success.' Any success I have had in life is due in no small part to the influence of my mother.

My mother inherited my grandmother's fine features: clear blue eyes, long dark eyelashes, fine hands, thick black hair and a soft oval face. She looked every inch an Irish colleen. As a child I imagined all mothers washed clothes, ironed shirts, pressed trousers, darned socks, did the shopping, cleaned the windows, swept the carpets, baked cakes, cooked the dinner, paid the bills, organized parties, attended school parents' meetings, went to the school plays, looked after their children when we were ill, sat with them at the dentist's and did innumerable other things, as well as holding down a full-time job. I thought all children like me had brothers who let them play with their toys, mended their bikes and taught them the guitar, and sisters who showed them how to sew and paint and helped them with their homework. I imagined that all homes had books and stories, music and laughter, courtesy and good manners, honesty and love. It is only now I am older and have met countless numbers of children in the schools I have visited that I appreciate just how very special my parents were and how hard they tried to bring the four of us up to be honest and decent young people. Now, in later life, I know for sure that the earliest influences of home and environment and the special relationship of a child with his or her mother have a deep and long-lasting effect on the character of the future man or woman.

I was raised to believe in myself, to never pretend to be something I was not and never deny my roots or be ashamed of my humble origins. 'Remember,' my mother was wont to say, 'whoever exalts himself shall be humbled and whoever humbles himself shall be exalted.' Mum disliked pomposity and people with affectations, was never judgemental, never held me up for mockery or ridicule and, most importantly for a shy and idealistic child of average ability, never derided my dreams. I always felt that she wanted me to have a mind of my own, to stand out from the crowd and not be like everyone else.

Much has been written by psychologists and 'child experts'

about the significance of birth order in a family. Last-born children, it is said, are generally very different from their siblings, particularly when compared with those who are born into a family first. The last child to arrive in an established family is said to be more altruistic, emotionally secure, empathetic and when small is more likely to relate to other children. He or she is said to be less conscientious and more good-humoured, less conventional and more unpredictable, more open to experiences, more affectionate and at times more rebellious. It is said that the last-born is more likely to embrace risk-taking and excel in contact sports. Well, the experts certainly got it wrong with me. As a child I was nearly the very opposite – shy, under-confident, conscientious, conventional, well-behaved, an ordinary little boy of average intelligence who was pretty hopeless at all contact sports.

I have many vivid memories of my mother when I was little. She was a tall, full-figured woman but she moved vigorously and laughed easily, stroked my head tenderly as I passed, called me a dozen endearing names and never missed an opportunity of telling me how very special I was. Behind her constant good humour and practicality, she possessed that special quality of making others feel good about themselves. She had an unswerving religious belief. Hers was a simple faith based on the words of Jesus that we should do unto others as we would wish they would do unto us. Another favourite biblical quote was, 'I was hungry and you gave me to eat . . . insofar as you did this to one of the least of these brothers of mine, you did it to me.'

So I grew up against a background of care and gentleness, good humour and discipline. She pinned my first pictures from the infant school on the cupboard in the kitchen, admired my feeble attempts at playing the piano, told me what a good reader I was and I knew what it felt like to be proud. She laughed at my jokes, made me birthday cakes with white icing and coloured candles and always kissed me goodnight and I knew what it felt like to be loved. What I learnt from my mother was that love, genuine love, unconditional love sees goodness and constantly emphasizes it. It is about compassion and care, support and encouragement, and every child is entitled to that.

Of course there are those in the world who will be sceptical of what I say, that no one could have had such a happy, untroubled and loving childhood. In *They F*** You Up: How to Survive Family Life* (the title taken from the poem by Philip Larkin), the psychologist Oliver James posits that the passing of the years allows memories to be selective and often fictionalized.

My childhood memories may indeed be a little rose-coloured, at times patchy and somewhat selective, but I recall with clarity so many occasions when my mother demonstrated her love for me and her compassion for others. I remember once, when I was six and we were on holiday in Blackpool, I wet the bed. Mum had told me not to drink too much that evening but I had carried on downing a good few glasses of lemonade. 'You'll be sorry,' she said, and left it at that. I was indeed sorry because I awoke in the middle of the night distraught to find my pyjamas sopping and a warm wet patch in the middle of the bed.

There were no recriminations. 'Don't get all upset,' said Mum, giving me a cuddle. 'We all wet the bed at some time in our lives. It's not the end of the world. Accidents happen.' She washed me, changed me, put me in a clean pair of pyjamas and popped me in her bed next to Dad. I slept between my parents that night and felt safe and secure and loved.

I also learnt from my mother very early on what kindness was. One day, when I was about six or seven, a fearsome figure arrived at the back door. She was old and wrinkled, with swarthy skin, dark shining eyes and a long beak of a

nose. I remember well the heavy boots, the threadbare cardigan and the coloured scarf wrapped around the scrawny neck.
For the entire world she looked like the wicked stepmother
in *Snow White*.

'Is your mother in, dearie?' croaked the crone in a strange
deep voice.

My mother chatted with the woman for some time before
buying from her a strip of lace and some crude wooden
clothes-pegs. I eavesdropped behind the kitchen door and
heard the woman tell my mother that she would have a long
and happy life and her generosity would be rewarded.

'Bless you, lady,' said the gypsy. 'You have kind eyes. May
your three sons and dark-eyed daughter prosper and may your
husband's other children too reap the riches of the world.'
There was an interesting conversation at the tea table that
afternoon when my father got home from work.

I was told later that gypsies were travelling people who lived
in caravans; they were not bad but simply poor and moved
from house to house selling their wares, trying to make a living.
My mother told me they were disliked and were often driven
away, but they had as much right to settle on beautiful lands
as the oldest families in their fine houses. My mother had a
profound belief that dustmen, cleaners, road sweepers, window
cleaners and shop assistants were all worthy of respect. Indeed,
anyone who came to the door was greeted courteously.

My mother was such a generous woman and never turned
anyone away. Even when the Jehovah's Witnesses knocked on
the door for the umpteenth time, intent on enlisting new
converts, Mum would never be rude but would listen patiently
and finally smile and shake her head and tell them she too was
a Christian and happy in her own faith. One Saturday morning an elderly man and a young woman arrived at the gate as
Mum was taking me to Miss Worrell, the dentist. I had a really
painful tooth and had been up most of the evening before,

biting on a bit of cloth soaked in whisky. Like most children I hated the dentist. It was the large rubber mask that was placed over your face and that noxious smell you had to inhale until you sank into unconsciousness. I was in a tetchy mood and needed some coaxing and a few firm words for me to put on my coat and go with Mum. So at the gate stood these two zealots, the man in a pristine suit, highly polished black shoes and carrying a briefcase, the woman in a smart jacket and both with great smiles across their faces.

'May we have a minute of your time, madam,' asked the first, 'to explain a little about what we believe?'

'Not now,' said Mum, brusquely. 'I'm in a rush.'

'It will only take a moment,' persisted the second.

'I'm sorry,' snapped Mum, 'but not now! I have heard what you have to say before and have told you not to keep coming round. As I have told you, I don't agree with any of your views. Now, I don't wish to be rude but I am in a hurry.'

'At least will you take a moment to look at our literature?' asked the man, looking rather deflated.

'No, thank you,' said Mum. 'I've read it before and I have to say that the only thing we have in common is God.'

'I see,' said the man, rather disconcerted. 'I take it then you will not be voting Conservative?'

I was nine years old in 1955. The *Daily Express* carried a story of two black girls, Claudette Colvin and Rosa Parks, who refused to give up their seats to white people on a bus in Montgomery, Alabama. At teatime I recall my mother and father discussing the racism that existed in America. I can see my mother's face now, red and angry, and can remember her sense of outrage at the injustice of making the two little black girls give up their seats for white folk. 'And they claim to be Christian,' my mother said, shaking her head.

Being a trained nurse and midwife, my mother was in

constant demand on the street for medical advice and to deal with accidents and emergencies. My father said once that we should have a sign on the front door saying 'Casualty Department'. Mum would leave the house willingly, sometimes mid-meal, to look at a fractious baby, dress a wound or see if a doctor needed to be called out. On one occasion we were in the middle of tea and there came a frantic knocking on the door. A distraught neighbour, carrying a choking child, was ushered into the kitchen. My mother took charge with great calmness, applied pressure to the little boy's chest and the offending peanut popped out. She then sat the trembling mother down with a cup of tea while I was deputed to keep the little boy occupied. A week later the mother reappeared with the child. He had swallowed a sixpence. Mum reassured the mother again and told her to give the child Syrup of Figs and the money would 'find its own way out'. In due course, that's exactly what it did.

Another time a casualty arrived from the council estate at the bottom of the road. A little boy, crying piteously, stood on the doorstep with his mother. He was sporting a huge blood-soaked bandage, which was wrapped around his head like a turban.

'Eric's fallen into t'cold frame at t'back of t'house,' announced the mother. "Is 'ead won't stop bleedin'.' Mum took charge. 'And when you've seen to 'im, nurse,' continued the woman, 'can you come and see to 'is dad? 'E's fainted.'

Bobby lived with his mother on the big council estate of Broom Valley. In the days when I was growing up, descriptions of those with special needs were blunt and insensate. Down's syndrome children were 'mongols', those with cerebral palsy 'spastics' and those with specific learning difficulties 'backward' or 'mental'. Bobby was a large, moon-faced, red-headed boy of about my age who talked through his nose and had a vacant expression. He attended the Newman Special School at Whiston and never came out to play with the other children in the street because I guess his mother knew he would be picked on and laughed at. Children can be corrosively cruel at times.

When my mother agreed to look after Bobby one Saturday afternoon I was dragooned into occupying him. I found it a great ordeal. He arrived with a large bag of boiled sweets (we called them 'spice'), which he refused to share. He filled his mouth with the sweets until his cheeks bulged out and clutched the confections to his chest, all the while shaking his head. He broke two of my Airfix models, and when he had consumed all his sweets he commandeered the swing at the top of the garden and would not budge. To my angry demand that he get off the swing and let me have a go, he picked his nose thoughtfully and shook his head.

It was with a great sense of relief that I saw his mother waddling down the garden path to take him home. She coaxed him off the swing with the promise of more sweets.

It was just before my tenth birthday when Bobby arrived at the gate at the back of my house. He was red in the face and waving his arms about him. I could just make out in the garbled nasal rambling that he wanted 't'nurse'.

I ran and fetched my mother. He flung his arms around her and buried his head in her chest. She patted the boy on the back like someone winding a baby.

'It's all right, Bobby,' she said quietly. 'Now you tell me what's the matter.'

'It's my mam,' he wailed. 'She's dying. Tha's got to come.'

I wanted to make myself scarce, embarrassed by this performance, but was told I had to accompany them in case I was needed to telephone for a doctor.

We found Bobby's mother in the front room of the house, stretched out on the settee gasping for breath and crimson-faced.

'What is it, Mrs Stockton?' asked my mother, kneeling down beside her.

'It's mi chest, nurse,' moaned the woman. 'I can't breathe and I've got this terrible pain just here.' She patted her heart. 'If I bend it gets worse.'

'Take Bobby outside,' ordered my mother, 'and keep him occupied.' She closed the door. A few minutes later she emerged, trying to suppress a smile

'Is she gunna die?' asked Bobby, his cheeks wet with tears.

'No, Bobby, she's not going to die. She's fine.'

'What was wrong?' I asked my mother as we made our way back home.

'She had her corset on too tightly,' she told me, 'and when she bent over one of the metal stays must have snapped and dug into her chest. She thought she was having a heart attack.'

Later that evening, having recounted the encounter to my father, my mother shook her head sadly. 'Whatever will happen to that poor lad when she dies?'

My mother was particularly kind to an elderly widower who lived a few streets away. Mr Parry lived at the bottom of Gerard Road, in a rather more exclusive area than the one in which we lived. The houses were older, larger and had a great deal more character to them compared to our redbrick semi-detached houses a few streets away. Most Sundays, after I had consumed a large lunch, I was despatched to Gerard Road with two metal plates on which a full roast dinner with all the trimmings was put. This was Mr Parry's dinner.

I never minded this particular errand because I loved visiting Mr Parry. He was an elderly, incredibly wrinkled man who lived alone in this tall, dark, imposing house with its peeling paint and overgrown garden. Mr Parry must have been in his eighties when I first met him but he walked, albeit slowly, with a straight back and without a walking stick. His appearance – the heavy, dark, hooded eyes, hatchet nose and teeth the colour of antique piano keys – could very well have been rather frightening for a young boy, but not to me, for when he spoke with that soft Welsh lilt he was mesmerizing. He was a deeply intelligent man and greatly interesting, and I would sometimes sit on the old sofa fascinated by the timbre of his voice and his wide knowledge and extraordinary memory. My mother described him as 'a real gentleman'.

Mum had known Mrs Parry through Church, both being stalwart members of the Union of Catholic Mothers. Mr and Mrs Parry had been in what the Catholic Church called a 'mixed marriage'. He was from Welsh nonconformist stock, his wife from an Irish Catholic background, and the marriage service had taken place quietly in a side altar at the Catholic church with no special Nuptial Mass and without any fuss. My mother told me that theirs was a tragic story. Mr Parry's family had nothing to do with him after he married a Catholic and they learnt that he had agreed to raise the children in her faith. Her family had little to do with her after she took up with a Protestant. Their only son had been killed in Italy during the war, and my mother told me Mrs Parry had died not long afterwards, probably of a broken heart.

Going into the house was like stepping back in time. There was an all-pervading smell of dusty carpets and damp. You entered through a heavy front door with a coloured glass window in the centre, into a shadowy hall where a grandfather clock with a painted dial ticked away reassuringly. You walked through into a cluttered parlour with an ageing and sagging horsehair sofa, a green leather-covered armchair, an antique sideboard and a huge oak Welsh dresser. There were two bookcases crammed with leather-backed tomes and neatly stacked magazines and newspapers. In winter a huge fire would be blazing away. I remember there was always a large blue bowl on the dresser filled with shrivelled apples, and on the wall a black and white print of Lord Nelson as he lay dying on the deck of the *Victory*, a pale, pathetic figure in a white shirt, his breast exposed. Mr Parry told me the admiral's body had been brought back to England in a cask of the finest French brandy and when, months later, it was taken out, it was perfectly preserved. A heavy and faded coloured cloth covered the table. But what fascinated me most about the room was the line of identical, highly polished black shoes that had been placed beneath the dresser – a pair for each day of the week.

The mantelshelf was crammed with all sorts of treasures: two great twisted stemmed brass candlesticks, a pair of strange, fat-faced porcelain dogs veined with age, a silver-framed photograph of a man and a woman and in the centre an ornate carriage clock. I was most interested in the small ivory tusks with designs of sailing ships carved on them. I learnt that these were called scrimshaws and were done by French prisoners-of-war at the time of Napoleon. Above the shelf was a gilt-framed mirror with an eagle, its wings outstretched, set in the frame at the top.

Mr Parry would take his lunch into the kitchen and put it into the oven to eat later, and then he would sit in his large armchair and light his pipe. I would spend the first part of the hour talking to him, mostly about what I had read and how I was getting on at school, and then he would tell me stories about when he was young. Despite my asking, he always steered well clear of talking about the war apart from the time he let me borrow a gas mask to take to school. He told me he had been a soldier in the Great War of 1914, when so many men had died in the trenches.

I guess one of the reasons I liked to visit him was that I never left without a small present: a silver Victorian shilling, a German military button, a brass paper knife made from a cartridge shell by a prisoner-of-war, a shiny belt buckle with a double-headed eagle on the front, a dull grey medal with a faded red and black ribbon. Once he gave me a small brass scale for weighing gold sovereigns. I still have his presents today. I always had my eye on the scrimshaws, which were displayed on the dresser, but sadly none came my way.

When I left the musty atmosphere of the house, I would take Mr Parry's washing with me in a canvas bag and my mother would drop it back, washed and ironed, the following week, when she would also collect the tin plates.

'Your mother is a very special woman, you know,' he never tired of telling me, 'and her rewards will be great in heaven.'

He was right.

5

Although a loved child, I was not indulged and my mother could be firm and intransigent at times. She was no soft touch. There were boundaries I could never cross. These included: no swearing, being rude, dropping litter, fighting with my brothers, being cheeky and leaving the bedroom in a mess. If I had come home to tell her I had been in trouble at school I would have been in twice as much trouble. Rules had to be kept and occasionally I would feel the chilly wind of her disapproval. My mother never viewed parenthood as a popularity contest.

No family is entirely free of disagreement and discord; every deep relationship has its tensions, moments of anger and annoyance, and there were times when I fell out with my mother. I can't say, however, that I was unduly rocked by the storms of adolescence, but I did have my moments.

One Christmas – I must have been about fifteen at the time – my mother bought me a corduroy jacket from W. Muntus, Outfitters, of Rotherham. It was a horribly thick, heavy garment with wide lapels, velvety ribs and a string of brass buttons on the cuffs. It was the sort of jacket old men wore. I hated it at first sight and told my mother so. She had a pale, hurt look on her face, as if she couldn't believe what she had heard. I had wanted a tight-fitting suit like the ones the Beatles wore, and a black turtleneck jumper, and I had been given this shapeless, old-fashioned jacket the colour of dog dirt. I wouldn't even try it on. There was no way I was going be seen wearing this monstrosity and I stomped off upstairs.

I emerged when Christmas dinner was on the table but sat in simmering silence and picked at the turkey. I felt everyone in the family was against me for being so ungrateful. No one spoke to me, which made it all the worse. My father took me aside later in the day and told me how disappointed he was in me, how I had upset my mother and how I should apologize and accept the coat with good grace. But I wouldn't, and sat for the rest of the day in the front room, silent and morose and listening as the rest of the family enjoyed themselves next door. Of course, sulking is the last refuge of the powerless and gets you nowhere, but I stubbornly stayed in the front room and was ignored. It was a long and dispiriting Christmas Day. I never did apologize and the coat, which I guess was returned to the shop, was not mentioned again. Needless to say I never got the suit like the one the Beatles wore, or a black turtleneck jumper.

On another occasion, around the same time, I asked if I could go on the school trip to Switzerland. My two best friends at school were going and I was desperate to go too. Mum read the letter from the school and, folding it carefully, placed it behind the clock on the mantelpiece.

'Well, can I go?' I asked excitedly.

'No,' she said bluntly, 'it's too expensive.'

I tried to reason with her but to no avail.

'You are not going,' she said, firmly, 'and that's the end of it.'

'But –'

'No buts.'

When Dad came in from work I tried persuading him.

'What did your mother say?' he asked.

'She said I can't go,' I said glumly.

'Then you can't go,' he said simply.

I went on and on about the school trip for a good week, and felt like many an adolescent who feels his parents are being grossly unfair. Perhaps I thought the persistent nagging would wear my mother down and she would eventually concede. Not a bit of it. She calmly told me every time the subject was raised that I would not be going on any trip to Switzerland so not to waste my breath. Her refusal to raise her voice made it more irritating. Finally, in one desperate attempt for her to change her mind, and with a dramatic outburst of anger and frustration, I told her she was mean and selfish and no doubt various other things as well and made a grand exit, slamming the door behind me. I waited for her to come up the stairs and concede but she never did and Switzerland was not mentioned again.

Later that evening I heard my mother discussing my unreasonable behaviour with Mrs Rogers, a neighbour who often called in for a cup of tea.

'He'll grow out of it,' my mother told her. 'His two brothers went through that difficult stage. It comes with adolescence. It's just his hormones playing up.'

'Well, Pat,' said Mrs Rogers. 'I'm glad there's no history of hormones in our family.'

As with all disagreements in our family it eventually blew over and I learnt a lesson that we cannot always have in life what we want. Children need more than unconditional love. They need boundaries and parameters, otherwise they will never come to fully appreciate what they have and strive to earn their parents' love. When thwarted, children may very well argue and sulk and throw tantrums, and it is easier for parents to concede, to have a quiet life and preserve the domestic harmony rather than confront them with the word 'No', but I am certain that refusing children's unreasonable demands brings with it long-term rewards. After forty years in education I have seen only too clearly the results of inconsistency, lack of supervision and indulgence in the home. The rise in knife crime, teenage pregnancies, alcohol and drug abuse and anti-social behaviour has its roots in the permissive manner in which some children are reared.

Of course there were times when I felt my mother was

indeed unreasonable. When I was at college training to be a teacher we were set an essay on the novels of D. H. Lawrence and given the task of reading several of his books, including *Sons and Lovers*. At home for the weekend, I left the book in the front room but later, search as I might, I could not find it. Enquiring of my mother if she had seen it, she told me with pursed lips that it was in the dustbin and there it would stay.

'You are not bringing dirty books into *this* house,' she said.

'Mum!' I protested. 'I have to read it for my course.'

'Well, you are not reading it in this house,' she told me firmly.

'Anyway, it's not a dirty book,' I informed her.

'It's by that man who wrote that book about the game-keeper.' She couldn't even bring herself to say the title: *Lady Chatterley's Lover*. The book stayed in the bin and when I was back at college, I bought another copy.

When I was young, the facts of life were never a subject for discussion with my mother in any overt sense, but she skirted around the subject on occasions. I was twelve and we were sitting in the front room. Dad was at work, Christine at a dance class and my brothers were in town. My mother, darning socks in a casual manner, told the story of a young girl in Canklow, a dark and disadvantaged area of the industrial Don Valley. The girl, who was a few years older than I was, had become pregnant. Some lad had 'taken advantage of her' and she had now, as the girl's mother had told her angrily, 'got herself up the spout'. My mother, as the health visitor for the area, was given the case. I was surprised at my mother's blunt, matter-of-fact observations: 'It's not usually the ones who carry on with boys who end up becoming pregnant,' she told me. 'It's the naïve ones.' She described this frail and frightened child, wearing her school blazer, eyes red with tears, trying to cope in a less than supportive family and facing what for her was a terrifying future. 'What will it feel like, nurse?' she asked. 'How long will it be before the baby is born? Will it hurt? What will happen to the baby?' The child would, of course, be adopted and the girl would, no doubt, carry the stigma of a bastard birth and be reminded frequently of it by her unsympathetic mother. Mum had seen this before. The girl would hold the baby in her arms, kiss it, love it, take it to her heart and not wish to part with it. The bond formed with her child when in her womb would be strengthened when she fed and cuddled it. Then she would be forced to give it away. Someone else would bring it up. All her life the girl would think about that child. 'It will be a torture,' said my mother. Then, looking up from the darning and staring at me, she added, 'And, of course, the boy who got her into all this trouble will get away scot-free.' I felt like saying, 'It wasn't me who got her pregnant, you know,' but I just nodded wisely. I knew what my mother meant.

In the 1950s sex was seen as something of a secret, not a topic to be talked about. It was the subject of rude jokes and seaside postcards full of innuendo. In some comedy films, like the *Carry On* series, it was something cheeky and naughty, where the characters were full of winks and nods and knowing looks. By twelve I had a good idea where babies came from, but until I started secondary school and the big boys 'educated' me, I was pretty naïve. Of course, like all boys, I bluffed. I was ten years old and wandering around Broom Valley Junior school yard one bright sunny lunchtime with Jimmy Everett and Terry Gaunt, my best pals, when Roy Evans sidled up.

'Guess what?'

'What?' we chorused.

'My next door neighbour's lass, Soppy Sandra, is up t'spout!' There were many descriptions of pregnancy and Roy knew the whole dictionary of them – 'up the spout', 'in the pudding club', 'a bun in the oven', 'in the family way', 'up the duff', 'eating for two'.

'Oh,' we replied, trying to sound uninterested.

'S'right. There was a right old ding-dong last night when 'er old man found out. You should have 'eard 'em shouting. All t'street could 'ear. Soppy Sandra were rooaring 'er eyes out, 'er old man were blowing 'is top and 'er old woman were tellin' 'em both to shurrup cos all t'neighbours could 'ear. It were great.'

'She should have been more careful,' said Terry, sounding like his father.

Roy tried to impress us. 'You can't get pregnant, tha knows, if t'bloke 'as an 'ot shower before he does it.'

'We know that!' snapped Jimmy, as ignorant as I was.

'But you can if you swim too close to somebody at t'swimming baths and they pee in t'watter,' said Terry.

'And if you put your tongue in their mouth when tha snoggin'', that's a sure way,' Jimmy informed us, chancing his arm.

'Or have a bath after somebody,' declared Roy confidently, not wishing to be outdone by the other two experts.

'Who told thee that?' asked Terry, fascinated.

'Our kid.' Roy winked. 'This buffer lass in t'cutlery section where he works 'ad twins after 'avin' a bath after t'lodger. He told me.' Roy then added, to give some authority to his brother's interesting information, 'He's cooartin', our Barry, tha knaws.'

I had remained silent and then three pairs of eyes turned in my direction. 'Have you been told t'facts o' life then, Phinny?' asked Roy.

'Course I have,' I lied, attempting to sound blasé. 'My dad told me last year.'

Dad never discussed anything of that sort. I am sure he would have been acutely embarrassed, as I certainly would have been. There was no sex education at school, nothing remotely sexual on the television, no books on the library shelves about 'the facts of life', and most parents shied away from broaching the subject, so we learnt in the playground from the supposed experts and heard many a fanciful story. My mother left a few medical books strategically placed about the house, perhaps hoping I would learn that way, but they were written in small cramped print and the contents were tediously detailed and uninteresting. I much preferred Biggles, who never ever got up to that sort of thing. He was too busy winning the war.

School was, of course, no help at all in preparing us for the onset of adolescence. One morning after assembly we were shown a short black and white film about 'the birds and the bees'. It *was* literally about the birds and the bees and made no sense at all. All I recall was a man lying on his back in a corn-field and the wind dispersing the seeds of a dandelion clock as he stared into a clear sky. The symbolism was completely lost on me. Nowadays, of course, schools have sex education built into the curriculum and very little is left to the imagin-ation. I recall once sitting in on a sex education lesson in a primary school. The visiting expert gave a very graphic account, illustrated with an animated film, of where babies came from to a hall of very attentive children. At the end he asked for questions. A boy at the back, a cheeky-faced little individual, the one you might predict would ask the difficult or embarrassing question, raised his hand. I saw the teachers give each other a look that said, 'I might have guessed it would be him.'

'Yes, young man?' asked the visiting expert cheerfully. 'What would you like to know?'

'Will we still be having rounders this afternoon?' asked the child.

It strikes me as very strange now that my mother – a midwife – never discussed such things with me but was prepared to let me find out for myself. We talked about many, many things around the kitchen table but there were certain things she must have felt were unsuitable. After her death in 1979 strangers would stop me in the street to offer their condolences and tell me stories about Nurse Phinn, how she had delivered a baby in the upstairs room of a public house, how she had saved the life of a toddler who was choking on a chip, how she had rushed round to a neighbour's house when a distraught father sought her help for his daughter who had been badly scalded, how she had reassured a worried parent after their baby had been circumcised. I learnt from a headteacher that she had toured schools to give talks to schoolgirls about 'the time of the month'. But she never told me anything about growing up and the changes of adolescence.

My earliest memory of my mother was sitting at the kitchen table making gingerbread men. The gingerbread men in the Grafton's Bakery in Rotherham all looked exactly alike and formed from a template. Mine were individuals. Some had large ears, others long noses, some were small, others fat and squat and some had long thin legs and spidery arms. I remember stirring the light brown mixture and then forming the figures, pressing in the currants for the eyes and nipples and tummy buttons. With a large wooden spoon I would scrape out the bowl as I waited for the gingerbread men to cook. When they came out of the oven I would line them up like soldiers. I was always loath to eat them. Mum would chant:

> Run, run as fast as you can,
> You can't catch me,
> I'm the Gingerbread Man!

Periodically she would have a big bread bake. I would help mix the flour and milk and yeast, then knead the dough in a large bowl before it was placed before the open fire in the living room with a damp teacloth over the top and left for the mixture to rise. I loved the bread, soft and warm with melted butter on the top. When I smell the aroma of baking bread I think of my mother.

She was not a great cook and her dishes were never fancy. Casseroles and chops with mashed potatoes and tinned garden peas or carrots, rissoles, shepherd's pie, egg and chips, minced beef – this was our staple diet. Scrag-end and brisket were popular, and many people, like my father, liked plenty of fat on the meat. The main course was followed by a pudding or a crumble. Rice puddings were my favourite. My mother would put a pint of milk in a metal dish with sugar and suet and sprinkle nutmeg on the top. I loved the brown skin that formed on the top and was usually the one who scraped out the tin afterwards.

On Sunday it was a small roast joint augmented by mashed and roast potatoes, cabbage, carrots and parsnips, all covered in thick gravy. Before we tucked into the joint, however, there was Yorkshire pudding and onion gravy. A thick slab of Yorkshire pudding was always consumed before the meal to fill us up, and could also be eaten at the end with treacle drizzled on top as an alternative to dessert. For Sunday tea there was a selection of sandwiches – Shippam's fish paste, egg and cheese, potted meat, Marmite and sandwich spread, the last and my least favourite consisting of chopped-up vegetables in a sticky mayonnaise, a concoction closely resembling vomit. The second course was always Wagon Wheels (large round chocolate-covered marsh-mallow biscuits), scones with jam and a trifle. Sometimes a tin of peaches in sweet, sticky juice would be served and covered in Carnation milk. My father would sit with a large napkin tucked into his shirt front and after the repast would announce he had had 'an excellent sufficiency'.

Mealtimes were important occasions in our house. We children took it in turns to set the table and we were responsible for clearing away and washing 'the pots' afterwards. We would never sit, as many youngsters do today, in front of a television set with our dinner on our knees but shared a family meal together when we would talk, say what we had been doing that day, relate anecdotes, tell jokes and air our opinions. Sometimes they were lively affairs when we argued and disagreed, but if voices were raised, my mother would promptly put a stop to it with 'That'll do!' It is not nostalgia to say that we have lost something with the demise of the family meal. When as a family we cease to interact over a shared meal, come together at the table and talk, we cease to enrich each other's lives, to articulate needs, share feelings and ideas, stimulate, inspire and support each other.

Mum trained at Blackburn Royal Infirmary from 1928 to 1931 as a state registered nurse. She did well in her examinations and left with a sparkling reference from the Matron, a Miss Gibbon, who described Nurse Mullarkey SRN as 'highly efficient, conscientious and loyal'. By the time I arrived on the scene she had added various other nursing qualifications to her name; she had become a state certified midwife and been promoted from school nurse to health visitor, touring homes in a deprived part of Rotherham. Canklow, her 'patch', was an area of endemic poverty, of densely packed rows of mean, back-to-back, redbrick terraces.

Very often I would search through my toy cupboard for a Dinky toy or a lead soldier, for a ball or a game, only to be told by Mum: 'It's gone to Canklow.' It was the same with clothes. My brother Michael would ask where a particular tie had gone, or Alec would comment on the disappearance of his favourite shirt, to receive the predictable reply: 'It's gone to Canklow.' Soon we became so used to hearing the familiar phrase that Mum would start: 'It's . . .' and we would all chorus: 'Gone to Canklow.'

In the airing cupboard my mother kept a pile of clean new vests and underpants of various sizes, neatly folded and kept at the back. These were the 'Canklow undies' which, over the winter, she would take for the children on her patch. Some children, she told me, were sewn into their vests for the winter and arrived at the clinic dirty, smelly and verminous. She always sent them away clean, disinfected and with a new vest and underpants. 'It's the least I can do,' she told us.

At tea my mother would tell us stories about her visits on the Canklow estate. One stays in my mind. It was of a young man, the eldest of six, who worked as a bellhop at one of Sheffield's top hotels. The house was dark and dirty and the father, a 'ne'er-do-well', as Mum described him, would slouch in front of the fire smoking and grunting. The internal doors of the house had been replaced by the council so many times they probably lost count, because when the inhabitants had run out of coal, anything which would burn was chopped up and put on the fire. Three or four scraggly-looking chickens clucked away in a pen in the back yard surrounded by piles of rubbish. Mum would call to see the new baby to find the young man carefully pressing his uniform. He looked as if he had scrubbed himself with wire wool, for his face shone as red as a polished apple. He was always cheerful and whistling as he ironed. The white gloves, the polished shoes, the red belt with the silver buckle, the pillbox hat were arranged on the table. Each day he would catch the bus to the city and at the end of the week would hand over his wages and tips to support the family.

'He'll go far, that young man,' Mum told us. She didn't need to spell it out. We were made to feel very privileged.

6

The bane of my mother's life when she visited the houses in Canklow were the dogs. She always assumed the worst in any canine until, in later life, she acquired one of her own. As someone who had been bitten by a savage little terrier early on in her career as a health visitor and still carried the scar on her ankle, she assumed they were 'up to no good' when they came trotting down the path madly wagging their tails, and she was deeply suspicious of the owner's predictable claim that the creature was 'only playing'. My mother would come home with graphic tales of these huge and ferocious beasts guarding the gates of the houses. The dogs were trained, or so she said, to attack anyone in a uniform or a dark suit; police officers, electricity meter readers, rent men and bailiffs were especial objects of attack and never got through the front gate or, if they did, very soon departed at great speed with the dog snapping at their heels.

My mother in her dark blue health visitor's coat and brown leather case was an obvious target for dangerous dogs. When the inhabitant of a particular house, with its trained canine sentinel standing at the gate, saw it wasn't an unwelcome visitor, he would shout an order to the snarling cur, which would then obediently flop down and let my mother pass. Then a disembodied voice from the direction of the house would shout, 'It's all reet, nurse, it'll not 'urt thee. It's as daft as a brush.' I guess my mother smiled nervously at the inappropriateness of that simile. My mother always carried a substantial leather bag, which she was adept at wielding like a weapon, and a large pepperpot, just in case of an attack, and on more than one occasion she had had recourse to use them both in warding off a vicious guard dog.

Once a particularly vicious beast called Major, a huge red-haired mongrel, attacked a small girl while my mother was visiting the area, seizing its victim by the leg until the child's mother warded it off with a broom handle. The angry mother carried the distressed child to Nurse Phinn for first aid, saying she had told the police umpteen times about the dog but they had done nothing about it.

'T'police never like coming down to Canklow, you know, nurse,' she observed. This came as no surprise to my mother.

On her way back to Ferham Clinic that afternoon my mother called into the police station and laid it on thick, saying that the child could have been savaged to death by this rabid dog and that something had to be done urgently. She would be reporting the incident to the Chief Medical Officer. As a result of my mother's intervention and her great gift for storytelling, the owner of the dog was summonsed and told to take the beast to the vet to have it 'put down', otherwise there would be a substantial fine. The authorities would pay a visit in the near future to make sure he had complied with the order.

Several weeks later Mother happened to call at the man's house. At the door stood a dog. It was the same size as Major, with the same pricked-up ears, tail, face and cold eyes. It was an identical creature but it was jet black.

'Down, Colonel,' ordered the owner.

'Where is the other dog,' asked my mother, 'the ginger-haired one?'

'Oh, 'e ran off, nurse,' the man told her bare-faced. 'Must 'ave sensed that 'is days were numbered. Not seen 'im this side of a week.'

'And this dog?' enquired my mother, eyeing the shiny black mongrel suspiciously.

'Oh, this is another one,' said the man. 'His name's Colonel and 'e's as gentle as a lamb.' The dog displayed a set of teeth like tank traps.

My mother later discovered that the owner had dyed the dog black to evade its execution.

She accompanied a social worker to the house some weeks later when she wanted him to look at a baby who was under-nourished and whom she thought might be neglected. My mother warned him about the dangerous dog and suggested he rattle the gate to see if the beast was about.

'No need, nurse,' said the man casually. 'I can handle dogs.'

As she walked nervously behind him while he sauntered up the path, the Hound of the Baskervilles appeared from round the back.

'Be careful,' my mother warned her companion, reaching for the pepperpot and ready to swing her bag. 'That dog's vicious.'

'Don't worry, nurse,' he replied nonchalantly. 'I have come across many dogs in my time.'

The creature, the size of a small bear, bounded towards them, teeth bared, tail in the air and ears back. The social worker, whom my mother described as a small insignificant-looking man with a bald head and large ears, remained perfectly motionless until the dog leapt up. He then promptly punched it on the right hinge of its jaw, knocking the beast out cold. 'You have to know how to handle dogs,' he told her calmly. 'I was a boxing champion in the army.'

After that, Major or Colonel was indeed 'as gentle as a lamb'.

At a parents' meeting at Canklow Woods Junior School when I was an education adviser in Rotherham, I met a grand-mother who remembered Nurse Phinn with great affection. She related to me the time my mother dressed the wound of another child who had been bitten by a stray dog on Canklow Road, how she calmed down and reassured the whole family and told them she would report the matter to the police when she had returned to the clinic. My mother, so the woman told me, left the house to find the rabid-looking creature snarling and slavering at the gate. She reached into her bag, produced the pot of pepper, took off the top, proceeded down the path and threw the contents into the face of the dog. The creature coughed and sputtered and ran off whimpering. At this point the man of the house emerged and asked my mother rather sheepishly, 'Has it gone, nurse?'

My mother would tell me tales about when she was training to be a nurse and would bubble with laughter. Mischievous doctors would send young trainee nurses up to the pharmacist for a couple of 'fallopian tubes' or a packet of 'Bowman's capsules' (Bowman's capsules are tubes in the body surrounded by blood vessels). They would send the innocents up to Sister (never to Matron, who took a very dim view of these pranks) for some 'islets of Langerhans' (the inside cells of the pancreas which produce hormones) or a couple of 'unciforms' (the hamate bone of the wrist). My mother herself, as a young nurse, had been subjected to such a trick when a doctor asked her to fetch his 'anatomical snuffbox'. She later discovered this was an area of the wrist surrounded by tendons and not an actual container.

When she became a theatre sister, part of her role was to induct the new recruits into the profession. She warned the trainee nurses to be wary of such tricks. One particular surgeon, not noted for his sense of humour, was an irascible, impatient and rather rude man but my mother said he could be forgiven for his personality defect because he was such a skilful surgeon and had saved many lives. My mother warned the new recruits to be very wary of this particular surgeon, not to address him at all but if he were to speak to them to always answer him as 'Mr', rather than 'Doctor', for in the medical world surgeons and consultants are correctly referred to as such. They were told that if he gave them an instruction they should follow it to the letter. He had been known to throw a whole tray of instruments on the floor of the operating theatre in a furious outburst. On one occasion he asked a young nurse watching proceedings nervously from the door of the operating theatre to make herself useful and 'fetch sister's coat'. Thinking this might be a ruse, she asked him if this was some sort of joke. The surgeon exploded and demanded that she 'fetch sister's coat immediately' as instructed.

'Do as you are told, nurse!' ordered my mother, as red-faced as the surgeon. The young nurse scurried off and returned carrying my mother's coat. The surgeon looked heavenwards and, controlling his temper, informed her it was the 'cystescope' that he required.

One trainee nurse, a permanently cheerful Jamaican woman with a beaming smile and sunny disposition, was assisting the anaesthetist in another operation.

'Arm board,' he said, meaning the device on which the patient's arm rests prior to the administering of the anaesthetic. The nurse nodded and smiled but made no move.

'I said arm board, nurse,' repeated the anaesthetist sharply.

'Ah'm bored too, doctor,' she replied pleasantly, 'but we'll soon be going home.'

My mother would, on occasions, commit her stories to paper and read them to me, and I still possess her lively accounts written carefully on white unlined foolscap paper. A favourite character who appeared in many of her accounts was Jinny. In one she wrote the story of their first meeting.

I first met Jinny whilst on my rounds as a health visitor. My superintendent had requested that I call at the young woman's house as there had been complaints from neighbours regarding Jinny's welfare. I duly called at the mean little terraced dwelling and knocked tentatively on the paint-peeling door. After what seemed to me a great length of time the door slowly opened and a face with large, sad grey eyes, a runny nose and an open expression peered at me. It was clear that the poor woman was mentally deficient. She was dressed in a shabby and heavily stained long black dress and her greasy hair, in need of a good wash, was tucked up untidily inside a sort of tam-o'-shanter.

'Who is it?' came a voice from within.

'It's a lady,' replied the woman, staring at me as if I were some strange exotic creature.

'What does she want?'

'What do you want?' she snapped.

'I need to speak to your mother,' I told her.

'Got no mother,' she said bluntly. 'She's dead.'

'Your father then.'

'Got no father,' she said. 'He run off.'

'Who looks after you?' I asked.

'Granddad.'

'Well, I need to speak to him. Tell him I'm a nurse.'

My words were conveyed to the person inside the house. 'She's a nurse and she wants to speak to you.'

'Tell 'er to come in,' said the voice.

'Have you a dog?' I asked.

'No.'

'Then I shall come in.'

Inside the dwelling, which had an unpleasant musty smell, sat an aged man as close to a blazing fire as physically possible, his feet in a bowl of steaming water. He ignored me.

'Jinny, fetch me some more 'ot watter, will tha?' He looked at me. 'It's good for my rheumatics, tha knaas.'

The young woman scurried off, returning a moment later with a large blackened kettle full of boiling water, which she proceeded to pour into the bowl. 'Slowly!' snapped the old man. 'I don't want bloody scaldin' to deeath!'

The old man informed me that his granddaughter was 'not reight in t'head' and had been allowed out of Middlewood, the mental institution in Sheffield, to attend her mother's funeral and had never been collected. 'Anyroad,' he said, 'what does tha want?'

I told him, as tactfully as I could, that the authorities felt he should have some help with Jinny. He grunted, then turning to Jinny said, 'Get t'nurse a cup o' tea.'

I thanked him but declined the offer for I saw the unwashed crockery on the table, the dust and dirt and the untidy state of the room.

A young man then appeared in the scene, stripped to the waist. 'If she dunt get weshed,' he told me and pointing to Jinny, 'I'll bloody swing for her. She stinks!' He then left the room as quickly as he had entered.

'Lodger,' said the old man. 'Fine figure of a man, isn't he, nurse?' He winked.

I didn't reply but told him I would take Jinny to the clinic and make sure she had a bath and her hair washed and I would arrange to have her feet, which seemed to cause her some distress, seen to by the chiropodist.

'Tha not tekkin 'er back to mental place then?'

'I'll speak to the doctor,' I told him.

I collected Jinny the next day, watched by several curious neighbours, and at the clinic saw to it she had a good hot bath, had her hair washed and was given a change of underwear and some fresh clothes. She looked a different person and beamed when she caught sight of herself in the mirror.

Then the chiropodist arrived, a big, bumptious man who always managed to appear at the clinic in time for tea. None of the nurses liked him for he was a lazy man and a snob to boot. He stood by the window, staring out and fingering his silver watch chain with one hand and in the other holding the small cup between a fat finger and thumb.

'The medical officer asks if you would please attend to this person,' I told him. The chiropodist surveyed Jinny with distaste. 'Are her feet clean?' he asked me.

'They are,' I replied.

'I am rather busy today,' he told me, extracting the watch from his waistcoat pocket and glancing at it. 'Can it wait?' I had an idea he was intending to send an assistant to deal with this particular client.

'No, it can't,' I told him, sharply. 'The medical officer says she is in need of urgent attention.'

When Jinny uncovered her feet the chiropodist gasped in disbelief and gave me a look which would freeze soup in pans. 'Dear God,' he mouthed, staring at the talons which were displayed before him.

'Doctor won't hurt me, nurse, will he?' groaned Jinny.

It was with great satisfaction that I informed her that, 'This is not a doctor, Jinny, it's the man who will cut your toenails.'

The chiropodist gave another grimace. The job having been done, I enquired of him when he would like to see Jinny again.

'Never! Never! Never!' he growled, pushing his instruments roughly into his bag and making a hasty departure.

My mother's stories, written in meticulous longhand, show a real talent for storytelling. There is sharp observation, lively dialogue, an authenticity and attention to detail which make her stories very entertaining. I am sure that if a certain editor at Penguin had not seen some potential in my own writing and opened a door for me when she read the first drafts of my Dales books, my stories about the life of a school inspector in Yorkshire would, like my mother's, have remained unpublished.

7

My mother loved music and could play any popular melody on the piano. Although she could read music, she tended to play by ear and if a tune came on the wireless she could replicate it in no time at all. There were many evenings and Sunday afternoons when we would go into the front room to listen to her play and we would sing along. My father's favourite song, which he used to sing in a deep bass voice, was 'If I Were a Blackbird'. I would crouch under the piano with my back to the mahogany and whistle along.

Mum had a collection of large black vinyl 78-rpm gramophone records which she played on the radiogram in the front room. There were one or two classical pieces – Chopin and Mozart – but mostly they were popular melodies and songs performed by Josef Locke, John McCormack, Kenneth McKellar, Alma Cogan and David Whitfield. She prized 'If I Were a Blackbird', sung and punctuated with whistles by Ronnie Ronalde. For the Christmas party at Broom Valley Juniors the children were asked to bring along a record and I was allowed to take the precious 78. It says a great deal about my mother that she trusted an eight-year-old boy with one of her most treasured possessions. Of course, the inevitable happened. I used to take a short cut to school through the allotments, and that day was just emerging through the iron gates leading on to Broom Valley Road when two boys from the estate jumped out on me, grabbed the record and flicked it like a Frisbee high over the green sheds and cold frames until it shattered on a far wall. I flew at them red with fury, but being much bigger and stronger than I, they punched me

hard in the chest, pushed me into the nettles and ran
off laughing. I was distraught and spent the whole of the
Christmas party sulking in a corner and wondering whatever
I should tell my mother. When I arrived home I didn't go
into the details of how the record had been smashed. I just
said I had dropped it and I was sorry. Some parents would,
no doubt, have berated the child for his stupidity and lack of
care, but my mother merely said, 'It's only a record. We can
get another.' But we never did get another.

My mother's reaction to the broken record was typical. On
another occasion, my brother Alec and I were wrestling in
the front room and I fell backwards into Mum's china cabinet.
In the large reproduction piece of furniture Mum kept her
bits of precious china, her tea service given as a wedding
present, assorted Coronation mugs, small cut-glass trays,
commemorative plates, a small porcelain figurine of a lady
with a parasol given to her by her friend Mrs Gill, a paper-
weight brought back by Dad when he was in Egypt with the
army and other delicate items well out of reach of the children.
I crashed back into the cabinet, smashing the glass and most
of the contents.

Two miserable boys waited in trepidation at the bottom of
Richard Road for the Cowrakes Lane bus to stop on Broom
Valley Road. Mum, in her blue health visitor's coat and clutching the brown case, saw us and rushed to meet us. 'Whatever's
happened?' she asked, a frightened look in her face. We
explained as we followed her up the hill heads down, not
wishing to meet her eyes.

'That's a very silly thing to do, isn't it?' she said after an
interminable silence. 'A silly and dangerous thing to do.' We
continued to stare at the ground. 'Are either of you hurt?' We
shook our heads. 'Well, I hope it's taught you both a lesson.'

On our hands and knees we collected together all the bits
of broken china and, with pathetic expressions on our faces,

deposited them in the dustbin. We gave up our pocket money for two weeks to help with the repair. My sister now has the cabinet with its tell-tale signs of damage.

The experience did not teach us a lesson. A couple of weeks later, Alec and I were at it again, wrestling – this time in the living room. Alec, who staggered back and fell, tried to regain his balance, reached out and knocked the large orange vase kept on the mantelpiece. It shattered into a thousand pieces. We had a short discussion and this time we decided to lie and blame Whisky the cat. When Mum came in we told an elaborate tale about how the cat had jumped from the chair, frightened by a backfiring car in the road.

When my mother was eighty years old I finally told the truth. I was at her house, just around the corner from where I lived, with my three little boys on our Saturday morning visit and the vase came into the conversation.

'Do you remember that very ugly vase that I used to have, the bright orange one?' she asked me.

'I think so,' I equivocated. 'Why?'

'There was one of these antique programmes in the television and one just like it sold for quite a lot of money. It was a Clarice Cliff and they're very collectable.'

'I have to tell you the truth,' I told my mother, finally. 'It's been on my mind for many years. I broke the vase. The cat was innocent.'

She thought for a moment before replying and then, much to the delight of my children, she said, 'Well, you had better go up to your room and say a prayer of contrition for blaming the poor cat. And,' she added, wagging a finger, 'you can go without your tea.'

In my parents' front bedroom was a large and ugly dressing table with three deep drawers. The bottom drawer was a veritable Aladdin's cave where my mother squirrelled away all sorts of presents. If any of us wanted a gift for a teacher or a girlfriend Mum would find something suitable from her bottom drawer. It was full of boxed lace handkerchiefs, bottles of scent, scarves, gloves, small leather purses, pieces of jewellery, cufflinks, bath salts, tablets of sweet-smelling soap and small china figures and dishes. We were not allowed to delve into her store of precious items. One teatime we were asked about the gloves. Mum had been given a pair of pale brown kid gloves with fur lining and had searched her bottom drawer for them but to no avail. Her friend Mrs Gill, who always bought tasteful and expensive presents, had given them to Mum at Christmas. Mum felt they were just too nice to wear and put them away. We all pleaded ignorance. One morning, some weeks later, my mother was visiting the primary school which my brother Michael attended, to assist with the TB injections. She looked through the headteacher's window to see her eldest son in the playground, in goal, wearing her prized gloves. She never said a word until he got home and then a few sharp words were said. He was an adult when she mentioned it again in passing. The following week Michael presented her with a brand new pair of pale brown kid gloves with fur lining.

One abiding memory of my mother was when she had a very dramatic nosebleed. I arrived home from school, I must have been eleven or twelve at the time, to find her in the living room with a blood-soaked towel pressed to her face. My father was at work and there was no sign of a brother or a sister to help me.

'Can you go and fetch Mrs Rogers,' my mother said calmly. I noticed that her hand was trembling. She must have seen the horrified look on my face and reassured me that it was just a nosebleed.

Mrs Rogers was a friend of my mother's and lived at the bottom of the hill on Broom Valley Road with her husband (Big David) and son (Little David), the latter being twenty-one and all of six foot two. She was a good-hearted, down-to-earth woman who possessed a loud expressive laugh and a dry wit, someone my mother described as 'the salt of the Earth'. She often called in for cup of tea and I would eavesdrop as she put the world to rights. Mrs Rogers was a woman noted for her memorable malapropisms and amazingly inventive *non sequiturs*. She spoke of her new 'sanitary unit' (sic) and the rude individual who 'testiculated' at her son when he was learning to drive. In any emergency she was the one to call upon. I rushed off and soon, in apron and fluffy bedroom slippers, Mrs Rogers accompanied me back to Number 19.

'I think we had better get the doctor,' she told me after attempting to stem the flow of blood. 'Tell Little David to go and fetch him.'

Dr Hagen was a large, distinguished-looking man with silver-white hair, a round red face and an air of authority. I had seen him at Mass, for he attended St Bede's with his wife and large family and always appeared to me a rather daunting figure with his serious face and penetrating eyes. That day he was good-humoured and chatty.

'A cup of tea would be very welcome, young man,' he said to me, as he proceeded to plug bits of lint up my mother's nostrils.

'I'll get that,' said Mrs Rogers. Before departing she whispered in the doctor's ear. 'I hope she's not one of those hermaphrodiziacs.'

Dr Hagen smiled and shook his head. 'Mmmmm,' he hummed after a while. 'It's not staunching the flow. I think we shall have to take you to the hospital, Mrs Phinn.' Then he turned to me. 'You can keep your mother company, eh?'

'Yes, doctor,' I said, my eyes filling up.

He patted my head. 'She'll be all right.'

Dr Hagen, who had other calls to make that day, dropped us off outside the Casualty Department on Doncaster Road.

We were told by a nurse to sit and wait and my mother would be attended to soon. I watched the clock on the wall and prayed it would not be too long. The time dragged and the blood continued to flow. Then my brother Michael arrived, parking his sports car directly opposite the entrance. He was on his way out that night and was dressed, as always, impressively smartly. Thoughtfully Mrs Rogers had left a note saying where we were.

'Why isn't she being attended to?' he demanded of me.

'I don't know,' I told him. 'We were told to wait.'

'Are you all right, Mum,' he asked my mother. She nodded but looked very pale and frightened.

'How long have you been waiting?' my brother asked me.

'About ten minutes,' I replied.

Michael strode off to the counter. I could hear his raised voice as he demanded some attention, and I saw him stabbing the air with a finger. He told me years later that words like 'medical negligence', 'blatant disregard' and 'the NHS Code of Conduct' had done the trick. His outburst certainly worked, for a moment later my mother was taken in a wheelchair down the long corridor and the blood vessel in her nose was cauterized.

'I'm sorry,' I said to my brother. I felt that I should have made more of a fuss and complained as he had done instead of just sitting there, but I'd felt afraid and helpless. 'I didn't know what to do,' I told him.

'You did all right,' he said. Michael ordered a taxi to take us home and my mother, cheerful after her ordeal, told him to go and meet the girl with whom he had a date.

The incident had a profound effect upon me. I had never seen my mother ill before, never seen her so helpless and pale, never really contemplated that one day she would not be around. As children we expect that our parents, like the weather, will always be with us. Then they go and there is such a void in our lives.

After I had taken my O levels Mum and Mrs Gill took me for a weekend to Paris as a reward for working hard. My excitement was palpable. It was the first time I had been abroad and the first time I had been on an aeroplane. The tour group consisted of largely elderly people who made a great fuss of the only youngster, pressing sweets and small amounts of money into my hand.

We spent three days in the Bon Accord, a cramped little hotel down a dark and rather smelly backstreet, but to me, who had never stayed in a hotel in my life, it was such an adventure. I loved the breakfast of sweet hot chocolate served in huge white cups, the crusty rolls with soft warm insides and the flaky croissants served with creamy butter and apricot jam. We saw the sights and I marvelled at the Sacré Coeur, the Eiffel Tower and the Louvre, but my favourite place was Notre Dame. This was not like St Bede's, the church I attended in Rotherham. The cathedral was vast, atmospheric and stunningly beautiful, with huge arches and magnificent stained-glass windows. On the Sunday morning we attended High Mass in Notre Dame, crowded with worshippers. I breathed in the incense-filled air and the heavy aroma of lilies, stared spellbound at the procession of the bishop and the attendant priests dressed in great embroidered gold cloaks (copes), listened to the overwhelmingly beautiful music, and joined in with the chanting of the Latin responses, which I knew by heart. I felt part of some very special coterie. I had seen the black and white film based on the Victor Hugo classic *Notre Dame de Paris*, starring Charles Laughton, and, as I stared heavenwards to the huge arched roof and heard the great tolling of the bells, I could almost imagine somewhere beyond, high in the tower, the hunched figure of Quasimodo swinging madly on the ropes.

During our visit we had our photographs taken on the banks of the Seine. The photographer was a con-man, a friendly, attentive, well-dressed individual. He pretended to take photographs, telling us they could be collected from the kiosk, which he pointed out, the following day. Mum paid him but when we went to collect the photographs they were, of course, not there and neither was the photographer.

My mother's poor opinion of the French didn't improve when we went for dinner that evening. Mrs Gill took us to a smart restaurant in Montmartre. It was a sumptuous place with white tablecloths, shining silver cutlery and great glittering chandeliers. I suppose we looked an odd trio: Mrs Gill in her elegant suit with the fur collar, my mother in her far-from-fashionable outfit, accompanied by a gawky long-haired youth in baggy flannels and a shapeless jumper.

A rather snooty waiter, attired in a black apron which very nearly touched the ground, presented us with the menus – huge, square, fancy-looking folders with all the dishes written inside in French. None of us could speak a word of the language and we stared for an inordinate amount of time until Mrs Gill, taking the initiative, called the waiter over and, pointing to the set menu, placed the order. The waiter returned to the table some time later carrying a bowl of cut lemons in small glass dishes, a large bottle containing a liquid which looked a lot like vinegar and a huge plate of oysters, open and sparkling in the bright lights and resting on a bed of brown shiny seaweed. Then the snails arrived on a special china plate with small hollows to accommodate the little shelled creatures. I stared in horror as the waiter placed the small fork before me to enable me to extract the garlic-smelling gastropods and said, smirking, *'Bon appétit!'*

We were cautious eaters in our house back in Rotherham and tended to look with great suspicion on the rare occasions when we were faced with food with which we were unfamiliar. We never ate spaghetti (unless from a tin soaked in tomato sauce), any cheese (other than Cheddar); we never touched garlic, mayonnaise (we ate salad cream), veal, shrimps, yoghurt, noodles, brown bread, sweet potatoes, pâté, any spices other than salt and pepper or anything else deemed 'foreign'. Fish was invariably cod and came perfectly rectangular in shape and smothered in bright orange breadcrumbs. When the fish arrived that evening, head, skin, tail, fins, eyes and all, I lost my appetite. The third course, cubes of white meat suspended in a pale yellow jelly, made me feel sick.

Some say that memories, even the most precious ones, fade surprisingly quickly with time. Well, the recollection of my mother's face when she saw the oysters, the snails and the fish with the popping eyes will never fade. Her mouth dropped open.

I watched the other customers, who were downing their own oysters with gusto, holding each shell between finger and thumb, tipping the contents into their open mouths and smacking their lips. I stared in fascination as they poked away at the snail shells with the little forks and cracked open the claws of bright pink lobsters.

We sat upright and motionless, staring at the untouched food with expressions of distaste. Mrs Gill called for the bill, which she paid hurriedly, and we left, I am sure much to the amusement of the waiter and the other diners. The whole meal had remained untouched. Leaving the restaurant my mother observed, 'I'd rather drink a phial of prussic acid than face that again.'

A couple of weeks after our Parisian adventure Mrs Gill persuaded my rather reluctant mother to accompany her to Harrogate for the day and I went along too. It was an altogether grander place than Rotherham – elegant, genteel, rather full-of-its-own-importance. There were wide tree-lined streets, impressive Georgian mansions, opulent hotels, majestic churches, expensive antique shops, fields and parks and the famous Royal Baths and Pump Room. The discovery of a

chalybeate in the sixteenth century changed this small insignificant town into a spa to rival Bath, Cheltenham and
Tunbridge Wells. The fame of its healing waters spread
and soon the rich and fashionable were flocking to Harrogate
to 'take the waters'.

We had afternoon tea at Bettys Tea Room on Parliament
Street. It was the most elegant place I had ever been to. Everything was bright and clean and stylish. We waited in a queue
until we were shown to a corner table covered in a spotless
and stiff white cloth and set out with delicate china cups,
saucers and plates and heavy silver cutlery. In the centre was a
single flower in a small glass vase.

A man sat at a grand piano playing classical music, smiling
waitresses in pristine white blouses, starched aprons and
dainty caps moved serenely from table to table, and refined
people drank from their china cups and dabbed the corners
of their mouths with pure white napkins. Tea was dispensed
from a heavy silver teapot, and a tiered set of sparkling white
plates arranged with delicate wafer-thin cucumber and
salmon finger sandwiches, tiny iced cakes, butterfly buns,
squares of heavy fruit cake, meringues and custard tarts was
placed before us.

'This is more like it, Madge,' said my mother, looking
around approvingly. 'When I caught sight of those winking
oysters and fish with their heads still on and their eyes. Oh,
their eyes —'

'Don't, Pat,' interrupted her friend, reaching for a sandwich,
'Least said.'

I returned to Bettys Tea Room some twenty years later
and I was delighted to see that it had changed little. On this
occasion I was accompanied by an American professor who
wished to visit 'the best teashop in the country'. As we walked
through the grand entrance to the restaurant, Quentin looked
as overawed as I had done as an adolescent all those years before.

'This is truly British,' he said, before heading for a table by the window already occupied by two elegantly dressed, elderly ladies who were taking afternoon tea.

'May we join you?' Quentin asked one of the ladies pleasantly.

If looks could maim, my American colleague would have ended up on crutches, for the face that stared up at him was that of a latter-day Medusa. 'Certainly not!' snapped one of the women. 'You hev your own table at Bettys. Furthermore you should queue.' She indicated a discreet little brass plaque on a stand which instructed customers to 'Please wait to be seated.'

We were shown to a table next to the one where the two women were sitting. I could tell as I commented on the surround-ings that Quentin was clearly more interested in the conversation on the adjacent table than he was in listening to me.

'Tell me, Gervase,' he whispered, nodding his head in the direction of the two women, 'is this rehearsed? It's like an Alan Bennett monologue.'

I eavesdropped too.

'Do you know, Joyce,' one of the women was saying, 'I was up and down those steps like a shuttlecock.' I imagined she meant a yo-yo. 'If I vomited once, I vomited five times. Mountainous, that was what the sea was like. Up and down like a fiddler's elbow. I was stuck in the ladies' lavatory with my head down a toilet bowl, heaving and splashing and the sea was outside heaving and splashing.' She paused for effect. 'And where was Sidney?' I assumed that the Sidney in ques-tion was the woman's long-suffering husband. 'I'll tell you where he was. He was in the restaurant with a French bap, a wedge of Camembert cheese and half a bottle of red wine.' Her companion nodded and grunted encouragingly. 'I'll tell you this, Joyce, if he'd have been on the *Titanic* he would be all on to raise himself up. Then he appears on deck asking me if I was all right and patting me on the back. I won't repeat what I said. I can't tell you how relieved I was to get my feet back on terra cotta.'

I recall chuckling and thinking that some time in the future that conversation would appear in one of my books. And indeed it did.

After my father died, my mother would be a regular visitor to our house on Sunday and would stay for lunch. I would ensconce her in a comfortable chair and give her a large sherry and the Sunday newspapers. One Sunday my third son, Dominic, had not done as he had been told – to tidy his bedroom. I was wagging my finger and playing the stern father when he started to smile, then laugh, and finally he collapsed on the floor in paroxysms of laughter. I ballooned with anger and was ready to smack his bottom for laughing at his daddy. As I looked up I caught sight of my mother in the mirror. She was in her chair behind me, pulling the most ridiculous face and waggling her fingers in front of her nose.

'Mother!' I exclaimed, no doubt rather pompously. 'I am endeavouring to instil some discipline here. You are not being very helpful at all.'

'Oh, do be quiet,' she sighed. 'You're not talking to teachers now.'

'Mother!'

'Don't "Mother!" me. Dominic's a lovely little boy. He's kind, considerate, well-behaved. You should thank God you've got such a child. My goodness me – an untidy room. Big deal! As I recall, your room was a tip when you were a child and I never went off alarmingly as you are doing now.'

'Mum –' I began.

'You will find that there are far more important things in life than an untidy room, I can tell you.'

'If I could –'

'I've come round for my Sunday lunch and a bit of peace

and quiet and all I get is you sounding off like Hitler on a soapbox.' I didn't say anything. Dominic stared at his grandma with his mouth wide open. Christine, my wife, tried to suppress a smile. 'I don't suppose I should be telling your daddy off in front of you, Dominic,' my mother continued, 'but he's wrong.' Then with a twinkle in her eye she added, 'And he sometimes forgets that he's my little boy.'

Following a massive stroke my mother was nursed for several months by my sister Christine. It was a tragic sight to see the suffering of such a strong-minded, generous and loving woman, paralysed and unable to speak and feed herself. She died one cold November afternoon like her mother, clutching her rosary beads. Her funeral was a quiet affair at St Mary's Church, Maltby, near Rotherham. We knew what hymns she would have wanted: 'O Sacred Heart of Jesus', 'O Bread of Heaven' and 'Star of the Sea'. They were the traditional hymns she'd grown up with and ones that are now rarely sung or even remembered. My sister read Psalm 121 from the Bible and I read a favourite prayer by Cardinal Henry Newman:

O Lord, support us all the day long, of this troubled life,
Until the shadows lengthen,
And the evening comes,
And the busy world is hushed,
And the fever of life is over,
And our work is done.

Then in your mercy,
Grant us safe lodging and a holy rest
And peace at last.

My brother Alec read at the graveside an American First Nation prayer:

Do not stand at my grave and weep;
I am not there, I do not sleep.
I am a thousand winds that blow.
I am the diamond glints on snow.
I am the sunlight on ripened grain.
I am the gentle autumn rain.
When you awaken in the morning's hush
I am the swift uplifting rush
Of quiet birds in circled flight.
I am the soft stars that shine at night.
Do not stand at my grave and cry;
I am not there. I did not die.

8

My mother's grandmother, Mary Touhy (née Brothers), a native of Portumna, County Galway, and her new husband arrived from rural Ireland to seek a better life across the water shortly after the Great Irish Potato Famine of the 1840s. She used to tell the story of how as a girl she would wade into the River Shannon and catch salmon between her knees. Her husband, Michael, hailed from Clonmel, County Tipperary, and came from a family of carpenters who supplied the coffins for the poorhouse in Nenagh.

In the early days of immigration from Ireland in the second half of the nineteenth century, the newcomers to England often made a poor impression and were disliked, even despised. Signs like 'No Irish, No Dogs' were common in boarding-houses. The Irish immigrants were likely to be very poor, lonely and ill-fed, and only wanted the chance to work and lead better lives, but the depth of their poverty and deprivation frequently degraded them and it is true that many sought an escape in the public houses. There developed a widespread view, reflected in the newspapers and periodicals of the time, that the Irish were noisy, dissolute and prone to drunkenness. But there were many who didn't fit this stereotype. My forebears who settled in Sheffield were far from undernourished, destitute or uneducated. They had a small amount of money and were proud, ambitious and determined folk who worked hard and settled well into their new life, eventually buying a small terraced house in Attercliffe, on the outskirts of Sheffield.

Attercliffe was a heavily populated part of the city, with row upon row of back-to-back, redbrick terraced housing with front doors leading out directly into the street, small, square back yards and outside privies. The landscape was devoid of trees and empty of colour but the houses appeared well kept, with white doorsteps and clean windows. This was where my grandmother was brought up.

My maternal great-grandparents, with help from their parents, had managed to save up to buy a passage to England and buy the modest terrace, determined to start a new life away from the devastation of a famished Ireland. Many Irish emigrants settled in Liverpool and Lancashire, but the Touhys moved further east and joined a small expatriate Irish community in Sheffield, centred on the recently built Catholic church of St Charles. It was clear that they both had a firmness of purpose and a driving ambition. Great-grandfather, a clever man who was largely self-taught and a tall, good-looking figure to boot, secured a job in the Sheffield Police Force, becoming P. C. E56 and rising to the rank of sergeant. His wife remained at home to bring up the five children.

Great-grandmother would make sure the windows and sills blackened by the grime of the industrial valley were wiped clean every morning and the front step was whiter than white when she had finished with the white chalk 'donkey stone'. She prided herself on keeping the smartest house in the street. Washing was done on Monday. All dirty clothes were washed in a large metal tub in the back yard, Great-grandmother using what she called a 'poncher' – a long, wooden-handled gadget with a perforated copper dome on the end. Washing would then go through the hand-operated mangle and be hung across the street on a long clothes-line. It couldn't be left out for too long otherwise it would be flecked with soot.

Once a week the large tin bathtub, kept upturned in the back yard, was brought into the house, placed before the fire and filled with warm water. The children, behind a makeshift curtain, would be bathed before the adults, scrubbed with brush and flannel impregnated with pink carbolic soap until their skin was red. The youngest would be first in, then the rest of the children, and finally, topped up with hot water boiled in a large copper kettle, it was Great-grandfather's turn. He would be allowed to soak.

Mrs Touhy was a fiercely proud woman who kept her children and herself clean, neat and tidy. She took such pride in the family's appearance that neighbours sometimes referred to her as 'the Duchess' and thought she considered herself a cut above them. They were a little wary of her husband because he was a policeman, but they were not too proud to call him out to settle a domestic dispute or have a quiet word with some of the local 'hobbledehoys' who made themselves nuisances.

One story my grandmother was fond of telling was when her father, on duty on Fitzwilliam Street in Sheffield, called into a grocer's shop to buy some eggs, which he placed for safe keeping in a paper bag underneath his helmet. He was then called to an altercation between a man and a woman who were causing a disturbance. He arrived to find the woman shrieking and her aggressor shaking her violently. When cautioned by P. C. Touhy, the man refused to give his name and ran off. My great-grandfather gave chase but slipped at the street corner and, falling to the ground, banged his head and helmet, cracking the eggs in the process. The woman stopped her wailing and promptly fainted, thinking that the slimy egg whites and bright yellow yolks dribbling down from underneath the policeman's helmet were his brains.

On another occasion he was called to help a drunken man who, having dropped his watch chain down a drain, had tried to recover it and in the process got himself wedged. Reaching down into the drain, the man lost his grip and slipped. When P. C. Touhy arrived he found a crowd of curious onlookers surrounding a pair of legs which were pointing heavenwards. He heaved and tugged and finally extricated the injured man, removing his trousers in the process. Rather than thanking him, the man pulled up his trousers angrily and demanded to know what my great-grandfather was intending to do about the lost watch and chain.

My grandmother, Anne, the youngest of the four sisters, was a bright, lively child by all accounts, excelling in English at school and leaving to train as a secretary. A picture of her shows a tall, immaculately dressed woman, straight-backed and stern, with dark Irish eyes. She met John Mullarkey, a young apprentice engineer at the local steelworks, fell in love and was soon married at St Charles's Roman Catholic Church, Attercliffe, on 4 August 1900. They set up home in Clough Street in Rotherham, where they started a family. The eldest child was Nora, born 1903, then came my mother, Margaret Patricia (Pat), born on St Patrick's Day, 1908, then James (Jimmy), born 1912, and last of all Mary Winifred, born at the outbreak of the First World War. Another child, Lawrence, died at the age of four. Mary was always known as Winnie – she was the 'apple of her mother's eye' and used to sit on the front step, a little princess in her white dress with her doll on her lap. Passers-by would comment on what a beautiful child she was. On one occasion a well-dressed woman offered to adopt her. My cousin Jane lent me a picture of her mother as a child, and Winnie was indeed unusually pretty with her great curls, dark eyes and pale skin.

Mary Winifred won a scholarship to Notre Dame High School in Sheffield. The uniform had to be purchased from the designated school outfitters near the school on Cavendish Street but my grandmother, being thrifty and with little money to spare, had the uniform made. When her youngest daughter came home from school that first week to tell her a nun had rounded on her in front of the other girls for not wearing the specified uniform, my grandmother paid Notre Dame a visit and told this particular nun in no uncertain terms that should she humiliate her daughter like that again in front of others she would do the same to her. She also reminded her of her vocation and that she was very fortunate to teach such a bright child.

The Mullarkey family was by no means well-off, but my grandmother managed the small amount of money meticulously. She would shop judiciously and was always on the look-out for a bargain. Once, my grandmother told me she recalled visiting the fish counter at Sheffield Market. Looking elegant in her Sunday best, she asked for any fish heads going free, which she would use to make the most delicious soup. 'For the cat,' she told the fishmonger.

'We haven't got a cat,' my mother piped up with all the honesty of a young child.

'Yes, we have,' said Grandma, giving her a knowing look.

'No, we haven't,' persisted my mother. Then she announced proudly to all in earshot that her mother boiled up the fish heads in a big pot over the fire for their tea.

Alma Road was the local school, but being from a Roman Catholic family the little Mullarkeys trekked across town to Masborough to attend St Bede's School, a dark, stone structure next to the church. Originally built in the late nineteenth century to meet the educational needs of R.C. children of all ages, it looked more like a prison or a workhouse than a school, with its blackened walls, greasy grey slate roof, small square windows and enveloping black wrought-iron fence.

Life for the small close-knit Catholic community in Rotherham centred on St Bede's Church, the school and the Catholic Club, and was dominated by the priest. The priest's word was law, and he was held in reverential respect, mixed with fear and wonder. Should any one of his flock miss Mass or leave Confession for too long he would be round asking why, and should a child not be at school it would be noted and mentioned to the parents after Mass.

John Mullarkey, my maternal grandfather, whom sadly I

never knew, was by all accounts a practical, industrious and ambitious man and worked hard to become a valued engineer at the great steelworks of Steel, Peach & Tozer in the Don Valley. I have a sepia photograph of him sitting proudly in a Windsor chair, staring at the camera with piercing eyes. He looks imposing with his large beard and high cheekbones, in a dark suit and a white shirt with starched collar. Soon he was 'on better money' and was able to move his growing family to a larger house with a garden on Gilberthorpe Street. The Mullarkeys were on their way up in the world.

My grandfather's brother, Patrick Mullarkey, who settled in the north-east of England, fought in the First World War. Something rarely quoted is that more Irishmen died in British uniform during the first two days of the Somme offensive than took part in the Easter Rising. Neither Irish Nationalist nor Ulster Unionist politicians are keen, I guess, on broadcasting this fact, but it is true nevertheless. In 1914 the Irish Volunteers enlisted almost en masse to fight for Great Britain, and Great-uncle Patrick joined up along with 140,000 other Irishmen, from the north and south of the island, to fight for the country in which he had come to live. A sergeant in the Tyneside (Irish) Battalion, he survived the war and went on to work in the shipyard. The only surviving picture of Patrick is on a small crumpled photograph showing a group of laughing young soldiers sitting among their kitbags. How I wish that they could reveal their chatter and lively humour. How I wish I knew more about him.

Such was John Mullarkey's skill and expertise as an engineer that he was promoted at the steelworks and sent to India to supervise the installation of blast furnaces, taking his son Jimmy with him. Jimmy's daughter, my cousin Monica, told the story (I can't vouch for the veracity, for she was a great storyteller, as indeed were all the Mullarkeys) that my grandfather caused a riot soon after he arrived there. The building of the blast furnaces was held up by a passive demonstration against

British rule. A thin, bald, insignificant-looking Indian wearing thick round glasses sat in silent protest, blocking the path of the workers to the steel foundry. My grandfather, a large and muscular man, was having none of this and when the small protester refused to move he carried him to the river and threw him in. The man was Gandhi. The troops were called out and mayhem ensued. Shortly afterwards my grandfather returned to England. None of the family spoke about what had happened, but I have a sneaking feeling he had a bit of a temper and enjoyed his Jameson's whisky a little too much. Most disappointed about his unexpected return was his eldest child, my Aunt Nora, who was all packed and ready to join him.

Aunt Nora and my mother trained as nurses. In the 1920s many of the trainees were Irish or of Irish extraction. Both my mother and my aunt had a natural aptitude for study and soon qualified as state registered nurses, with high marks in their examinations. Nora was quite a beauty and had a succession of eligible beaux. At the time when she was Sister-in-Charge of the Casualty Department at Doncaster Royal Infirmary she was walking out with a doctor, much to the delight of my grandmother, who had very high hopes for her children. She brought them up to believe that they were special and could achieve anything. My mother used to repeat Grandma's words: 'Aim for the moon and you might just go through the roof and reach the stars.'

I can picture Aunt Nora now, with her pale, penetrating blue eyes and affable smile. She could be charming, witty and entertaining but, like her two sisters, she had the sharp Mullarkey tongue and did not suffer fools gladly. She disliked in particular people who pretended to be something they were not. She was also fiercely defensive of those in her family, as I was soon to find out.

One Friday (I was about ten or eleven at the time) my mother kept me off school. I had been sick that morning and she said I could stay in and read my book. My father was on the night shift, so he was at home and could look after me. By lunchtime I was feeling much better and my father, thinking a bit of fresh air might do me good, asked me to go on an errand to the butcher's shop on Wellgate and fetch a couple of pounds of pork sausages for tea.

I was on my way back home, my mouth full of sweets and the sausages wrapped in greaseproof paper tucked under my arm, when a football bounced across Wellgate Road and landed in front of me.

'Chuck us t'ball back!' came a shout from behind the black iron railings that surrounded the playground of Wellgate Junior School. I picked up the ball, crossed the road and was about to throw it over the railings when an angry man bellowed at me from the school entrance.

'You, boy! Get in here!'

'Me?'

'Yes, you! Get in here now.'

Clutching the sausages in one hand and holding the football on the other, I approached the scowling figure. He reminded me of Mr Punch with his sharp chin and long beak of a nose.

'How many times do I have to tell you boys?' he asked.

'What?' I asked.

'What? What?' he repeated angrily. 'What what?'

'What?'

'What, sir, that's what! And empty your mouth. When you speak to a teacher you say "sir". I have told you boys time and time again not to kick footballs near the road or go outside the school playground at breaks.' His gullet rose and fell like a frog's. 'Now get into school.'

'But . . .' I started, trying to tell him that I was not a pupil at this school, but he raised a hand like a traffic policeman.

'No buts. Into school.' He pushed me towards the entrance and I was carried along with a group of boys and girls my age as they crowded through a door. I ended up in a tall-ceilinged classroom with high windows, standing at the front with forty pairs of eyes trained upon me.

'Are you the new boy?' demanded the teacher.

'No,' I replied.

'No, what?'

'No, I'm not.'

'No, sir! And what have you there?' he asked, stabbing a bony finger at the package which I held.

'Sausages,' I told him.

There was a ripple of laughter from the class.

'Sausages!' he roared.

'For my dad's tea.'

He thrust his face into mine. 'You are an insolent and disobedient boy,' he said, 'and you will soon learn that I do not like insolent and disobedient boys. Any more out of you and I shall cane you.'

There was no way this man was going to cane me, I thought, and could feel anger rising inside. 'I don't go to this school,' I blurted out. 'I go to Broom Valley Juniors. I'm off because I'm sick. I was on my way home with my dad's sausages and I was only trying to return a football. Now I'm going home.' I then headed for the door. Then as a final riposte, I added, 'And you are not my teacher.'

When I related the story (suitably embellished of course) to Auntie Nora she told me the man had no business detaining me and she would be 'having a word' with this particular teacher when she visited the school the following week to undertake the inspection for head lice. I should have loved to have been a fly on the wall when she made her visit.

Auntie Winnie was a bright and lively child and followed in her father's footsteps to work at Steel, Peach & Tozer as a comptometer operator. Jimmy, athletic, good-looking, always an adventurer and a charmer, joined the Irish Guards. The family was flourishing, and then tragedy struck. Grandfather

Mullarkey succumbed to a disease which he had probably contracted in India, and died a relatively young man, having seen only two of his seven grandchildren – my sister Christine and my cousin Audrey.

When Grandfather Mullarkey died, my grandmother, Anne, went to live with my Aunt Nora and her husband, my Uncle Ted. This seemed the best solution, since Auntie Nora and Uncle Ted had no children and owned a spacious house on the outskirts of Rotherham overlooking Herringthorpe Playing Fields. I would visit most Sundays, to find this formidable, striking-looking woman sitting in the front room at Number 38 Wickersley Road in her wing-backed armchair, watching the passers-by, listening to the wireless or reading a book. She was the archetypal matriarch, ensconced in her chair as if on a throne, presiding over the comings and goings of daughters and sons, grandchildren and cousins, friends and neighbours. On a small table she would have a large china cup and saucer, which I was deputed regularly to top up with good strong tea. If it was not 'strong enough to trot a mouse across it', and was 'as weak as dishwater', I would be told in no uncertain terms. If I left the spoon in the cup she would comment, 'That's how Lord Nelson lost his eye.'

I still recall her, in a dark woollen dress and thick brown stockings, with a cardigan draped over her shoulders and a red scarf around her neck fastened at the throat with my grandfather's silver tie-pin. She looked rather fearsome at first sight, but when she saw me her eyes lit up and she became this warm smiling figure who treated me with infinite patience and a sort of amused tolerance. From her Irish parents she had inherited a natural charm, a sharp wit, an absence of pomposity and an innate generosity. She clearly enjoyed the visits of her grandchildren and I, being the youngest, always felt she had a soft spot for me. I loved her company, for she was a great storyteller with a dry sense of humour combined with the graceful knack of being a very good listener.

9

My grandmother spoke a great deal about my grandfather but rarely about her own parents, except one Sunday when she told me how lucky they had been to escape the terrible famine in Ireland. Thousands died when the potato blight devastated crop after crop; many others emigrated to America and Australia and some came to England looking for a better life. Perhaps she felt some shame that her parents had survived the terrible suffering and distress through their flourishing trade in making coffins for the poor victims. Her parents had taken quite a risk, she told me, leaving everything behind, but then she added, 'If you don't take some risks in your life, you never get anywhere.'

When my third son, Dominic, was studying for his degree at Hull University, he had an assignment to complete on the Great Irish Potato Famine. He became increasingly interested in the topic and we would have long discussions well into the night. 'Did Grandma ever talk about it?' he asked. 'Did she tell you anything about her parents and how they managed to leave Ireland?' When he asked, both my parents were dead and I could be of little help because they had never mentioned it. There was only the vague memory of that long-ago conversation with my grandmother. This sudden interest in the Great Famine seemed to me to be an ideal opportunity for us to visit Ireland for a long weekend, so that Dominic could gain a more intimate knowledge about the disaster and at the same time I could undertake some research into my forebears, the Touhys.

We stayed at a small boarding-house in Portumna. The

landlady, one Mrs McCrudden, was a mine of detailed and gruesome information. Pursing her thin lips she described to my wide-eyed son how, a stone's throw from her very house, thousands had died at the side of the road, little children eating grass in a desperate attempt to stem their pitiful hunger, frail old women begging for crusts, weeping fathers and emaciated mothers, fields of rotting potatoes stinking to high heaven while the rich English landowners gorged themselves silly in their castles and big houses, sucking the very lifeblood out of the poor Irish people. She shook her head sadly and then asked, 'More toast, any of yous?' With polite smiles, we declined.

The first day we walked along part of what Mrs McCrudden described as the 'Old Famine Trail'. It was a hot, dry, dusty day, unusual for Ireland in the spring, when the country is usually enveloped in a soft rain and the sun is hidden behind billowing clouds. After a mile of gentle walking and interesting conversation, we caught sight of a strange obelisk some way off the track.

'This is probably a memorial to the many thousands who died in the Famine,' I observed. 'Shall we go and have a look and say a prayer?'

We headed along the dusty narrow path, which skirted a ploughed field, and very soon realized that the distance to the monument was deceptive. It was a great deal further off than we had thought. Tired and thirsty, we finally arrived at a large but incredibly crude construction. It looked as if a pile of old rubble had been cobbled together, bricks of all shapes, sizes and colours, bits of paving, broken breeze blocks, lumps of limestone, misshapen rocks, all held together tenuously by great gobs of cement and mortar.

'Don't get too close,' I warned Dominic.

The ugly, looming tower looked remarkably unsafe, and one hefty kick would have brought the whole lot tumbling down. A few yards from the amazing structure was a house-cum-hostelry with one rusting metal table and three old wooden chairs outside. At the door stood a friendly-looking individual with red cheeks and a fuzz of white hair. He nodded and smiled as we approached.

''Tis a lovely day,' he said.

'Yes, it is,' I replied.

We approached the memorial gingerly. At the base was a slab of pale concrete and written into it in large crude letters were the words: 'On this spot on the 17th March, 1857, nothing happened.' Dominic looked at me quizzically.

'What's it mean, Dad?' he asked.

'I've really no idea,' I replied.

We decided to sit outside and have a drink before we set off back down the dusty track, so we ordered two pints of Guinness. After an inordinate amount of time I popped my head around the door of the hostelry. The landlord was behind the counter reading a newspaper.

'Have you forgotten about us?' I asked.

'Is there a fire?' he asked.

I returned to the table outside. After another long wait, the friendly landlord emerged with the stout and, much to my amusement, deposited two cardboard beer mats on the rusting metal table, on top of which he placed the two pints.

'You have to let the Guinness settle,' he told me.

'I see,' I said, before taking a large, thirst-quenching gulp.

'You'll be from over the water then,' observed our host.

'Yes,' I replied, wiping my lips.

'Whereabouts?'

'Doncaster, South Yorkshire.'

'Would you be knowing my cousins the Flahertys? They live in Yorkshire.'

'I'm afraid not,' I said. 'Yorkshire is a big place. It's the size of Israel.'

'Is that so?'

'There are said to be more acres in the county than words in the King James Bible.'

'Now there's a thing.'

'What is this monument for?' asked Dominic, pointing to the strange tower of bricks and stone.

'Now, if I had a penny for every time someone asked me that,' the landlord replied, smiling widely. He drew up a chair and straddled it. 'You see, it's like this. As you can see, I'm a bit off the beaten track here and don't do a whole lot of business. In the summer we gets whole tribes of Americans, lovely people with a whole lot of money to spend and desperate for a bit of history. They don't have it in their country, you see. So they come over to Ireland and to this part of the world looking for their roots. They're not likely to divert in my direction, me being so far off the road. Now my tower here — I built it with my own hands a few years back — is a great draw, so it is. Seeing it from the road, aren't they thinking that it's some owld memorial to the Great Famine or the like and wouldn't it be a good idea for them to get a few photographs to take back home? And after they've walked along that dusty owld track on a hot summer's day aren't they as tursty as a camel in a sandstorm and just gagging for a drink?' There was a twinkle in the dark eyes. 'Just like yous. I got the idea from the monument at Recess, just opposite the owld craft shop there. Tourists in their coaches stop to look at the great needle of stone and then they call into the shop. "On this site in 1897," it says, "nothing happened." Then there's another monument in Connemara dedicated to Conn, Son of the Sea, which says, "Erected for no apparent reason." The Irish aren't as stupid as some folks like to think, you know.'

The following morning I enquired at the post office if anyone knew of the Touhys who had lived thereabouts. The postmistress, a round, red-cheeked individual, thought for a moment, nodded sagely and then directed us to a small, derelict cottage a little way out of Portumna where she told us she thought the Touhys had once lived. She was certain that the Touhy family had lived thereabouts once, before setting off for a new life in England, or was it Scotland, or it could have been Australia, or maybe it was America. After some searching Dominic and I found the cottage in question. Only three walls were standing, and the coats of whitewash no longer shone as they would have done in years gone by. The roof had partially caved in and weeds sprouted from the remaining sodden thatch. The floor was littered with broken glass, the remnants of a table and a ladderback chair and everywhere were rabbit droppings. It was an emotional time for me. I stood there for a moment trying to imagine what it would have looked like all those years ago. I pictured a group of poorly dressed children clutching their few possessions, a weeping mother closing the old wooden door for the last time, a father staring grim-faced over the sweeping emerald green of the fields stretching for miles under an eggshell blue sky that he would never see again.

Dominic, who had been poking about in the rubble, found the remains of an old sepia photograph in the drawer of the table. Years of rain and wind had discoloured it, but the faded face of a bearded individual still stared from the paper. Could this be my ancestor? Was this the same Michael Touhy, the proud-faced man with the piercing eyes who had taken his family to Sheffield to escape the Famine?

We called in at the post office to thank the woman who had helped us find the cottage.

'I'm so grateful,' I told her through the wire mesh at the counter. 'I can't tell you how indebted I am to you to have found where my ancestors once lived.' I pushed the faded portrait through the grill. 'I guess this must be one of my ancestors.'

'Aaahhh,' said the woman smiling. 'Now there's a thing I should be telling you. I was pleased to be of help, but after you had gone I was speaking to Mrs O'Halloran. She's ninety-five if she's a day and has a memory like an elephant with a degree from Trinity College, Dublin. She comes in here every day, rain or shine, and without so much as a stick to hold her up. Fourteen children she had and every one made something of themselves. I was telling her about you were after looking for the Touhy cottage and how I'd directed you. Now, Mrs O'Halloran was telling me that the cottage I sent you to was not the Touhys at all, but belonged to the Toweys.' She glanced at the photograph and nodded sagely. 'And sure, wasn't she right. This is a picture of old Ignatius Towey's grandfather, whose four grandsons became holy priests and went saving the souls of the heathens in Africa. White Fathers they were and the pride of the village. They have his eyes, so they do.'

I felt deflated. 'Did Mrs O'Halloran mention where the Touhy cottage was?' I asked.

'Touhy,' the postmistress told me. 'She said she'd nivver heard of them. She said I must have been thinking of the Toweys. You could try Father Sullivan up at the church.'

We did indeed try Father Sullivan, an aged priest in a threadbare cassock and sandals and sporting white stubble.

'Touhy,' he mused, 'Touhy,' taking a deep breath. 'Now there was a Gerry Touhy, if my memory serves me right.'

I took out my notebook and, with pen poised, waited for the revelation.

'He died of the drink, poor man. But that was well before my time.'

'Oh.'

'Then there was Tommy Touhy. He lived at the time of my grandfather Duffy. Great storyteller he was, by all accounts.'

Now this is getting better, I thought scribbling down the name. 'A storyteller,' I mouthed, 'a great Irish traditional storyteller, a seanachie?'

'More of a liar,' said the priest, stroking the stubble on his chin. 'He could talk the hind legs off a Connemara pony, so he could. A man blessed with the Blarney by all accounts and his romancing got him out of a lot of scrapes.'

'Do you know what happened to him?' I asked.

'Deported,' the priest told me. 'Poaching I think it was. He can't have been that persuasive in the end.'

And that is as far as we got in trying to trace the family Touhy over in Ireland.

10

Grandma Anne Mullarkey was a striking-looking woman. She had clear, penetrating blue eyes, high arching brows, long dark eyelashes, thick lustrous silver hair, fine hands and a sensuous oval face. Of medium height, she was neither thickset nor thin and until age crept up on her she held her body stiffly upright. Like many of Irish stock, she possessed that Celtic combination of levity and seriousness. Laughter and tears were never far apart. She was a fine storyteller, a keen and discerning reader and an avid letter-writer. The correspondence with her relations in Ireland, some of which survives to this day, displays her gift with words and strong command of the language. The letters are written in the most beautifully formed copperplate handwriting; the grammar is exact and there isn't a spelling mistake to be seen. In this letter, written in 1951, she is writing to Mary Stanton, one of my mother's cousins, whose husband had recently been committed to a psychiatric hospital. It demonstrates a clever turn of phrase that was characteristic of her use of English.

Dear Mary

I received your very sad letter and am deeply grieved for you. As you requested, I have prayed to our Blessed Lord and all the Saints constantly for his speedy recovery. May you have better news on your next visit to the hospital and may God give you the strength to carry on. I have an idea of the numerous jobs you have to contend with but there is a saying that 'God fits the back for the heavy burden.'

You might recall Mrs Murgatroyd of Beechwood Road. You

helped Nora to lay out her mother. A few years ago her husband was taken in the same way. He was moved to Middlewood Hospital and was there for a while until he was given the electric shock treatment. It was immediately successful and he is now back at work as large as life and twice as natural. For those who can stand it, I hear it is the best treatment but it is drastic.

I wrote to Noreen to tell her of your great trouble and she will acquaint Eileen. You may remember the latter had her own trouble when her husband was taken away and had seven ribs removed to clear his tuberculosis. It was thought that he would not last long for this world for he had the smell of clay upon him. I saw him a few weeks ago and to look at him he would be chosen as the healthiest man in a day's walk. Do keep your courage up Mary and, if God spares your health, you will come through it all right. I am certain of that.

Nora was very sorry to hear of your trouble and so was Pat. Winnie is on holiday in Cornwall but I know she will be distressed as they to hear the news on her return.

Kathleen Mullaney sent me an invitation to her wedding. I didn't go. I've done with her. She brought her brother to see me, the one who hopes to be ordained priest next year. He strutted in the room in his clerical dress like the Pope himself. He hopes to train at the English College in Rome. Let's hope it doesn't go to his head. Pat Flynn gets married any day now. It was said that John Flynn was the wild one of the family.

Do write to me soon, Mary, for I am very anxious.

With love,

Auntie Anne

As this letter reveals, my grandmother was a devout Roman Catholic, a great believer in the power of prayer and, until the time came when she became infirm and housebound, a regular attendee at Confession and Mass. The letter also reveals a healthy attitude to the clergy in an age when the priest's word was law and to question it was close to sacrilege. Although she accorded priests deference and greatly valued their work, she was never in awe of them and was not afraid of questioning the edicts of the Church.

On one occasion – I must have been about fifteen at the time – I entered into a discussion with her about Heaven and Hell. It was prompted by a wireless programme in which the pundit and commentator Malcolm Muggeridge challenged an eminent Catholic theologian about the concept of Limbo. As a Catholic, I was taught quite unequivocally what happened after death and where I would end up. If I lived a blameless life and truly repented of all my sins, I would end up in Heaven. If I didn't, I would be condemned to the flames of Hell for all time. Then there was the other place – Limbo. This was the abode of the souls of unbaptized infants and of the just who died before Christ. Those in Limbo suffered no pain or consciousness but would never see the face of God. It seemed to me, a questioning adolescent, that this arrangement was rather unfair and not in keeping with this benevolent God. Surely He would not consign these innocents who, through no fault of their own, had died unbaptized or lived before the time of Jesus to such a cold and empty place? My grandmother listened to what I had to say and effectively ended the discussion with the words, 'He's a wise man is Malcolm Muggeridge, and like him, I take Limbo with a pinch of salt.' I was pleased to learn some years later that the Catholic Church no longer propounds the idea of Limbo.

Interestingly, at the age of eighty Malcolm Muggeridge knelt before an altar and was received into the Roman Catholic Church. When asked why, he replied: 'The day will come, dear boy, when you must decide whether to die within the Church or outside the Church. I have decided to die within the Church.' A few years later he did and so may I when I am summoned to eternity.

Grandma's use of English would have fascinated the connoisseur of the colloquial; she had the rich variety of speech often possessed by the Irish – lively, colourful and vibrant – and shared with her three daughters an acerbic turn of phrase when speaking of those she disliked. Her comments on the failings and the unfortunate appearances of others were never mordacious or malicious because in their humour there was a sort of warmth and the listener could not help but smile. Her idioms were legendary in the family:

She's that good, she bites the altar rails.
He has eyes like a couple of cold, fried eggs.
She has a mouth like a torn pocket.
He's as much use as a grave robber in a crematorium.
If she died with that face on her, nobody would wash the corpse.
It runs in the family like Kitty O'Hara's nose.
A shut mouth catches no flies.
He's so fond of work, he'd lie down beside it.
She has an expression like last year's rhubarb.
If he was thrown after you, you wouldn't turn around to see what the clatter was.

I once took a friend to see her, a boy with red hair and very prominent front teeth. 'Poor lad,' commiserated my grandmother, 'that young fellow could eat a tomato through a tennis racket.' On another occasion, on seeing a particularly fractious and unfortunate-looking pair of twins creating havoc on a bus, she was said to have remarked: 'The mother, poor woman, would have been better off with a pair of jugs.'

My Uncle Ted, sometimes unfairly I have to say, came in for his share of criticism, and when Grandma wanted to divulge something to my mother that she didn't want Ted to hear, she would close the door. 'I don't want old loppy-lugs listening,' she would say. 'That man comes into the room as quiet as a drop of soot.' Deep down of course she had a strong affection for her son-in-law, and as she grew older and more infirm her comments about Uncle Ted were more approving.

I looked forward to the Sunday visits because Grandma Mullarkey took a particular interest in my reading and writing. I cannot pinpoint the precise moment when I came to the decision that I wanted to be a writer, but certainly on those occasions when I sat with my grandmother listening to her stories and anecdotes, her reminiscences and commentaries, the seed was sown.

One of the most vivid early memories I have of Grandma was when she would read to me from a small hardbacked picture book about a shrewd little boy who outwits a greedy tiger. I soon knew the story of *Little Black Sambo* by heart. Conceived and written by Helen Bannerman in 1889, while passing away the long hours on a train journey between Madras and the hill town of Kodaikanal in India, the book is viewed by many today to be a racist text. The visual stereotype of the central character – a semi-clad, thick-lipped, frizzy-haired little boy with bulging eyeballs – is clearly a caricature of a native child seen through the eyes of a white colonial woman and is not appropriate to present to young children in this day and age. The illustrations apart, however, the story for me was and still is captivating. There was such power and emotional strength in the imagery, such skill and pervasiveness in the language, that this simple little story stirred my imagination. *Little Black Sambo* was the first black child I encountered in a book and I delighted in his sheer joy, courage and cleverness.

As an older child I would take along with me on my visits the book of the moment – *Moonfleet* or *The Children of the New Forest* – and Grandma and I would read quietly together. At other times she would read to me from one of the large illustrated books she kept on a shelf near her bed. One favourite was *The Swiss Family Robinson*, with its garish coloured plates and big print. I loved the story, where all the members of the shipwrecked family worked happily together under the benign guidance of a father who was both strong and wise and sported bulging muscles and a long chestnut beard.

When Grandma read, I thrilled at the sound of the words, the rhythms and the rhymes and would sit goggle-eyed at the power of her voice and her extraordinary memory. She knew passages of verse by heart and had a natural feel for measure and stress; I still recall snippets of verse she would recite:

> And down the long and silent street
> The dawn, with silver sandaled feet,
> Creeps like a frightened girl.

I learnt later that these were lines written by Oscar Wilde, one of her favourite writers. She might not, I guess, have approved of his personal life but she loved his poems and stories, as I do.

Children in the schools I visit frequently ask me which is my very favourite story. I tell them I have read a good many books in my time but the story I love the most, one which brings back such happy memories of my childhood and one which I wish I had written myself, is 'The Selfish Giant' by Oscar Wilde. It was my grandmother's favourite story and was read to me when I was small. It is a powerful, poignant and simply written narrative about a Giant who forbids the little children to enter his beautiful garden.

One Eastertime when visiting a small rural primary school in Nidderdale, North Yorkshire, I read 'The Selfish Giant' to a group of eight-year-olds. The children sat in a semi-circle around me on the carpet in the reading corner, and listened intently as I recounted the tale of the mean-minded Giant who forbids the little children to come into his garden to play. 'My own garden is my own garden,' he tells the children, 'and I will not allow anyone to play in it but myself.' When spring comes, the Giant's garden remains cold and barren and a great white cloak of snow buries everything. The Giant cannot understand why the spring passes his garden by. Summer doesn't come and neither does autumn and the garden stays perpetually cold and empty of life. One morning the Giant sees a most wonderful sight. Through a little hole in the wall the children have crept into his garden and every tree has a little child sitting in the branches among the blossoms. They have brought life back to his garden and the Giant's heart melts. He creeps into the garden but when the children see him they are frightened and run away. One small boy doesn't see the Giant, for his eyes are full of tears. The Giant steals up behind the child and gently takes his little hand in his. Many years pass and the little boy never comes back to play in the garden. Now very old and feeble, the Giant longs to see his first little friend again. One day the small child returns.

Downstairs ran the Giant in great joy and out into the garden. He hastened across the grass, and came near to the child. And when he came quite close his face grew red with anger, and he said, 'Who hath dared to wound thee?' For on the palms of the child's hands were the prints of two nails, and the prints of the two nails were on the little feet.

'Who hath dared to wound thee?' cried the Giant; 'tell me, that I may take my big sword and slay him.'

'Nay!' answered the child: 'but these are the wounds of Love.'

'Who art thou?' said the Giant, and a strange awe fell on him, and he knelt before the little child.

And the child smiled on the Giant, and said to him, 'You let me play once in your garden, today you shall come with me to my garden, which is Paradise.'

And when the children ran in that afternoon, they found the Giant lying dead under the tree, all covered with white blossoms.

At the end my little listeners were clearly moved, as I was when I first heard the story, and they sat in silence. The teacher dabbed her eyes. Then a small girl sitting at the front declared, 'I'm a Methodist, Mr Phinn, and I'm going to Paradise one day.'

'I am sure you are,' I told her, smiling.

'I'm Church of England,' volunteered another child, 'and I'm going to Paradise as well.'

I nodded. 'Of course.'

A wiry-looking little boy at the back stood up and announced loudly, 'Well, I'm nowt – but I'm gerrin in!'

You will probably be first in the queue, I thought to myself.

It was Grandma Mullarkey who bought me my first dictionary when I started secondary school, and the treasured portable Olivetti typewriter with the black and red ribbon. I would sit with it on my lap feeling like 'a real writer'.

Grandma would listen as I read my early efforts, while my mother would be in the kitchen talking to Aunt Nora. Sometimes she would nod in the manner of a dowager and make a small noise of satisfaction, but at other times there would be a slight raise of the eyebrow, a brief lift of the chin, a small shake of the head and she would tell me gently that the story or the poem could be improved. I learnt about plot, character, style and other textbook concepts well before I came across them later in my schooling. I was never undeterred by my grandmother's comments, disappointed but never deflated. I learnt a lesson for all would-be writers: if you cannot accept constructive criticism and if you are unwilling to persevere with your work, then give it up. Grandma, interested in world events, politics and religion, was also fascinated by people and taught me another invaluable lesson for the would-be writer: to be curious and observant. 'If you don't understand something,' she would say, 'then ask somebody and if they can't tell you, go to the library and get a book.'

Charles Dickens, in *David Copperfield*, said that 'the power of observation in numbers of very young children is quite wonderful for its closeness and accuracy'. From an early age I became adept at observation, encouraged by my grandma to question, watch, listen, seek out, and as a consequence I became a curious child, eager to know things. I would never intrude in a conversation but would like to observe and eavesdrop; I would steal, glean, collect information and anecdote, and always felt that in some strange way I was storing these impressions for a future date. To this day I still love to watch people and to listen to them and continue to record my impressions in a writer's journal. I am fascinated by human behaviour, people's mannerisms, accents, nervous tics, facial expressions, a curl of the lip, the arching of an eyebrow, a throbbing vein: significant details which are so invaluable for a writer. I will sit behind a couple of gossiping elderly women on the bus, overhear a snippet of conversation in the doctor's waiting room, discreetly observe an angry customer berating a poor shop assistant, and store them at the back of my mind for possible future use. I can't do anything about it; after so many years, I am programmed to do it. I am still like a magpie, obsessively collecting interesting material and feeding off memories.

Grandma Mullarkey opened a door in my early childhood and changed my life for the better, and when she died she left a great gap. When I was sixteen I accompanied my mother to Doncaster Gate hospital, where my grandmother, aged eighty-one, was dying of stomach cancer. There is no image in my childhood that I carry with me more clearly than the one of my grandmother in the hospital bed. She looked pale and weary, propped up in the bed clutching her rosary beads, but her eyes were as bright and intelligent as ever. She told me not to look so miserable. 'Remember,' she said, 'a smile will gain you ten years of life.' She died the following day, clutching her rosary beads.

11

My grandmother always spoke very fondly about her own father, who seemed to me to be very much like my own. Through Connie, a character in one of my Dales books, I expressed the sentiments I feel about my father.

He was the best father you could hope for, was Dad. Never raised a hand to me, never used a bad word. He was always there for me, he was . . . You never really appreciate your parents when you're young. It's only when they're dead do you realize you never can get away from them. They're always going to be with you in your thoughts and in your memories. And when they're dead, you stop being a child, don't you?

My father was a gentle-natured man who taught me much of what I know about integrity, honesty and taking pleasure in the simple things in life. He was not a demonstrative person when it came to outward signs of affection; I guess like most Northern men at that time he would have felt embarrassed hugging his son or kissing him goodnight, but for all that he was a warm, compassionate man, full of life and laughter, and gave me the sense of being loved. He rarely exercised discipline, seldom shouted and never smacked me. By mutual consent 'tellings off' were allotted to my mother.

It was my father who developed (for what it is worth) my sense of humour, indeed my sense of fun. It is said that we do not really get to know our fathers until we are adults ourselves and only then do we come to understand just what sort of person they are. This was not the case for me. I knew my father when I was young. I watched him, listened to him, spent time with him, was entertained by him and wanted to be like him. He was an extremely amusing and witty man.

Dad was typical of many Yorkshire folk: industrious, plain-speaking, generous and good-humoured, with strong views and a wry sense of humour. But there was much more to his character than that. He had a strong sense of justice and a real depth of sentiment. I can never remember him speaking ill of anyone or expressing a racist comment. He was a good father who provided for his family without fail. He was never out of employment and rarely had a day off work.

I was immensely proud of my father's army service. He never won the military cross or got mentioned in despatches or achieved an officer's rank, and from what he said he never saw any real action, but I treasure the photographs of him that were taken in a studio in Cairo. He poses, this handsome, clean-shaven man, hair neatly combed with a sharp parting, his beret tucked in regulation fashion under his shoulder strap. When my Grandmother Phinn remarried and his stepfather, Mr Craig, came into my father's life, I guess things were not entirely happy for him or his siblings at home. My grand-mother, still a relatively young woman, went on to have two more children so I guess the house became rather crowded. On the death of his mother my father left to live with an uncle before enlisting and eventually becoming a despatch rider in the Royal Artillery. I didn't know until after his death, when I was looking through some old photographs, that he was a member of the Army Equestrian Team. He could be a dark horse, my father. There's a picture showing him posing proudly in full uniform in front of a huge stallion.

On leaving the army he became a steelworker at Steel, Peach & Tozer. This huge works, where molten steel was poured from 100-ton cradles into ingot moulds and later rolled into billets and bars, is where my father spent his early working life. He then moved into the 'finishing shop', where his job was to chip out faults (scarfing) in the metal as the steel billets rolled out in the finishing bank. His correct title was 'de-seamer'. As the steel emerged it might have a 'seam' or a defect that had to be removed, otherwise when the metal was rolled out there would be a fault. Nowadays a sophisticated machine, using oxygen jets, blows the debris away and the de-seamers can remain relatively clean. In my father's day de-seaming was a filthy job.

He hated the night shift, having to go to work as it was getting dark when people were settling down to an evening, listening to the wireless, sitting in front of the television or going out to the pub. He would go quiet and we children knew to be on our best behaviour.

My father was not an ambitious man, otherwise he might have become a foreman and entered management. He certainly had the ability and the personal skills to be in charge of others, but perhaps not the drive nor the desire for wealth and position.

When I worked as an education adviser in Rotherham, the Education Department moved premises from the old Wellgate School to the new open-plan offices at Norfolk House. There was a great deal of clearing out, and many old files and records were sent to the Rotherham archive at the public library, computerized or disposed of. During the clear-out I discovered the scholarship scores, school certificate and Eleven Plus results of generations of Rotherham children, including those of myself and my father. I had performed well in the general knowledge and English part of the Eleven Plus but indifferently in the arithmetic and problem-solving sections of the paper. My father, in contrast, had achieved high scores in all parts of the scholarship examination he sat and was clearly grammar school material. My mother's reaction when I told her was unexpected.

'You must never tell your father,' she said firmly. 'It would only upset him.'

At the time I could not understand the logic in this, but reluctantly agreed and never disclosed what I had discovered to my father. Thinking about it now, maybe it would have distressed him to know that he had passed for the grammar school and, given the chance, could have gone on to greater things.

After his death, when I broached the subject of his scholarship examination, my mother told me that my father had been quite content with his lot in life and never aspired to anything more. I cannot believe that. I cannot believe that he was happy working in the steelworks with all the noise, heat, oil, dust and dirt. As a boy, on my way to watch Sheffield United (my eldest son, Richard, is, thank goodness, an avid fan), I remember well the bumpy bus ride from Rotherham to Sheffield via Attercliffe, past the place where he worked for thirty or more years. Down the depressing Don Valley rattled the blue and white double-decker bus, past dirty corrugated iron sheds, yards of scrap, rusty cranes and huge overhead transporters. It was an area that contained little but dust, dirt and an incredible ugliness. This is where my father spent all his working life. I knew, as I surveyed that grim environment, as young as I was, that I wanted more out of life than this and therefore from that point on I developed a tenacity and ambition that would drive me to work hard at school and achieve.

Years later, when I visited the magnificent Magna, the industrial museum now sited in the Don Valley, it was only then that I fully realized what an unpleasant and dangerous job my father had and what a very special man he must have been to have endured that smoky smouldering hell day after day, night after night, and never complain. Most of us want a job that offers some variety and challenge – to go in to work in the morning and look forward to something different. But the de-seamer had to go in to work day after day with the same predictable, monotonous and intensely dirty job to do. And the fact that my father did that work without moaning or getting moody or angry with us children seems to me to be remarkable.

My father was a man of routine. With six of us in the house all vying to use the bathroom, he would use the kitchen in which to wash and shave. I liked to watch him cover his face with shaving foam and then slowly and meticulously scrape away at his chin with an old silver safety razor. Then he would trim his moustache and comb what wisps of hair he had across his largely bald head. I never saw him in his work overalls, for he would set off for the foundry in a sports jacket and neatly pressed trousers as if he were going to work in an office.

I remember Mrs Harrap, who ran the post office on Badsley Moor Lane, once asked me if my father was 'that dapper little man with the nice smile'. This is how others saw him and it summed him up pretty well.

Dad, along with my grandmother and my mother, was instrumental in developing my love of and fascination for language. Although he had left school at fourteen, he was a clever man with a sharp, comic talent for description; a man who read, told stories and recited poetry. He loved to tell amusing tales, employing as he did all the techniques of facial expression, timing and accent of the professional comedian. I imagine that some stories were invented, others were apocryphal, but I always believed implicitly in them. He would come home from his couple of pints in the Masons Arms in Wellgate following the afternoon shift and announce, 'I heard a funny story today,' and then he'd be off.

One story he told was of the elderly woman who had a pet canary. It would sing to her each day, chirruping away on its perch. When the plumber, a friend of my father's called Reg, came to fix her gas fire he turned on the jet to test the appliance and accidentally killed the bird (canaries being very susceptible to gas). Not wishing to face the old lady and tell her what had happened, he stuck the bird back on the perch with a bit of putty and departed. It was some days before the poor woman, who had wondered why the canary had ceased singing and wasn't eating its seed, discovered that the bird was dead.

Another story concerning Reg was when he arrived at a house to fix the gas oven. At the bottom of the back door was what he thought was a draught excluder: a long piece of stuffed multi-coloured cloth with a snake's head at the end. Needing to get into the yard at the back, the plumber casually picked up the length of material only to find it was a real snake: a python which he later discovered was part of the act of the exotic dancer who lived at the house.

Then there was the story of the man who had all the luck in the world. He was born into an affluent family and never had to worry about money; he was clever, handsome, charming and popular. He was lucky to have a beautiful wife whom he loved and lucky to have happy healthy children and many friends. His only misfortune was that he had a nut allergy, but he had learnt to live with that and he carefully avoided any food containing nuts. Unfortunately one day in a restaurant he began to choke on a fishbone. Luckily for him there was a doctor at the next table who knew how to administer the Heimlich procedure and he was quickly able to dislodge the obstruction from the man's windpipe. Luckily the manoeuvre was successful, but unluckily the doctor had applied too much pressure and broke a rib, which punctured the man's lung. The man stopped breathing. Luckily the doctor knew about mouth-to-mouth resuscitation and revived the man. Unluckily the doctor had been eating nuts.

Growing up in an environment of such extravagant anecdotes, clever wordplay and brilliant comic patter, it is no surprise that I became fascinated with language at an early age and developed some skill at story-telling myself.

12

I still recall with great pleasure the occasions when, as a small child, I stood with my father at the kitchen sink while we washed and dried the dishes (which we called 'the pots'). He would launch into a funny poem or a monologue; I thought my father made them up.

> There's a famous seaside place called Blackpool,
> That's noted for fresh air and fun,
> And Mr and Mrs Ramsbottom
> Went there with young Albert, their son.
>
> A grand little lad was young Albert.
> He was dressed in his best, quite a swell,
> With a stick with an 'orse's 'ead 'andle,
> The finest that Woolworths could sell.

The following week, after hearing this monologue which, I discovered later, was called 'Albert and the Lion', I was listening with the other children to Miss Wilkinson, headmistress of Broom Valley Infant School, telling us in assembly to sit up smartly and rub the sleep out of our eyes.

'You are a lot of sleepyheads this morning,' she told the six-year-olds sitting crossed-legged before her on the hall floor. Then she asked, 'Does anyone know another word for 'sleepy'?' I imagine she was looking for a word like 'tired' but I raised my hand.

'Yes, Gervase?' she asked.

'Somnolent,' I replied, with all the precocious confidence of an infant.

She was quite taken aback. 'Wherever did you hear that word?' she asked.

She had perhaps never heard of the narrative poem 'Albert and the Lion', in which the sleepy old King of Beasts lies 'in a somnolent posture' until mischievous little Albert pokes the stick with the ''orse's 'ead 'andle' into the creature's ear and is promptly eaten up. In the monologue Albert's mother does not appear unduly shocked that the lion has devoured her son, 'and him in his Sunday clothes too', and looks for compensation. She is told by the equally unconcerned zoo keeper not to upset herself and that she can always have other children, to which she responds, 'To feed ruddy lions? Not me!'

I cannot recall ever having said this but I was reminded of it by Miss Wilkinson when I visited her a couple of years ago in the Clifton Meadows Residential Home in Rotherham, where she lived. I shall have more to say about the remarkable Miss Wilkinson later on.

The narrative poems and monologues in my father's repertoire were not always of the amusing variety. He could perform exciting, sad, poignant and sentimental ballads and verses too, like 'Brown Boots', 'The Fireman's Wedding', 'The Charge of the Light Brigade', 'Christmas Day in the Workhouse', 'Dangerous Dan McGrew' and 'The Boy Stood on the Burning Deck'. A favourite which he performed with great gusto and accompanied by facial expressions and extravagant gestures was 'The Green Eye of the Little Yellow God':

There's a little yellow idol to the north of Kathmandu.
There's a little marble cross below the town.
There's a broken-hearted woman tends the grave of Mad Carew
And the little god forever gazes down.

The language, rhythms, rhymes and colloquialisms of speech in this dramatic poem thrilled me; they rolled and vibrated. Words like 'Kathmandu' conjured up wonderfully exotic visions of azure seas and golden sands peopled by great heroes and dark villains. I would escape the gloom of a cold wet winter's day or the dirt and grime of industrial Rotherham and enter the world of Mad Carew, the young subaltern who prises out the jewelled eye from the little yellow god to give to his sweetheart on her birthday, only to be found later draped across his bed with a dagger plunged into his breast.

I enjoyed all the poems my father read, but it was the amusing material that I loved the most. I would crack out laughing when he suddenly read the blackly humorous poems of Harry Graham and R. C. Sherriff, and I would repeat the verses to amuse my friends at school:

> Tell me, mother, what is that
> That looks like strawberry jam?
> Hush, hush, my dear, 'tis only Pa
> Run over by a tram.

Sometimes, after a fair bit of persuasion, Dad would recite my favourite poem, 'The Irish Pig', written in 1934 by Bower and Best:

> 'Twas an evening in November,
> As well I can remember,
> I was strolling down the road in drunken pride,
> And my knees were all a flutter,
> As I landed in the gutter,
> And a pig came up and lay down by my side.
> Now I lay there in the gutter
> Thinking thoughts I could not utter,
> When a colleen passing by was heard to say:

'Sure you can tell the man who boozes,
By the company he chooses,'
And the pig got up and slowly walked away.

This is still my party piece, which I recite at regular intervals, embarrassing my own children, and it is a poem my brother Michael can declaim *par excellence*.

When I was fifteen I was asked to perform a piece of verse for the Christmas concert at school. My English teacher, Mr Pike, commented several times when I had been reading a poem in class that I had natural timing, good expression and excellent pace. I had clearly learnt this from my father. Several poems were suggested but they were all pretty depressing stuff. I wanted to perform something amusing and make people laugh – a poem like the ones my father would recite. Mr Pike was one of those teachers susceptible to persuasion, and he was finally prevailed upon to let me pick my own piece providing that the word 'ruddy' was substituted by 'flipping'. I readily agreed and was allowed to recite a Yorkshire dialect poem my father used to perform and which I've always assumed he wrote himself. I was dressed in flat cap, muffler and corduroy trousers tied at the knee with string, and performed the verse with a friend, dressed in a tail coat and top hat, who interrupted the narrative at intervals to provide the Standard English translation.

Letter to Mi Dad

I wekkened up in t'mornin'	When I woke up one morning
An' I ached in every booan.	I had a splitting headache
Mi 'ead felt reight wammy	And felt an all-round lethargy
Enuff to weigh a stooane.	And an aching in my joints.
'Th'as got t'influenza!'	'I think you may have a touch of flu,'
That's what our Mam, she said,	observed my mother,

'An' theers knowt to mek thee berrer	'So I suggest you take to your bed
Than a couple o' days in bed.	for two days. I'll send for your Aunt
I'll send for thee Auntie Eva	Evaline. She's extremely helpful when
She'll know what's to do,	it comes to family illness and will tend to
She's ne'er been round a-lately	your needs. I have not seen her for quite
She'll 'elp to pull thee through.'	some time.'
She cum just after dinner,	My aunt arrived after lunch.
(She could 'ave come afoor)	I thought she might have appreciated the
An' she slapped a poultice on mi 'ead	need for some urgency and come earlier.
As thick as t'oven dooar.	She placed an extremely thick hot moist
She med a pan o' greaasy soup	flannel on my face and made a substantial
Enough for fotty men,	and reviving broth. When I had eaten
An' when I'd 'ad mi fillin'	sufficient she partook herself.
Whay, she etten rest hersen.	She filled a hot water bottle
She filled 'ot watter bokkle	and placed it in my bed. She felt
An' she bunged it in mi bed,	it would bring out the fever.
Full o' boilin' watter,	
To mek me sweat, she sed.	
Well, she's ant been gone a minit,	It can't have been more than a moment
P'raps a tick or two,	before the stopper on the bottle worked
When cork flew out on t'bokkle	itself loose
An' wet all t'beddin' through.	and saturated the

I were reight sharpish

In jumpin' out of t'bed
An' I gives mi Auntie Eva
Such a crack across 'er 'ead.
Well, she gor 'old of mi noggin

An' she gives it such a thump.

She turned mi round and
   smacked mi face
An' kicked me 'ard up t'rump.
Then red in t'face and spittin'
   blood
She's up and out o' t'dooer.

"E can cure hissen!' she shouts

'I'm stoppin' 'ere na moore!'
I shouted out, 'Good riddance!'
To me Auntie flippin' Eva,

'And I'll not be seein' thee
   ageean,
If I'm down wi' Scarlet Fever!'

But the funny thing was when
   she'd gone
I felt a whole lot better.
Well, I hopes I find you in
   good health
And wi' that, I'll close this letter.

sheets, scalding me in the
process.
I leapt from my bed and, in a
   state of some distress,
   foolishly resorted
to violence and assailed my aunt.

She reacted violently by
   striking me
forcibly on the head and
   buttocks.

I could tell she was extremely
   angry,
for she departed forthwith,
   vowing
very volubly that she could be
   of no
further assistance.
I felt this to be the best course of
action and welcomed her
   leaving.

The strange outcome of this, is
   that
after she had departed I felt
   quite
recovered.
I trust you are keeping well,

With best wishes, etc. etc.

The performance was very well received and I had an early taste of what it felt like to stand on a stage under the bright lights with all eyes upon me, hearing the sound of laughter. It was exhilarating.

I learnt early on how important laughter is in life. Without doubt it makes you feel good and it does you good: it takes you out of a bad mood, lifts your spirits and offsets the impact of stress. Research has shown again and again that there is a deal of truth in the old axiom that 'laughter is the best medicine' and that 'a chortle a day keeps the doctor away'. Laughter is like a glue that bonds a group of assorted people together. There is something very pleasurable and reassuring about sitting in a theatre or at a film laughing along with everyone else in the audience. Laughter is infectious.

Before he went on the night shift my father would sometimes come up to the back bedroom which I shared with my two brothers, sit on the end of the bed and tell me a story. It might be one he had made up himself, but more often it was a re-telling of one he had heard or read. Sometimes he would read from a novel. I recall sitting propped up by the pillow completely spellbound. My father never claimed to be advanced in learning and yet the vividness of his language, the descriptive detail, the range of voices he employed for the different characters, were something that the more educated would find hard to achieve. My father knew, perhaps intuitively, the importance of suspense in a story. He would reach an exciting part – for example where Rob Roy, concealed in the heather, sees the King's men who are searching for him getting closer and closer, or the part where young Jim Hawkins is hiding from the mutineers in the barrel of apples and spies through a knot-hole the approach of the villainous pirate Long John Silver – and he would pause. 'Go on, Dad,' I would urge. Once, when he was reading from *Great Expectations*, he arrived at the point where young Pip meets the convict in the cemetery. My father adopted a pathetic, frightened little voice for Pip and a deep growl for Magwitch, the escaped convict.

'Hold your noise!' cried a terrible voice, as a man started up from among the graves at the side of the church porch. 'Keep still you little devil, or I'll cut your throat!'

A fearful man, all in coarse grey, with a great iron on his leg. A man with no hat, and with broken shoes, and with an old rag tied around his head. A man who had been soaked in water and smothered in mud, and lamed by stones, and cut by flints, and stung by nettles, and torn by briars: who limped and shivered, and glared and growled; and whose teeth chattered in his head as he seized me by the chin.

'Oh! Don't cut my throat, sir,' I pleaded in terror. 'Pray don't do it, sir!'

I listened entranced, my eyes 'like chapel hat pegs' as we say in Yorkshire. Then my father stood up, snapped the book closed, said, 'Well, goodnight,' and departed.

'Daaaaad!' I cried after him.

'Tomorrow,' he said.

I fell asleep dreaming of the misty cemetery, the dark fields beyond, the crouching shape of the toothless convict who suddenly emerges from behind a gravestone.

The following year my father took me to the Tivoli Cinema in Rotherham to see David Lean's 1946 adaptation of *Great Expectations*, with its brilliant use of eerie settings, close-ups and long shadows. Finlay Currie's truly terrifying Magwitch and Martita Hunt's crazy, misery-soaked old crone, Miss Havisham, had me glued to my seat. When he asked, 'Did you enjoy the film?' I guess he must have felt a certain warm pleasure when I replied that I preferred his reading from the book.

13

My father loved his garden. I would spend many a happy hour with him pulling out weeds, digging the borders, pruning, collecting the mown grass, watering the tomatoes in the greenhouse and burning the dry wood. He grew roses, lavender, lilacs, columbines, poppies, pansies, snapdragons, wallflowers, catmint, forget-me-nots, irises and many other flowers, so that in summer the garden was a blaze of colour. He built a trellis for the sweet peas, a rustic wooden archway spanning the path for his climbing roses and made cold frames out of old window frames, where he would grow his marrows. Beyond the garden was the allotment, where he grew potatoes, parsnips, Savoy cabbages, onions, sprouts, beetroots, runner beans, broad beans and carrots, though 'nothing fancy' like his neighbour Mr Hirst, whose wife had a penchant for garlic, asparagus and spinach. At the top of the allotment were blackcurrant, blackberry and gooseberry bushes, which were frequently raided by the local boys.

As we went about our business Dad would be explaining, showing me things and asking questions. He was well ahead of his time when it came to recycling and had two large brick-built compost heaps where the grass cuttings and vegetable waste were religiously heaped to rot down. If he heard the rag and bone man on the street with his horse and cart I would be sent out with a bucket and shovel to collect the horse manure for his roses. I found this deeply embarrassing, but there was no argument, I was instructed to get it before anyone else. Sometimes I would have to follow the cart down the hill waiting for the horse to perform and then shovel the steaming pile into the bucket. On my return, Dad would store the manure and later sprinkle the rich crumbly dung on the soil with his broad fleshy hands. He had the finest roses in the street.

If anyone stopped to pass the time of day, Dad would wink at me and tell one of his tales. One Saturday morning I was helping him in the front garden when a woman stopped to admire his efforts.

'Lovely garden,' she said.

'Thank you,' my father replied.

'What's that plant?' she asked, pointing to a bushy fern.

'Alopecia,' Dad replied with an impassive expression. 'Variegated.'

'Alopecia,' the woman repeated. 'Really?'

'And this one's a hysteria,' he continued, pointing to a healthy-looking shrub.

The woman moved on.

It was some time later that I discovered that 'alopecia' is the absence of hair from the body and 'hysteria' a psychological disorder.

The allotment was a neat patch of dark brown earth bordered by a tangle of briars, raspberry canes and gooseberry and blackberry bushes. There was an old green shed, the paint peeling and the roof sagging, where Dad kept his seeds and plant pots. On the top was a small wooden figure that moved as if digging when the wind blew.

Dad loved to go out on the allotment, digging and pruning and planting in a world far away from the dust, filth and heat of the steelworks where he spent his working day. He was a devotee of the gardening programmes on the wireless and when we got our first television in 1959 he rarely missed programmes like *Gardening Club*.

I shared my father's appetite for gardening and loved the musty, earthy smell of the shed, the dark corners, the privacy and complete freedom from disturbance. It was a place where I could find complete peace and quiet. I would sometimes creep into the shed to read, stretching out on the bit of dusty old carpet. I read *Ivanhoe* and *The Arthurian Legends*, struggling with the words as the light began to fade, forgetting all that was around me and escaping into an adventure where brave knights jousted and fought pitched battles in front of great towering castles. From an early age I always felt there was something magical about books, the way that as soon as you opened the covers you were transported beyond the constrictions of time and place and could escape into an entirely different world.

When I was seven or eight I helped Dad create a small crazy paving patio under the French windows at the back of the house. I was appointed to break the larger slabs with a heavy hammer and then like a jigsaw we put the pieces together. Me with my small spade and he with his large shovel, we measured out the mixture of sand and cement, then hollowed out the centre of the mound and poured in the water slowly and carefully before mixing it all up. Then we sat on the grass admiring our handiwork and Mum appeared with two mugs of tea for the workmen.

Years later, after my father's death, I visited Number 19 Richard Road. The owners invited me inside but I declined. I just wanted to sit for a moment on the back step, looking at the crazy paving which Dad had so lovingly created and which had survived all those years. I just wanted a moment to remember my childhood.

Near the River Don in Rotherham were the 'old baths', and some Saturdays, when he wasn't at work, Dad took me swimming. There were none of the health and safety notices seen in swimming baths today – 'No bombing, running, shouting, jumping, ducking, splashing, pushing'. We would spend an hour in the warm, steaming, pale green water, so strong in chlorine that our eyes streamed for a good half hour after we had dried ourselves. In the entrance, where we queued to get in, was a large bronze bust of Captain William Webb, a national hero, the first person to swim the English Channel in 1875. His healthy moustachioed face used to appear on the front of matchboxes. It seems odd, of course, in this day and age, that such an athlete and national hero should be used to advertise safety matches, the smokers' constant companion. On the way into the changing rooms, children would rub Captain Webb's nose for good luck, so the only part of the noble effigy that shone brightly was the aquiline proboscis.

It was not unusual, as we were getting into our trunks (those terribly itchy woollen affairs with canvas belts and metal clasps), to see a rat, a visitor from the nearby canal, running between the cubicles.

'Watch tha feet!' the attendant would bellow from the side of the pool. 'Theere's a rodent on t'premises!' This would be followed by the screams and yelps of terrified children, frantically scrambling up on to the wooden seats in the cubicles.

'Geeaw, wi' all that racket, yer daft 'aporths!' the attendant would shout. 'It's more freetened o' thee than thy are of it.'

As I cowered on the wooden seat, I wasn't at all convinced. We would hear scuffling and running as the attendant chased the intruder with the long bamboo pole with which he used to teach the children to swim. 'Come 'ere, yer little bugger!' he would shout.

The pool would be a screaming mass of adolescent bodies swimming in all directions as we twisted and turned, dived and side-stroked to avoid collisions.

Following our swimming sessions, skin wrinkled and pink-eyed, I would be taken by Dad into the café for mugs of hot sweet tea and teacakes. I would pick out the currants before eating the soft bread, while watching the swimmers emerging from the changing rooms with slicked-down hair and red shining faces, giving off an overpowering smell of chlorine.

My father was an incredibly patient man and taught all three of his sons to swim in record time. It was because we all had such implicit trust in him that we willingly let go of the side of the bath. 'It's all right,' he would say, 'I'm here. I won't let you drown. You'll be fine.' It wasn't long before I was splashing up and down the baths. My brother Alec was the swimmer in our family, though, and could slice through the water like a knife. Later he swam for the school and won most of the races, much to the delight of our father, who never missed a gala.

On one occasion – I must have been about eight – Dad said we were going to the baths with a friend of his called Peter and his son, Francis. In the car he told me that Francis went to a special school and was about my age. I was warned to be on my very best behaviour and make a bit of an effort with Francis, who hadn't many friends. I thought this Francis would be like the boy at the top of the hill who went to Rudston, the posh private school on Broom Lane, that he would be toffee-nosed and full of himself. I had no idea what a 'special school' was. When we arrived at Peter's house, I fully expected to see this boy waiting on the step dressed in coloured blazer and wearing his fancy cap. I followed Dad into the front room, to find Peter's wife sitting on the settee with the boy face down across her lap. She was rubbing some ointment into his bottom. The boy wore nothing but a thin white vest. I didn't know where to look or what to do, so I stayed rooted to the spot. None of the adults seemed the slightest bit awkward or self-conscious and continued to chat away. The boy himself didn't appear at all embarrassed and looked up at me and smiled. If Mum had done that with me I would have prayed that the floor would open and swallow me up. I could see now that the boy was what in those days they called 'handicapped' or 'mentally deficient'.

'Nearly done,' said Peter's wife, pulling on these sort of plastic pants. 'Francis has been so looking forward to today. He loves the water.' She stroked the boy's back. 'There's a little friend here,' she told him. The boy smiled and gurgled and threw his head back. 'This is Gervase,' she continued, 'and he's come to take you swimming.' My heart sank into my shoes. I was unsure and frightened. At school the word 'spastic' was used as a term of abuse. 'You spastic!' boys would shout if you missed a shot at the goal or did something stupid. So many times I had passed the life-size plaster figure of the smiling boy with callipers on his legs, holding the charity box, that stood outside Davy's Café in All Saints' Square, but I'd never met a real disabled person. And now I was to go swimming with him. Suppose my friends were at the baths? What would they say? And why hadn't Dad told me?

The wheelchair was put in the boot and we set off for the swimming baths with Peter next to my father in the front of the car and me sitting with Francis in the back. The boy smiled a lot and pulled funny faces, and when he tried to speak he dribbled. I remember feeling so embarrassed at the baths, seeing people staring at us as we headed for the water, and I quickly swam on my own in the deep end instead of playing in the shallows with Francis. I made no effort at all to be friendly or kind. When Dad waved for me to come and join them, I flipped beneath the water and ignored him.

Dad didn't say a word as the four of us left the baths. Peter thanked me for coming and pressed a two-shilling coin into my hand. Francis smiled and nodded. I felt awful. On the way home I could see that my father was angry with me. I don't think I had ever seen him so angry. He dropped off Francis and his father and after we turned the corner, he pulled over and switched off the engine.

'I think you should be ashamed of yourself, young man,' he said quietly. He only called me 'young man' when he was mad at me. 'I am very disappointed in you.'

I hung my head and mouthed, 'I'm sorry.'

'I should think you are,' said Dad. 'It costs nothing to be

friendly, and Francis is just like any other boy but he's got a lot more than most to put up with.'

'I'll play with him next time,' I promised.

'I shouldn't think there will be a next time after the way you behaved today,' said Dad, starting the car, and that was all he said on the matter. He was a product of a generation that didn't acknowledge the value of self-exploration. He was not in the business of explaining why it was thoughtless and mean of me to behave as I had done. He didn't need to – I knew. He drove home without another word on the subject and I felt guilty and dejected. I can't recall my father getting angry very often, but on that occasion I remember well his quiet voice and the look in his eyes and I still feel bad about that day at the swimming baths. I never did get to play with Francis again.

Christmas was for me, as I guess it is for most children, a very special time, and my father made a great effort in our house to have everything just right for the occasion. He would increase my pocket money for me to buy presents and before the big day take me shopping into Rotherham. I loved those visits into town just before Christmas, when the shop windows were stacked with Christmas goods, when coloured lights lit up the streets and carol singers and the Salvation Army band filled All Saints' Square with music. It was even more special when a light dusting of snow covered pavements and roof-tops, making the dark town seem so much cleaner and brighter. I loved it when the air became so icy it burnt your cheeks and your exhaled breath came in great clouds.

The old imitation Christmas tree would be taken from its dusty box and erected in the front room to be decorated with coloured balls, little wooden figures and tinsel, and we children were allowed to drape streamers in the living room and put up balloons. The crib with the small plaster Nativity figures was given pride of place on the mantelpiece and the crucifix on the wall was taken down until the New Year.

One year my father was persuaded by Mr Evans to have a real Christmas tree. Our neighbour said he had a contact in the Forestry Commission at Clumber Park and could provide one at a fair price. He didn't mention just how big the tree would be. We were expecting a small affair, so when this strangely shaped monstrosity arrived my mother was less than pleased and stared in disbelief as it was manoeuvred through the back gate. It was all of eight foot high, with great spreading lateral branches and twisting roots.

'We won't get it in the house, never mind the front room,' my mother complained.

'Not to worry,' said Dad. 'I'll chop a bit off when I get back from work.'

Alec, my brother, prevailed upon Dad to let us cut the bit off, and when he had departed for the afternoon shift, we set to work with the saw. The bit we lopped off the tree was from the top, so we had this strange-looking truncated Christmas tree that shed its needles the very day it was placed in the corner of the front room. It was to be the very last real Christmas tree we bought.

Christmas morning I would wake up to see the bulging pillow-case at the bottom of the bed. There would be tangerines and string bags of assorted nuts, chocolate coins encased in gold and silver foil, a box of rose-scented Turkish delight covered in powdery icing sugar, glistening dates on a bony stem in a box with three camels on the front. There would be crystallized fruits, a selection box of chocolates, coloured pencils, a John Bull printing set, roller skates, a penknife, lead soldiers and always a book.

Every Christmas and every birthday my father bought me a book. These formed a precious collection, my own little library, and I have them still. As I look up from my desk now

I see a shelf full of those adventure stories my father bought for me when I was a child: Anthony Hope's swashbuckling *The Prisoner of Zenda* and *Rupert of Hentzau*, John Buchan's gripping *The Thirty-Nine Steps*, Chesterton's thrilling *The Man Who Was Thursday*, Edgar Rice Burroughs's *Tarzan of the Apes*, Erskine Childers's masterpiece *The Riddle of the Sands*, and, of course, *Treasure Island*. My father would write a small message or adage in the front.

I cannot remember my father ever shouting or swearing or smacking me. I just picture a small, quietly spoken, loving man with fingers as fat as sausages, a shiny bald head and a smile that lit up my world. The qualities he hoped to instil in us were politeness, kindness, obedience, patience, unselfishness, fortitude, courage, truthfulness, self-control, application, modesty and reverence. Plus, of course, a sense of humour, for he was a massively amusing and witty man.

My father died one sultry summer afternoon. He had just returned from the Royal Oak, where he had enjoyed a pint of bitter and a game of dominoes. He was feeling tired and told my mother he would have a rest. She found him later draped across the bed. He had had a massive heart attack.

On his death I collected together the little sayings he had written in the front of every book he ever gave me and composed a poem for him. In it I tried to put into words some of the things this remarkable man, for whom I had a profound love and respect, tried to teach me.

A Father's Advice to his Son

Always smile at those you meet
And they will do the same.
Look for good in others, son
And don't waste time on blame.
Never be ashamed of crying,

It's not a sign you're weak,
And don't be quick to criticize
And think before you speak.
Give more than you take, my son,
Do no one hurt nor harm
And don't be afraid of being wrong
And always chance your arm.
Stick firmly to your principles,
Don't follow fads and trends,
And always answer to your heart
And value all your friends,
And keep that sense of humour
It will help you to survive,
And don't take life too seriously, son,
For none come out alive.

14

I am five. The photograph shows a chubby little boy with a round pale face, a mop of black hair and large eyes, standing on the back step of the house in Richard Road just before he sets off for his first day at school. He does not look at all happy. In fact, he seems on the verge of tears. He is wearing a crisp white shirt and a little tartan clip-on tie, short grey trousers which he eventually will grow into, socks pulled up to the dimpled knees and large polished black shoes and a blazer. A rose is pinned to his lapel.

When I look at the photograph I wonder just what my mother was doing sending me to school looking like a little adult attending a wedding. The class photograph taken at the end of my first year shows that my mother's taste in my clothes had not altered, for again I am dressed like a little dandy. The girls are all dressed in similar clothes: pale cotton, knee-length dresses, cardigans, white ankle socks and sandals. The boys too are dressed in virtually identical outfits: white shirts, jumpers, grey shorts, grey socks and black shoes. I am the exception and stand at the end of the row in a jacket and bow tie. I suppose even at such a young age I looked, and must have felt, different.

The most indelible impression of my early childhood was when I started school. Broom Valley Infant School appeared to a small boy of five as a vast, cold and frightening castle of a building, with its huge square metal-framed windows and endless echoing corridors, shiny green tiles, hard wooden floors and the oppressive smell of stale cabbage and floor polish. The very doors at the entrance looked gargantuan, and everything beyond seemed ten times bigger than normal. There was an asphalt playground full of the disconcerting animal din of a large group of children occupied in manic activity – running, skipping, leaping, jumping, chasing, screaming, shouting – which is still to be heard in primary schools up and down the country today. Outside each classroom was a row of neatly spaced hooks and I recall wondering what they were for. Maybe the children were hung on them if they were naughty. It was a daunting place. I didn't like it at all and wanted to leave.

On my first day, so my mother told me years later when my own children started school, when I arrived at the infant classroom I screamed and shouted, tugged and writhed as she held my small hand firmly in hers. I hated it and wanted to go home and sit at the table in the kitchen and help her make gingerbread men and listen to her stories. When I saw her head for the door, leaving me in the school entrance, I thought I would be abandoned for ever and couldn't be consoled. 'I want to go home!' I cried. 'I want to go home!' But I was made to stay, and Miss Wilkinson, the headteacher, took my hand and led me down a long cold corridor to the infant classroom where I met a young, slim, smiling teacher standing at the door to greet me.

I spent the whole morning whimpering in a corner, resisting the kind attentions of the infant teacher, Miss Greenhalgh. At morning playtime I couldn't be coaxed to eat the biscuit or drink the milk on offer and continued to sniffle and whimper. But by lunchtime I had become intrigued and soon dried my tears. Just before lunch Miss Greenhalgh opened a large coloured picture book and began to read. I loved books, and the bedtime routine was my mother or father or sister snuggling up with me to read. I knew all the nursery rhymes and the fairy stories and, although I couldn't read, I knew if a word was changed or a bit missed out and would tell the reader so. When Miss Greenhalgh opened the book on that first morning, I stopped sniffling and listened. She looked to me like someone out of the pages of a fairy tale: long golden hair like Rapunzel's, large blue eyes like Snow White's, and such a gentle voice and lovely smile, like the Sleeping Beauty's. When she started reading the story, I was completely captivated.

In the afternoon I was keen to hear the rest of the story but the teacher went through a few basics on how we should behave, about going to the toilet before the lesson, washing our hands, saying 'Please' and 'Thank you', calling her Miss, raising our hands if we wanted something and not shouting out. I was desperate for her to finish the story, but then we were all told to lie down on little canvas beds for a nap.

'When will you finish the story?' I asked glumly when it was nearing home time.

'Tomorrow,' replied Miss Greenhalgh, smiling.

The following morning I wolfed down my breakfast, keen to get back to school and Miss Greenhalgh.

I loved those early years at school. We moulded little clay models, dug in the sandpit, played in the water tray, counted with little coloured beads, sang the nursery rhymes, danced with bare feet in the hall, made models with toilet rolls and cardboard boxes, splashed poster paint on large sheets of grey sugar paper, chanted poems and learnt to read. Most of all I loved the fairy stories read by Miss Greenhalgh, stories which celebrated goodness of heart, compassion, kindness to animals, consideration for the poor, weak and elderly and which abhorred greed, selfishness and cruelty. I remember that when the wicked stepmother or the ugly sisters got their come-uppance, we children cheered.

Miss Wilkinson had the shining eyes of the great teacher. As I recall, she was a small vigorous woman with a sharp sense of humour and a striking appearance. Although she had a kindly smile, clearly loved the company of young children and was rarely impatient or cross, there was no way any child would question her decrees.

I visited this remarkable woman in 2006. She was a resident at the Clifton Meadows Residential Home in Rotherham and had reached the ripe old age of 101. Dressed in a pale woollen suit, her eyes twinkling with incipient good humour, I recognized her immediately and, to my surprise, she recognized me.

'Hello, Gervase,' she said.

'Miss Wilkinson,' I replied.

'Stand up properly, don't slouch,' she said with mischievous affection.

We talked for an hour about education. Teaching, for her, she told me, was hard work but the pleasures were great. The real joy, she continued, was to see the hard work take root and flourish, to see children grow in trust and confidence and come to love learning.

'And do you recall when you wet yourself?' she asked me mischievously, her eyes dancing with merriment.

'Of course I do,' I replied. How could anyone forget the first time people had laughed at them? It had been a deeply upsetting experience.

I made my first appearance on stage at the age of six in the Broom Valley Infant School Nativity play. Miss Wilkinson had convinced me that I was just as important as Joseph or the Archangel Gabriel, despite that fact that I didn't say a word and I didn't move. I was the palm tree. Encased in brown crêpe paper with cardboard fronds and with papier-mâché coconuts dangling around my neck, my little face peering out of a pale green woollen balaclava that my mother had knitted for me, I stood stiff and erect by the cardboard stable as the curtains opened. I was so excited and there was a lovely glow about me until I saw and heard the audience. At first there was a faint titter and a few suppressed laughs and then I realized everyone was laughing at me. They were not supposed to laugh at the palm tree. I scanned the faces in the hall for my parents and saw my mother and father in the second row, with expressions on their faces willing me to carry on, but I couldn't. I froze under the bright lights and then – I wet myself. A dark brown stain spread at the front of my trunk and bits of the crêpe paper dropped off to reveal my electric blue underpants. I was distraught and, crying piteously, the little palm tree exited stage right clutching his papier-mâché coconuts.

Having spent a lifetime in education, I know that some teachers would have stabbed the air with a finger and berated that child. 'Why didn't you go to the toilet before you went on stage?' some would have demanded angrily. But not Miss Wilkinson. She put her arm around my shoulder and comforted me. 'Don't worry,' she told me gently. 'It's not the end of the world.' Her voice became conspiratorial. 'I'll let you into a little secret. When I was your age, I used to wet my knickers.' As I sat reminiscing with my former headmistress, she looked across her teacup and smiled. 'Yes, Gervase,' she chuckled, her eyes glinting with humour, 'and it comes full circle.'

In 1984, when I was appointed General Adviser for Language Development with Rotherham Local Education Authority, the first school on my list of visits was Broom Valley Infants. I was to examine and report on the teaching of reading. There was a great feeling of anticipation that morning as I strolled up the drive of the infant school I had attended as a small child, in my dark inspectorial suit and with my black briefcase in my hand.

The school was no longer a vast and frightening place but just a small, square, featureless building with a flat roof, like so many post-war schools. I stood for a moment in the entrance hall, staring down the corridor and thinking of my childhood. I recalled the lukewarm milk, the skipping-ropes, hoops and hopscotch, the dressing-up corner, the afternoon naps when each infant would retire to a small canvas bed for half an hour, the shiny Izal lavatory paper with the unpleasant disinfected smell and the bars of lemon-smelling Sunlight soap. I learnt at that infant school the value of memory, the importance of reading, respect, clarity of speech, to be wary of angry eyes and furrowed brows, to raise my hand when I wanted something, to go to the lavatory at playtime, to wash my hands, not to call out, not to be a show-off, not to play with the girls, to share my sweets, leave a clean plate, drink my milk, enjoy make-believe, to avoid bullies and to watch and listen.

Before informing the school secretary on my return visit all those years later that I had an appointment with the headteacher, I took a deep breath and looked down the corridor. The smell of cabbage and floor polish had lingered . . . and so, I was soon to discover, had my teacher – Miss Greenhalgh.

'Well, well, well,' she said with a wry smile when I met her. The long golden hair had gone, but the large blue eyes stared into mine and the smile I knew so well appeared on her lips.

'I'm lost for words,' I gasped. 'It's Miss Greenhalgh.'

'Lost for words!' she repeated. 'Well, there's a first.'

'I can't believe it,' I said. 'I just can't believe it. It's Miss Greenhalgh.'

'Under the circumstances, Gervase,' she said, maintaining the small smile, 'I guess you can call me Dorothy.'

'I couldn't possibly call you Dorothy,' I spluttered.

'Why ever not?'

'Because you were my teacher, Miss Greenhalgh,' I said. Then I added, 'And I should tell you that I loved every lesson that you taught. I couldn't wait to get to school. I loved being in your class. I still remember the Reading Corner and the great round reading cushions and the little puppet theatre and the stories, all those wonderful stories you told us.'

'Well, it's just as well you have such fond memories of me and thought so highly of my teaching, Gervase,' she told me, 'because I haven't changed my methods.'

'It's so good to see you,' I said, still taken aback at meeting her after so many years.

'It's a funny old world, isn't it?' she sighed. She smiled with curious wistfulness, as if she had recalled something fondly from the distant past. 'I taught you to read, and here you are, checking up if I do it properly. I can't have done such a bad job – you've got more degrees than a thermometer and write books yourself now, don't you?'

'I do,' I said, 'and my love of books and reading started at home with my parents and with you in the infant classroom.'

'Get away with you.'

'It really did. You were a wonderful teacher.'

She looked at me for a moment and smiled. 'Would you like the book you learnt to read with?' Miss Greenhalgh asked me. 'Your first reading book?'

'You surely still don't have it?' I asked.

'Oh, I never throw things out,' she replied. 'You never know when they'll come back in. I've been in education long enough to know that things swing in and out of fashion like a pendulum. Mind you, I guess the *Happy Trio* reading scheme will not make a comeback. I'm up with all the modern reading schemes now. We've been through *Janet and John*, *Nip and Fluff*, *Peter and Jane*, *Dick and Dora*, the *Rainbow Readers*, the *Beacon Readers*, the *Gayway Readers* – of course they changed that name to *New Way Readers* when it was reprinted. Oh yes, I'm all contemporary now. Before you go you can have a copy of *The Happy Trio* – it will bring back memories.'

'*The Happy Trio*', I murmured. 'Yes, I remember *The Happy Trio*.' This scheme was the staple reading for learner readers in the 1950s and it was pretty dull stuff. The brightly coloured watercolour illustrations which accompanied the short phrases and sentences depict a sparklingly clean little girl with golden curls and red ribbons and dressed in a spotless pink dress, snow-white socks and sturdy sandals. The little boy is equally pristine and beautifully dressed. Father (never Dad) is ever-cheerful, young, good-looking and prosperous and spends most of his life dressed in a suit and tie and reading the newspaper. Mother (never Mum) is a slim, permanently smiling, equally attractive individual who spends most of *her* life in the kitchen, beaming contentedly and dressed in a brightly patterned floral dress and frilly apron. Her hair is flawlessly in place. The house is amazingly spacious and tidy, with a perfectly kept garden and a big shiny black car parked outside the large garage. Everyone seems to be idyllically happy (including the well-behaved dog) and beams from the page. This is a perfect world, clean and wholesome, free of injury, upset and suffering. At five I already had a head full of words. I was used to rhymes and stories at home and did not take to the tiresome children in the reading scheme, who seemed so far removed from my own life. Nobody ever fell over and cut a knee, quarrelled or shouted, had a nosebleed, wet the bed, cleared the blocked sink, was sick, overslept or went to the toilet.

The first book in the series, a thick, sturdy, fabric-covered tome, shows a small boy and girl on a bright yellow background, dancing in delight. There are seventeen 'stories' in the collection, the first of which is titled 'Come':

Come, Sally.
Come. Come.
Oh, Sally.
Come, come.
Come, Sally, come.
Oh, see.
See Sally go.
Go, Sally, go.
Go, go, go.

The remaining stories hammer home the key words and have the same paucity of plot, character and language.

I was using the text at a lecture some years later at the North of England Conference in York to demonstrate how these old schemes were unrelated to the world in which most children lived, and how poor they were in arousing my curiosity and interest when I was young. At the end of my lecture I was approached by a headteacher who told me that she still used the scheme to good effect, and that had I put a bit more feeling into the reading of the text, it wouldn't have sounded so bad. When I tried reading it with 'a bit more feeling' at home, for my wife's benefit, she told me, 'If you read it like that you're likely to get arrested.'

When I visited Broom Valley Infants all those years later, Miss Greenhalgh reminded me that I was no high-flier. 'I'm very pleased you have done so well, Gervase,' she told me. 'Yes, you've done very well, very well indeed.' There was a short pause before she added, 'Because you weren't on the top table, were you?'

She was right; I was not on the top table. I suppose I would have been described in those days as an average child, one of the unremarkable majority, a part of the big bulge in the academic bell. I never came near the top of the class, I found mental arithmetic hard, I never gravitated to the football team, I sang at the back of the choir and in the school Nativity I had the part of the palm tree. I did do well later at school because of the combination of loving, supportive parents and dedicated, patient and enthusiastic teachers, but during those early years I was an ordinary, average little boy, not one of the bright little buttons on the top table.

I believe that the two keys to success in education are high self-esteem and great expectation, and I was fortunate to possess both. It would have been easy for Miss Greenhalgh to write off that biddable, quiet, ordinary little boy with the funny name who came from a humble background, one whose parents were unlikely to storm into school and make demands. She could have concentrated just on the top table, the Eleven

Plus certainties, those destined for academic success, and let the average children coast and those with special educational needs struggle. But she didn't because, like all great teachers, all children mattered to Miss Greenhalgh.

Being of average ability I learnt, from an early age, how to study. Learning did not come as easy to me as it did to the brighter children, but I was determined and ambitious to do well. I worked hard, applied myself and dreamed of one day moving on to the top table to sit next to the first love of my life, Susan Barlow.

15

Susan Barlow was the top of the top table. She smelled of flowers and lavender soap and wore snow-white stockings and sensible pale leather sandals. She had large inquisitive eyes behind Elastoplast-pink framed glasses, her hair was tied up in bunches with red ribbons and she was always smiling. There was a list of names on the infant classroom wall and silver stars were awarded against each for really good work. I was somewhere in the middle, but Susan was way out in front. She was the first to get the coveted badge, which she pinned on her pink cardigan. It said to the world: '*I AM A FREE READER.*' This meant she had completed every boring book in the *Happy Trio* reading scheme and could now select her own from the small library in the reading corner. How I longed for that little tin badge. Then came the day when Miss Greenhalgh pinned the coveted award on my cardigan. I remember running down the school path punching the air and shouting for the entire world to hear: 'I am a free reader! I am a free reader!' Striding home down Broom Valley Road, I really expected all the adults I passed to stare in awe and announce in hushed voices: 'He's a free reader.' Of course no one did. But, at home, my mother reacted as all mothers should.

'What have you got covered up?' she asked. I had concealed the badge with my hand. 'Let me see.' I removed my hand so she could read what was printed in large red letters on the badge. 'Where did you find that?' she teased.

'I didn't find it,' I announced proudly. 'I'm a free reader.'

'You can't be, love,' she told me with a twinkle in her eye. 'You have to be a very, very clever boy to be a free reader.'

'Well, I am,' I said proudly.

'You will have to prove it,' she said. So, sitting on my mother's knee, I read from a small square book with a little rabbit on the cover, *The Tale of Peter Rabbit*.

When I had finished I received a great hug and a kiss. 'You *are* a free reader,' she said. 'Wait until your father gets home.' I waited by the gate at the top of Richard Road until I saw Dad making his way up the hill after the afternoon shift. I ran to greet him and told him the fantastic news.

'A free reader,' he said, lifting me high in the air. 'Well, well, well, a free reader.'

That afternoon I walked on clouds.

Since that day *The Tale of Peter Rabbit*, the children's classic by Beatrix Potter, has been one of my all-time favourites. As I travelled around the schools as an inspector I would often test children's reading skills by asking them to read from that small, square, rather battered book which I always carried with me in my briefcase. When I started to visit schools in the Yorkshire Dales, however, I soon discovered that this particular story was singularly inappropriate.

In an infant school in Nidderdale, John, a serious little boy of about seven or eight with a tangled mop of straw-coloured hair, was clearly not very enamoured of the plot. He arrived at the part of the story where poor Peter Rabbit, to escape the terrifying Mr McGregor who was searching for him in the vegetable garden, had become entangled in the gooseberry net. The frightened little rabbit gave himself up for lost and shed big tears. It was the climax to the story, and when my mother had read this part to me when I was small, my eyes had widened like saucers and my mouth had fallen open in expectation of the capture of the poor little rabbit by the cruel gardener. It was Mr MacGregor who had caught Peter's father, and his wife had put him into a pie. But John stared impassively at me with tight little lips and wide staring eyes.

'What a terrible thing it would be,' I said, hoping to encourage

1. 'From your darling Pat.' The photograph of my mother that my father kept in his wallet.

2. The Mullarkey children posing in their Sunday best: Aunt Nora, Uncle Jimmy, Aunt Winnie and my mother. Don't they scrub up well?

3. My mother modelling her new shoes on the steps at Blackpool.

4. 'When shall we three meet again?' The formidable Mullarkey sisters, Nora, Winnie and my mother, at brother Michael's wedding.

5. 'Off to war!' My father is the good-looking one, third from the left.

6. 'The hero of the Western Desert.' My father sitting out of the sun in Egypt during the war.

7. 'Love's Young Dream.' My father soon lost that wonderful quiff.

8. 'I shall not say it again!' Dad's expression, even at seventy-five, could silence a banshee.

9. My father and mother on their wedding day. I borrowed the bowler hat when I made my first appearance on stage at thirteen, singing the Sandy Powell number.

10. The happy couple. Mum and Dad in Scarborough.

11. The proud grandparents, my father and mother, with my first child, 'little tricky Dickie'.

12. PC 56, Grandfather Mullarkey.

13. Grandma Mullarkey.

14. Grandfather Touhy. Despite his reputation as a raconteur, he doesn't look a barrel of laughs in this photograph.

15. Uncle John (my father's brother) with his fiancée. She set the trend in hats.

16. Uncle Alec (my father's brother), the decorated RAF officer.

17. No wonder the doctors chased after her. Nurse Mullarkey, my beautiful Aunt Nora, at Doncaster Royal Infirmary.

18. Aunt Hessie. She could read a book from cover to cover at five.

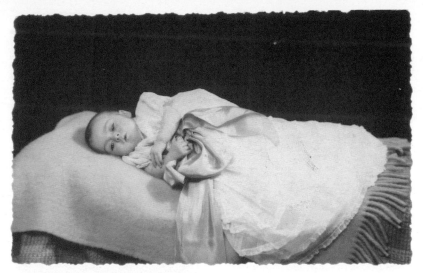

19. 'However did you manage, being called Gervase and growing up in Rotherham?' Me at my christening at St Bede's Church.

20. Gervase Richard Phinn at his christening. I reckon my mother promised to name her fourth child after the obscure Roman saint if he interceded on her behalf and she had a safe delivery.

21. Grandma in her latest beachwear, paddling with me in Blackpool, 1948.

22. When it comes to good looks my brother Alec wins hands down. But I smile more than he does.

F. SHAW
ROTHERHAM

23. 'Don't you think this pram's a tad too small?' Me at six months.

24. Walking along the promenade in Blackpool with my Uncle Alec and my father.

25. My father at Blackpool (with my brother Alec). He is wearing the latest thing in sunglasses.

26. A Blackpool fishing trip, 1954. Fish caught: Alec 5, Gervase 0. I was not smiling when we got back to shore.

27. Two little legionnaires (Alec and me) in Blackpool, 1954.

28. Alec got the two twins, I got the girl in the goggles. Blackpool, 1955.

him on again, 'if poor Peter Rabbit should be caught.'

'Rabbits! Rabbits!' cried the angry-faced little lad, scratching the tangled mop of hair in irritation. 'They're a blasted nuisance, that's what my dad says! Have you seen what rabbits do to a rape crop?' I answered that I had not. 'Rabbits with little cotton-wool tails and pipe-cleaner whiskers,' he sneered, 'and fur as soft as velvet. Huh! We shoot 'em! They can eat their way through a rape crop in a week, can rabbits. Clear nine acres in a month! Millions of pounds' worth of damage when it's a mild winter. No amount of fencing will stop 'em.'

'We gas ours,' added a little girl of about ten with round cheeks and closely cropped red hair whom I'd met earlier, and who was sitting nearby. 'That stops 'em, I can tell you.'

'Nay, Marianne,' retorted the boy, curling a small lip, 'gassin' doesn't work.' Then, looking me straight in the eyes, he added, 'Never mind poor old Peter Rabbit. It's Mr McGregor I feel sorry for – trying to grow his vegetables with a lot of 'ungry rabbits all ovver t'place!'

'Perhaps we should look at another book,' I suggested feebly.

There is a lesson here for all adults who select books for children, which is that books that an adult enjoys may not necessarily appeal to a child. Many children's writers (including J. K. Rowling) have had their manuscripts rejected by editors only to go on to have massive success with their work when it is finally published. But I digress. Back to my badge.

Badges awarded to children for effort I believe to be important. They give recognition, which is something we all strive for. They show achievement and make a child feel good. After my mother's death, my sister, Christine, was sorting through some personal effects when she came across an old box in which my mother had kept her prized possessions. There at the bottom, with my swimming medals and cycling proficiency pin, was an old tin badge: '*I AM A FREE READER.*'

One inspector and former colleague once told me that he

had a real dislike of the practice so common in infant schools where teachers awarded 'these silly little badges with smiley faces on – "Headteacher's Award", "Good Work", "Well done".' I disagreed. One should never miss an opportunity of celebrating young people's accomplishments, however small, for we all thrive on recognition and success often leads to greater success. I have so many memories of being congratulated on the things I did well and can still recall the great sense of achievement and pleasure when I was awarded that little badge at the age of six, the sensation of success I felt years later when I was awarded my O and A levels, my Certificate in Education and my degrees.

A month after a school inspection I was giving an address at a very prestigious charity dinner at the medieval Merchant Adventurers' Hall in York. It was attended by the Lord Mayor, the Lord Lieutenant, the High Sheriff, the Masters of the Guilds and all the great and the good of the city. Printed on the tickets was the instruction that 'decorations will be worn'. Those attending all sported their badges. They happened to be CBEs and OBEs, elaborate chains of office, golden insignia, knighthoods and various medals and awards. Like the badges given to small children, they gave recognition, showed achievement and, I am sure, made the wearers feel good. I was sitting next to a heavily be-medalled individual who enquired of me what the small enamelled badge was that I was wearing rather discreetly on my lapel. I told him it was the only decoration I possessed: '*I AM A FREE READER.*'

'Really,' he said with a bemused smile.

'I do have another decoration,' I informed him seriously, 'but I felt it a little pretentious to wear it.'

'And that is?'

'Cycling Proficiency,' I said.

'I guess we are in for an amusing evening,' said my colleague.

In the year 2004 an Honorary Doctor of Letters was conferred upon me by Leicester University. The ceremony was in Lincoln Cathedral, and, prior to all the graduands ascending the platform to receive their degrees, I was presented with my award and asked to say a few words. I told the assembly that I was greatly honoured, that I only wished my parents could have been there that afternoon to see me receive such an accolade and to celebrate my success. I told them I was an average scholar who tried my best and worked hard and that there are many, many children in schools, like me, described as average but with parents and teachers who believe in them, encourage them to aim for the moon and delight in their success. With this kind of support, I told them, young people can achieve something in life. I described my own early schooling and mentioned my wonderful parents, dedicated teachers and the little girl who sat at the top of the top table. 'For those exceptionally bright children,' I told the congregation, 'it must be hard for them to understand why other children aren't as quick on the uptake. Some of us have to work hard and persevere but we can get there in the end.' I then mentioned Susan Barlow, the bright little girl who was top of the top table and no doubt went on to great academic success. Following the degree ceremony, I progressed down the aisle of the hall to the thunderous strains of the organ. At the door a small, crimson-gowned figure turned to face me.

'Hello,' she said.

'Hello,' I replied smiling. 'Have we met?'

She returned the smile. 'I'm the little girl who sat at the top of the top table,' she said. 'I'm Susan Barlow.'

It was such a pleasure to meet her again after so many years. She had – which came as no surprise to me – gone into academia and was a professor at the university.

One memory of Broom Valley Infants that stays in my mind is when Miss Greenhalgh organized Book Day. All the children were to come dressed as characters from books, and along Broom Valley Road that morning could be seen Peter Pan,

Paddington Bear, Noddy, Pooh Bear, Heidi, the Wicked Witch of the West, Snow White, Pinocchio, Humpty Dumpty, Long John Silver and a host of other characters from fiction.

My sister, Christine, made me the most magnificent red and yellow outfit from crêpe paper for this fancy dress event. I went as the Pied Piper of Hamelin and set off for school with her in my colourful doublet and little red and yellow hat, clutching a recorder. People on the top deck of the bus craned their necks to get a view of the little figure that strutted along, passers-by stared and then smiled, and old ladies peered through the curtains. I felt the centre of attention and so proud. Half-way there, the sky opened and the rain fell as thick as umbrella spokes. In seconds the crisp crêpe paper turned into one soggy, orange mess and I arrived at school soaked to the skin and sobbing uncontrollably. Miss Greenhalgh took charge immediately and I was dried and given a clean pair of shorts and a yellow T-shirt to wear. By this time, my great heaving sobs had become a pathetic sniffle and snuffle, but when I saw myself in the mirror I returned to the howling. The dye from the red and yellow crêpe paper had run, and looking back at me in the mirror was a small boy with brilliant orange streaks down his face, arms, hands and legs. Miss Greenhalgh calmed me down, gave me a cuddle and ushered me into the hall where all the other children were waiting in their colourful costumes. I remember their smirks and grins and the whispering and giggling and felt desolate.

'Who's he come as, miss?' one of the children asked.

'Well, can't you tell, Susan Johnson?' Miss Greenhalgh said with exaggerated surprise in her voice, while putting her arm protectively around my shoulder. 'He's come as the Gingerbread Man. Fancy you not knowing that.'

I returned to Broom Valley Infants just before the Christmas of 1985. I had been asked by Miss Greenhalgh, now Mrs Ross and the deputy headteacher, to play Father Christmas, as the caretaker, who usually took the role, was in Moorgate Hospital. What could I say? I will let Mrs Ross take up the story:

And of course I remember too a certain Father Christmas who arrived in brown shoes and, when told by the Deputy Head (me) that Father Christmas didn't wear brown shoes, he promptly removed shoes and socks and walked into the hall in bare feet. He then told a wonderful story about Rudolph and his antics, giving a very plausible explanation of his lack of footwear. The sceptics amongst the children then became believers!

That is not quite how I remember the visit. As I recall I donned the costume and after a strong cup of coffee entered the hall to find row upon row of open-mouthed, wide-eyed children. They squealed in delight when they saw the familiar red coat and white cotton-wool beard. Everything went well until a bright little spark announced loudly, 'You're not real, you know.'

'Oh yes, I am!' I replied in a deep, jolly Father Christmas voice.

'Oh no, you're not,' she persisted, 'your beard's held on by elastic. I can see it. And Father Christmas has big boots. You're not wearing boots. You've got bare feet.'

'Ah, well, I got stuck in a snowdrift on my way here and my boots were so filled up with snow that I had to take them off to dry them.'

'Well, where are they then?' asked a child.

'The school caretaker is drying them out in front of his fire.'

'He hasn't got a fire,' piped up another child. 'It's smokeless on the estate.'

'Well, on his pipes then.'

'You're not the real Father Christmas!' continued the first child, obstinately shaking her little head.

'Oh yes, I am!' I said in my loud, jolly voice, and heard a whole school hall shout back: 'Oh no, you're not!'

Mrs Ross intervened and bailed me out by starting the singing. After three verses of 'Rudolf the Red-nosed Reindeer' each child came forward to receive a small present.

'What are the names of your reindeers?' asked a little boy.

'Well, there's Rudolf,' I started, 'and Donner and Blitzen and er . . . er . . .'

The deputy headteacher, seeing that I was struggling, helped me out again by explaining that Father Christmas was rather deaf.

'Some of the snow from the snowdrift is still in his ears,' she said.

One child asked me if I knew her name and when I replied that I did not, looked crestfallen. 'But I thought Father Christmas knows all the boys' and girls' names?'

Mrs Ross explained that Father Christmas's eyes weren't too good either and he had such a lot of letters to read.

One rather grubby little scrap asked if she could sit on my knee.

'No, Chelsea,' said the deputy headteacher firmly. 'I don't think –' She was too late; the child had clambered up and clung to me like a little monkey.

'Come on down, Chelsea,' said Mrs Ross. 'I don't think Father Christmas wants children on his knee. He's got a poorly leg.' Any more ailments, I thought, and I would be joining the caretaker in the Moorgate Hospital.

'Now, you be a very good little girl and sit on the floor, Chelsea,' I said in my jolly voice, 'otherwise all the other children will want to climb up.' Chelsea stayed put and held fast like a limpet. I chuckled uneasily until the child's teacher managed to prise her off. Mrs Ross shrugged and looked knowingly at the teachers standing around the hall.

After the children had sung me out to 'Jingle Bells' I was invited into the staffroom. It was extremely hot under the red suit.

'Father Christmas, you were a great hit,' said the deputy headteacher. The staff looked on and nodded. 'And we'd like to give you a little Christmas gift.'

'Oh no,' I said, 'it really isn't necessary.'

'Oh, but it is necessary,' insisted Mrs Ross, and presented me with a small bottle wrapped in bright Christmas paper.

I shook my gift and held it to my ear. 'After-shave?' I enquired. 'Is it after-shave?'

'No, Father Christmas,' the staff replied.

'Is it a little bottle of whisky?'

'No, Father Christmas,' they choralsed.

I tore off the wrapping to reveal a small brown bottle of medication. The label read: 'For infestation of the head.'

'Chelsea's just got over head lice,' said the headteacher. 'It's not advisable to be too close to her for the time being.'

'And she's just recovered from scabies,' piped up a beaming teacher. The rest of the staff then joined in with a hearty, 'Ho! Ho! Ho!'

My Miss Greenhalgh came to see me on stage in Rotherham. I shall treasure the note she wrote to me after the show:

My philosophy on children was that I wouldn't want them to be all alike but if you can dig deep enough there is always a redeeming feature to be found somewhere and they all deserve encouragement. I think some of the adverse comments I received as a child at school made me determined never to do that to children and I am pretty sure I never did. The experience of being told by one of my teachers that I was not good at all at her subject had a lasting impact; it helped me to become a better teacher.

I have to say Gervase you were a lovely little boy, very good-looking, very quiet, very neat. I always had a feeling that you were a thinker but didn't <u>always</u> do yourself justice. No, you weren't on the top table but you were a bright lad and you've proved me right.

16

Growing up I never thought of myself as being 'a bright lad'. In fact I felt rather in the shadow of my talented sister and brothers. Unlike them, very little came to me naturally – it needed application. Christine, the eldest, was the intelligent one in the family and passed her scholarship examination with flying colours to attend Notre Dame Convent High School in Sheffield.

Notre Dame (so my parents explained to anyone who would listen) was considered the best state grammar school in the area. Mum and Dad were very proud when my sister was offered a place.

'She's passed for the convent,' my mother bragged to Mrs Evans over the garden wall, the very morning she received the letter from Sister Monica, the headmistress, with the good news.

'A convent!' exclaimed our neighbour. 'Is she becoming a nun then?'

'No, no, of course not,' my mother told her. 'It's just a school. Well, not just any school. It has the best reputation in South Yorkshire.'

'I wouldn't like to be a nun,' said Mrs Evans, pinning another pair of large blue bloomers on the line. 'I'd find their habits very restricting.'

It wasn't just Roman Catholic girls who attended the convent. Well-to-do Protestant parents from Fulwood, Broomhill and other affluent areas of Sheffield happily paid the fees for their daughters to attend, certain in the knowledge that their girls would emerge educated, well-mannered, cultured and courteous and not be distracted in their academic endeavours by pubescent boys. Little did these parents know that often, once on the bus into the city, the ties, gloves and hats of the sixth-formers were stuffed into satchels, the white ankle socks were replaced with nylon stockings and lipstick and mascara were applied before the boys from De La Salle College boarded the bus.

I was in my last year at junior school when I visited Notre Dame Convent. My sister Christine was the Deputy Head Girl by then and was in the sixth form, and she informed me casually one morning, while I was playing with my lead soldiers in the wooden fort that my father had made for me, that I had been invited with her for tea the following Saturday by the headmistress.

'I don't want to go,' I told her, arranging my archers along the castle walls.

'Well, you're going,' she said firmly.

'Why?'

'Because you are!' she exclaimed. 'Nobody argues with Sister Monica, and if she's asked you to go for tea with her, then you are going.'

'She's not my headteacher. She can't order me about,' I said peevishly. 'Anyway, I don't like nuns.'

'Don't be silly. You've never met one.'

'Well, I don't like the look of them. They look like penguins.'

'Well, you are coming with me,' said Christine. 'I have to go and you're coming with me.'

'I'm not.'

'You are.'

'Not!'

'Mum says you have to.'

'Well, I'm not going!'

Christine tried a different tack. 'Please.'

'Why does she want me to go anyway?' I asked. 'I'm not going to a girls' convent when I leave junior school!'

'Sister Monica often asks the brothers and sisters of the prefects in the school for tea,' my sister explained. 'It's a custom. So you really have to go.'

'Well, I don't want to go.'

'If you do,' Christine said, 'I'll buy you that little brass cannon for your fort, the one that fires matchsticks.'

I had wanted that cannon for weeks. I had seen it in Coopers' toy shop on Doncaster Road. The bribe was too much to resist.

'OK,' I said, 'but I want the cannon.'

'And you have to be really, really good and polite and don't eat with your mouth open and you must say, "Thank you, Sister," and "Please, Sister," and remember to blow your nose and not yawn or fidget or speak unless you are spoken to.' It sounded a real ordeal, I thought, but it was worth it to get the cannon.

Before setting off for the convent I was washed, scrubbed, combed, brushed and dressed in my Sunday best. Then I was given a final warning from Christine: 'And remember, be on your best behaviour – or no cannon.'

Notre Dame Convent on Cavendish Street in Sheffield was a dark, forbidding building with small mean windows criss-crossed with thin iron bars. The entrance hall was cool and quiet and smelt of lavender floor polish and old wood. In the alcoves there were large, coloured plaster statues of saints with downcast eyes, a gentle-faced virgin with long thin white hands holding a lily and standing on a snake, and a figure of Jesus with a sad expression, touching his exposed vivid red heart. Placed high up on the far wall hung a huge dominating black cross with the contorted figure of Christ, staring down wide-eyed.

We were met by a large fussy nun called Sister Agnes, who showed us into a small spartan room with a plain wooden table and four hard-backed chairs. In the corner was a statue of a nun with a halo, a great black wimple and a huge white collar. She was a stout, homely-looking woman with a round cheery face and held a book on her lap. She didn't look like my idea of a nun at all.

'Who's that?' I asked.

'That's Blessed Julie Billiart,' Christine told me.

'Julia Billiards?' I said. 'It doesn't sound like the name of a nun to me.'

'Julie Billiart!' my sister snapped. 'She's the foundress of the Sisters of Notre Dame of Namur.'

I blew out my breath noisily. I could tell that this was going to be a prolonged and unpleasant experience, but I thought of my little brass cannon. 'I don't like it here,' I said, shivering theatrically. 'It's really, really spooky.'

'Don't be silly!' snapped Christine. I could see she was as nervous as I.

'I bet it's full of the ghosts of dead nuns walking the corridors moaning and groaning.'

'Don't be silly.'

'It's worse than the dentist's,' I whispered.

'Be quiet, I can hear her coming.' I strained my ears but couldn't hear anything.

The door creaked open and Sister Monica swept through as if on oiled castors. She smiled a small thin-lipped smile. With her long black cloak and hood, sharp beak of a nose and small black glittery eyes, she reminded me of a blackbird. I almost expected her to trill when she opened her mouth. We stood up.

'Christine,' she said in a hushed voice. 'How very nice to see you. Thank you for coming.'

'Good afternoon, Sister.'

She stared at me thoughtfully, like a customer considering a purchase. 'And this must be your young brother, Gervase.' She held out a long white hand and I touched it nervously.

Her hand was as soft and cold as snow. 'And how are you, young man?'

'I'm very well, thank you, Sister,' I replied politely. I could feel myself beginning to tremble.

'Do sit down,' said the nun quietly. 'We shall be having tea a little later. I hope you are hungry. I'm sure you are. Boys are always hungry, aren't they?' How would she know, I thought. I don't suppose she sees all that many boys. 'Sister Mary Francis has been very busy in the kitchen.'

Sister Mary Francis couldn't have been all that busy in the kitchen because when the tea arrived it was little more than a plate of cold meat and salad. The thin slice of anaemic ham had a halo of fat around it, the leaf of lettuce looked as if it had been left in the sun all day and the half tomato looked as if someone had trodden on it.

'For this bounty, O Lord,' said Sister Monica, 'make us truly thankful and help us always to remember those who are less fortunate than ourselves who have little to eat. Amen.'

'Amen,' I repeated, thinking that those less fortunate were welcome to this food.

'Do start,' said Sister Monica, lifting up her knife and fork and giving the thin-lipped smile. She cut the meat into tiny squares and posted them carefully into her small mouth.

I hated ham, and this excuse for meat tasted like cardboard. The fat lined the roof of my mouth and I could feel bits of gristle on my tongue. I chewed and chewed but I just couldn't swallow the revolting bullet of food.

'Do you like school?' asked the nun.

'Oh yes, Sister,' I replied, spitting out bits of ham and lettuce. Christine tapped my ankle under the table.

'And at what are you good?' asked the nun.

'Pardon, Sister?'

'What do you like doing at school?'

'Well, I like stories,' I told her.

'Really?'

'He enjoys reading and writing,' Christine interrupted, 'and he plays the piano.'

'That's very good,' said the nun, dabbing her mouth with the napkin. 'Jesus liked stories too. And do you take after your sister? She's our brightest star in art.'

'I like drawing, Sister,' I replied, pushing a lump of fatty meat to the side of my mouth, 'but I'm not very good.'

'I'm sure you are.'

'No really, I'm not,' I replied. 'I do like drawing but I'm not very good.'

The nun popped a piece of ham into her mouth and chewed slowly. There was a long and embarrassing silence. 'And do you say your prayers?'

'Yes, Sister.'

'And go to Mass?'

'Yes, Sister.'

'And Confession?'

'Yes, Sister.'

'And do you serve on the altar?' she asked.

'Pardon?'

'Sister,' Christine hissed.

'Pardon, Sister?' I repeated. It was strange calling this woman 'Sister'. She looked more like a mother.

'Do you assist the priest at Mass?'

'You mean an altar boy, Sister?'

She nodded.

'No, I'm not an altar boy,' I told her.

'And you attend a Catholic school?'

'No, I go to Broom Valley.'

'A non-Catholic school.' She arched an eyebrow.

I wondered how long this quizzing was going to go on for. I'd seen war films at the cinema where the Gestapo interrogated English prisoners. Sister Monica would have been really good at that. I am sure if she had asked me I would have told her anything.

There was a long pause. She continued with the meal, occasionally dabbing her mouth with a small lace handkerchief. 'And do you think you might have a vocation?' she asked suddenly.

'We go to Blackpool,' I said, my mouth still full of the fatty wodge.

Sister Monica's smile was now pained and ironic. 'A vocation, not a vacation.'

'I don't know what you mean,' I said.

'Sister,' prompted Christine prodding me in the side.

'I don't know what you mean, Sister.'

'To become a priest?' asked the nun.

The thought had never entered my head. Be a priest like Father Hammond? Not a chance. I wanted to be a soldier or a policeman or a fighter pilot.

'No, Sister,' I said, and then as an afterthought I added, 'I think you have to be really brainy to be a priest. I don't think I'm clever enough.'

The answer obviously impressed her. She rested her knife and fork on the plate and fixed me with the small black eyes.

'Humility is one of the qualities of the priest,' said the nun. 'Many young men have thought themselves unworthy but have become very great priests. If you work hard and say your prayers and attend Mass regularly, you may get the calling.'

'The calling?' I repeated.

'God might call you to become one of his priests,' said the nun. 'A great privilege, the greatest honour – to administer the blessed sacraments.'

I had this picture of God, a large, white-haired figure, popping up from behind a cloud and calling down to me. 'Pssst! Pssst!' he would hiss. 'You down there.'

'Me?'

'Yes, you, the boy with the hair sticking up, the runny nose and the scuffed shoes. Do you want to be a priest?'

'No, thank you very much,' I would reply, 'but thank you all the same for asking.'

I could see my sister was not very pleased with me as we made our way to the bus, but I still got my little brass cannon.

Having trained as a teacher in Liverpool, Christine returned to teach at Notre Dame and subsequently became Head of the Art Department. I cannot count the number of times I've been approached over the years by her former pupils, who tell me what an amazing teacher she was.

My sister is a talented artist, and as a teenager she would spend hours sketching, drawing, painting delicate watercolours, producing the most vivid oil paintings. Dad bought her a cabin (which she euphemistically called 'the chalet') which he erected at the end of the garden behind the garage, and Christine would spend hours in her studio on her art. Should I come anywhere near, to peer through the window and see what she was up to, she would tell me in no uncertain terms to go away. I have vivid memories of Christine's chalet. It was a colourful, interesting place and I loved it when I was invited (on rare occasions) into her private haven. In the centre was a large paint-spattered easel, behind which was a long trestle table with every bit covered in tide-marked jam jars, crumpled rags, discoloured and stiff, clusters of bottles filled with white spirit, turpentine substitute and honey-coloured linseed oil. There were pottery jars full of long-stemmed brushes, boxes of charcoal, tins of watercolours and little silver tubes of oil paint, their necks crusted with the most exotically named colours – magenta, scarlet, violet, coral, viridian, ultramarine.

Every conceivable wall space was covered with posters, prints, portraits, sketches, paintings and photographs. It was a riot of shape and colour. From the ceiling dangled multicoloured mobiles – squares, circles, diamonds and triangles.

The windowsills were crammed with plants, some of which had given up the ghost weeks before, feathers in jars, clay figures, carved boxes, animal skulls, shells, fragments of pottery and glass and all manner of strange objects and artefacts. The bookshelf was entirely covered with a clutter of dog-eared folders and files, sketchbooks, teaching texts, thick dictionaries and numerous art history books.

Sometimes on a wet Sunday afternoon Christine would try to show me how to sketch and paint, but, sadly, it was clear I had little of her talent.

17

Michael is my eldest brother and, as younger brothers often do, I looked up to him. Although nothing was ever said, I always had the feeling that he was our father's favourite. He was more like Dad than any of us, I guess. Michael has always been gregarious, good-humoured and extremely good company, and no one can tell a joke as well as he. When he speaks, the whole room listens. He was also extremely practical, like our father. While I had my nose in a book and Alec, my other brother, played his guitar and Christine painted, Michael would be making models, taking things apart, fiddling in the engine of the car with Dad, activities which held no fascination at all for me. Michael could make and mend anything. I would spend a couple of frustrated hours trying to fix my train set and then my brother would come along and it would be working in no time. The zip would stick on my jacket and try as I might I couldn't move it, then Michael would fiddle with it and it would work even better than before. I would be struggling over my maths O level, and he would sit with me for five minutes and I would soon grasp the concept. He was fascinated with machines and gadgets. At seventeen he built his own motorbike, and at twenty a small sports car which he drove around Rotherham, usually with a girl next to him on the front seat.

My other brother, Alec, was the proud owner of a bicycle, which he had saved up to buy and purchased second-hand through *Exchange & Mart* magazine. He had painstakingly re-enamelled the machine in bright purple paint and had painted '*gran turismo*' in silver lettering on the crossbar. He

polished and oiled the bike each week, and had fixed these
large chrome cow-horn handlebars on the front. The machine
was in fixed gear with a naked chain, which meant that the
pedals turned automatically as the bicycle moved and the rider
had little control apart from the brakes. I was not allowed to
use it.

One Saturday I saw Alec set off for town and a few minutes
later I was up at the top of Richard Road on his prized *gran
turismo*. As I cycled down the steep hill the bicycle gathered
speed. I applied the brakes but to no avail. There was a screech,
a shudder and the smell of burning rubber as the brake pads
attempted to grip the wheel casings. The pedals rotated alarmingly and I hung on for dear life as I careered down the hill.
At the very bottom of Richard Road was the busy main Broom
Valley Road, and thoughts ran through my mind that I would
end up under the Cowrakes Lane bus if I didn't do something.
I turned the cow-horn handlebars, collided with a gas lamp
and was thrown up in the air, ending up flat on my back. The
world turned round above me. With a raging pain in my head
and with something wet dribbling down my forehead, I
managed to wheel the bike with the buckled wheel and twisted
handlebars back up the hill and arrived at the back door.

'I've fallen off Alec's bike,' I managed to tell my mother
before everything went black.

I came round to find myself seated in a chair in the living
room with a damp towel around my head and my mother
holding my hand.

'Thank God,' she said.

Then I heard Alec's voice. 'Is he going to die?'

My mother assured him I was not. He then informed her
angrily that I had buckled a wheel on his bike and bent the
handlebars and that I would have to pay to have them fixed.

When Doctor Johnson arrived I was propped up in bed in
a pair of clean pyjamas, a fresh towel wrapped round my head.

He examined the wound, now matted with dried blood, lifted an eyelid and peered into my eyes, took my pulse and declared that my brain was pretty well intact and it was too late for stitches and the cut would heal itself. Then he passed the towel to my mother and said, 'He can dispense with the turban.' Later that day Mrs Rogers, a neighbour, arrived with a jar of cow's-foot jelly and an egg custard, both of which remained uneaten.

Alec loved animals, and until he left home at the age of twenty to emigrate to Ireland, he kept a whole menagerie of creatures. He had the usual pets youngsters like to keep – rabbits, tortoises, hamsters, mice and budgerigars – but he also kept a ferret in a small hutch and a grass snake in a glass tank. Then he became fascinated with birds of prey. It started when he discovered two baby owls that had fallen out of a nest. He brought them home, reared them and released them. Then he found a young kestrel, which he trained to hunt, like the fictional Billy Casper in Barry Hine's classic *A Kestrel for a Knave*. Alec would take the kestrel, which gripped on to the large leather gauntlet he wore, up Moorgate Road to Boston Park, where he would let the bird fly free. It would wheel and flutter in the air until my brother swung the coloured lure (a bunch of feathers with a lump of meat attached to a long string) above his head and the bird would return to his gloved fist. It was thrilling to watch. Once the kestrel, high in an empty sky, hovered and then plummeted downwards. The next minute a small bird fell tumbling to the ground in a flurry of beating wings. The kestrel sheered away and then dropped to the ground on to its prey. It wasn't long before the bird, having had the taste of freedom, took off and never returned. Alec spent hours in Boston Park looking for it, but without success.

My father was immensely tolerant of Alec's pets, even following the time when the ferret escaped and was discovered in Mrs Evans's kitchen baring its needle-like teeth, but he was very wary of the falcon after the 'incident'. Alec brought home a peregrine falcon which he had bought from somebody at the Art School where he was studying. The peregrine was a much larger bird than the kestrel and far less predictable. It would sit on its perch in the back garden, a beautiful and powerful creature with huge shining black eyes, curved beak and sharp talons. Children in the street would call just to look at it. One memorable day Alec removed the little leather hood with the bright plume on top from the bird's head and began to fiddle with the jesses (the short leather straps that fastened around each leg of the hawk) just as Dad emerged from the garage. The bird took off and landed on Dad, digging its claws into his bald head. At Doncaster Gate Hospital the young doctor looked perplexed.

'A bird?' he said. 'You say a bird did this? What sort of bird?'

'Well, it wasn't a budgie,' Dad told him, irritated.

'Budgie!' the doctor exclaimed, preparing a tetanus injection.

'It was a falcon,' Dad told him. 'A falcon landed on me.'

'Whatever for?' asked the doctor.

'I don't know,' said Dad. 'Perhaps it wanted to carry me off to its nest to feed me to its chicks.'

When Alec moved to Ireland he continued his interest in falconry and appeared, as the king's falconer, in the film *Alfred the Great*, starring David Hemmings as the eponymous hero, which was being filmed near Galway.

Most parents, I guess, would dissuade a youngster from keeping such creatures but my parents never seemed to mind. When Alec arrived home one day with a liver and white puppy with doleful eyes and floppy ears they merely took it in their stride, telling him that Dan (the name given to the dog) was his responsibility. Neighbours had dogs, little snappy terriers, fat slobbering labradors, fearsome alsatians and frisky mongrels, but Dan was different. He grew to be an elegant, gentle-natured creature, a pure-bred German pointer. There were no threatening rumbles or sharp yapping, no growls or show of sharp teeth. He was such an amiable beast we all grew to love him. At the park few dogs could keep up with him. He would bound off into the distance but return immediately at the call of his name. He would snuffle in bushes and then on scenting game he would freeze. His tail would shoot up, his nose would dip to the floor and he would raise one paw and 'point'.

Once, on a trip to Bridlington in my sister's VW Beetle car, we stopped in a lay-by for Dan to stretch his legs. The man in the car parked behind enquired what breed he was.

'He's a German pointer,' I told him.

'And you're in the Volkswagen?'

'Yes.'

'Bloody patriotic, aren't you,' he said.

There was one occasion when I saw my mother at her formidable and angry best. A policeman arrived at the back door. I was in the living room but could hear the conversation.

'Does an Alec Phinn live here?' he asked my mother.

'Yes,' she told him.

'I'd like a word with him.'

'What about?' she asked.

'We have reason to believe that he was involved in the theft of some sweets from the corner shop on Gerard Road.'

'Says who?' asked my mother.

'If I could have a word with him,' said the policeman.

'Not until you tell me who's made this accusation.'

'Are you the boy's mother?'

'I am.'

'The owner of the sweet shop thinks your son might have been involved.'

'Thinks?' repeated my mother.

'Yes.'

'Did she see my son take some sweets?'

'No, but –'

'Did somebody else see him take some sweets?'

'Not exactly,' said the policeman, 'but another boy said he thought it might be your son.'

'So some boy says he thinks that it may have been my son and you have wasted your time coming all the way up here on information which cannot be adequately substantiated, on the word of another boy who *thinks* it might be my son, on a rumour?'

'Madam,' said the policeman, 'may I have a word with your son?'

'No, you may not,' said my mother. 'He is not a thief and I strongly resent the implication that he is. I should have thought that the police had better things to do than waste their time on tittle-tattle. Good morning.'

The policeman departed.

My mother put on her coat. I could tell she was really angry. 'I'm going down to the corner shop,' she said. 'I won't be long.'

I wished I could have been a fly on the wall when she gave the shop owner a piece of her mind.

On another occasion, a sunny afternoon as I was helping my father paint the garage door, two soldiers strutted up the drive.

'Good morning, sir,' said the man with the three stripes on his arm.

'Morning,' said Dad.

'Does an Alec Phinn live here?' asked the sergeant.

'Yes, he does,' said Dad.

'I believe he is interested in joining the army.'

My father put down his paintbrush and smiled. 'I very much doubt it,' he said.

'We have a completed application form,' said the sergeant.

'I think it's somebody's idea of a joke,' said my father.

'May we have a word with him?'

'Be my guest,' Dad said, 'he's in the back garden.' Then he added, 'Watch your uniforms on the gate. It's just been painted.'

On the lawn at the back of the house stood my brother with his falcon on his arm. Alec was a student at the Rotherham Art School, and like most art students at the time was dressed in rather colourful and individual clothes: a brightly flowered shirt, tight jeans and cowboy boots and with his hair shoulder length.

The soldiers stared at him for a moment, then at each other and without a word retraced their steps.

'Good morning,' they said, and marched off down the path.

My two brothers are both very musical. Michael has a fine tenor voice and Alec, who went on to become a professional musician, could play any instrument with strings on it. Neither had any formal lessons – they were just possessed of a natural musical talent.

During Mass at St Bede's one Sunday, my mother began to weep. At the Communion, the soloist in the choir sang 'Panis Angelicus' in a beautiful clear tenor voice. After the service the curate, Father Daly, stood at the door of the church shaking hands with his parishioners.

'You must be very proud of your son, Mrs Phinn,' he said.

'I am, Father,' said my mother, looking down and smiling at me.

'No,' said the priest, 'I meant your other son, Michael. It was he who was singing the solo part at this morning's Mass.'

My mother had never recognized her son's voice.

Once discovered, of course, Michael was encouraged to display his talent. My mother would invariably cry when he sang: 'Danny Boy', 'I'll Take You Home Again, Kathleen', 'Galway Bay', 'Macushla' and other sentimental Irish ballads.

Alec isn't a singer but a talented guitarist. When he was ten and we were on holiday in Blackpool, our father bought him a cheap wooden ukulele. Alec mastered the basic chords of the instrument during the week, so well in fact that on the Friday he was entered for the children's talent competition. Jolly Uncle Peter Webster hosted the show on the pier, and lines of children were keen to show their talents. At the audition Alec was picked to take part. The judges were selected from adult members of the audience who didn't have a child performing. I guess we would have won (we were runners-up) if Alec hadn't been burdened with me singing along with him. The winner was a precocious Shirley Temple look-alike, dressed for the part in a frilly dress and curly hair and carrying a great stuffed dog. She rendered the song 'How Much is that Doggie in the Window?' in a loud and shrill voice and finished with a tap dance. Departing with her prize and a smug expression on her face, she informed everyone within hearing that she had won the contest last year and the year before. I bet Jolly Uncle Peter Webster felt like chucking her off the pier. I know I did.

That cheap wooden ukulele never seemed to be out of my brother's hands until his birthday, when he was given his first guitar. Then came the skiffle craze. At fifteen Alec formed a group: guitar, double bass (made out of a tea chest with a broom handle and a thick piece of twine for the string) and washboard. Richard Road became an open house for Alec's friends, and the group would congregate in the garage and practise endlessly the Lonnie Donegan hits: 'Does Your Chewing Gum Lose Its Flavour on the Bedpost Overnight?', 'Last Train to San Fernando', 'My Old Man's a Dustman' and 'It Takes a Worried Man to Sing a Worried Song'. The garden was full of Bill Haley, Little Richard, Tommy Steele, Adam Faith and Marty Wilde.

At twenty Alec moved to Ireland, and some years later, with the fiddle player Frankie Gavin, he formed De Dannan, one of Ireland's leading traditional Irish folk groups. His solo albums *Innisfree* and *Blue Mountain*, with tracks arranged by himself, have become classics.

Since I couldn't sing like Michael or play a guitar like Alec, it was decided that, at the age of eight, I should have piano lessons. When I was little I would love to sit beside my mother's feet as she played the piano, my back resting in the polished wood, feeling the vibrations run through my body as she plonked away. Her feet would go up and down on the pedals and her body would sway from side to side. She would play sentimental Irish ballads, popular songs, favourite melodies and hymns, rarely using music but wonderful at improvisation. Sometimes on Sunday after Mass the family would retire to the Catholic Club and Mum would be persuaded to play. I was so proud of her as I sat in the corner with my bottle of ginger beer and a bag of crisps, the sort with the little blue twist of salt in the bottom. I wanted to play like that.

Each week I went for an hour's lesson to Miss Platt. Miss Platt lived in a large semi-detached house on Worrygoose Lane. The 'parlour', as she called it, where she kept the large polished mahogany piano, smelt of cats and lavender furniture polish. I would catch the bus from town to Wickersley with my thin leather music satchel tucked underneath my arm, feeling very grand. Before my lesson I would wait in the hall listening to the expert playing of her star pupil, Ieuan Walsh, whose lesson was before mine. Listening to his flawless performance of 'Für Elise' and the 'Moonlight Sonata' didn't make me feel all that confident.

Miss Platt had two Siamese cats. They would hiss and arch their backs when I entered the room, then leap on to the sofa opposite and purr softly, all the while keeping me under careful observation with their green almond eyes. I once made the mistake of trying to stroke one of the beasts and was rewarded with a vicious scratch.

Miss Platt was a small, cheerful woman with a lilting birdlike trill in her voice. As I banged away on the keys she would occasionally nod in the manner of a dowager at a soirée, craning an ear and keeping a fixed smile on her round face. If I managed to play the piece through without a mistake she would smile beatifically and raise her small hands like Jesus sermonizing. Miss Platt had a small stock of comments: 'Delightful, dear,' 'A little more practice I think, dear,' 'Very nice, dear,' 'Careful with the crotchets, dear,' 'Coming along nicely, dear.' She wasn't one of those piano teachers who rapped your knuckles if you made a mistake or shouted at you if you hadn't practised. She was a paragon of patience, particularly with a small heavy-handed boy who had little aptitude at the piano. While other students rose through the ranks of the pianoforte examinations, I, much to my chagrin, didn't. 'I want him to play the piano for enjoyment,' my mother told her, 'not pass examinations.' I had no natural talent for playing the piano but I persevered for a time, until O levels reared their heads and then I stopped. Today I play haltingly but with enthusiasm any tune which happens to be in the key of D.

18

Uncle Alec was Dad's elder brother. His dream was to become a pilot, and he passed all the ingenious tests by which potential air crews were selected but trained for the secondary role as a navigator and flew with the bombers during the war. I have his eight medals, which include the MBE, on my wall. Uncle Alec looked and spoke like a character out of my Biggles books. He was tall and lithe, with a great ginger handlebar moustache and hands like spades. He would appear at the door un-announced, with his brown canvas kitbag, stay for a few days and then depart. Once he arrived in the early morning and climbed through a window to gain entry. He settled down on the settee in the front room, only to be confronted later by my father brandishing a poker, assuming we had burglars.

On leaving the RAF Alec became a civil servant in London and travelled by train daily to his office with brolly and brief-case. When he retired he spent most of his time tending his garden and making wooden boxes for the blue-tits. It was such a different life from the RAF. I still have on the desk in my study a beautiful polished trinket box he made from the propel-ler of a crashed Blenheim bomber in which he had flown. I guess he must have had some close shaves, but, like many who had gone through the war, he would never talk about it.

Aunt Nora was my Mum's elder sister and she, like my mother, had trained as a nurse. A striking-looking woman with large dark eyes and a winning smile, she was extremely witty, with a dry sense of humour and an amusing turn of phrase. For many years she worked in Rotherham as a school nurse, accompanying the doctor around schools to assist with the TB injections, the polio inoculations, the hair inspections for head lice and to undertake the regular medical assessments of the children. On one occasion, when visiting a school in Kimberworth, she discovered that a child, rather than having gained height since his last assessment, had in fact shrunk. The doctor was rather bemused, for the child was clearly not under-nourished. He expressed his anxiety to the headteacher, who was not at all concerned and quipped, 'The lad seems to be settling down nicely, then.' The doctor was not amused.

One of Aunt Nora's main jobs as she toured the schools was the relentless search for nits. The 'nit nurse' featured large in school folklore, and every child dreaded the humiliation of being singled out as a carrier of these unwelcome little visitors. We lined up to have our scalps examined and when one child started to scratch his scalp we were all at it. Should any vermin-ous creatures be discovered in a child's hair, a letter would be sent home with the instruction that he should be deloused before being sent back. Headteachers would show her notes from parents, which included:

Ethel's off with nits which are all down our street. I'll send her back when she's been fumigated.

Our Maggie came home with nits last night and they're not hers.

Nurse says she's found nits in her head, well I've looked in her head and can't see any because I don't know what they look like.

In one school a new and rather naive young teacher was told by my aunt that it was not really a sensible idea to let her long hair cascade over her shoulders.

'But I'm very proud of my hair,' she told my aunt, clearly stung by the comment.

'Well, I suggest you tie it back,' suggested my aunt, 'unless, of course, you wish to be infested with head lice.'

The young woman very nearly fainted.

Some children would present themselves to Nurse Lloyd smelling to high heaven. They had been sewn into their vests for the winter and emanated a most unpleasant smell, of which they had become oblivious. One child's chest had been rubbed liberally with fatty, evil-smelling goose grease by his grandmother, who believed that it would ward off all known germs. My aunt was less tactful than my mother in these circumstances. She removed the vests and made no bones about telling the youngster that he smelt and needed a good wash, and should tell his mother to put him in a bath and get out the carbolic soap.

Uncle Ted was Aunt Nora's husband. He was a quiet, rather shy man with a pronounced stutter and was firmly under his wife's thumb. Aunt Nora called the shots in their home and no mistake. Ted had a rather mysterious past. Mum and Dad never talked about it and I can't recall Ted ever saying anything about his childhood. I formed the impression, probably quite wrongly, that he was the illegitimate son of a wealthy man who had had an illicit liaison with one of his servants. I was reading Catherine Cookson when I came to this conclusion. It was very probably a fanciful notion, but on my twenty-first birthday I was presented by Aunt Nora with a set of the most beautiful inlaid gold cufflinks in a red-leather-covered box. 'These were Ted's father's,' she told me. 'Ted never wears them and we would like you to have them.' When I asked about his father Aunt Nora evaded the question. Then there was the silver-topped Malacca walking cane, which was kept in the umbrella stand in their hall. I asked about it once. 'Ted's father used to walk out with that,' said Aunt Nora. Then she added, 'Apart from the cufflinks and the china bowl, it's the only thing that he got.' She left it at that. Just before his death a half-brother appeared to claim the stick.

My father was a very generous man and he found Ted's

meanness irksome. When he joined my father in the Masons Arms, Ted was invariably last at the bar to buy his round, and on other occasions he evaded paying for any of the drinks. When his nephews and nieces visited he had to be prompted by Aunt Nora to dig into his pocket and give us a shilling. Mum put a charitable gloss on this tight-fistedness and told us it was down to his childhood, when money had been in short supply. 'I guess he had very little when he was young and therefore is careful with his money.'

After coming out of the army, Ted set himself up as a plasterer working for a number of building firms. He drove a small white van which came in very useful when I started college and needed to transport all my things to Leeds. Aunt Nora and Uncle Ted did look rather incongruous when they went out for the evening, all dressed up, climbing from the small white van.

Grandma Mullarkey clearly thought Nora could have done better for herself. When she was a ward sister and stunningly pretty, doctors had queued up to take Nora out. Mum used to tell me how distraught her well-connected suitors were when Nora grew bored with them and moved on. She settled eventually for Ted, who was hard-working, reliable, even-tempered and adored her. There's no doubt he was a handsome man in his youth, and a picture of him in his army uniform shows a dashing, dark-haired young man with a generous smile. I recall him once telling me he 'fell on his feet' when he met Nora and couldn't believe his luck that she had fallen for him.

The only lengthy conversation I had with Uncle Ted that I recall was when I was in the sixth form and we walked from Bridlington to Flamborough village across Bempton Cliffs. He told me that as soon as he was able he joined the army and rose through the ranks to sergeant in the Royal Army Medical Corps. After a drunken night out and being late reporting back at the barracks, he was stripped of his stripes, so his time in authority was short.

When he went with the British Expeditionary Force to France he was angry that priority was given to constructing the officers' toilets. Of course, it was inconceivable that officers and other ranks should share the same facilities. Ted told me that the French thought it laughable that the British officers had to have their own private little lavatory when everyone else performed under the trees or in a large smelly hole in the ground.

The experience of Dunkirk stayed with my Uncle Ted all his life. That dramatic escape from the clutches of the ravaging German army, when more than 300,000 British and French troops were rescued by a ragtag flotilla of naval vessels, fishing boats and paddle steamers, was a vivid memory for him, but one that was rarely spoken of. Winston Churchill had called that retreat a 'miracle of deliverance', and to rally the troops said the spirit of Dunkirk would endure as 'an example of triumph in the face of adversity'. Ted didn't quite see it like that. For all the heroism involved, he viewed the conflict as a colossal military defeat and it brought back painful memories. What he witnessed on those French beaches I never discovered, but it must have been traumatic because his stutter started from the day he left Dunkirk.

Along with many of his comrades he was stranded without food or water on the Dunkirk beaches at the end of May 1940. In spite of a rearguard action, the British and Allied troops had been practically driven into the sea by the numerically superior and better equipped German forces. Ted had lived in a cellar on puddle water and a pound of sugar for a week, finally escaping on 4 June. Crammed with other soldiers into a French fishing smack, he tried to tend to the wounded as the boat navigated a precarious course out of a harbour littered with the wreckage of half-sunken ships. He told me he had seen sights no man should see, how he looked back and saw thousands of troops still on the beaches, many wounded and dying, and felt helpless. It was chaos. As they were pulling out of the harbour the German planes circled like vultures overhead and then dived, and Ted, looking up at the empty sky, thought his time had come. To his amazement not a bomb was dropped or a machine gun fired. The Stukas dipped their wings and saluted the retreating British army.

When he died, Ted left me his medals. There was one he never sent for: the Dunkirk Medal.

Aunt Nora was a devout Roman Catholic and each Sunday morning Ted would drop her off at the church for eleven o'clock Mass. He would then go and have a pint at the British Legion and collect her later. I was the executor for Ted's estate, and his strong desire was to be buried with his wife in the Catholic section of the cemetery in Bridlington and have Nora's priest, Canon Plunkett, say a few prayers. I promised him when he was nearing the end that I would endeavour to carry out his wishes. When he died I made an appointment to see the priest, a large, forceful character with a pronounced Northern Irish accent. I imagined, as I was shown into his study by the housekeeper, that I would have a real job persuading Canon Plunkett to agree to a service for a non-believer, but I was wrong. I remember sitting facing the priest across his large mahogany desk, listening to his monologue.

'Ted Lloyd was a good man,' the canon told me, 'and he deserves a Requiem Mass. I always had the feeling he wanted to come into the church when he dropped off your aunt. God will look upon him in a kindly light, for he was a devoted husband, a hard worker and a thoroughly nice man.'

I arranged with Ted's former comrades from the British Legion and the Dunkirk Veterans that they would attend the funeral, and on the day a large group, many in blazers and berets, some with flags, others wearing chestfuls of medals, assembled outside the church. Not unsurprisingly, no one appeared from Ted's side of the family. Just before the coffin was carried into the church the housekeeper could be heard complaining to the priest in the small porch.

'It's disgusting, Canon, disgusting. You open your porch for the down-and-outs and this is what they do.'

I asked what the problem was.

'The vagrants who congregate in the porch of a night have urinated in the holy water font, that's what,' the housekeeper snapped, screwing up her face into a terrible grimace. 'The good canon here leaves the porch open so those who have nowhere to go can shelter from the cold and rain. Many is the time he's been knocked up, haven't you, Canon, by one of these down-and-outs asking for food and money and I don't know what. And this is how they repay his Christian charity – by urinating in his holy water. It's disgusting.'

More holy water was blessed and the contents of the font replaced. Then the priest appeared resplendent in black cope and biretta.

After the Mass I had arranged for a reception in the church hall. Sandwiches and sausage rolls, pork pies, salads, cakes and desserts filled the tables, all overseen by the priest's house-keeper. Only five of us stayed. The British Legion contingent departed and the Dunkirk veterans had other appointments to keep. My sister, wife, myself and two others surveyed the vast spread. It was a sorry little group.

'What are you going to do with all this food?' the house-keeper asked me.

'Perhaps you might give it to the down-and-outs,' I suggested.

'Over my dead body,' she replied, 'not after what the dirty devils did in the canon's holy water font!'

19

Uncle Jimmy was Mum's younger brother. He was a slim, strikingly good-looking man with pale blue eyes and a captivating smile, so it came as no surprise that he was 'one for the ladies'. He would always arrive at the door with a great smile and a present for me – I guess of all his nephews and nieces he had a bit of a soft spot for the youngest. I still have his presents: the pair of binoculars in the simulated leather case, the pencil box with the sliding lid, the Dinky toys, the picture book of famous British heroes, the *Thomas the Tank Engine* books. He was a romancer was Uncle Jimmy, an adventurer, a risk-taker and one of the most generous and loving men it has been my good fortune to meet. When only seven he left home, caught a bus to the station in Rotherham and went on to Liverpool, where he boarded a ship for Ireland. How he managed to get all the way from Yorkshire to Galway at that tender age without a penny is quite amazing. I was told that even at the age of seven he had 'a touch of the Blarney', for he convinced a group of friendly soldiers to take him under their wing and that his parents were waiting for him on the quay in Dublin.

He made his way from Dun Laoghaire and across Ireland to Galway, arrived at Auntie Maggie's cottage and stood at the door as large as life, telling her that his mother knew where he was and had sent him over for a holiday. My Grandma, of course, had no idea where he was and got in a state of great panic. The police were called and then a telegram arrived from her cousin telling her that: 'Jimmy is with us. All is well. We'll get him home.'

Jimmy had only been found out when Aunt Maggie asked him to write a postcard telling his mother he was safe and well. The postmistress read the postcard and promptly informed Aunt Maggie. Jimmy's postcard home read: 'Dear Mother, don't worry about me. I am in London. Love Jimmy.'

One Sunday young Jimmy set off to Mass but never arrived at St Bede's. He was spotted by a neighbour of my grandmother's swimming in the canal. In the dirty brown stretch of polluted water Jimmy was seen diving and splashing away merrily. His parents never mentioned it, but the following Sunday his father followed him at a discreet distance. When Jimmy plunged under the water, the neatly stacked clothes on the bank were snatched by his father, who then waited until the truant emerged. If he expected his son to panic, Grandfather was greatly mistaken. Jimmy searched for a while and then, unable to find his clothes, set off for home attired only in a dripping pair of cotton underpants. He was intercepted near the Chapel on the Bridge and made to get dressed, much to the amusement of passers-by. Unfortunately for Jimmy his father did not see the funny side of things and gave his son a good hiding when he got him back home.

As a young man Jimmy went to India with my grandfather and astounded the other passengers and the crew when, on sight of land, he dived off the ship and swam ashore. He was entirely fearless and worked for a while as a steeplejack, always relied upon to climb to the very top of a building without turning a hair.

The story of Grandfather's stolen silver and china became well known in the family. Certain valuable items had gone missing and the Indian servants were lined up so that the culprit could be found. Jimmy finally came clean and admitted selling the things to buy presents for various lady friends he had in the nearby village. Grandma often wondered if she had mixed-race grandchildren somewhere in India. He got in with the

army set in India and on returning home joined the Irish
Guards, where he distinguished himself before being invalided
out with damage to his ears caused by the loud guns. For most
of his life he had impaired hearing, but never complained.

. I always hoped Uncle Jimmy's visits would coincide with
the arrival of the fair, for he would take me there. Great
coloured wagons and huge lorries would trundle through
Rotherham, and tents and stalls, roundabouts and rides would
set up at the stretch of spare ground just outside the town. I
loved the noises, the smells, the bustling crowds, the bright
lights and the excitement of the fair. I can still see the stallhold-
ers with their red noses and hear their loud voices, grown
raucous over the years through constant shouting.

The whole area was a noisy, wildly colourful experience,
full of stalls where you could throw balls or darts or hoops in
the hope of winning a garishly pink cuddly rabbit or shoot
popguns to win a goldfish trying to swim in a little see-through
plastic bag with an inch of water in the bottom.

Such was my uncle's generous nature that he insisted I went
on nearly every ride – rollercoaster, carousel, Big Dipper,
Mighty Slide and merry-go-round. The one exception was
the Tunnel of Love. The Ghost Train was pretty tame compared
with the modern-day equivalent. It wouldn't frighten a toddler
today. A small train with hard wooden seats rattled around a
single track in a darkened tent, accompanied by taped screams
and ghostly noises. On the walls were a few plastic skulls and
pictures of headless corpses, and occasionally an iridescent
skeleton or a giant spider would drop from the roof. The
rollercoaster was seriously scary. Those daring enough to go
on it would sit in an open cabin with a crossbar across the
centre to stop them falling out. It rattled and trembled slowly
upwards on wavy tracks to a point high in the sky and then
plummeted downwards at incredible speed. Ear-piercing
screams of terror would come from the occupants of the cabins,

occasionally supplemented by 'uurrghhhs' and 'ahhhhs' when a waterfall of vomit covered those unfortunate enough to be in the car in front of the perpetrator.

My favourite ride was the dodgems. In a small car Uncle Jimmy was adept at weaving and dodging; he would slam his foot on the pedal and we would speed wildly around the small metal floor, sparks raining down on us. He would wait for his opportunity to crash into another vehicle and send it careering into the side. Collisions and head-on crashes were permitted, indeed actively encouraged, by the two fairground youths who dodged between the cars to keep them moving. They can't have been much older than fifteen, those youths with greasy black slicked-back hair and dark complexions, and they always seemed to give the girls more attention than anyone else. Slow cars and those driven by the inexperienced were obvious targets and were soon identified, and the poor occupants had the stuffing knocked out of them by six or seven aggressors who descended upon them at high speed. I guess many tottered on home after the experience with severe whiplash.

Feeling (or being) sick at the fair was part of the ritual. It came as no surprise that at the end of the evening I, like most of the children, had consumed a sickly concoction. Attracted by the savoury intoxicating aroma of the food stalls, I had eaten hot dogs smothered in ketchup and drizzled in greasy onions, toffee apples, candy floss, ice cream, syrupy waffles and all washed down with sickly sweet lemonade. On my way home, holding my Uncle Jimmy's hand, white-faced and wet with perspiration, I felt the sheer happiness of youth.

Uncle Jimmy ended his days in Ireland with his two daughters Audrey and Monica, who adored him, by his bedside.

My mother's cousin, Auntie Mary as we called her, lived on a small farm in Ireland. Mum was a great letter writer; most

Sundays she would write to Mary with all the news and on occasions she would send a parcel of clothes. Once, when my brother Michael went to stay with Aunt Mary, he came downstairs ready to set off for the long walk to Mass as our Irish cousins appeared attired in their Sunday best. Michael recognized the jackets, ties, shirts, jumpers and jackets but didn't say anything. Each St Patrick's Day a parcel would arrive for Mum from Ireland from Aunt Mary with a large clump of shamrock and a holy picture of St Patrick, dressed in green vestments as a bishop and standing on a snake. On the reverse of the card would be one of Mum's favourite prayers, the Irish Blessing:

> May the road rise up to meet you,
> And the wind be ever at your back.
> May the rain fall soft upon your fields,
> And the sun shine warm upon your face.
> May the roof above you never fall in,
> And those of us beneath it never fall out.
> And until we meet again
> May God hold you in the hollow of His hand.

March 17th was a special St Patrick's Day because it was my mother's birthday, and she always insisted on the saint's card (which invariably contained the prayer) rather than a birthday card.

A week before Christmas the turkey would arrive from Aunt Mary. One Christmas there was no sign of the bird. The man behind the parcels counter at the railway station told us, as if we didn't know, that it was Christmas and there were lots of parcels in the post. The turkey, much to our relief, finally arrived on Christmas Eve. On getting it home we discovered that it was complete – head, neck, feathers, legs and claws. It had been killed, boxed and posted as it was.

Christmas dinner was served at eight o'clock the following evening.

Auntie Noreen was a second cousin of my mother's and lived in Gainsborough, where she ran a corner shop and off-licence. I loved the Sunday afternoon visits, because Auntie Noreen was a larger-than-life, massively good-humoured woman with an infectious laugh and she kept us royally entertained with the exploits and the observations of her customers. She always prepared a banquet of a tea – triangular egg and ham sandwiches, cheese straws, buns with white icing and glazed cherries on the top, chocolate cake, scones and tea cakes, crumpets and almond slices, jelly and ice cream. She would ask customers to save up the cards in the tea and cigarette packets for me and I would come home with a good wodge to trade in the playground the following Monday.

Auntie Noreen had a parrot. It was an African grey called Percy and it had a vicious temper and a wide and colourful vocabulary. It lived in a large brass cage in the corner of the shop and would grip its perch with great yellow talons, noisily cracking walnuts with its shiny black beak. Walnuts were always the ones left after Christmas because they were impossible to get into even with a nutcracker, but the bird split them with ease, dropping the shells into the tray beneath it.

'Be quiet!' Percy would squawk as we entered the shop. 'Put t'wood in t'hole! What are you up to? Ee, by gum! Play up your own end!' The parrot was a clever way of enticing children into the shop, where they would then buy sweets. None went near it, of course; they just stared from the shop doorway or by the counter and marvelled at the creature's facility with words.

There was also an old dog called Rusty that sat behind the counter and would sometimes bark at the sound of the shop bell. The parrot, in a perfect imitation of Auntie Noreen, would squawk, 'Shut up! Shut up! Shut up!' The dog would immediately stop barking.

One Sunday Percy was taken out of his cage, brought into the back room on his perch and placed on a long metal stand, but he was soon getting on everyone's nerves with his constant barrage of noise.

'Be quiet, Percy!' Auntie Noreen said sharply.

'Be quiet, Percy!' the parrot mimicked with the exact intonation and accent, and then began to make the most ear-splitting high-pitched squawking.

Auntie Noreen, taking hold of a small spray that she used to water the plants, squirted the parrot. Percy immediately ceased his noise and began to preen himself. Unfortunately, after a few minutes and when he was dry, he started up again.

'You'll go out in a minute!' threatened Auntie Noreen.

'You'll go out in a minute!' repeated Percy.

'Silly bird,' said Auntie Noreen.

'Silly bird,' echoed the parrot.

The parrot continued to interrupt the conversation, so Auntie Noreen consigned the bird, perch and all, to the small downstairs toilet, where it could be heard going through its repertoire.

Some while later, after several large glasses of lemonade and a surfeit of food, I went to pay a visit. As I sat there, the parrot watched my every move with its small shiny blackcurrant eyes, occasionally opening and closing its beak and showing a slug-like tongue.

'What are you doing?' it asked.

'What does it look like?' I replied. I was now conversing with a bird.

'What are you doing?' it asked again.

'Mind your own business.'

I couldn't do anything as I sat there with the wretched bird scrutinizing me, so I turned the stand and the perch and the parrot around to face the wall. I then resumed my seat. As I did so the parrot swivelled around to face me again. I repeated this several times but the parrot merely turned around when I was seated. It was unnerving. Eventually I managed, with closed eyes, to complete my ablutions and opened the window to let in some fresh air. The parrot, sensing freedom, flapped its wings madly and headed for the wide blue yonder. I slammed the window shut just in time, but the bird hit the glass with a sickening thud and fell to the floor, where it lay prostrate and completely still. I was mortified and rushed out to tell Auntie Noreen. I just hadn't the courage to tell the truth.

'I think Percy's had a heart attack,' I lied. 'He's just fallen off his perch.' The comatose bird was brought into the living room and brandy was spooned through his beak. The small black button eyes opened a fraction and it gave me an accusatory stare. Then the shiny black beak opened. 'Well, I'll go to the bottom of our stairs,' it squawked.

20

Writing in 1928, the author and poet A. R. Wright, in his *English Folk Lore*, sums up in verse some of the towns and cities of Yorkshire:

> Bradford for cash,
> Halifax for dash,
> Wakefield for pride and for poverty.
> Huddersfield for show,
> Sheffield what's low,
> Leeds for dirt and vulgarity.
> Barnsley for ale,
> Doncaster for rail,
> And Rotherham for great singularity.

I knew from an early age that there was something rather different about the town in which I was born. I was vaguely aware that there was something distinct about Rotherham. In the popular mind it was (and I guess still is) the butt of the comedian's joke ('Rotherham doesn't have a twin town, it has a suicide pact with Grimsby', 'It's like a wet weekend in Rotherham', 'The town's like a cemetery with lights'). Rotherham is viewed in the popular mind as a dark, depressing, brooding Northern industrial place with little to commend it. The image is one where steelworks belch out acrid smoke, pit heads ruin the landscape, men in flat caps and mufflers, cigarettes dangling from their mouths, drag whippets behind them, grubby urchins play on narrow cobbled streets, muscular women donkey-stone the steps of their mean terraced houses and running though the centre is the pungent-smelling polluted river the colour of khaki. It's grim up North.

In *Pies and Prejudice: In Search of the North*, Stuart Maconie describes Rotherham as 'Sheffield's smaller, sourer, more ingrown neighbour' and says that 'when Rotherham looks down on you, some would say you're in trouble'. He continues:

An American visitor I knew watched a head-scarved Rotherham woman who could have been anything between thirty and seventy walking home with her shopping, leaning into a gale, carrying cheap plastic bags over a concrete bridge between two of Rotherham's uglier estates. She said that it was like a bleak vignette from one of those forgotten chemical towns in the former Soviet Union.

This is not the picture I have of the town of my birth. Rotherham in the 1950s had the real gritty Yorkshire character to it – solid, uncompromising, unostentatious – a vibrant, friendly, hard-bitten place, and there was nowhere in the country where the inhabitants were warmer or more hospitable. I grew up surrounded by people with an unflagging generosity, a sharp humour and a shrewd insight into human nature which I learnt to love.

The gloomy, depressing image of this dark industrial town in the Don Valley, a place of dust and dirt, of noisy steelworks and ugly pitheads, was not wholly true. There were, of course, the smoky mornings, impenetrable smog and an unpleasant odour that sometimes emanated from the canal and the river, but a bus ride out of the centre of the town took you in minutes into open country. Such beauty so close to heavy industry still comes as a great surprise to visitors to the area. Over the past two or three decades the landscape has undergone massive changes for the better. Heavy industry has declined, fish have returned to the rivers Don and Rother, and along the banks willows grow and shrubs flourish. The steelworks where my father spent most of his working life has been turned into a magnificent museum.

In the school holidays I would explore the area around the town. I would set off in the morning on my bike with 'a bottle of pop' and a sandwich and cycle out of the town and into the country, returning only when it began to get dark. One of my favourite destinations was Roche Abbey. I would cycle out to Wickersley, famous for the grindstones used in the Sheffield cutlery trade, through the mining town of Maltby and into the open country, eventually arriving at the crumbling remains of the magnificent Cistercian abbey. The monks had picked a perfect location, and in 1150 they built this impressively beautiful structure in a verdant, peaceful, rock-bound valley with clear streams. It stood for 400 years, until the Dissolution of the Monasteries during the reign of Henry VIII, when it was pillaged for the stone. Only the east of the abbey remained, but one could sense by the outlines of the stones how huge and imposing this building must have been. I recently returned on a cold winter's morning, when there was a light dusting of snow on the ancient stone and watery sunshine struggled to make its way through the heavy December sky. There was no sound or movement and I was at once again aware of the spirituality and tranquillity of this awesome place. Some things we see in life are soon forgotten, others never leave us. The memory of my first view of Roche Abbey has stayed with me, like an oil painting, an enduring masterpiece.

My father once told me a story about Roche Abbey. The ruin and grounds became part of the Earl of Scarbrough's Sandbeck estate. In the eighteenth century the then Earl commissioned the noted landscape gardener Lancelot 'Capability' Brown to create a beauty spot in the ruined area, which involved the planting of woodland and the setting of lawns. Until the abbey and grounds were presented to the nation in the early twentieth century, the area was not open to the public.

The story goes that some time early last century the then Lord Scarbrough, walking his dogs through the woods bordering the abbey, came upon a large hairy individual at the entrance to a shabby tent.

'Who are you?' he asked abruptly.

'Jack,' the man replied. 'And who are you?'

'I am Lord Scarbrough and you are on my land.'

'Am I?'

'Yes, you are. Would you be so good as to decamp, pack up your things and depart.'

'Why?'

'Because, as I have said, this is my land.'

'I'm not doing any harm,' the man said amiably.

'That is beside the point. This is my land.'

'Where did you get it from?'

'I got it from my father,' the noble Earl explained calmly.

'Well, where did your father get it from?' the man asked.

'From his father.'

'Well, where did he get it from?'

'He got it from his father who got it from his father who got it from his father, right the way back many centuries ago when my ancestor acquired it.'

'Well, how did he get it?' the man asked, making no effort to move.

'He fought for it,' Lord Scarbrough replied.

'Well, I'll fight you for it!' came the reply.

It is an amusing account, but I guess it was one of my father's tall tales.

After I had read Walter Scott's epic story *Ivanhoe,* I cycled out one bright Saturday morning to Conisborough Castle, near Doncaster, where the novel is set. This towering Norman fortress with its ninety-foot circular keep and six mighty buttresses was a deserted roofless shell when I was a boy, but it had retained its grandeur. The castle rises majestically from a mound overlooking the River Don, and for me it is the most impressive medieval building in South Yorkshire. I recall sitting on the perimeter wall staring up at the imposing edifice and imagining knights in glittering armour, gallant Crusaders, dastardly villains, jousting and sieges, dark dungeons and great battles.

Other places of interest around the town to which I would cycle included Cusworth Hall, which now houses the Museum of South Yorkshire; Keppel's Column, a towering pillar with a viewing platform at the top, erected in 1778 by the second Marquess of Rockingham to commemorate the acquittal of his friend Admiral Keppel, court-martialled after a naval defeat at the hands of the French in 1777; Hoober Stand, a strange triangular and tapering 518-foot structure with a hexagonal lantern, built in 1748 to celebrate the victory of the Duke of Cumberland at Culloden Moor in 1746; and the Needle's Eye, a bizarre folly dating from 1780 and sited at the edge of Lee Wood on the Wentworth Woodhouse estate. The Needle's Eye is a strange triangle of stone with a huge urn on the pinnacle and a gateway through the centre. The story is that the second Marquess of Rockingham, who appears to have been very fond of follies, once boasted that he could ride a coach and horses through the eye of a needle. To prove his point he had this quite useless monument built and galloped through it in his carriage. I was intrigued by such fanciful tales.

The town centre of Rotherham was and still is dominated by the great red sandstone church of All Saints, with its magnificent 180-foot spire. Built in the thirteenth century, it is one of the finest examples of Perpendicular architecture in Yorkshire. A walk away was the Bridge Chapel of Our Lady, with its battlements, parapets and pinnacles, a rare survivor of medieval times. There are only four surviving bridge or chantry chapels in England, and Rotherham's is reputedly the finest example. For a time it was used as a prison, with a cell in the crypt, an almshouse, a dwelling and a tobacconist's shop. I remember in a history lesson being told that the retinue of the ill-fated Queen of Scots intended to break their long journey to Fotheringhay Castle at Rotherham, but her regal group was stopped as it crossed the bridge. The worthy burghers of the town, in true Yorkshire fashion, refused Her Majesty entry when they discovered they had to pay for her board and lodging. She was sent on her way to Hardwick Hall in Derbyshire, where she received greater hospitality.

As a teenager I was rather different from other boys my age in finding such old stone structures – castles and churches, follies and abbeys – of interest, and the stories behind such buildings fascinated me. I still feel a thrill when standing on a battlement or amidst the ruins of an abbey or in a great cathedral, imagining times past.

Of course I didn't spend all my time searching for ruins and visiting churches and monuments. Other destinations for me were Elsecar Reservoir, Worsborough Dam, Sprotborough Canal, Swinton Lock and the 'hell hole' (a dark and sinister stretch of water) at Whiston Meadows. I would visit the surrounding villages of Hooton Roberts, Firbeck, Tickhill, Laughton, Letwell, Thorpe Salvin and Wentworth, all with their own distinctive characters and set among open country.

There are two parks in Rotherham and both were favourite haunts of children in the 1950s and 60s. Clifton Park, on the corner of Clifton Lane and Doncaster Road, was created to serve the leisure needs of a growing population. The opening ceremony was by all accounts a memorable affair, attended by thousands who were entertained with fireworks and bands. The high point of the festivities was perhaps not the ascent by Captain Whelan in a hot air balloon but when one of the town councillors became entangled in the ropes and was unceremoniously lifted off the ground by his legs as the balloon rose. Fortunately, the poor man managed to disentangle himself.

The park had a children's paddling pool, a cenotaph, gardens, lawns and picnic areas. Sometimes on warm summer Sunday evenings my parents would take me to the park to sit by the domed and pillared bandstand and listen to the Salvation Army or one of the colliery bands.

I preferred Boston Park. There were fewer park-keepers hovering around to tell children to keep to the path, and more space and freedom. At the entrance stood a small squat building, 'Boston Castle', with battlements and small square mullioned windows, erected as a hunting lodge by the Earl of Effingham, who originally owned the land. The local newspaper, the *Rotherham Advertiser*, once described the folly as 'a castellated pigeon cote'. The Earl was something of a maverick and supported the American cause in the War of Independence. When he leased the area to Rotherham Corporation for conversion to a park he insisted that the opening ceremony took place on 4 July 1876, the centenary of the Declaration of Independence.

Certain memories stick like burrs. When I was fifteen I had my first and last camping experience. With two of my friends, John and Paul, I took the bus to Sheffield and then the train to Bamforth station in Derbyshire. We equipped ourselves from the Army and Navy Stores in Rotherham with all that was deemed necessary for our expedition – sleeping bags, groundsheets, rucksacks, large khaki ex-army anoraks, boots, woollen balaclava helmets and substantial gloves. We also invested in a compass, metal water flasks and billycans. John brought the tent, which he had borrowed from his Uncle Norman, a seasoned camper.

'Don't you think it's a bit cold to go camping?' Dad asked me, as I was packing my rucksack.

'No, we'll be as snug as bugs in a rug when we're in our sleeping bags,' I told him, confident that this was going to be a really exciting experience.

'I should have thought you'd have been better waiting until the summer,' said Mum. 'It gets very cold in October, you know.'

The same advice was proffered when we were on the train.

'Camping, are you?' asked the ticket collector. 'Not the weather for camping.'

I have to admit, as I stared out of the steamy carriage window at the cold, grey autumn sky and the dark clouds hovering ominously overhead, to some slight apprehension.

After a brisk walk from the station we decided to erect the tent in a field. I had had an idea, when I had first seen the rather compact canvas bag which John had brought with him, that Uncle Norman's tent might be a trifle small for the three of us. When it was taken out my fears became all too real.

'Is that it?' I asked.

'It's a bit small,' added Paul.

'We'll be all right once we're in,' said John, trying to sound cheerful.

We set up the tent under a tree at the side of the field after some difficulty. It had not occurred to any of us to bring a hammer to knock in the metal securing pins and we spent a largely unsuccessful hour bashing away with a large rock. After we had gathered some wood for a fire it began to rain, so that was abandoned and we clambered into the tent cold, wet and hungry. This was not turning out as we had expected. It rained and rained all night, the ground around us became a quagmire and a cold wind shook the tent. We huddled together inside our sleeping bags, hardly speaking and praying for the morning. I lay awake listening to the pattering of the rain on the canvas, and this was accompanied, when my two friends fell into deep sleep, by a nocturnal chorus of gurglings, snortings, wheezings and trumpetings. Then, when I eventually drifted off, I was awoken by a movement below me. Some creature was burrowing underneath the groundsheet. I shot up and out of the tent, waking my friends in the process. In the half-light I caught sight of glistening eyes. The ground was wet, the morning a cold misty grey and before me stood these mysterious shapes with shining eyes. I shot back into the tent and in a strange, muffled voice told my companions what I had seen. It took some courage for all three of us to stick our heads through the tent flap some time later, shaking with cold and fear. The mist had cleared and the cows observed us impassively with big sad eyes.

I arrived back home later that afternoon. Mum met me at the kitchen door and asked, 'Did you enjoy your night under canvas then?'

'It was marvellous,' I lied.

Bonfire Night was always a special time. A month before 5 November, along with my friends, I would collect branches, tea chests, boxes, old chairs, rickety tables, crates, planks of wood, anything that would burn, and we would start constructing our bonfire. We had the ideal place at the back of the house – the allotment – and on a patch of earth the conical structure soon took shape.

We would make a guy out of old clothes, stuff screwed-up paper in the arms and legs and paint a face on a piece of cardboard. He would be wheeled through the streets on a trolley made of pram wheels and two planks and we would ask passersby: 'Penny for the guy?' With the money we collected we would buy fireworks.

In October fireworks were for sale at the newsagent's and I would buy a thin rectangular box on the front of which, in garish reds and blues, the caption 'Light up the Sky with Standard Fireworks' was emblazoned. This small collection would be added to over the coming weeks up to 5 November. There would be Catherine wheels, blockbusters, squibs, jumping jacks, traffic lights, penny bangers, Roman candles, golden fountains, silver rain and rockets in brightly coloured cardboard tubes with a cone on the top and a thin wooden stick down the side.

Mr Morgan devoted a special assembly at Broom Valley Juniors to the terrible dangers of Bonfire Night. His dramatic account told of boys (it was always boys) who had been maimed, disfigured, burned and scarred for life by not taking sufficient care. His cautionary tale was told each year of the foolish boy who had been dared by his friends to put a penny banger in an empty oil drum which had subsequently blown up, searing his face to such an extent that the whole of the skin had melted. It was a horrific picture. The message about the dangers of fireworks was rammed home by my Auntie Nora, who had been sister-in-charge of the Casualty Department at Doncaster Royal Infirmary and related yet more stories of accidents and tragedies.

When it was dark, children and parents assembled on the allotment and gathered around the bonfire. The air was full of wood smoke and cordite and the rockets shot up into the dark sky and burst into sparkling rain. The adults supervised us as we took it in turn to light the twist of touchpaper on the fireworks and the sparklers. There was always a sense of disappointment when the wonderfully described firework fizzed and there followed a modest few seconds of showering sparks. Sometimes a firework failed to ignite and after a short period we would approach cautiously, prod it with a cane and place a bucket over the top. Later we would throw it into the bonfire where it would explode.

The rockets were always saved for last and were put into milk bottles and lit with a small twist of rope. They shot into the night sky, to explode to the accompaniment of 'oooohs' and 'aaaahs'.

My father would not countenance a guy being put on the fire. It might have been a decision he made when I, as a small child, had been terrified by the image of a human form in the

flames. I had been taken to the municipal bonfire at Herringthorpe playing fields when I was six and, sitting on my father's
shoulders, had watched fascinated as the huge bonfire crackled
into life. And then I saw him in the half-light – a man perched
on the very top, with fat legs and a floppy hat. I could just
make out a smiling face. I screamed and screamed and pointed
to the figure in the flames.

'There's a man, there's a man on the fire!' I cried, as the
flames licked around him. People laughed.

'It's just a guy,' my father told me. 'It's not real.'

Perhaps that was why my father never allowed us to put a
guy in the bonfire, or perhaps he found the image of a human
form burning distasteful. Whatever the reason, when I had
children of my own, having a guy on our bonfire was taboo.

21

When I was growing up the favourite place to visit, particularly if the weather was cold and wet, was the cinema. Rotherham and the area around had a goodly number of picture palaces – there was the Tivoli, the Empire (later renamed the Essoldo, then the Classic and finally the Cannon), the Whitehall, the Cinema House, the Regal (which became the Odeon and then the Scala) and the Hippodrome, and a bus ride away in neighbouring Sheffield there were a good few more. In the late 1950s and early 60s, when television got a firm foothold on people's leisure pursuits, the cinemas all closed down save for the Odeon, which became a bingo hall.

On Saturday morning I would meet my friends at Adams' General Store and stock up on sweets prior to going to 'the pictures'. Sweet rationing had ended in 1953, so I was just the right age to sample the delights of what we called 'spice'. Adams' corner shop stocked a whole range of delicious confectionery: liquorice sticks and liquorice strings, pear drops, lemon drops, thick chewy brown slabs of McGowan's toffee, Sherbet Dabs, penny Arrow bars (strips of soft toffee), humbugs, aniseed balls, jelly babies, extra strong mints, boiled sweets, lollipops, chocolate bars, dolly mixtures, blackjacks, gobstoppers that changed colour when you sucked them, aniseed balls, halfpenny chews, all of which we ate with no concern for our teeth or our weight. In the week of the Coronation Mrs Adams said we could choose something on the house – but costing no more than threepence.

With our pockets stuffed with sweets we walked into the town or caught the bus to Sheffield and joined a jostling, noisy queue

of children outside the cinema. The manager and usherettes must
have had some sort of masochistic streak to take on hundreds of
noisy, lively, misbehaved, excitable urchins every week. It must
have been a nightmare for them, but for me it was irresistibly
attractive. In the musty darkness of the cinema I could escape
from the real world for a couple of hours and into the domain
of pirates and princes, cowboys and explorers, aliens and villains.

The manager of one cinema, a tall thin man in a baggy suit
and wearing a black dickie bow tie, would appear just before
the doors were opened and shout down the queue. He would
never complete the sentence because we would all shout out
the last word at the top of our voices.

'Any messing about and you're . . .'

'OUT!'

We would file in through the foyer under the watchful eye
of the manager, who would have a martyred expression on his
long lugubrious face. Should he see a boy (it was always a boy)
whom he had sent out the week before for misbehaving, he
would grip the miscreant's collar and say, 'Out!' If the boy's
friends came to his assistance they would be threatened with
expulsion as well, and they soon quietened down. None would
want to miss the next exciting episode.

Once inside the cinema the noise was indescribable, and
various missiles – peanuts, sweets, popcorn – would fly through
the air until the manager strode to the front accompanied by
two beefy usherettes to warn us again.

'I've told you once,' shouted the manager, red-faced and
angry, 'any messing about and you're . . .'

'OUT!' we all roared.

Once the lights dimmed the cinema became a wild affair,
with children shouting, cheering, jeering and jumping up in
their seats, running up the aisle and spitting orange pips and
shooting rice and rock-hard peas through pea-shooters. The
lights would come on.

'Now look,' shrieked the manager, his voice an octave higher, 'I've told you once, any more messing about and you're . . .'

'OUT!' we all shouted back.

The film-show at the Sheffield ABC would start with a raucous sing-song to the music of a Souza march:

> We are the boys and girls,
> Well known as the minors of the ABC,
> And every Saturday we line up
> And see the films we like
> And shout aloud with glee.
> We love to laugh and have a sing-song,
> What a happy crowd are we.
> We're all pals together,
> The minors of the ABC.

The black and white films would include a cast of brave and gallant heroes: the Lone Ranger and his side-kick, Tonto, Hopalong Cassidy, Roy Rogers, Zorro, Tarzan – all handsome, clean-living, clean-shaven, God-fearing, good-natured heroes who only resorted to violence (and then never to kill) as a very last resort. I liked Flash Gordon the best. Each thrilling episode would finish just as our hero was about to be crushed to death or blown up or zapped with a death ray. 'Will Flash Gordon escape?' came the zig-zagged letters across the screen. Of course I knew he would, he always did, but I couldn't wait until the next episode.

During one performance I was gripped by my collar and heaved out of my seat by the manager, charged with skimming the top of an ice cream carton. I had been guilty of throwing things in the past, but on this occasion I was innocent of the crime and felt the unfairness of the accusation deeply.

'It wasn't me!' I protested.

'Out!' the manager ordered.

'I didn't do it!'

'I saw you.'

'How could you see me in the dark?' I argued.

'Out or I'm stopping the film,' he threatened.

This was guaranteed to rally support for him from all the children in the cinema, for the last thing they wanted was an interruption to Flash Gordon. There was no camaraderie there. They all started the chant, 'Out! Out! Out!'

I stamped for the exit unaccompanied by my valued friends, who I imagined would come to my support or at the very least leave with me in protest. I learnt early on that friends will only go so far.

I told my father when I got home. 'It's not fair,' I grumbled.

'Life's not fair,' he replied.

'Are you going to see the manager and tell him?' I asked.

'Tell him?'

'Tell him it wasn't me and get my money back.'

It was one of the few occasions when I remember getting angry with my father. He threw his head back and laughed. 'I've got better things to do on a Saturday morning than traipse down to the cinema. Put it down to experience.'

The following week, masked by Jimmy and Terry, I managed to evade the manager's eagle-eyed scrutiny of the children filing past him but gave him an evil look as I passed.

In the late 1940s the Ealing Studios produced a series of films, such as *Passport to Pimlico* and *Kind Hearts and Coronets*, which became massively popular. They were typified by their restrained humour and gentle tolerance. Then there was a series of films centred on the good-hearted but accident-prone Norman Wisdom, the gormless George Formby, and the 'Lancashire lass with the big voice and large heart', Gracie Fields, which depicted the working class in an affectionate but patronizing manner. None of these interested me. They left

little to the imagination. I loved films, particularly the flamboyant and daring adventures that came across the Atlantic.
'Movies,' said Alfred Hitchcock, 'are just like real life with all
the dull parts taken out.' This is what made the films so interesting. There was Gregory Peck as the noble and heroic
Captain Horatio Hornblower, in the sprawling swashbuckler
adapted from the C. S. Forester books, who sails on a secret
mission to deliver weapons to the treacherous and bloodthirsty
Spanish rebel, El Supremo. There was Errol Flynn as the notorious Captain Blood and Margaret Lockwood as the scheming
Lady Barbara Skelton, the wicked lady of the title who takes
to highway robbery, prissy Cary Grant as the stiff-upper-lipped
British officer, and Frank Sinatra, wonderfully miscast as the
Spanish guerrilla fighter who, with a band of motley freedom
fighters, drags a massive cannon across Spain in 1810 to blow
up the French stronghold. Then there were Janet Leigh and
Tony Curtis in *The Black Shield of Falworth,* complete with Ye
Merrie Olde Englande backdrop and ridiculous Brooklyn
accents, intent on saving Henry IV from a fate worse than
death. My favourite was *The Adventures of Robin Hood,* in which
the flamboyant Errol Flynn has a splendid showdown with the
villainous Basil Rathbone's Sir Guy of Gisbourne. It was all
stirring stuff, where goodness, honesty, integrity and compassion were rewarded in the end and evil got its just desserts.

It was to the Tivoli Cinema that I took Brenda. She was
my very first date. I was fifteen and I met her through my
friend Peter. He was 'walking out' with a strikingly pretty
dark-haired girl called Lynne, and she had this friend, a small,
round-faced strawberry blonde called Brenda. I agreed to meet
Brenda in the Ring o' Bells Café in Rotherham town centre,
next to the parish church, and go to the cinema.

I spent a good hour getting ready, scrubbing my face until it
shone, covering up the two angry red spots with some of my
mother's flesh-coloured face powder, brushing my teeth violently,

slicking my hair with Brylcreem, splashing my brother's after-shave liberally over my face and body, changing my shirt umpteen times, squeezing into tight drainpipe trousers and polishing my winkle-pickers to a high shine. When I looked in the bathroom mirror I thought I looked quite presentable.

Brenda sat in the corner of the café, dressed in a shocking pink knitted cardigan and wearing sensible brown sandals and white ankle socks.

'Hello,' I said brightly.

'Hello,' she replied. There was no trace of a smile.

'Want a drink?' I asked.

'Milkshake,' she said. 'Strawberry. Large one.'

This is going to be an expensive evening, I thought to myself, mentally counting the money in my pocket.

'I thought we'd go to the pictures,' I told her as she took a gulp of the milkshake, leaving a pink moustache above her lips.

'OK,' she said.

'Do you like films?' I asked.

'Depends.'

'It's science fiction.'

'I don't like science fiction,' she told me.

'Do you want to go somewhere else?'

She sighed. 'No.' She drained the glass. 'Have we time for another milkshake?'

'No,' I said.

That was pretty much the extent of the conversation until we arrived at the cinema to join the queue for the film.

'So what do you like doing?' I asked her.

'Knitting.'

'Oh.'

'I've knitted this cardigan. Do you like it?'

'Yes,' I lied. It was a horrendous pink affair. She stood out like a huge shapeless ball of candyfloss.

'Don't your feet hurt in those shoes?' she asked.

'No.'

'I'll knit you a scarf if you want.'

'Great,' I mouthed. This girl, I thought to myself, has the personality of petrified wood.

In the cinema there was a row of double seats at the back. The arm rests had been removed so couples could snuggle up to watch the film and more likely have a good snog when the lights went out. Brenda, armed with a large carton of popcorn and a bag of liquorice allsorts which I had bought for her, headed for the rear seats.

'I like it down the front,' I said, striding down the aisle before she could argue.

Brenda sat through the first part of *The Amazing Colossal Man* munching away merrily. The film was a version (and a very poor one at that) of the *King Kong* classic but set in the atomic age. The eponymous hero was a colonel who had been exposed to a massive dose of radiation during a nuclear bomb test and had mutated into a fearsome giant.

In those days girls were inclined to scream and boys to whoop really loudly when anything frightening appeared on the screen. If there was a romantic part, particularly one involving kissing, there would be great jeers, howls and smooching noises from the audience and some brave boy would shout out, 'Gerrem off!'

Brenda sat there motionless, her eyes glued to the screen, posting popcorn into her mouth. She crunched away noisily. When she had consumed the contents of the carton she started on the liquorice allsorts. Just as the monster appeared on the screen Brenda suddenly thrust her face forward and planted her lips on mine. This occurred a few times before the lights came up. It was a quick, unexpected, jerky, liquorice-popcorn tasting experience and not particularly pleasant.

'Are we having chips?' she asked, as I walked her home. I

noticed that her teeth were black from chewing the liquorice allsorts.

'If you want,' I sighed.

'I like scraps,' said Brenda.

Scraps were the bits of fried batter which came away from the fish and they were given away free. I asked for two-pennyworth of chips and scraps.

'Do you like scraps?' asked Brenda.

'Not really.'

'What fish are we having?'

'Fish?' I repeated.

'I like haddock.'

'I'm not that hungry,' I told her, thinking of the dwindling resources I had in my pocket.

'You can have a bit of my haddock if you want,' she said.

'I'm not that bothered,' I replied.

'Are we having mushy peas?'

I sighed again. 'I suppose so.'

I said goodbye to Brenda at the gate of her house. I saw the curtains move inside and a face appear at the window. Her parents had no need to worry, I thought to myself. There was no way I was going to try anything on. I kept a good distance because I didn't want to be pounced on again.

''Bye,' I said.

'I'll start on your scarf,' she told me.

'Great.'

'What film are we going to see next week?' she asked.

'I'll let you know.'

She puckered her lips.

''Bye,' I said walking off, touching the few odd coppers left in my pocket.

That was my first fleeting romance. It was a 'brief encounter', for I found that scraps were the only thing Brenda and I had in common.

22

In the 1950s Rotherham town centre was a colourful, bustling place with a wide range of shops: butchers, bakers, confectioners, herbalists, opticians, greengrocers, jewellers, haberdashers, grocers, chemists, cobblers, outfitters, sweet shops, bookshops, shoe shops, sports shops, toy shops, nearly every conceivable retail outlet. Blue and white double-decker buses could be seen everywhere, and trolley-buses with electric overhead cables that sparked in the rain like fireworks trundled down the main streets. Today the centre of the town is a rather sad and sorry place, like an old dowager who has fallen on hard times, still a place with character and history but rather faded and neglected. Many of those varied and individual shops of the 1950s – Mason's jewellers, the great stores of Muntus and Speed's, Waddington's men's outfitters, Tattersall's fruiterers, Glover's fishmonger's, Cooper's toy shop, Danny Williams sports – have disappeared, as people prefer to visit the vast nearby Meadowhall complex or one of the superstores that have sprung up near the town, where they can buy every conceivable product in comfort under the one roof, in the warmth and out of the rain. Something special has been lost, I feel.

Some Saturdays I was taken by my parents into Rotherham to help with the shopping, get kitted out with new clothes and have the dreaded haircut. Dad often called in at the Masons Arms on Wellgate 'just for a half' on the way into town, agreeing to meet us when all the shopping had been done, and he would help us carry it back. I often wished I could go into the pub with Dad. It was an intriguing, noisy, bustling world, thick with tobacco smoke, where men argued and laughed and told jokes, played darts and sat at sticky tables playing dominoes. There seemed to be a glow of contentment inside the doors.

'Not for you, young man,' Dad would tell me. 'Wait until you're older. You help your mother with the shopping and I'll see you later.'

Our neighbour, Mrs Evans, had her shopping delivered from Beaumont and Stevenson's, 'quality grocers', but we never did. It was much more interesting to take a trip into town, walking from shop to shop, meeting people and on occasions ending the visit with a coffee and a cake in Davy's Café. On my sortie into Rotherham with my parents I should have much preferred staying with my father in the pub, where a row of men propped up the bar talking and laughing and putting the world to rights, but I had to go with my mother into the town centre.

Like many people at that time, my mother shopped for her groceries at the Co-op because she could get her 'divvy'. The idea of the Co-operative Society was that customers should share some of the profits, and for a small initial payment (I have an idea it was two shillings and sixpence) you became a member and were given a dividend number. I guess many people my age can still recall their Co-op divvy number. Mum's was 29305. As my mother queued, waiting to be served, I was intrigued by the method of payment for goods. The shop assistant placed the money in a small metal cylinder which was attached to an overhead wire, and with a sharp pull on a lever, the missile would shoot off at high speed to a cashier who would deal with the purchase. After a short time the cylinder would shoot back on the wire with the customer's change and a receipt inside.

We would invariably call into Boots the Chemist, where patent medicines were dispensed. My mother, ever health-conscious, purchased jars of cod liver oil and malt, a brown, viscous, not unpleasant tasting concoction, and a strange mixture called Fennings, guaranteed to ward off colds, influenza, coughs and other chesty ailments. There was also a small library in Boots and we rarely left without a purchase. Then on to Schonhut's, the high-class butcher's, housed in a mock Tudor building, for the Sunday joint of beef or, for a change, a cut of pork. The butcher, a broad-shouldered, big-chested man with great beefy arms and wearing an immense apron, was a frightening figure who wielded a giant cleaver over a blood-stained block of wood. His red cheeks shone as if they had been scrubbed. I remember my father telling me that during the First World War with the prevalent anti-German hysteria a mob had attacked Schonhut's, smashing the windows and making off with the meat and the pork sausages, until the police arrived in force. I remember thinking that the looters would not have dared try that on if this giant had been behind the counter. Next stop was Stanilands or Graftons for the bread, and if I was lucky, a doughnut or a custard cream, Stockdales for the fruit and finally W. Muntus and Co., the large department store, a rabbit warren of a place, where my clothes were purchased. We would then meet my father outside F. W. Woolworth on College Street. The bulk of the shopping was passed over and my mother would leave us to buy the last few items and later to meet us outside Davy's Café, while I went with Dad for the dreaded haircut.

On Saturday mornings there would be a row of men and glum little boys waiting for their haircuts. Reg, the barber, was a small bald-headed man with a fleshy face, a red nose the shape of a turnip and fat white hands. He was irritatingly jaunty and garrulous, and what was more annoying was that he was inordinately slow. It wasn't that he spent a long time on the job in hand – namely cutting people's hair – it was because he never stopped talking. There were long pauses between cutting the hair or shaving a customer when he would discuss national and local events. The barber's was an exclusively masculine world where the topics of conversation centred largely around football and work.

Even as a child I was fascinated by other people's language. Reg had a rich repertoire of sayings which peppered his conversation. Of the goalkeeper at Rotherham United he once remarked, 'He's about as much use as a poultice on a wooden leg'; of a recently deceased neighbour, 'Well, that's another page turned in the great book of life'; of the meanness of a customer, 'He could peel an orange in his pocket'; of the boy who broke wind, 'Close t'back door'; of the woman of ample proportions who served in the hardware shop and was noted for wearing a low-cut dress beneath her overall, 'Her suet dumplings are boiling over.'

My father was first in the barber's chair, this large swivelling throne of a thing with a simulated brown leather covering and an adjustable footrest, and he remained there while Reg snipped a bit off the back and trimmed the wisps of hair that were combed across his otherwise bald pate. He then scraped the back of his neck with a cut-throat razor, trimmed the moustache and eyebrows and removed any stray hairs in the ears.

'Now then, young fella-mi-lad,' the barber would say when it came to my turn, 'let's be having you.'

He placed a plank across the arms of the chair, lifted me on to it, wrapped a large sheet around me which smelt of shaving soap and a sickly sweet cologne and asked, 'How do you want it?' Before I could tell him I just wanted a trim or 'a tidy-up', he turned to my father and asked, 'Short back and sides and good bit off t'top?'

'That's fine,' said Dad.

'Could I have it a bit longer this time?' I would ask plaintively. I hated going to school on the Monday with a head like a coconut and everyone asking the same inane question: ''Ave you 'ad your 'air cut?'

'No problem, young fella-mi-lad,' Reg would say, but would then proceed to scalp me.

I just wanted this prolonged and painful experience to be over as soon as possible, so when he started on the interrogation I would answer the questions he fired at me in monosyllables.

'How's school then?' he'd ask.

'OK.'

'Behaving yourself, are you?'

'Yes.'

'Do you play football?'

'No.'

'Cricketer then, are you?'

'No.'

'What do you play?'

'Nothing.'

'Been on holiday?'

'No.'

'You're a right little chatterbox, you, aren't you?'

'No.'

Sometimes he would ask an embarrassing question with a sort of snigger, such as, 'Got a girlfriend yet, then?' I wouldn't even deign to answer and would shake my head. The only occasion I said anything above the one-word answer was when I saw him reach for the electric clippers, which buzzed like a frantic bee. I would then mention the spot on the back of my neck, touching it with my finger to indicate the location, and ask him to be careful. My request would come to nothing, for invariably he would slice off the top of the spot, whistling as he did so. I would yelp and wonder if he had done it on purpose because I'd been less than friendly when he interrogated me. Then the barber would reach for a strand of cotton wool, dip it into some liquid and press it on my neck. The stinging sensation was indescribable and there would be a sharp intake of my breath. This was followed by some word of wisdom from Sweeney Todd, such as, 'Wait till you're shaving, young fella-mi-lad, you'll get used to a few cuts.' This produced a few laughs from the customers, which made me colour up with anger and embarrassment. The final part of the ordeal was to have talcum powder puffed on to my neck, followed by a vigorous brushing down.

On one occasion a Teddy Boy was sitting on the bench when we entered the shop. He was leaning back casually, legs apart, chewing. The other customers stared at him as if he were an exotic specimen in a museum case, but he was unconcerned. The style of hair and dress that he affected said to the customers that he was an idler, a troublemaker, a ne'er-do-well. But I was irresistibly drawn towards this character, whose sophistication elevated him above the conventional teenagers of the time. I was full of admiration for someone who had the courage to walk around the town in his powder blue suit, string tie, crêpe-soled shoes, yellow socks and with this wonderful coiffure. He sported a hairdo that was a work of art. His shiny, black, heavily brilliantined hair was slicked back on both sides, rising from his forehead in one smooth wave and tapering at the nape of his neck. I knew there was no way that Reg was going to give *him* 'a short back and sides' and 'a good bit off t'top'. When he asked the barber to be careful of his DA and leave his sideburns alone, being an inquisitive child and seeing Reg's lips purse with disapproval, I asked my father later what a DA was, but he was evasive. It was a friend at school who told me it stood for 'duck's arse' – the shape of his hair at the back.

My father, I recall, equivocated on another occasion. As he paid the bill, Reg would invariably ask Dad a question, always the same one, to which my father always shook his head. Reg spoke in a sort of sly, whispery voice, the sort spies used in the radio plays. I was intrigued.

'Something for the weekend, sir?' he would enquire.

I asked my father what it meant as we left the shop one Saturday. He reddened and dismissed my enquiry. 'Something you don't need to know about,' he told me. 'And don't go asking your mother.' Once, when out of my father's hearing, I asked Reg. He tapped his nose. 'That's for me to know and you to wonder,' he told me. This made it really mysterious.

Clustered around All Saints' Square were cafés and shops,

banks and offices. The building I remember most was Davy's Café and Restaurant, where we used to meet my mother after the scalping at Reg's. The restaurant was above the food emporium, which smelt of ground coffee and smoked bacon. In the shop, sugar was dispensed from open sacks with a silver scoop, weighed in great brass scales and the contents poured into stiff blue paper bags. Butter was uncovered in a huge mound, and the shop assistant would pat the creamy slabs into squares of the required weight using a wooden spatula. There was a huge bacon slicer, and joints of bacon and legs of ham wrapped in white muslin. The shelves were stacked with jars of pickles and jams, boxes of biscuits and cereals. I remember being fascinated by the long strip of brown flypaper that hung down from the roof and gathered struggling insects on its sticky surface.

When I was in the sixth form a group of us would hurry out of school after the bell had sounded for the end of morning lessons, run down Moorgate and Ship Hill, and on to the High Street to Davy's Restaurant. There we would have meat and potato pie or cod and chips, beef with Yorkshire pudding or two fat chops. This would be followed by spotted dick or jam roly-poly, bread and butter pudding or apple crumble. I always seemed to get very generous portions, because my Aunt Nora's best friend, Ivy, was a waitress there and always made a fuss of me. Following the substantial lunch we would catch the bus back to school and attempt to keep our eyes open during the lessons that afternoon.

It was in Davy's that I developed my skill at eavesdropping – an important attribute if one is to become a writer. Ladies who lunch, businessmen and lawyers, shoppers and salesmen would be on neighbouring tables and their conversations intrigued me. I would often entertain my friends by mimicking these people. Sometimes my Uncle Doug, who worked in the finance department at the Council Offices, would appear with his colleagues, and on those occasions I made sure I was on my very best behaviour, lowering my voice and not laughing too heartily. He was a rather severe-looking man was Uncle Doug, with white winged eyebrows, and was of 'the old school', who believed that young people should be seen but not heard.

Food played an important part in our family life. I was not a fussy eater but I turned my nose up at some of the delicacies to which my father was partial: black pudding (a black sausage containing pork, dried pig's blood and suet with chunks of white fat in it), pigs' feet, liver, cowheel, polony (a fat sausage made of bacon, veal and pork suet), 'penny ducks' (a mixture of cooked offal heavily spiced and seasoned) and chitterlings (the intestines of a pig). Dad's favourite meal was tripe and onions. Mum would cook it in milk and drizzle chopped onions on the top. Of course, none of us children could be persuaded to try any. We would watch with screwed-up faces as Dad devoured the sickly white concoction and then licked his lips dramatically.

There was a tripe shop in Rotherham and on Saturday, if I didn't go into town with my parents, I was sometimes sent to get a large piece of the white rubbery honeycombed delicacy for Dad's tea. I never minded going to the shop because the owner was a most interesting woman. She had steely white hair, a round red face and large salmon pink hands and would stand behind her counter, arms folded implacably under her impressive bay window of a bosom, which wobbled like a bouncy castle when she moved. I became accustomed to waiting in the queue and privy to the proprietor's observations on life. Specific members of the locality were openly discussed, their opinions, prejudices, secrets, daydreams, aspirations and, of course, what they got up to. I would be quite content to wait and listen as the proprietor took her time, slicing a piece of tripe, weighing it ('It's just a bit over, love, is that all right?') and wrapping it in white greaseproof paper, all the while holding forth and entertaining her clientele. I enjoyed the patter, listening to the rhythms, the turns of phrase and colloquialisms of speech. I think people would have been quite happy to go there for the conversation alone. Her observations were vividly illustrated with expressions, idioms and a dry Yorkshire sense of humour, which was delivered in the deadpan manner of a comedian.

Her caustic comments on other people's appearance were legion: 'He's like a streak of tap water'; 'She's a face like a parish oven'; 'He comes in here like a sack of spuds, tied up ugly'; 'She's no oil painting herself, I can tell you'; 'He looked as if he was dragged through a hedge backwards'. It occurs to me now, looking back on my days in the tripe shop, that three words come to mind – 'pan', 'kettle' and 'black'. There were expressions the proprietor used which made no sense to me at all: 'She's all kid gloves and no drawers'; 'There are more ways to kill a cat'; 'I've not sat down since I got up.' A frequent turn of phrase, if she was told some interesting news, was, 'Well, I'll go to the bottom of our stairs!' The proprietor of the shop was a mistress of the non sequitur: 'He wants to get down on his knees and thank God he's still standing up,' she would announce, or 'Nobody ever goes there these days, it's too crowded.' Such vibrant, colourful use of English was a paradise for the connoisseur of the colloquial, and I enjoyed the constant patter. Here was the precursor of Norman Evans's gossipy neighbour, 'over the garden wall', and Les Dawson's wonderfully comic characters Cissie and Ada, with their sharp observations, dry humour, deadpan delivery and amusing banter, all accompanied by expressive facial contortions.

I would often enter the shop at some crucial part of a story: 'Of course, if she'd have tied it up with a piece of string, it wouldn't have happened'; 'And I said to him, if you think I'm doing that with my bad back, you've got another think coming'; 'When the police finally arrived, you will never guess where she'd put it'; 'I'll tell you, if it was me, I'd give her a piece of my mind, and no mistake.'

Ailments, operations, confinements, illnesses, medical problems, all were discussed in graphic detail and inquests held. I heard about surgical removals and diseases, hernias and gallstones, arthritis and lumbago, tennis elbow and water-on-the-knee. If it was 'a woman's problem' or something she didn't want little ears to hear, the proprietor would lower her voice to a confidential whisper, ending with a tantalizing silence when she mouthed the particular condition or observation.

One story I remember well was when she related a visit to see her daughter in Listerdale Maternity Unit. The woman in the next bed was huge. 'Like a mountain she was. It's a wonder the bed didn't collapse under her. She lay there like a beached whale, heaving and puffing and moaning. "You'll feel a lot better, love," I told her, "when you've had your baby." "I've had it!" replied the woman. I wanted the floor to open and swallow me up.'

Another time a woman was foolhardy enough to complain about the tripe she had bought the previous week. 'I had to give it to the dog,' she announced in a loud voice for all those in the queue to hear.

'Is that so?' said the virago behind the counter. 'Well, I'll tell you this, if the Queen herself and the whole of the royal family were to visit Rotherham, they'd come here to this shop for their tripe and buy the bloody lot!'

Looking back to my childhood I reckon I was unusual in this interest I had in adults and their conversations. I was gifted with a fertile imagination and a good memory and soon became a keen observer and a dedicated listener, fascinated by people and by the language they used. I can still see in my mind's eye that large woman in the tripe shop, in her white nylon overall with her fat pink hands, holding forth to her customers and putting the world to rights.

One wet Saturday morning I was sent to buy Dad's tripe as usual but on the way out of the shop I dropped the parcel. It went splat on the pavement. Now dogs love tripe, and there was always some mangy beast hanging around near the entrance. On this particular day a bristly little mongrel shot out from behind me and snapped up the tripe, paper and all. I chased the dog, shouting and waving my arms, and finally managed to get the tripe back but not before it had been chewed and had rolled into the gutter and picked up a fair bit of dirt.

'Sorry, love,' said the tripe shop owner, when I returned to the counter hoping for a replacement. 'I can't be doing that. You'll have to buy another piece.' I explained to her that I had no more money. 'Well, it will teach you to be more careful with your tripe, won't it?' she told me, before resuming a conversation about the state of the public urinals in the town centre.

When I arrived back home I had already devised a plan. If I explained to Mum what had happened she would, no doubt, send me back to the shop, which was the last thing I wanted. I was keen to meet my pals at Herringthorpe playing fields that afternoon. So before Mum could take the tripe from my hands I shot up the stairs and into the bathroom.

'Have you got your Dad's tripe?' came her voice up the stairs.

'Yes,' I shouted back, 'but I'm desperate for the toilet.' I then washed the tripe thoroughly under the cold water tap.

Mum cooked the tripe, Dad ate it, and I watched with a screwed-up face.

'Delicious,' said Dad, licking his lips when he had finished. 'Best bit of tripe I've had in a long while. You must mention it, Pat, the next time you go into the shop,' he continued. I gulped and prayed Mum would do no such thing.

23

I was brought up in a devout Roman Catholic family and religion played a prominent part in my childhood. Most of the small Catholic minority in Rotherham (as indeed in the rest of the country) were of Irish working-class stock and could be best described as timorously conservative. The laws of the Church were to be obeyed and the priest's word was law. There was a certainty in the belief, for, after all, Catholics had a monopoly on the truth and others were out of line. Ours was the one true church, founded by St Peter, defended and preserved by his successor, the Pope, who was infallible.

It wasn't so much the practice of attendance at Mass and Confession that had the greatest influence on me, it was the pervading deep conviction of my parents that the best course in life was, as Jesus exhorted, to do unto others as we would wish them to do unto us, to treat people with kindness and compassion. This guiding principle was ever present in my life, and should I do something of which my parents disapproved, I would get the stock question: 'Would you have liked someone to do that to *you*?'

Each Sunday all of us children would be scrubbed and combed and dressed in our best clothes to attend Mass at St Bede's Church at Masborough, a strongly traditional parish. This was before the Vatican II Council when Pope John XXIII, son of an Italian peasant and third of thirteen children, reinterpreted the Catholic faith in the light of modern circumstances and unleashed within the Church a liberalization which many found disquieting. Within three months of taking office in January 1959, the new Pope summoned the General Council of the Church and things began to change, including the use of the vernacular, rather than Latin, in the services. I was thirteen at the time.

The whole family, all in our Sunday best, would walk down Wellgate through Rotherham town centre, with its great red sandstone church of All Saints, on past the dark weather-blackened buildings and row upon row of endless back-to-back terraces, over the rusting bridge that spanned the greasy green canal, with the pungent smell of industry and the taste of dust in the air.

On the exterior, St Bede's was an ugly dark stone church, but inside it was another world. It was in this church that I had my first introduction to indoor beauty, of ornament, ostentation, spectacle, sacrament and mystery. It was like entering a magical world, a world of burnished metal, gilt, stone and polished wood. As a small child I would sit on one of the hard wooden pews in the shadowy interior, the smell of candles and incense in the air, the rain beating against the windows outside, and look at the bright plaster tablets lining the walls depicting the 'Stations of the Cross'.

Christ's passion and death fascinated me – it was a violent, colourful, exciting story full of interesting characters. The places he visited had irresistibly attractive-sounding names too: Palestine, Jerusalem, Galilee, Jericho, Bethlehem and Gethsemane. Here was a compelling saga indeed. From humble origins this son of a carpenter attained exceptional power and influence, transforming so many people's lives, and he did it not by telling people that they were worthless and evil, by haranguing and disparaging, but by telling them little stories about a man who fell among thieves, a spendthrift son and a poor widow who gave her last coin.

Without any advantages of brute force, money, status or useful connections, he managed through his personality, his example and his oratory to put across his teachings so effectively that 2,000 years later they are still being followed. There were in Jesus the qualities of tolerance, compassion, innocence and courage which demanded my admiration. Jesus I never feared, for he was always to my mind the mild, caring man like the one depicted in my children's Bible and he gave his life for others. He was the Good Shepherd, the Lamb of God. His was the statue with a sacred heart, the outstretched hands and the gentle face. It was easy to love such a person. I wasn't so sure about God, though. He was a more mysterious, less forgiving figure, rather fearsome, like a white-haired, long-bearded head-master who was forever watching me. He saw what I got up to and knew what I was thinking.

I never found going to Mass burdensome. I loved the words, the pageant, the imagery and the rhythms of the strange language intoned by the priest and chanted by the congregation. I would wait in anticipation for High Mass to begin. It was theatre. The thundering organ would fill the church, the choir would raise its voice and then would come the procession from the rear of the church and down the central aisle. The senior server, holding before him a great golden cross, would be followed by four altar boys, dressed in scarlet and white and bearing lighted candles, and the solemn-faced priest in shimmering green silk swinging the censer. Clouds of sweet-smelling smoke would fill the air. In the sixth form I visited my first Protestant church, a Nonconformist chapel, and was amazed at the contrast. Where were the sweeping colours, the heady smell of incense, the stained-glass windows, the pictures and statues to which I had become accustomed? There was no mystery here in this dark and spartan building. It was as chilly and dimly lit as a cellar and about as unattractive, with its rows of long hard pews, pale plain walls, exposed heating pipes down the side, liver-coloured floor tiles, windows high and mean with plain glass and metal grilles. At the front was a wooden lectern above which, writ large, was the lettering:

'Fear the Lord.' This was a place of penance, not praise, cold, colourless, unwelcoming; it didn't seem to me to be the sort of place in which God would feel at home.

At St Bede's there were great brightly coloured plaster statues staring down serenely from their plinths, a flickering red light hanging in a casket of gold above the tabernacle, heavy wooden pews redolent with lavender polish and camphor, rows of shining candles, and the great high altar draped in white linen with the huge brass candlesticks and an ornate golden cross. Then there was the lingering smell of the incense and the chanting of the Latin, which for a child were so mysterious, so magical. I learnt all the Latin responses by heart – '*Dominus vobiscum*', '*Credo in unum deum*', '*qui tollis peccata mundi*', '*miserere nobis*' – without understanding very much, but I derived great pleasure from the sound of the words.

Children have a need for certainty in an uncertain world, and in Catholicism there was a real certainty. Nothing was left to doubt, there was no discussion. The stability of this highly structured but simple supportive faith gave me great solace. Everything was explained in the little blue-backed penny catechism which every Catholic child was given and required to learn, and for those prepared to conform and repent of their wrongdoings the 'one, true Catholic Church' was a comfortable haven, offering salvation.

I was brought up to believe that Catholics had the 'one true faith'; ours was an orthodoxy that had been passed down for centuries from Jesus and St Peter. There was heaven for those who had lived unblemished lives and eventually, after a period in Purgatory, for those who were truly sorry for their sins and sought forgiveness. Heaven was somewhere in the sky above the sun, in the clouds, where everything was light, happiness and peace. The great golden gates opened on to a paradise where God, like a genial old man with a white beard, sat on his heavenly throne. On His right was Jesus and on His left the Blessed Virgin. Hovering above were the angels, saints, the cherubs and seraphim. Deep below in the bowels of the earth was Hell, where an eternal fire raged and where the Devil, the fallen angel, held sway. Evil people, whose souls were damned, were in perpetual torment and denied the sight of God. In between there was Purgatory, where the not-too-bad people were purified of their sins before being promoted to Heaven to join the angels and saints. Then there was Limbo, full of grave-faced babies who hadn't been baptized.

Father Hammond, the parish priest, was a small, severe-looking man with a pinched mouth and dark heavy hooded eyes and reminded me of a hungry blackbird. I guess he wasn't really like that, but as a child that is the memory I have of him. Some people I have spoken to about him found this priest a difficult and intransigent cleric but others have a very different memory. In a recent St Bede's parish magazine one parishioner remembers him as a kindly man with a great sense of humour. I don't recognize this latter picture. For me he was a dour, uncompromising and serious-minded man who applied the letter of the law and not the spirit. He was intolerant of anything he considered disrespectful in church – noisy children, latecomers, those who were inappropriately dressed. Once he refused Communion to a young woman wearing bright lipstick.

My mother fell out with Father Hammond over my education. As a school nurse she had a very good overview of the teaching and learning which took place in the town's schools. She was fiercely ambitious that I should succeed, and felt that Broom Valley Infants (a state school), five minutes' walk away from our house, would be more appropriate for me than St Bede's, the Roman Catholic school, and decided to send me to the former. Father Hammond was not best pleased and told my mother in no uncertain terms that she had a clear duty to provide me with a Catholic education. My sister Christine, who sat in on the discussion, remembers him sitting in the front room, with cool immutable gravity, straight-backed, his lips drawn together in a tight thin line when my mother told him her mind was made up. He had refused a cup of tea and sat with his biretta on his knee, head on one side, fingertips pressed together. It was clear that few in his congregation challenged his authority. My mother clearly did not take to his harsh sermonizing tone and told him, in a polite but firm way, that she would do as she thought best for her own children. She was adamant that I would attend Broom Valley Infants. To question the priest in the 1950s was tantamount to sacrilege, and he was very displeased. Father Hammond warned her of the consequences and left. He then did something singularly cruel. He forbade my mother Communion. He refused to give her the sacrament and told her he would continue to deny her so long as her child was at a non-Catholic school. It hurt her deeply and she felt the injustice but she did not change her mind about my schooling. I find it surprising now that she obeyed the priest's directive and never received the sacrament at all until my schooling was over.

One Saturday my mother caught the train to Leeds to petition the Bishop. Bishop Heenan, later Cardinal Heenan, was an exceptionally able, kindly and sympathetic man and listened quietly to my mother's *cri de coeur*, but he refused to intervene on her behalf. His response was that it would be 'unwise' for him to 'undermine' the parish priest. The Bishop informed my mother that the only way of preserving the faith in children was to ensure that they received a good sound Catholic education. That was the motivation of her parish priest in taking such a hard line. My mother assured the Bishop that she would ensure that I was brought up in the Catholic faith, I would go to Confession, be confirmed and attend Mass regularly, but the Bishop declined to intervene. My mother thanked the Bishop for seeing her but informed him that, in her opinion, the priest was wrong to deny her such a precious thing. Her idea of the priesthood was that the priest, a servant of God, lived a blameless life and that he was a mediator between God and man, both by example and ministration. Being a priest demanded that the principles of justice and charity be translated into action. This was what Jesus stood for. I suspect the Bishop found it hard to deal with this thoughtful, strong-minded and determined woman who knew her Bible, and I guess he would have been quite taken aback when she reminded him of the words of Jesus: 'Be merciful, just as your Father is merciful. Don't be a judge of others, and you will not be judged; do not condemn or you will be condemned; forgive and you will be forgiven.' There was, she felt, little justice, mercy and charity in Father Hammond's diktat.

'Your priest may very well be wrong,' Bishop Heenan told my mother, 'and for that he will, as we all will, have to answer to God.' So the Bishop would not overrule his priest and for thirteen years my mother never approached the altar rails at Communion.

Father Hammond was certainly on the solidly conservative wing of the Church, and we only felt the rustle of a reforming breeze following Vatican II with the arrival of a new young and enthusiastic curate, Father Delaney. When Father Hammond processed down the central aisle at High Mass, draped in coloured silk and preceded by the servers and altar boys, I always felt slightly afraid of him. I wasn't alone. On one memorable Sunday, Father Hammond, at the conclusion of the Mass, picked up the chalice draped in a small square white cloth, donned his biretta with priestly precision and slowly descended the altar steps. Seeing the priest heading for the side door, a group of men clustered at the door at the back of the church made their move. They would be heading for the Catholic Club for a few pints prior to lunch. Father Hammond, catching sight of them, stopped in his tracks and shouted the whole length of the church, 'The Mass has not ended until the priest has left the altar!' The men froze in their tracks like a group of recalcitrant schoolboys told off by the headmaster.

The priest was of the opinion, prevalent at that time, that in certain circumstances and in certain places, children should be seen and not heard. During Mass, if a baby cried or a toddler was noisy, the parent was informed by Father Hammond to take the offending child out of church. Times have fortunately changed. I was thinking of Father Hammond when I attended Mass recently. The young priest, on seeing a parent leaving the church with a noisy infant, asked her to return to her pew and then recited a little verse he had been given by his tutor during his training:

> Though picture books may fall beneath the pew,
> And childish voices rise above the prayers,
> Spare them rebuke, for God's house is their own
> And his incomparable gifts are theirs.

Being a collector of interesting snippets and verses (you never know when they will come in handy), I prevailed upon Father Devine (what a wonderful name for a priest) to have a copy.

Once Mass started, the back door of the church was closed and bolted. Father Hammond would not allow anyone to come in late. One Sunday there was an almighty banging on the back door just after the priest had intoned, *'In Nomine Patris . . .'* The door was hastily opened and there stood Mr Ryves, a large and formidable man, leaning on a sturdy walking stick. 'No one bars God's door to me!' he shouted, and entered the church to the amazement of the priest and the congregation. He limped slowly down the central aisle to the very front pew, his usual seat, genuflected with some difficulty, made the Sign of the Cross and stood looking the priest in the eye. This was theatre at its best. There was an unearthly silence, with all eyes fixed on the priest's stern face. Then Father Hammond coughed and proceeded with the Mass. I wondered what the priest would have to say when Mr Ryves next went to Confession, what penance he would dole out. Some years later I met Mr Ryves's son, Peter. He came to teach at the same school and we became good friends. We would reminisce about our schooldays. Peter told me that the priest never mentioned the incident, but neither did he lock the back door of the church again to his father or anyone else.

Sometimes Mass was equally entertaining. When Father Hammond processed around the church at High Mass, he would splatter holy water to the right and left, dipping the aspergillum (a brass stick with a round knob on the end) in the receptacle and proceeding to drench the congregation. He seemed to do this with a vengeance, spattering faces and clothes with liberal amounts of water. On one occasion, he thrust the brass stick into the holy water and had begun to splash everyone when the ball on the end shot off. Rumour had it that one of the altar boys, noticing that the knob screwed on to the top of the stick, had unscrewed it so that it was held on tenuously by a single thread. The brass ball flew through the air, and with a resounding crack hit an elderly woman telling her rosary beads smack on the back of her head.

'Jesus, Mary and Joseph!' cried the old woman, falling to her knees. 'I've been struck!'

Such was Father Hammond's authority and hold on his congregation, no one dared laugh. He continued to process, apparently unperturbed by the interruption. The following week I noticed that the aspergillum had been replaced by a sort of pastry brush.

24

I made my First Holy Communion at seven, the time judged by the Catholic Church when children have reached the age of reason and can tell right from wrong. Dressed in my new blue suit, white shirt, white ankle socks and new black shoes, I joined the back of the procession down the central aisle at St Bede's with a bevy of little boys dressed like me and girls looking like miniature brides dressed in white silk with veils. With my hands pressed firmly together I knelt at the altar rails and stuck out my tongue ready to receive the Body of Christ in the form of a small dry round wafer, which we were told not to chew but to swallow whole. The priest's breath smelt of the sherry my mother sometimes put in the trifle at Christmas. In his magnificent green silk vestments and bearing a silver chalice before him, he processed down the line of children repeating, 'Corpus Domini nostri Jesu Christi custodiat animam tuam in vitam aeternam. Amen,' again and again. Under my chin a grave-faced altar boy in red and white put a silver plate in case the priest dropped the host.

On the way out of the church people pressed coins into my hand, ruffled my hair and patted my back. Back home there were sausage rolls and scones and cakes. That night I knelt with my mother beside the bed and said my prayers and felt very grown-up.

Being at a non-Catholic school, I had to prepare for my First Communion by attending a class on Sunday after Mass. The lessons were taught by a sweet-faced woman. She was a good-humoured and sympathetic teacher, with bright eyes and a ready smile, who made us feel special, as though each one of us was the one person she wanted to see. She brought biscuits and cake, which the few children receiving instruction would eat after the hour's session. She would tell us about Jesus and how he died for our sins, and read the parables from a children's Bible, which she explained. I didn't mind attending her class at all, for she was kindly, could tell a good story and answered my questions. For homework we had to learn sections from our small penny catechism and colour in pictures from a large colouring book featuring characters from the Old Testament and the life of Jesus.

Occasionally Father Hammond would appear to test us on what we had learnt. I have always been able to remember things, and even when I did not understand the content could rattle off a piece of text parrot fashion in such a convincing manner that it would appear that I was knowledgeable.

'Who made you?' the priest would ask.

'God made me,' we would chant.

'Why did God make you?'

'God made me to know Him, love Him and serve Him in this world, and to be happy with Him for ever in the next.'

'To whose image and likeness did God make you?'

'God made me to his own image and likeness.'

I recall that once we were asked about the Blessed Trinity and Father Hammond singled each of us out in turn. This was a real ordeal, because we had to stand in turn and answer the question that was directed at us. He never shouted or looked angry if we got it wrong but it was clear from his eyes that he was displeased. There was a rather grubby boy in the class who had an unusual name like mine. His name was of the good Catholic variety like Ignatius or Xavier and he attended irregularly. No one wanted to sit near him because he smelt. I remember Miss Martin being particularly kind to him and smiling as he wolfed down the biscuits and cakes. I wonder now if he came just for food, for he rarely bothered learning his catechism. The poor lad was not only unfortunate-looking, with jug-handle ears, a face full of spots, cross eyes and a long thin neck, but he had a speech impediment.

Once the priest asked us why it was important for us to be quiet in church.

'Because people are trying to sleep?' enquired Ignatius innocently.

Father Hammond's eyes looked heavenwards and he sighed.

On another occasion we were told by Miss Martin, 'We must all be good children and aspire to be like Jesus.'

Ignatius scratched his head. 'Well, I don't know about that, miss,' he said. 'Jesus was a good boy and look what happened to 'im!'

'What is the mystery of the Three Persons in one God?' Father Hammond asked me one Sunday in the class.

'The Mystery of the Three Persons in one God is called the Mystery of the Blessed Trinity,' I replied smugly.

Father Hammond nodded. Then his eyes settled on Ignatius (or Xavier). 'What do we mean by a mystery?' he asked.

The boy spluttered something completely unintelligible.

'I have no idea what you are talking about,' said the priest.

'That's because it's a bleedin' mystery, innit?' the boy replied.

Sometimes the curate, Father Delaney, would join the class and talk to us. I liked Father Delaney because he smiled a great deal and told interesting stories. Once he told us about when he was young in Ireland, living on a farm in the middle of nowhere and always wanting to be a priest, something we might later want to consider, that is, if God called us. I prayed that God didn't go calling on me. I had my sights set on another career.

On one occasion Father Delaney asked us if there was anything we wanted to know about the life of a priest. 'Why was he called "father" when he had no children?' he was asked. 'Why didn't he get married?' 'Had he met the Pope?' Then

Ignatius (or Xavier) piped up. 'It must take you ages to go to the lavatory,' he said. There was a stunned silence before the teacher snapped, 'That's not the sort of question to ask Father,' she said.

The priest smiled. He knew exactly what Ignatius (or Xavier) was thinking. His black clerical garment had a long line of small buttons down the front.

'It's a fair question,' said the priest, laughing. 'Even priests have to go to the lavatory.' He turned to us. 'This, children, is a cassock,' he explained, 'and I don't have to undo every single button to remove it.' He demonstrated by unhooking the top. 'There are small hooks at intervals down the front. Most of the buttons are there just for show. So I don't have a problem when I want to spend a penny.' The teacher's face was scarlet.

I was really pleased to see that it was Father Delaney who was to hear my first Confession. I was frightened of Father Hammond and didn't fancy telling him what I had been doing wrong. In the Sunday class we had practised what we would say on the special day and had to have a sin ready to confess. On Saturday morning those receiving instruction sat in a line on the pew opposite the confessional. It was like a big black wardrobe, was the confessional, with small curtained windows and a heavy brass handle on the door. When it came to my turn, I took a deep breath, entered the dark stuffy box and knelt facing a grille. I could hear the priest breathing on the other side.

'Bless me, Father, for I have sinned. This is my first confession,' I whispered.

'Speak up, my son,' said Father Delaney.

I waited. I wasn't sure whether I should begin or not. 'Shall I start, Father?' I asked tentatively.

'Yes, my son,' came the voice from the other side of the grille.

'I've used some rude words, Father,' I said.

'I see,' said the priest. 'And do you know why it is wrong to use rude words?' he asked.

'Yes, Father. The teacher told us that every time we swear, Jesus weeps.'

'That's right,' said the priest. 'What did these rude words begin with?'

'I used the "b" word, Father and the "h" word,' I told him.

There was long pause. 'The "h" word'?' said the priest.

'Yes, Father.'

Looking back, I guess the priest was very curious as to what the 'h' word was.

'What is the "h" word?' he asked.

'I'd rather not say, Father, it's very rude.'

This must have been even more intriguing for him. 'Whisper it through the grille,' he told me. His voice was hardly audible.

Leaning closer, I replied, 'Harse.'

Father Delaney made a little snorting noise. 'Harse,' he repeated and I saw him hold a handkerchief up to his eyes. He looked as if he were crying.

My bottom lip began to tremble. I had made the priest cry. I didn't realize it was so serious a sin. 'I'm sorry, Father,' I whimpered, 'I won't ever say it again. I promise.'

Almost choking, the priest told me to say one 'Our Father' and three 'Hail Marys' and make a good act of contrition, which I did whilst wiping my eyes.

'*Ego te absolvo in nomine patris, et Filii, et Spiritus Sancti. Amen,*' he managed to say before holding up the handkerchief again to his eyes. Then he added, between sobs, 'Pray for me, my son.'

When it came to my confirmation some years later, Father Hammond informed my mother outside church after Mass that I would need to attend Saturday morning classes in preparation.

'There's really no need for that, Father,' my mother told him. 'My daughter Christine will be teaching him.'

'He needs instruction from a teacher qualified,' said the priest. 'I am afraid a relation, however well intentioned, cannot prepare the boy sufficiently well for confirmation.'

'Father,' my mother replied. 'My daughter Christine is a fully qualified teacher and holds the Catholic Teaching Certificate with distinction from Mount Pleasant Roman Catholic Teacher Training College in Liverpool.'

Father Hammond never approached my mother again, neither did he quiz me on my religious knowledge.

The Bishop confirmed me on a bright Sunday at Mass. A photograph of me on the day shows a rather gangly, self-conscious boy of fourteen in a smart suit and white tie, posing outside the church with a parent on either side. I took the confirmation name of Benedict and was presented with a missal, a book of texts used in Catholic Mass, by Mum's friend Mrs Gill, some black shiny rosary beads by Christine, money by my brothers and a large crimson-covered book illustrated in vivid colour called *Stories from the Bible*. Some years later, when I was a school inspector travelling round the schools of Yorkshire, I read from this large crimson-coloured volume given to me on the day of my confirmation.

'This book was given to me when I was a boy by my mother and father,' I told the children in a school assembly. 'It is a very special book, full of wonderful stories which were told by a very special man. In the story I am about to read, which is called "The Story of the Lost Sheep", Jesus tries to help us understand how we should feel about the poor and weak.'

I read the parable and then I explained how such stories taught us all how to lead better lives.

'And what would you say to Jesus,' I asked, holding high the red book like some preacher of old, 'if he were to walk into the hall this morning?'

A boy on the front row thought for a moment, then raised

his hand and said loudly, 'I'd give 'im that book, Mester Phinn, and I'd say, "Jesus Christ – this is your life!"'

Every third or fourth Saturday morning I went with my sister to Confession at St Bede's. We would kneel outside the dark wooden wardrobe and wait our turn to tell the priest about our transgressions. 'Pray Father, give me your blessing for I have sinned. It is three weeks since my last confession.' I guess the sins of a small boy were tediously familiar to the faceless figure behind the grille. I would tell him the peccadilloes of childhood: I had been bad-tempered, forgotten to say my prayers, shouted at my brothers, not done as I was told – all pretty tame stuff. I sometimes thought of spicing it up a bit with, 'I've had these impure thoughts', but never dared. Imagine if he asked me to go into details. Father Hammond would be there on the altar the next day staring at me and knowing my innermost secrets. I certainly wasn't giving too much away. I often wondered what he would say if I said I had pushed an old woman off the bridge or murdered our next-door neighbour, Mrs Evans, while she was hanging out those big blue bloomers on her washing line. I knew he couldn't tell the police, he was bound by the confidentiality of the confessional. I'd seen it at the Regent Cinema, in an American film where the priest was bound to secrecy.

On one occasion the rectangle of wood that was slotted into a frame on the front of the confessional box, telling would-be penitents which priest was in residence, was different. Instead of announcing that Fr Hammond was at home, it said that Mgr Wheeler was in situ. The woman in the pew in front of my sister and before us in the confessional stakes was clearly unaware, as I was at the time, what the Mgr (Monsignor) stood for. She entered the box and said in a loud voice, 'Bless me Mugger for I have sinned. It is four weeks since my last confession.' The priest, I discovered later when he emerged stony-faced from the confessional, was an ancient Irishman with little outcrops of wispy white hair. He clearly was not prepared to have a list of bland, venial sins rattled off, for him to dispense the predictable penance of, 'Say one Our Father and three Hail Marys.' He asked her to slow down, speak up and provide more details. Those waiting in the queue were entertained by a most colourful and detailed description of the woman's marital situation, how her over-demanding spouse would arrive home the worse for drink, expect his 'conjungal rights' and not leave her alone. She continued to tell the priest that she had six children and couldn't cope with any more. We all waited in excited anticipation for the priest's judgement, straining our ears. My sister still relates the story in vivid detail and how, all the way home, she would burst into fits of giggling but not tell me what was so amusing.

25

At seven I moved up from the Infants, where I had been very happy and made good progress in my work, and into the adjacent building of Broom Valley Junior School. My school reports, which my mother kept in a blue folder, show that I was 'fairly good' or 'good' in most things and rather better in English. Reading through them now, I get the impression that my teachers saw me as a decent enough boy but one of average intelligence and limited prospects. I am described in tones that strike me as deeply condescending, a way of saying I would not achieve much in life. As can be seen from my final Junior School report, my form teacher's comments and the headteacher's observations are far from extensive. Teachers these days, obliged to write detailed assessments of a child's achievement, effort, progress and conduct which cover a good few pages, must view such an unforthcoming end of school report with a wry humour.

Broom Valley Primary School Rotherham
School Report for Gervase Phinn
July 25th, 1958
Class 4

Number in Class : 43

SUBJECT	Maximum Marks	Marks Obtained	Comment
ENGLISH:			
Reading	20	20	Very Good

Composition	20	18	Good
Spelling	20	12	Needs care
Language and			
Literature	20	15	Fair
Comprehension	20	17	Quite Good
ARITHMETIC			
Mental	20	11	Must try harder
Accuracy	50	44	Good
Problems	30	25	Good
HISTORY	20	14	Very interested
			Disappointing result
GEOGRAPHY	20	17	Very Good
NATURE STUDY			
SCIENCE	20	18	Very Good
NEEDLEWORK			
CRAFTWORK			Fair
MUSIC			Fair
ART			Fairly Good
PHYSICAL TRAINING			
AND GAMES			Fairly Good
CONDUCT			Very Good

PROGRESS Gervase is a steady worker, always trying his best.
He shows an interest in all activities.

Head Teacher: .... J. Leslie Morgan ....

This is a revealing report, not because it tells you very much
about the pupil's attainment and progress, but because it indicates, in its paucity and restraint, the sort of information parents
were likely to receive about their child's education in the 1950s.
It was perhaps thought by the teachers that it was not good
for pupils to be too cocksure, so there was no fulsome praise
or hearty congratulations. However, I should have thought
that the full marks I achieved for English might have merited

an 'excellent' and the 18 out of 20 for composition a 'very good'.

The report indicates that I needed to try harder in mental arithmetic. I hated mental arithmetic because I was frightened of the large, craggy-faced teacher in the tweed jacket and shiny black shoes who smelt of tobacco and shouted. He would fire questions around the classroom like a Gatling gun and I would stutter or freeze when he got to me. It wasn't that the teacher humiliated me or smacked me, as some teachers undoubtedly did in the 1950s, but he failed to inspire me.

Christine, my wife, loved arithmetic at school and the challenge of numbers. Her 'party piece' is adding up the prices of the items in the supermarket trolley as fast as the assistant at the till can enter them in the cash register. She then gives the exact money. 'How do you do that?' asks the person on the checkout. Richard, my eldest son and an accountant, as one might guess, loves figures and became fascinated with mathematics when his teacher at secondary school, the brilliant Mr Hopley, came into his life. He told them in that very first lesson: 'I am going to show you the magic of mathematics.' This enthusiast, with the smiling eyes of the dedicated teacher, generated in his students a real excitement for mathematics. Had I been taught by such a teacher I would undoubtedly have enjoyed the subject, perhaps performed better in the Eleven Plus examination and my life might have taken a completely different course.

I do remember the weekly elocution lesson that took place in the last term of the final year at the Juniors, when it was the teacher's avowed aim to improve the way we spoke. I have an idea that the woman with the thin grey hair scraped savagely over her scalp and the steely grey eyes who appeared in the classroom was some sort of supernumerary brought in for the sole purpose of teaching us to speak 'properly' like the BBC announcers. When she spoke, she sounded to me as if she had a hot potato in her mouth or, as the woman in the tripe shop might have said, 'a plum in her gob'. The idea of getting us to speak 'properly' no doubt was well-intentioned, but the poor woman was, of course, on a hiding to nothing. We were Yorkshire children growing up in a world where everyone seemed to drop their aitches and pepper their speech with 'sithee' (see thou), ''ey up' (hello), 'geeore' (give over), 'naaden' (now then), 'shurrup' (shut up), 'thawhat' (pardon) and 'gerron' (get away with you).

Each Monday morning we would chant our sentences, and I have to admit I quite enjoyed the lessons and discovered I had something of a talent for mimicry.

'We have a nice hice in the country, you know.'

Of course I would never use this affected voice when I was outside the classroom, unless it was in the playground to enter-tain my peers. That would have meant certain ridicule at best and severe bullying at worst.

Recently I discovered the grey-covered exercise book in which I had copied out the various 'Speech Exercises' all those years ago, and smiled at the memory of sitting behind a hard wooden desk chanting the silly sentences and doggerel with forty or so other children.

Gertie Gordon grew a gross of gaudy gay gladioli.
Careful Katy cut and cooked a crisp and crunchy lettuce.
They thought they fought to defend the fort.
It was Harry Harding's habit to help his uncle in the haberdashers.

Down the path and across the grass,
The little children run,
To see the bird bath by the bower
And the tall trees in the sun.

In the book I have copied down some notes from the black-board and have added a small drawing. The illustration shows a man in a top hat and another in a flat cap. Between them, like a fence, stands a great capital 'H'. Underneath is the caption: 'When is an H not an H?' The notes that follow explain how important it is not to 'drop the aitch in speech.'

H is what we call the aspirate or breath sound and is often left out where it ought to be put in and put in where it is not supposed to be there. The H in the sounding of a word separates the well-educated from the less educated. Anyone who hopes to speak correctly must know when and when not to use it.

Then there were exercises to practise:

> Henry Hall hops on his heels.
> What an odd habit.
> How horrid it feels.
> Hopping on his heels
> Is not hopping at all,
> So why not hop properly, Henry Hall?

> Harry went to Hampstead,
> Harry lost his hat,
> Harry's mother said to Harry,
> 'Harry, where's your hat?'
> Harry said he'd lost it.
> It wasn't true at all.
> For Harry's hat was hanging
> On the hatstand in the hall.

> He hit him on his head
> With a hard and heavy hammer
> And it made him howl horribly.

I can just imagine the children of Rotherham practising their aspirates on their way home.

I was once told a story by a former headteacher that when he was a child living in Huddersfield there was the feared visit of the school inspector. He was a stickler for 'correct English' was this dark-suited, sour-faced individual from the Ministry of Education in London, and was dismayed to find that the children spoke in a strong regional accent. Having watched a lesson, the inspector observed that the young pupils were deficient in their speech and that the teacher must try to eradicate the use of dialect. He had noted, for example, that many of the children used the word 'putten' instead of 'put': 'I've putten it down' instead of 'I have put it down.' He suggested that remedial work was needed in this area. The teacher complied, and when the inspector made a return visit some weeks later assured him that the offending 'putten' had been eliminated from the children's vocabulary. To demonstrate this the teacher wrote on the blackboard the sentence: 'I've putten the apple on the desk.'

'Now children,' he said, facing the class, 'what is wrong with the sentence on the blackboard?'

One bright spark raised a hand and replied: 'Tha's gone and putten putten when tha should have putten put.'

Alban, a friend of mine who farms near Whitby, when a child, once asked his father which was the correct pronunciation of 'either'. Was it pronounced 'eether' or 'eyether?' His father replied, 'Owther'll do.'

The former school inspector Leonard Clarke described a visit to a Yorkshire School in the 1950s. The headteacher asked him if he wanted to hear the children sing and the inspector soon found himself in the school hall where the senior choir were assembled to perform for him. He enquired of the music teacher what the children were going to sing.

'"Wetherby Socks",' replied the teacher, a large, bluff Yorkshireman.

'I don't know that particular tune,' said the inspector. 'Is it a local folk song?'

'Nay,' replied the teacher, looking at him as if he were not quite right in the head, 'it's very famous. 'Asn't thy 'eard of it?'

'I can't say I have,' replied the inspector.

The music teacher turned to the choir, which then gave an enthusiastic rendering of 'Where the Bee Sucks'.

In the aftermath of the Second World War a high proportion of children had school dinners but our response to them was not one of gratitude. School dinners at Broom Valley Juniors were dire: thin cuts of pale meat with thick rims of white fat and pieces of gristle, lumpy gravy, lukewarm mashed potatoes, over-boiled carrots, watery cabbage, to be followed by insipid semolina, tapioca (frogspawn) or rice pudding with a splodge of raspberry jam in the middle. Sometimes dessert would be a rock-hard chocolate sponge square covered in sickly pink custard. In the playground, out of the teachers' hearing, of course, we would chant:

> Splishy, splashy custard,
> Dead dogs' eyes,
> All mixed together with giblet pies.
> See it on the dinner plate, nice and thick,
> And swallow it down with a bucketful of sick.

In those days there were no salads, fresh fruit, yoghurts or squeezed orange juice on the menu at school, just the same old fare served from large shiny tin containers by a dinner lady who, if we complained, told us we should think ourselves lucky because there were people starving in Africa who would be glad of it.

I recall one of my friends saying *sotto voce* that 'the Africans were welcome to it', and he was sent to Mr Morgan and had to stand outside the headteacher's room all dinner time for being ungrateful.

One memory of the Junior school was being forced to sit through school lunch while the lumpy gravy and fried parsnips slowly congealed on my plate.

'Come along,' said the dinner lady sharply, standing over me with her arms folded underneath her bosom. 'Get it eaten or you'll be sent to Mr Morgan.'

I thought of a wonderful ruse. 'I'm a Catholic,' I told her.

'What?'

'It's against my religion to eat parsnips on a Holy Day of Obligation. It's like not eating meat on Fridays.'

The plate was cleared away, much to my satisfaction. I decided that this would be one lie I would not be admitting next time I went to Confession.

I got my first real glimpse of a world of unimaginable privilege when, as a child of ten in 1956, I came upon Wentworth House. Our class of forty plus pupils was bussed out one bright sunny Monday morning from Broom Valley Juniors to Wentworth Woodhouse, a village twixt Rotherham and Barnsley, so that the female students training there to be P.E. mistresses could 'practise on us'.

Wentworth House was once the palatial residence of the Earls Fitzwilliam. Built in the 1720s for Thomas Wentworth, later Marquess of Rockingham, this vast, imposing stately home, with its 600-foot-long Palladian east front, the largest façade of any building in Europe, with its five miles of passageways and a room for every day of the year, took over sixteen years to complete. The surrounding park had upwards of 1,500 acres of vast lawns and majestic woods, ornamented by temples, columns and picturesque water features. After a colourful catalogue of family indiscretions, endless arguments, forbidden loves, contentious court cases, feuds and financial setbacks, the residence became a white elephant, too big and expensive to manage.

The redoubtable Lady Mabel Smith, sister of the sixth Earl Fitzwilliam, with the keen social conscience of the more liberally minded aristocrat, suggested turning Wentworth into a school, and in 1947 she used her not inconsiderable eloquence and influence to get the West Riding County Council to take on the house on a fifty-year lease.

This historic mansion subsequently became a training college for female P.E. teachers and was named the Lady Mabel College in her honour. In 1979, when the maintenance costs proved too prohibitive, the college closed, and nine years later Lady Elizabeth Hastings, the tenth Earl's granddaughter and beneficiary, put the house up for sale. Today the vast building stands in its lonely acres, stark and shuttered, the home of a recluse, its great iron gates closed to the public.

So in 1956 I got my first sighting of Wentworth. I had read about such buildings in the history books but had never seen such an immense edifice. I recall climbing down from the bus in my P.E. kit of white vest and black shorts and plimsolls (which we called pumps), to see what looked like a huge cardboard cut-out. It was breathtaking. I marvelled at the great stone pillars, ornate pediments, porticos and domed pavilions (although I had no idea what these were called at the time), and the many hundreds of windows. Of course, we small urchins were not allowed to ascend the flight of steep stone steps and enter into this palace. We were lined up on the lawns to the front of the house ready to be 'practised on'.

We were joined by a group of young female students, all identically attired in short navy blue pleated skirts (well, they were short for the 1950s, stretching from their waists to just above the knees), white short-sleeved blouses, pristine white ankle socks and remarkably white, unblemished plimsolls. I had become susceptible to girls since reaching double figures, and the sight of this bevy of athletic long-legged beauties in short skirts and tight blouses is one of my favourite memories! Behind the students strode a much older woman with short cropped hair, broad shoulders and massive arms and a face that could freeze soup in cans. She was attired rather differently, in a white jacket with sleeves and a more capacious white pleated skirt. Later we discovered that this Amazon was the students' teacher and she called the shots. The bossy woman in white put the fear of God into us as she boomed out various orders, telling us to line up smartly, be on our best behaviour and listen carefully to all instructions. Even our teacher looked frightened of her and stood like a spare part, watching proceedings but venturing no comment.

Each student was assigned five pupils on which to practise her skills. It was not an unpleasant experience for me and my pals to have our own personal fitness trainer – this tall willowy blonde with a soft smile and long legs who helped us with our physical exertions: star jumps and squat thrusts, hand springs and forward rolls, handstands and press-ups. After half an hour of stretching and jumping, leaping and running, we were allowed to rest and get our breath.

That morning I lay on my stomach staring across the parkland dotted with grazing deer, avenues of tall cedars, dense woodland of ancient oaks, manicured lawns, wide borders bursting with colourful flowers, pale statues and spouting fountains. I had never seen anything like it.

On our way back to school, our teacher, now in rather a chatty mood, told us that the house had once been the home of just one fabulously rich man and his family, a grand and very wealthy lord, and that he would have had 700 servants to look after him – gardeners and grooms, coachmen and carpenters, kitchen maids and cooks, brewers and butlers, stewards and housekeepers, lamplighters and a man to wind up the clocks. He even employed a mole-catcher. A hundred thoroughbred horses would have been kept in the stable block, which resembled a huge Georgian house. With all the precocious confidence of a ten-year-old, I asked him why would anyone want to live in such a big place and was it not unfair that someone should have all this while others have so little? I cannot recall the teacher's reply, but I guess that he merely shrugged as he always did when one of his pupils asked an awkward question.

I returned to Wentworth House some thirty years later and this time I went inside. I was General Adviser for Language Development with Rotherham Education Department at the time, and was given the task of disposing of the remnants of the college library. In 1979 when Lady Mabel College closed, Sheffield City Polytechnic took over the property, but by the mid 1980s, when the local authority gave up its lease on the house, all educational materials and equipment of any value were transferred to the city campus. A residue of several hundred unwanted books, teaching texts, guidelines and journals was left behind and it was my job to dispose of them. Rather than just sending them to a waste paper company for pulping, I initially circulated all Rotherham schools inviting interested teachers to come and take what books they wanted for the school libraries. I would be there all day on a Saturday I specified, to supervise matters.

On the day when Wentworth was open for the collection of books, it snowed heavily. I drove up the long gravel drive, now thick with snow, and parked the car in front of the house. I describe the scene which I beheld as I sat looking out over the expanse of white, in one of my Dales books.

All around the hall stretched a strange white world stroked in silence. No wind blew the snow into drifts, no birds called, no animal moved and, save for the sporadic soft thud of snow falling from the branches of the towering dark trees which bordered the drive, all was silent. There was a stillness, as if life itself had been suspended.

The caretaker responded to my banging after some time and the great door was opened and I stepped inside. I followed him through a vast pillared hall which must have been sixty feet square and forty feet high, with a gallery supported by huge fluted marble pillars. In its day the grandeur of the dimensions, the ornate decoration, the magnificent paintings and statues and the lavish furnishings would have been unparalleled in their beauty and opulence.

The books had been stacked in the Marble Saloon. It was here in 1912 that the great ballerina Anna Pavlova had danced for King George V. I set myself up on a hard-backed chair in the Ante Room, an area which must have been at least forty feet in length and half as much wide, with an immense stone fireplace guarded by a pair of fearsome-looking carved stone griffins. It was strange and rather unsettling for me, sitting there on a shabby hard-backed chair amidst the piles of old books in this cold, empty building, thinking of what this house must have been like in its heyday.

As I left that winter afternoon, having dispensed the books to those hardy teachers who had braved the weather, I paused for a moment at the top of the stone steps and looked out over the snow-covered lawns and I pictured that little scrap of a boy in his P.E. kit doing star jumps on the grass.

26

'No childhood,' writes Philip Roth in *The Plot Against America*, 'is without its terrors.' My terror came in my last year at junior school in the form of the bully. I was a popular pupil with my teachers. Most were kindly, smiled a great deal, rarely shouted and clearly enjoyed the company of children. I also found them mines of information and would not be afraid of asking them questions or reticent about sharing my own thoughts and feelings. From what my school reports say about me, I was 'well-behaved', 'a steady worker' who 'tried his best', a boy who was 'good-natured and helpful' and one who caused his teachers no trouble. I wasn't a high flier, nor was I a child in need of special help with my work; I was just an ordinary sort of boy. When I visited Broom Valley Junior School as an education adviser in Rotherham many years later, the present headteacher, Philip Crutchley, informed me he had looked through the old punishment book prior to my visit to see if my name appeared when I was a pupil at the school. Thankfully, there was no mention of me. Nor was there a mention of my achieving anything of note either.

Schools are places where children acquire much more than the principles, ideas and processes of a subject. They are formative little worlds where children develop their social skills, learn to get along with others, make friendships and sometimes enemies. They are places where rules circumscribe their every move, where they discover, are hurt, feel lonely, experience success and failure, and where teachers loom large. In the good schools they learn about love, beauty, compassion, goodness, cooperation, care and other positive human emotions and feelings. Children, however, even in the good schools, also learn the hard lessons of life; lessons about injustice, humiliation and cruelty and sometimes, if they are unlucky, they come across the bully. A measure of rough and tumble in a school builds a degree of immunity and teaches us to stand up for ourselves. One can't expect children to be permanently pleasant with each other. We have all been name-called and called others names ourselves, but systematic cruelty in the form of constant bullying is a very different matter.

Bullies seek out their victims, those who are likely to be in some way different. It might be skin colour, physical appearance, a disability, the colour of one's hair or the way one speaks. For me it wasn't just my name that set me apart. Perhaps it was that to some in my class I must have appeared something of a 'goody-goody'. I enjoyed most of the lessons (the notable exception being mental arithmetic), readily volunteered answers to the teachers' questions, offered to tidy the books, clean out the hamster cage and act as milk monitor. I little thought that my behaviour would antagonize the large moon-faced boy who was frequently outside the headteacher's room for misbehaving.

Charlie, it was clear, was not popular with the teachers. His hopeless forgetfulness, his permanent scowl, his answering back and lack of interest in the lessons rubbed them up the wrong way. I guess I appeared to him everything he was not, and he singled me out for his special attention. He would delight in mispronouncing my name, much to the amusement of some of the other children, who were no doubt as afraid of him as I was and thankful they were not his victims. 'Gervarse! Gervarse!' he would shout after me down the corridor. I would carry on walking, afraid to face him and feeling everyone's eyes upon me. Children can be a delight, but they can also be corrosively mean and spiteful, and those of us who become the object of the bully's unwelcome attention remember for a lifetime those periods when it was our turn to be picked on and our most secret insecurities exposed and held up for ridicule.

Charlie developed a real, almost obsessive dislike of me. He was a tall, fat, round-faced boy with lank black hair and scowled constantly. Maybe if it had been just him who picked on me I might have summoned up enough courage to challenge him, but he enlisted two other boys to make my life a misery. Charlie and his two fellow bullies would stop me going to the toilet and tip everything out of my satchel, write cruel notes and leave them on my desk and spit at me when my back was turned. He would poke and push and call me names at every opportunity. His speciality was the Indian burn. At breaktimes he would sidle up with his two cronies, who would grab me and hold me while he would wring a bare wrist with his hands close together until the skin chafed and stung.

The bullying soon began to affect my school work. I became very quiet in class, stopped volunteering to help the teacher and at breaktimes found a quiet corner in the cloakroom rather than go into the playground. I kept my head down, not wanting to attract attention. I tried to keep out of Charlie's way and ignore him as much as I could, believing in the old adage that bullies soon get tired of teasing once the victim ceases to react. This didn't work and the bullying continued.

I never said anything to either my parents or my teachers and to them everything must have appeared normal. But things were not normal. Those who have been bullied know only too well how vulnerable you feel, how your self-confidence diminishes and how weak and frightened you become, dreading going into school, filled with fear and apprehension in case your persecutor is lying in wait.

There are two ways of dealing with those who delight in others' suffering. You either enlist the help of an adult who might make it stop, or you confront the tormentor. I eventually took the second course. Recently I heard the legendary

Yorkshire athlete Lord Sebastian Coe speak at a dinner. He started his immensely entertaining talk with the words: 'When you are brought up in Sheffield and are called Sebastian, you soon learn to run.' Well, I grew up in Rotherham and was called Gervase and I couldn't run, but I soon discovered that words could be powerful weapons, more powerful than fists. I have never believed the sentiments in the children's chant: 'Sticks and stones may break my bones, but calling never hurts me.' Those who are bullied know only too well that 'Sticks and stones may break your bones, but words can break your heart.' For a while, I endured a miserable time at school, watching and waiting for the bully to pounce, having to endure his constant name-calling and cruel comments. Bruises fade but cruel words stay with you.

I found that my words could hurt bullies too, and one day I gave as good as I got. I recall vividly the very first time I confronted him. It was on the way home. I usually waited a while in school until the rest of the children had set off for home. In doing so there was less likelihood of Charlie getting me. That day he was without his two cronies and had commandeered a girl's skipping rope. He waited for me outside school, then followed me down Broom Valley Road and began thrashing at my legs with the rope. I had had enough. I grabbed the rope, yanked it from his hands and told him to leave me alone. Then the words just spilled out. I told him no one really liked him and that they talked about him behind his back and laughed at him and everyone knew where he lived, not in a proper house but in a prefab.

Of course, it ended in a fight. I'd known it would happen one day, and at night in bed I had often wished I had the courage of Tom Brown, who flattened the cowardly bully Flashman to the cheers of the other boys, or David, who killed the Philistine giant with a sling and a pebble. It didn't quite work out like that for me. Charlie was a head taller and a good stone heavier. He thumped me hard in the stomach, which winded me, then grabbed me around the neck. I kicked his shins. He cried and swung a punch at me which split my lip. I felt frightened and angry and I hit him in the throat with all the force I could muster. He cried, gasped, coughed and spluttered, then lunged at me again, punching me in the chest. I remember picking up the skipping rope and throwing it at him. I heard the crack as the wooden pommel came in contact with his head. Then I turned on my heel. I was much smaller and thinner than he and a faster runner too, and I soon left him behind me, hurling insults and threatening to get me the following day at school. I had been well and truly thrashed and ran home with tears streaming down my cheeks, a bloody nose and cut lip.

I was pleased the confrontation with the bully had taken place well away from the school, without a baying audience to witness my shame. I had seen playground fights and had shuddered at the thought that I might one day be in the middle of a ring of solid spectators egging on each of the panting adversaries with roars and cheers of encouragement – 'Smack 'im!', 'Thump im!'– until the teacher hurried out to break it up.

At home I told Mum, as she wiped my face and rubbed Germolene on my lips, that I had fallen climbing up the gate of the allotments taking the short cut home. She knew, of course, that I was lying.

'Who did this?' she asked.

'I told you,' I said. 'I fell over.'

'Do I look stupid?' she asked, and repeated, 'Who did this to you?'

'A fat kid at school,' I admitted.

'Right,' she said, 'I'm up to the school tomorrow to sort this out.'

'No, Mum, please,' I pleaded. 'It will only make things worse.'

My brother Michael, who had been combing his hair in the mirror, said, 'Leave it to me, Mum, I'll sort it.'

'And how will you do that?' she asked.

'I'll have a quiet word with this fat kid. Tell him to leave him alone.'

The following day at school Charlie sauntered up to my desk. He was sporting a red bump on his forehead. He kicked my ankles under the desk. 'You're dead!' he told me, running a finger across his throat.

After school, as usual, I ran home but as I approached the allotment gate I slowed down. I knew the bully was stalking me. As I turned to take the short cut through the allotments, he ran up behind me, panting.

'Got you!' he shouted, grabbing my shoulder. Then my brother appeared. Michael was really good at sports and played cricket and football for his school. He was lithe and athletic, and in the sea cadets he had taken up boxing and proved to be a good amateur fighter. He had been waiting, out of sight. The bully stopped in his tracks, then reeled backwards at a blow to the base of his stomach. He landed with a thump on the ground. Michael, legs apart, stood over him, then dragged him to his feet and pushed him up against the iron railings. He pushed his face forward and grabbed Charlie by the throat.

'You're choking me!' gasped the bully. 'I can't breathe.'

'Touch my brother again,' said Michael, 'and I'll ram your bloody teeth down your fat bloody throat.' Then he pushed him away, kicking him up the backside and sending him staggering forward.

'I'll tell mi dad!' howled the bully, holding his throat.

'And I'll tell mine,' said Michael, 'and he's bigger than yours. Now scram!'

The next day at school I said nothing about the incident and neither did the bully. He kept well out of my way and wouldn't meet my eye when I stared at him in assembly. I suspect that like most bullies, Charlie was more frightened than frightening and as much in need of help as his victims. After that, to my great relief, he left me alone.

I feel passionate about anti–bullying and schools should acknowledge that it exists, is a real problem, and should actively do something about it. As parents we would all like our children to attend a school which is happy, optimistic and productive, because children thrive in this kind of environment. Bullying, both physical and verbal, causes children untold misery. I know it did for me. Persistent bullying affects a child's happiness, well–being and educational success and can result in permanent health and psychological damage. In my experience bullying causes enormous family stress and is responsible, in great measure, for truancy and depression. It can even lead to a child taking his or her own life.

In 1994, I was addressing a parents' meeting at a small primary school. At the end of my talk I was approached by a large man with a pale moon face and a great mound of a stomach. I recognized him immediately. He was with a tall, overweight boy of about eight or nine with lank hair and a round pudding face.

'Now then,' said the man smiling widely. 'Do you remember me?'

'Yes, I do,' I said, looking him straight in the eye. 'I remember you very well. Your name is Charlie.' I could feel my heart beginning to pound in my chest.

The man turned to the boy. 'I was telling my lad here that you were a pal of mine at school, wasn't I?'

The boy nodded and scowled.

'No, I wasn't,' I corrected him. 'I was no pal of yours. You were a bully. You bullied me and made my last few weeks in primary school a misery. You used to call me names, kick me and spit at me.' The man coloured up and shook his head but he didn't reply. The boy looked up at his father. 'I just hope,'

I continued, 'that your son doesn't have to put up with what I had to endure at your hands.'

'It must have been somebody else,' the man blustered.

'No, it was you,' I said calmly, but feeling my heart banging away in my chest. 'You see, the bully forgets, but the bullied never do.' With that I left him standing there. My wife later said that I perhaps should have resisted that temptation to say what I did. After all, it was such a long time ago and children can be very cruel. But then Christine was never bullied at school. I am afraid that I was unable to forgive and forget, since this particular bully showed no remorse, how could he? He had forgotten his cruelty.

27

On some wet Saturdays in winter, when the sky was slate grey and the air icy cold, I stayed at home in the living room, with a blazing fire in the grate, making model Spitfires from Airfix kits while listening to the light programme on the Bakelite wireless. I spent a great deal of time listening to the wireless; the entertainment programmes, plays and quizzes were my favourites. I recall the soft Dublin accent of Eamonn Andrews and the strong Yorkshire twang of Wilfred Pickles. Wilfred Pickles presented a quiz show called *Have a Go*, which was popular with all the family and at its peak attracted an audience of twenty million. He would ask his wife, 'How much money is there on the table, Mabel?' and if the contestant won he would shout, 'Give 'em the money, Barney.' Those taking part were often asked, 'Are you courting?' or 'Have you had any embarrassing moments?'

The quiz programme *Top of the Form* intrigued me. It began with the stirring 'Marching Strings', played by Ray Martin and his Orchestra, and then teams of boys and girls with frightfully posh accents, all of whom seemed remarkably well-informed, battled it out to see who was the brainiest. I could visualize them sitting behind a long table in pristine white shirts, school ties and fancy blazers with gold beading, earnest expressions on their faces. I never missed the exciting adventures of Dick Barton and his Cockney sidekick 'Snowey' White, the serial in which each episode began with the fast-moving 'Devil's Gallop' by Charles Williams.

I would listen to *The Goon Show* with Peter Sellers, Harry Secombe, Michael Bentine and the outrageous Spike Milligan. I loved the characters: Hercules Grytpype-Thynne with the fruity British upper-class accent, the ex-Indian Army officer, Major Dennis Bloodnok ('Damn those curried eggs'), and the British jobsworth ('You can't park that 'ere, mate'). I used to amuse my friends by mimicking the silly Goon voices of Eccles, Bluebottle and Minnie Bannister.

Most Sundays before lunch (which we called dinner) I would listen to *The Billy Cotton Band Show* or *Two-Way Family Favourites*, with Jean Metcalfe and Cliff Michelmore, when service wives and sweethearts would request records for their husbands and boyfriends serving in occupied Germany and Cyprus. The room would be filled with Glenn Miller, Doris Day, Guy Mitchell, Rosemary Squires, Winifred Atwell, Russ Conway, and every week selections from *Oklahoma!* and *Carousel* would be played. A favourite request was for Ann Shelton to sing, 'Lay Down Your Arms and Surrender to Mine', with its dire lyrics.

In 1959 my father arrived home carrying a black and white television, with a small grey screen set in a shiny brown veneered and ungainly wooden cabinet with a pair of double doors at the front. He placed it in the corner of the living room and it changed our lives. Instead of playing games of Monopoly, chess or draughts in the evening, my father now, most evenings, spent a deal of time transfixed, facing the small grey screen. I have to say television initially held little interest for me. At first all I recall were the dreary documentaries, boring interviews with experts, political commentaries, newsreel programmes, cookery lessons from the heavily bearded Philip Harben, gardening hints from Fred Streeter, quasi-quiz shows like *Animal, Vegetable, Mineral* and *What's My Line?*, finishing with the po-faced clergyman reading the *Epilogue*, whom I rarely saw because I was in bed by the time the television shut down at eleven o'clock. Books still held sway in my life.

Of course, I had seen televisions before. The big national event of my childhood was the Coronation on 2 June 1953, a day the *Daily Mail* called the 'Crowning Glory', and we were invited, along with other selected neighbours, into Mr and Mrs Marshall's house three doors down from us to watch the ceremony on their newly acquired television set. Two million people had television sets at the time but few of them lived on Richard Road.

This seven-year-old, clutching his Coronation mug, crown piece and little cloth Union Jack on a stick, saw very little from the back of Mr and Mrs Marshall's 'lounge' but was given a running commentary and a selection of personal asides from Mrs Evans, our other neighbour, about the dress, the coaches, the horses, the abbey, the guests and anything or anybody else that appeared on the screen. The rain poured down, so that many of the dignitaries, monarchs and heads of state were hidden behind umbrellas. One guest, Queen Salote of Tonga, endeared herself to those assembled in the Marshal's lounge by waving from an open-topped carriage, wet through but smiling as if the sun shone on her face. Occasionally Mrs Simcox from up the road, the least monarchist among the group, added her half-pennyworth – she would have no truck with kings and queens – which was followed by indignant outbursts. This was post-war Britain, of course, when we all stood for the National Anthem at the end of a film. No one would have dared remain seated or, even more unthinkable, walk out of the cinema while the band played. It was certainly not the era to make the slightest criticism of the royal family and the new young Queen.

The television in the corner of our living room soon began to be of interest to me when more programmes for younger viewers appeared. For small children there were *The Woodentops*, *Muffin the Mule*, *Andy Pandy*, *Sooty*, *Listen with Mother*, *Pinky and Perky* and *The Flowerpot Men and Little Weed*. There was not the surfeit of action films, reality shows, soap operas and cooking and antique programmes which make up so much of the television schedule today, but there were American situation comedies that amused me. I liked George, with the lugubrious expression, in *The Burns and Allen Show*, the dead-pan humour of Jack Benny and the dizzy but endearing blonde in *I Love Lucy*, but the programmes I really loved were the exciting cowboy and historical adventures: *Rawhide*, with the youthful Clint Eastwood playing Rowdy Yates, Casey Jones the eponymous engine driver who always managed to avoid disasters on the line, *Gunsmoke* and *Ponderosa*. *William Tell* was a favourite, and always started when the hero shot the apple from his son's head. It was accompanied by the lively music of the *William Tell* overture and the rushing sound as the bolt from the crossbow flew through the air and split the apple in half. I would sing along with the inane lyrics:

> Come along, come along with William Tell,
> Come along to the land he loves so well.

I guess in this day and age there would have been a warning for children not to try the feat with the crossbow at home. I loved to hate the outrageous and vastly overweight Lamburgher Gessler, a master of overacting, who did a wonderful facial expression which I used to imitate. Other programmes I never missed were *Zorro*, with the masked crusader, with his flashing sword and flashing teeth, and *Robin Hood*, in which a youthful Richard Greene, as the dashing hero, in extremely clean tights and with a jaunty feather in his cap, always managed to foil the goatee-bearded and permanently glowering Sheriff of Nottingham. On the way to school we would all sing the music that accompanied the opening credits:

> Robin Hood, Robin Hood, riding through the glen,
> Robin Hood, Robin Hood, with his band of men.
> Feared by the bad, loved by the good,
> Robin Hood, Robin Hood, Robin Hood.

Davy Crockett, King of the Wild Frontier, became something of a cult figure. When I was ten or eleven there was the craze for Davy Crockett hats. The television series started the wide-spread enthusiasm for this ridiculous headgear, and every boy on our street was soon sporting a large fur muff with a tail dangling down the back. The hats were made of different-coloured rabbit fur. Mine was a pale ginger. It looked as if I had a tomcat on my head. To go with my Davy Crockett hat my brother Michael made me a leather waistcoat, dyed black and with pale leather stitching. He bought thirty or so silver threepenny bits from Mrs Harrap, who ran the post office, drilled each one and sewed them around the edges. I was the envy of the street. Mr Fowler at the top of Richard Road made me a whip and, much to our neighbour Mrs Evans's irritation, I would practise cracking it and trying to whip tin cans off the wall which separated our two gardens.

I didn't take to some of the programmes. The precocious, clean-cut, cheeky-faced boy actor with the tinny American drawl in *Circus Boy* rarely got a word in before he was turned off. Another hero of the small screen who was given short shrift was the Lone Ranger. In his tight pants and his silly little mask which didn't fool anyone, he was too clever by half. He was always shouting, 'Hi-ho, Silver,' which was really irritating, and he never seemed to get dirty. He would be accompanied by Tonto, his buckskin-clad Indian sidekick, who spoke in strange broken English and was constantly saying 'Kimo-sabe'.

All the adventure programmes were deeply moral. Cruelty, greed, selfishness, unfairness and unlawful behaviour were never rewarded and good always triumphed. This was good clean fun, for the fights never ended in the horrific death of the villain. Nobody was maimed or lay writhing in agony on the floor. There was no loss of blood from a gunshot wound or a sword, for our heroes, who had high moral principles and were far too compassionate and well-meaning, merely disarmed their opponents. There might have been a bit of rough and tumble, a few thrown punches, but nothing too excessive or frightening.

Then came *The Six-Five Special*, *Crackerjack* with the small bespectacled Peter Glaze and Leslie Crowther with the irritating smile, *Juke Box Jury* with David Jacobs, and *Armchair Theatre*, which I was occasionally allowed to watch. It was all inoffensive material – no innuendo, rude jokes, bad language or gratuitous violence and certainly no sex. Mum kept a very keen eye on the programmes and banned me from watching anything she deemed unsuitable. She refused to allow me under any circumstances to watch *Quatermass*, the science fiction series, on the grounds that it was far too frightening for an impressionable boy. It is a wonder that she allowed me to read *Treasure Island*.

My mother had a habit which, when I recall, still brings a smile to my lips.

We would all be watching a programme, the children on the carpet beneath the television cabinet, my father in his armchair, and a love scene (very mild by today's standards) would appear on the screen. It might involve a semi-clad couple in an embrace, but little else.

'Turn it off, Jimmy!' my mother would snap, as if he were responsible for it. Dutifully my father would rise from his chair and turn the knob.

Most people my age will remember what they were doing when President Kennedy was assassinated and I am among them. There was a deep sense of shock in the house when the news came on the television, and I remember my mother weeping and my father sitting in a chair silent and serious-faced. Another television programme I have a vivid memory of was a documentary on the Holocaust. It was screened late at night and there was a warning that viewers might find some of the material distressing. I was sixteen or seventeen at the time, and Mum and Dad told me I should put away my books and come downstairs because there was something I should see, that all people should know about. We sat in silence staring at the small black and white screen and not a word was said. When the television was turned off, my mother was clearly deeply upset and said that what had happened in those death camps should never ever be forgotten, for it showed mankind at its most evil. I still see those recurring images of chalk-white, emaciated bodies, stick legs and arms, blank faces, deep-set eyes, shaven heads, semi-naked skeletons wandering aimlessly through the high wire gates. I still shudder at the memory of tangled masses of bodies shovelled into deep open graves and the traumatized faces of the liberating soldiers.

Today television has become integral in the lives of most children, and in this age many have a television set with DVD player in their bedrooms. They can watch from six in the morning to late at night, hopping from one channel to the next and often watching the most unsuitable material. But in the 50s and 60s television was not so important in children's lives, for there wasn't the variety on the screen and there were other things to occupy our time.

There was poetry in those early television programmes, squeezed in between the quizzes and the plays, the news and the variety shows. It was not traditional verse read by earnest poets; it was in the form of advertisements, which employed all the figurative language of poetry – repetition, rhyme, rhythm, alliteration, simile, metaphor, onomatopoeia. At the time these adverts were considered revolutionary, but far from destroying the fabric of the nation, as some would have us believe, they added to its richness, colour and gaiety and were memorable in their catchy tunes and clever lyrics. I remember the jingles to this day:

You'll wonder where the yellow went
When you brush your teeth with Pepsident (toothpaste)

Murraymints, Murraymints,
Too good to hurry mints (sweets)

You'll grow a little lovelier each day
With fabulous pink Camay (soap)

Opal Fruits – Made to make your mouth water (sweets)

We are the Ovaltinies, happy girls and boys (milky drink)

The Milky Bar Kid is big and strong
The Milky Bar Kid just can't go wrong (chocolate bar)

P . . . p . . . p . . . pick up a Penguin (biscuit)

A million housewives every day,
Pick up a tin of beans and say:
'Beans means Heinz' (baked beans)

I still have a great weakness for Marmite spread on a slice of fresh white bread and recall the clever little ditty that advertised this enduring product:

If Ma might give me Marmite for my breakfast,
If Ma might give me Marmite for my tea,
If Ma might give me Marmite for my supper,
How happy I and Pa and Ma might be.

I was so fascinated by the television jingles that I took to inventing some of my own and entering competitions. At eleven I tried my hand at the Brooke Bond PG Tips Competition, where entrants had to complete the sentence, 'I drink Brooke Bond PG Tips because . . .' in twenty words or less. The other entries can't have been very good, for I won the runner-up prize (a cheque and some packets of tea) with my effort:

> It perks you up,
> When you pick up a cup,
> And it's the only tea for me.

This small masterpiece was my first published effort. I was now a paid writer.

28

Like most boys I liked football and swimming (but wasn't much good at either), and I liked excursions on my bike. Some weekends in summer when I was ten or eleven, me and my friends (I was a member of the gang) would take ourselves up to the building site or to Archer's Farm on Moorgate. We would walk up through the allotments at the back of my house, along a path of beaten mud overgrown with nettles and across the fields, lifting the dried cowpats with sticks and disturbing a buzzing cloud of yellow horseflies. Then we would climb the five-barred gate and run across to a small copse where we had built a den out of dead branches, cardboard, bits of rusty corrugated tin and asbestos roofing. There were five of us and we would spend all day there, with our den as the base. We would climb trees and swing from the branches on a rope, daring each other to run through the stinging nettles. We would have mock fights, cowboys against the Indians, British against the Germans, Flash Gordon against the aliens, and run wild across the grass, dodging the wet cowpats and skimming the dried ones at each other.

To become a member of the gang everyone had to go through an initiation ceremony. It was Tommy, the self-proclaimed leader, who thought it up, and as new members joined they were sworn to keep secret what went on at the ceremony. I was the last to be initiated and had endured sleepless nights thinking of what terrors were in store for me. The members of the gang had already told me that it was a horrible ceremony but that if I failed to pass the three tests I couldn't become a member.

When the dreaded Saturday for the initiation arrived I

couldn't eat my breakfast and felt my stomach doing kangaroo jumps. On the way to Archer's Farm, where I was to meet the gang members at nine o'clock, I began to imagine all sorts of dire rituals.

Mr Archer was busy milking the cows when I arrived and the four gang members were waiting for me outside the barn. I was taken inside without a word and blindfolded.

'First you have to stroke a dead rat,' I was told by Tommy. My hand was guided to a cardboard box, the sort shoes come in, and the lid taken off. My hand was thrust inside. I touched something wet and furry. I could imagine the black shiny coat, the pointed face, the cold dead eyes, the needle-like teeth, the claws and the long grey tail. I had seen enough rats on the farm to know what they looked like. I took a deep breath and ran my fingers across the fur.

'He has passed the first test,' said Tommy.

Then I was taken across the barn to some ladders and told to climb up. I knew this part of the barn. There was a sort of balcony, not too far off the ground. Below were bales of hay. We had often leapt off and I knew the hay would break my fall. Blindfolded it was a different matter. Suppose they had put something in the hay beneath me? I was positioned on the edge and told to jump.

'There aren't any pitchforks or rakes down there in the hay, are there?' I asked.

'That's for us to know and for you to find out,' Tommy told me.

'There had better not be,' I said.

Before I could say anything else I was pushed forward and I landed safely in the hay.

'He has passed the second test,' said Tommy.

By now I was thinking that I had done rather well, and was pretty confident that I would sail through the third and final test.

'All you have to do is eat three maggots,' said Tommy.

'I'm not eating any maggots!' I cried.

'You 'ave to,' said Tommy.

'Well, I'm not!'

'Come on,' said Simon, 'we've all had to do it.'

'Well, I'm not!'

'Then you can't be in our gang,' announced Tommy firmly.

'Come on,' said Jimmy in a friendly voice, 'we've all 'ad to do it. Gerrem down ya.'

I gritted my teeth and forced my lips together but fingers were pushing in a maggot. It was soft and squelchy. My mouth filled with saliva and I poked the maggot to the side of my mouth. Then another was posted through my lips and another.

I felt I was going to be sick. The thought of those pale, wriggly maggots in my mouth made my gorge rise.

'Swallow 'em,' urged Tommy.

In one great gulp, they were gone.

'He has passed the third test,' announced Tommy.

The blindfold was taken off and hands were patting my back and telling me, 'Well done.' I felt a warm glow come over me.

Tommy held up a small furry toy rabbit. 'There's your dead rat,' he said, chuckling.

Simon held up a Heinz Baked Beans tin.

I cannot describe the relief at seeing what I had been eating. They were not maggots at all but three baked beans. Of course when you were blindfolded and your imagination was working overtime it was easy to convince yourself that they were real maggots you had swallowed.

I sat in the hay and laughed and laughed and that started everyone else off laughing too.

'So I was eating beans,' I said, lying back and staring up at the roof of the barn. 'Baked beans.'

'Eh?' said Simon.

'The beans in the tin,' I said. 'I thought they were real maggots.'

'You're daft, you,' said Tommy.

'Well, I was blindfolded,' I said. 'I couldn't see what I was eating.'

'No, I mean, you're daft,' he repeated. 'We just collected the maggots in the bean tin.'

It's a wonder that those of us growing up in the fifties managed to survive. We jumped off walls, climbed trees, wrestled on the damp grass, threw stones at cans, lit fires, fenced like knights of old, with switches cut from the great weeping willow tree by the pond, fished for tiddlers in muddy streams, swung across rivers on a rope fastened to a branch, drank water from a garden hose, shot each other with potato guns and catapults, played marbles in the dirt, chewed sticky toffee, and then returned home for deep-fried fish and chips, with bread and butter, stodgy puddings and mugs of tea with three spoonfuls of sugar in. We had never heard the phrases 'health and safety' and 'high in saturated fats and carbohydrates'.

The building site on Moorgate where the large detached houses on the Duke of Norfolk Estate were being built was the finest playground a child could ever wish for. Saturday and Sunday afternoons were the best times, when there were no workmen about to chase you away – only a bad-tempered watchman who spent a deal of his time sleeping in his little hut. His guard dog, a fat, lazy and stupid old labrador called Laddie, which, like its master, enjoyed lengthy naps, occasionally roused itself to give a single bark before slumping back into its somnolent posture. On the site, well away from the watchman's hut, there were cement mixers to climb into, mountains of sand to run up and down, bags of cement to jump on and create explosions of grey dust, nuts and bolts to lob, buckets full of slimy water to throw, ladders to scale, planks to balance on, ropes to swing on and scaffolding to climb up. It was much more fun than playing in Clifton Park. If I were to visit such a building site today I would have to wear a hard hat and a yellow jacket and sign some sort of indemnity. As children we would spend hours in this 'playground' and return home weary and grubby, with nothing but a scraped knee or a bruised shin to show for it.

At Archer's Farm we would help feed the hens, muck out the pigs, collect the eggs, ride on the back of the tractor, watch the cows being milked, cut down the swathes of stinging nettles, pretending they were ranks of enemy soldiers and, above all, stay away from Gertie, the old grey goose which would honk and chase you, neck forward, beak open, wings flapping. There was an old crossbred sheepdog which would follow us around, and a yapping three-legged Jack Russell terrier, appropriately named Jackie. A clouder of feral cats inhabited the barn and would catch the fat black rats and little fieldmice, and hiss and snarl and arch their backs if we came anywhere near. Both dogs and cats, very wisely, avoided Gertie. I much preferred to be inside the barn, that huge, shadowy, hay-smelling, mysterious place piled high with straw bales and full of strange rustlings. We would lug the bales around and make tunnels and caves; we would leap from the upper floor on to a mountain of soft hay or watch the cats stalking the rats.

Mr Archer, the farmer, was a small grizzled man of few words, with a sad countenance. He had a broken nose, a weather-reddened face and eyes as grey as the ocean on a winter's day. Invariably he wore old green overalls, heavy boots and a flat cap, oily and frayed, the inner rim blackened by dirt and sweat. His pronounced limp, it was rumoured, was the result of his tussle with Moses, the 750-kilo bull that roamed the top field. The great Friesian creature had, so the story goes, knocked him down, tossed him in the air, pummelled him with its head, caught his side with its horn and broken the farmer's leg and two of his ribs. He was very wary, as we all were, of this proud and fierce animal. Sometimes we would tease Moses, running across the side of the field, a good distance away, willing him to chase us, and when he did we would scream in fright as he pounded down the field. We would leap over the five-bar gate and watch fascinated as he charged right up to us before swerving away, snorting and bellowing and shivering with fury.

Of all the animals, I liked the pigs the best. 'A dog looks up to you, a cat looks down on you,' Mr Archer once told me when I was helping him to muck out the sties, 'but a pig, he looks you straight in the eye.' I learnt quite a deal about these intelligent creatures on those Saturday visits to Archer's Farm, for instance that they are essentially clean animals which defecate where they get water and leave the rest of the pen dry for sleeping.

Mr Archer never appeared particularly pleased to see this motley gang of boys appearing in the farmyard, but he never thought of us as nuisances and never told us to 'Clear Off!' or 'Play up your own end!' as so many adults did.

'Tha can collect eggs, if tha wants,' he would say morosely, or 'Them tools could do wi' a bit of a clean, if tha's a mind,' or 'T'cats need summat to eat,' or 'It's gerrin dark, gerroff hooame.' None of us liked one job the farmer asked us to do – to hold up the cow's tail when he was milking. Those of us who were commissioned to take on this potentially hazardous task were in fear that the restless bovine might decide to perform at the very moment when we were holding its tail aloft. It never happened, of course, but the fear was always there.

Sometimes I would go up to Archer's Farm by myself. I enjoyed the company of others but took pleasure in my own company too and enjoyed solitary walks in the park, the quiet of the public library in town and the peace and solitude on a crisp sunny day away from the smoke and grime of Rotherham. I would lie face down on the soft grass with a book, feeling the heat of the sun on the back of my neck, the smell of earth and grass in my nostrils and only the sounds of birds and insects around me. I would look up to see the swallows swooping and darting around their nests below the eaves of the old barn and watch the lazy-looking cows in the field beyond. The three-legged Jack Russell would sometimes find me out and snuggle up to me, but apart from my canine companion I was left in peace and could lose myself in my book. There in the sunshine I would read *The Red Badge of Courage*, *The Count of Monte Cristo*, *The Man in the Iron Mask*, *The Last of the Mohicans* and everything seemed right with the world. As darkness gathered I would watch the rooks, some settling to roost in the syca-mores, others flapping above the trees, circling and floating on the evening air like scraps of black cloth, or I would watch the rabbits bolting across the fields when they caught sight of me, their white tails bobbing. Then I would head off home, saying goodbye to Mr Archer on the way. 'Tha's off then?' he would say. He was a man of few words.

Only twice did I see Mr Archer show any real emotion. Once, when he came upon the chicken coop and found a fox had got in, he plucked his cap from his head and threw it to the ground angrily. Then he sat on an upturned orange box and surveyed the carnage, shaking his head. The fox had bitten off the heads of all the chickens and tossed the carcasses aside. Some townsfolk think foxes are rather attractive, elegant crea-tures, with their russet coats and bushy tails, but I learnt early on that they are vicious and dedicated predators and kill for the sake of it. Another time he lost his temper was when the cockerel went for him. The cockerel, called Jock, had a habit of appearing from nowhere and running up squawking madly with its wings flapping and its beak thrust forward. One day it picked the wrong moment to go for Mr Archer. When it rushed up to him in a flurry of wings, crowing frantically, the farmer lifted up his heavily booted foot and gave it an almighty kick which sent the bird flying through the air.

'That's the last bloody time it'll gu fer me,' he announced, and picking up the dead bird he added, 'And t'bugger will be in t'pot toneet.'

There was an old air raid shelter in one of the fields, and some of my happiest times were spent hiding in the smelly half-light among the discarded beer cans and soggy cigarette packets, pretending that the Gestapo (two of my pals) were looking for me. Just before dusk we would light a fire and roast potatoes that we never ate.

One day two friends and I found a large chest full of tools underneath a piece of old carpet in the air raid shelter. Mr Archer left his milking to examine our find and declared that the chest was probably stolen and had been hidden here by the thieves, who would return later to retrieve it. He would contact the police. The following week the *Rotherham Advertiser* printed a short paragraph relating how a group of children had discovered a cache of stolen tools. Our names were printed, and a commendation for our good sense. I was described as twelve-year-old Gervaisse Finn. Not only had the reporter spelt my name incorrectly, he had also added a couple of years on my age. This was an early realization that those who write for newspapers frequently get their facts wrong and that one should be sceptical about what is written by reporters.

I liked fishing for newts and sticklebacks, minnows and the ugly bull-headed fish at Whiston Meadows with my brother Alec, and flying my bright yellow box kite at Boston Park. I liked visiting Clifton Park Museum to see the great stuffed lion in the glass case dominating the entrance and the case-upon-case of birds' eggs all arranged in neat rows. We rarely went into the long room with the priceless collection of Rockingham pottery. At the very top of the winding staircase a stuffed golden eagle had pride of place, a bloody rabbit clutched in its bright yellow claws. The curator, as I recall, wasn't as tolerant of boys as Mr Archer. He would watch us keenly with eyes like the stuffed golden eagle, shushing us if we spoke too loudly. He was clearly very relieved when we left and he could settle down again to the cool peace and tranquillity in his small office in the marble-floored building.

Some Saturdays I would meet my friends at the New Baths on Sheffield Road. These were bigger, better and cleaner than the old baths where I went with my father. The floors and walls were tiled, there were showers and clean cubicles and the toilets didn't smell. As you paid your money to get in you were given a sort of large blunt nappy pin with a small key attached which you fastened to your swimming trunks. The greatest attraction of the New Baths was the diving blocks and boards. There was a long diving board with an adjustable roller and a diving block, and we spent most of the session jumping, plunging and bombing in an explosion of water. Sometimes a show-off would demonstrate a perfect dive from the very top block, surfacing to swim serenely to the side. I once tried to dive from the second block but landed flat on the water – the dreaded belly flop. I submerged in a rush of bubbles and spluttering, choking, drowning, I madly thrashed to the side thinking my stomach had been split open. I was sent out to get dressed by the attendant for acting the fool. Once I was dared to climb the steps to the highest block – a square flat platform with metal railings – and to jump off. Halfway up I got cold feet but there was no turning back, for a queue had formed behind me. With stomach churning, I edged to the end of the platform. The rectangle of pale blue water seemed miles down. I was terrified. Of course there were stories of boys who had plummeted from the top block and broken their necks, others who had cracked their heads on the bottom and drowned, which made the ordeal more terrifying. I stood there for five minutes considering what to do.

'Are tha goin' to jump, or what?' asked a boy half my size, who stood with his arms folded over his skinny chest. Behind him was a group of impatient boys. I had an audience. I stepped off the platform and, with eyes firmly closed, hit the water with an almighty crash and surfaced to the cheers of my friends. The following week I was with the best of them, running across the top platform and launching myself into the water with abandon.

My mother and father never seemed concerned about my safety unless I arrived home after the appointed hour, and then I would be in real trouble. They were not timid, anxious, risk-averse parents and no one harked on incessantly about health and safety and the perils of the wider world. Those days were so different. Parents didn't worry about where you were, who you were with, what you were doing, and never imagined that predatory paedophiles were lurking around every corner and behind every bush. It wasn't as if they didn't care about us. They belonged to the wartime generation and had lived through dangerous times, seen houses crumble before them, gas pipes split open, burst water mains, mounds of rubble, and perhaps understood the child's need for adventure and challenge. Amazingly, in all those early years, apart from a few scrapes and scratches, I never hurt myself and was never approached by the stereotypical 'dirty old man in a raincoat'.

29

When my children were growing up they must have been heartily tired of me telling them about my happy childhood, without all the films with special effects and fancy Disneyworld holidays, exciting computer games and sophisticated toys, expensive trainers and designer T-shirts. As a teenager, when asked to write a GCSE history assignment about the society in which his parents grew up, Richard, my eldest son, challenged me robustly about those halcyon days of my youth, that idyllically happy and peaceful time when smiling bobbies walked the beat, everyone was friendly and courteous, neighbours popped in for a cup of tea and a chat, children were well-behaved and could spell and punctuate properly, where there were no football hooligans, graffiti artists, litter louts, terrorists and paedophiles and we were happy with the simple things of life (and still get change from a ha'penny).

Some say that the mind has a great facility for retaining and exaggerating happy memories of childhood and erasing the more distressing and disturbing ones, that we choose not to remember those occasions when we were unhappy or depressed, we lock these out and tend to look back on a Golden Age which never really existed. Some might say that nostalgia is a form of homesickness, that our memories have been warped into a yearning for a previous life when everything was less complicated and stress-free. George Orwell wrote that 'only by resurrecting our own memories can we realize how incredibly distorted is the child's vision of the world'.

Maybe my remembrance of childhood is somewhat distorted. As my son reminded me, surely everything wasn't as perfect when I was a child as I imagined it to be. Children then, as now, he argued, took no great interest in the national and international events, they didn't listen to the news on the radio or read the depressing accounts in the daily papers; they were far too interested in playing out with their friends, going to the cinema, watching television and all the other things that youngsters like to do. While I might go some way to agreeing with him, I still feel that for me, it certainly seemed a far more peaceful, simpler and carefree world that I inhabited as a child than the one in which I live now. Of course I remember significant events: the 1958 air crash which killed seven Manchester United Players – the 'Busby Babes'– and three staff members, the assassination of President Kennedy, his brother Bobby and Martin Luther King, something about the Suez Canal debacle and a man called Nasser and the Bay of Pigs crisis and Mr Khrushchev, but not a whole lot else. There were the terrible Moors Murders, of course, but they stood out in their stark and unbelievable horror and brutality. Life in the 1950s and 60s no doubt had its darker side, but it was not a world where a nail bomb is placed in the Admiral Duncan public house to kill people whose only crime was to be gay, where a deranged man shoots dead sixteen children and a teacher in Dunblane, where an aeroplane full of innocent people is blown from the skies above Lockerbie, where a gun-toting madman wreaks havoc in Hungerford, where racist thugs set upon and kill a black boy standing at a bus stop, where a headmaster is stabbed to death outside his school, where twenty-nine people are blown to pieces as they are going about their shopping in Omagh, where a family doctor called Harold Shipman systematically murders his patients, where two ten-year-olds drag the toddler Jamie Bulger to a railway line to kill him, where two little girls are murdered by the school care-taker, where Sarah Payne's short life is ended by an evil predator and where suicide bombers on a London tube train claim fifty-two innocent lives and maim countless others. I can't recall such a catalogue of horror when I was young.

Things for an ordinary little boy growing up in Rotherham seemed so sunny and uncomplicated, and I, like all my friends, did indeed find pleasure in simple things. Games seemed to change as the seasons changed. In summer the boys in the street were out early on Saturday morning on the bit of dusty, uncultivated ground at the top of Ramsden Road playing 'taws', and with a bag of marbles we would play until it got to dinnertime. Girls liked skipping and pushing their toy prams or dressing up. There were games that both boys and girls played, and we were all keen on the fads like pogo-sticks, hula hoops, yo-yos, whips and spinning tops, but peashooters and potato guns were the preserve of the boys and no girls were allowed to play the rough games like British Bulldog.

Traditional pastimes survived long after we had put away the pogo-sticks and spinning tops. During the week after tea and with homework finished, I would be out on the street to meet my friends, Jimmy Everett, Terry Gaunt and Michael Wales. Richard Road was a steep hill and in summer we would race down on roller skates or on bicycles or, even better, on 'bogies', those crude trolleys we built from old pram wheels and slats of wood with a rope to steer. Mr Fowler, who lived at the top of the hill, made me and my friends catapults and we played for hours firing at tins and bottles until the offensive weapons were confiscated by Mr Wales (no relation to Michael), a teacher who lived a few doors away from me. When we broke a window in his greenhouse we owned up (we really had no choice, because he was in the garden at the time), apologized and asked him not to tell our parents. He took the catapults from us with the injunction, 'You could take somebody's eye out with one of these,' but never did tell our parents or ask us to pay for the damage. A week later he presented us with a large bag of marbles. We would then retire to the top of Ramsden Road to battle it out.

In autumn it was conker time. We would collect bags of conkers from Clifton Park, soak them in vinegar, bake them in the oven, leave them in the airing cupboard for a year, carefully skewer them and then spend hours competing in the street and in the playground. Children throughout the country tried to perfect the killer conker, and these hard shiny brown nuts were pickled, boiled, baked, varnished and pampered. The big round ones were not the best. They were soft and yielding and easy targets. We all looked for small, flat, sharp-edged specimens. I learnt about *schadenfreude* early on. It was such a pleasure to see a champion conker that had survived twenty or more battles smashed to smithereens by a newcomer, to be greeted by wild cheers from the onlookers.

In winter we would pray for snow so that we could position ourselves at the brow of the hill and sledge down at high speed. There were no trainers, denim jeans or bomber jackets in those days. We were kitted out in Wellington boots, hand-knitted jumpers, old school flannels, duffel coats and knitted woollen balaclava helmets (close-fitting hats covering the whole of the head and encircling the neck). The posh children had balaclavas made out of leather with a fur lining. My brother's was made of simulated leather, an unyielding pale brown plastic with a felt lining, and when I sneaked it out of his cupboard one winter it made me feel like Biggles as I sped down Richard Road on my sledge, shrieking at the top of my voice. We became skilled at steering the sledge on to the pavement just as we reached the bottom, because ahead was the busy Broom Valley Road and the Cowrakes Lane buses.

Of course if there was snow there would be snowmen and snowball fights. One snowman carefully sculpted in the front garden by a father for his little boy was something of a masterpiece. It stood six foot high, with chips of coal for the eyes, a carrot for the nose and a crescent of apple for the mouth. One evening one of the boys on the street rearranged the creation and the next morning, on our way to school, we passed a leering, one-armed figure. The carrot had been repositioned lower down to form a very prominent orange penis, above which was a tuft of grass for the pubic hair. The child's father, incensed by such vandalism, called on all the houses in the street to try to discover the culprit.

I abandoned cricket early on in my childhood. It was Uncle Alec, on one of his rare visits, who attempted to teach me the rudiments of the game when I was eight or nine years old, but his tuition didn't last above three coaching sessions. I have to own that I couldn't really take to the game. I failed to understand why anyone could enjoy hitting a really hard ball flying at great speed towards them with a stiff piece of wood so that someone else could run up and down. Uncle Alec, who loved cricket and played for the Royal Air Force, had had great success with my brother Michael (brother Alec just wasn't bothered), who went on to become a very skilful player, but after lesson number three with me, Uncle Alec gave it up as a bad job. I was an unwilling pupil and useless to boot and, unlike my eldest brother, had no ambition to play for Yorkshire. After the last and memorable session Uncle Alec returned to our house with his very apologetic nephew in tow and the appearance of one who had just clambered out of the boxing ring. My batting technique, despite my uncle's coaching, was to wield the bat like a deadly weapon as the ball approached, thrashing the air madly and leaping up and down. My bowling technique would have put the fear of God into a regiment of Gurkhas. In this, the last of my coaching sessions, I managed to crack the ball with such accuracy and speed that it hit my poor uncle smack in the face, dislodging a couple of teeth. In my poem, written some years later, I recorded the incident but do have to admit to a little poetic licence:

Unlucky Uncle Alec
When one day playing cricket,
Saw a four-leaf clover
And thought that he would pick it.
As he bent down
Towards the ground
To pluck the lucky leaf,
The cricket ball
Flew through the air
And knocked out all his teeth.
He shouted, 'Drat!'
And dropped the bat
Which landed on his toes.
It bounced back up
And cracked his chin
Then smacked him on the nose.
Smeared in blood
And caked in mud,
He said, 'I'm glad that's over.'
Then with a sigh
He held up high
His lucky four-leaf-clover.

I was not allowed to play out on Sunday morning because
there was church. In the evening, homework completed, the
time would be spent before bedtime completing a huge jigsaw
of Westminster Bridge or the *Cutty Sark*, or playing snakes and
ladders, draughts or chess with my brothers, or carefully painting in the little shapes in the 'Painting by Numbers' set. Then
there was the John Bull printing set with the little rubber letters
and ink pad. And sometimes I would spend many a happy
hour patiently gluing together the plastic components of model
aircraft – Spitfires and Hurricanes, Messerschmitts and Fokkers
– then laboriously painting them using little tins of enamel

paint and finally sticking on the transfers. However hard I read the instructions there was always a part left over at the end. I reckoned that the makers of the models did it on purpose.

Like most children I loved collecting things: postcards, toy soldiers, Dinky cars, coins, stamps, cigarette cards. All my friends would save the cards out of Brooke Bond PG Tips and cigarette packets, and we would swap them at school and stick them in a book you could send away for from the manufacturer. There were *Birds of the British Isles*, *Animals of the British Isles*, *Flags of all Nations*, *Great Sporting Heroes*, *Kings and Queens of Europe*, *Great British Regiments*. We would spend breaktimes at school bartering, and we were always envious of the boy who managed to complete the set first. Then there were the free gifts in the cereal packets. At the bottom of the box would be plastic figures to collect, badges and little coloured plastic submarines which when filled with baking powder sank to the bottom of the glass and then surfaced. In the comics (*Eagle*, *Beano* and *Dandy*) there would be free gifts – a cardboard Snapper which made the sound of a bang, a special agent's badge, 3-D glasses, cut-out models and posters. By collecting the labels on Robertson's jam and marmalade jars you could send off for a little enamel golliwog badge and it was every boy's ambition to get the full set.

In 1953 all the children in the country were given a Coronation mug and a crown, a shiny five-shilling piece in a small plastic box. I wasn't bothered about the mug but I treasured the large silver coin showing the young Queen on horseback. This started my interest in coin collecting and over the years I built up quite a collection. Mrs Harrap at the post office put aside anything that might be of interest to me, such as foreign currency or coins which were out of circulation which she had inadvertently accepted, and friends of my parents and neighbours were also dragooned into looking for unusual coins for me.

Some Saturdays I would take the bus to Sheffield and walk

up Glossop Road to Ford's Antiques. There was a small rack of trays in a side window displaying a selection of coins, each with a small circular tag on which was written in careful, spidery writing the monarch's name, the denomination and the price. The elderly owner, who smelt of mothballs and wore a stiff white collar, was always pleased to see me and would take out the tray of coins and tell me about the various kings and queens depicted. Charles I was shown with long curls and in elaborate clothes, Oliver Cromwell plain and dour, the aged George III with a great bull neck. Victoria, who reigned for sixty or so years, was represented in different issues as a young, middle-aged and old woman. 'You learn a great deal about the character of a particular king or queen from the coinage,' I was told. Further up Glossop Road was Jameson's Antiques, and I always called in on the offchance that the owner might have some coins. There were never any customers in the shop when I called, just Mr Jameson behind a large desk, poring over a book. He always smiled when I entered the shop and shook his head when I asked if he had any coins. One memorable Saturday he smiled and as I turned to go told me I was in luck. He produced a small canvas bag of coins.

'Five bob?' he asked.

I held the bag, heavy with coins, but didn't look inside until I was home. I rushed upstairs and emptied the contents on the bed. It was a treasure trove.

There were several Roman coins, a well worn George III shilling, some small silver sixpences, assorted pennies and four huge dull metal coins with the profile of George III on the obverse (I learnt later that these were called 'Cartwheel' two-penny pieces weighing exactly two ounces and were the largest British coins ever minted). There were also four or five tokens, a small silver medal, several American cents and dimes, a silver dollar and a thin brass coin with a shield like a spade on the reverse. The following week I visited Rotherham public library and scoured the coin catalogues. My heart was in my mouth when I discovered what I imagined one of the coins might be. On my way home I called in at Mason's jewellers. It took me a time to summon up the courage to enter the shop. I stood beneath the large clock at the entrance rehearsing what I would say. The interior was elegant and cool, with cabinet after cabinet full of rings and watches, bracelets and necklaces.

'May I help you, young man?' asked a young woman.

'I have a coin,' I said nervously. She arched an eyebrow and waited. 'I . . . I think it might be gold.'

She smiled and disappeared into the back. A tall man in a dark jacket emerged, took the coin from my hand and examined it with a small magnifying glass.

'It's what is known as a spade ace guinea,' he said. 'George III mintage, in fine condition, dated 1797. They were very common in their day and often forged in the form of gaming tokens. The brass copies often had "In memory of the good old days" on the reverse. But this is genuine.'

'It's gold?' I asked.

'It is,' he replied. 'Are you considering selling it?'

'No, thank you,' I said, taking it from him. On the way home, I walked on clouds.

Later that week I saw an advertisement in *Exchange & Mart*. My brother Michael, who was always building things, took this magazine and I was idly skimming through the pages when I came upon a small boxed item: 'Old U. S. Currency Urgently Required. Good prices paid.' I wrote to Major Monte B. Lambkin, who was based at an American air force base in North Yorkshire, sold the cents, dimes and the silver dollar for three pounds, eleven shillings and sixpence, and made a new pen-friend. Years later the golden guinea was made into a pendant for my wife Christine. It has been her favourite piece of jewellery, and whenever she wears it I recall the time I discovered it.

30

My parents were great day-trippers and most weekends found us – Mum and Dad, my two brothers and sister and myself – in a green Morris Oxford heading for the coast. It was always the seaside. Mum would pack the box of sandwiches and fruitcake and fill the flasks, Dad would check the car – tyres, oil, water – and we children would be waiting excitedly, crammed into the back seat of the car, keen to be on our way. We left the smoke and grime of Rotherham behind us and headed for Thorne, Driffield and Market Weighton. It was usually my brother Alec who would ask first, 'Are we nearly there yet?'

One Saturday morning we were late starting. Mum just could not find her false teeth. Each night before bed, she would leave them soaking in a glass of water on the small shelf in the bathroom. The next morning the glass was empty of water and teeth. We searched everywhere. Then Michael remembered that in the night the amorous meowing of our neighbour's tomcat had woken him up. He had leaned out of the bathroom window and thrown a glass of water at the noisy feline. The glass had contained our mother's false teeth. So a search was started and the garden combed for the missing dentures. It was Christine who spotted the teeth in the guttering.

'Bit early for cleaning windows,' observed Mr Evans, our next-door neighbour, when he spotted Dad up the ladder.

'No,' replied my father casually, 'just retrieving my wife's false teeth.'

As we sped along on our trip to the seaside Dad would be full of fanciful tales. On the way we always passed under a low bridge, and Dad would tell us about the driver of a double-decker bus who, misjudging the height, sheered off the top of the vehicle. 'And every single passenger on the bus was decapitated,' he told us. On the way home in the shadowy darkness we would pass over a small hump-backed bridge. As we approached he would tell us of the great green hairy monster which lived beneath, with its dripping fangs and red-rimmed eyes. He would slow down and nearly stop at the brow of the hill and announce in a mock-frightened voice, 'We've broken down.' We would all howl.

Once at the seaside we made straight for the quay for a trip around the bay on the *Bridlington Belle*. Another of Dad's stories was of how the leaking vessel had sailed to Dunkirk to rescue the stranded British troops. I have an idea that this particular story was true.

If it was Filey it would be a stroll along the Brigg, followed by fish and chips, smothered in salt and vinegar, eaten out of newspaper as we sat on the harbour wall. Sometimes we would go further afield: to Staithes, where time seemed to have stopped; Sandsend, where we would search for fossils and walk along the great stretch of golden sand; Robin Hood's Bay, where we would explore the narrow entries; Runswick Bay, where the cluster of cottages seemed to cling precariously to the cliffside; and of course, Whitby with its quaint streets, picturesque quay and imposing abbey. One memorable Sunday my parents insisted we visit St Mary's Church, situated high on the clifftop. We were told there was a magnificent view over the harbour from the church and we could see the famous box pews and the three-decker pulpit. We were deeply unim-pressed until Dad mentioned Count Dracula. It was just off the coast, he told us, that the ship bringing his remains to England had been wrecked, and in the graveyard he still roamed at midnight. One hundred and ninety-nine steps later, we arrived at the church but were not overly interested in the famous box pews and three-decker pulpit. We were in search

of the vampire. When the vicar, a tall, thin, white-faced individual in a flowing black cape, appeared at the door of the
church I was very impressed.

'Are you Count Dracula?' I asked innocently. My red-faced
parents hurried their little boy down the steps and back to the
car.

Scarborough was a favourite holiday destination. I loved
making sandcastles on the soft sandy beach, the donkey rides,
steering the chugging smelly little motor boats on the boating
lake, listening to the music at the Spa, walking along the promenade with lips sticky with candyfloss and the sweet pink sticks
of rock which lasted for hours and hours. I loved the climb
up to the castle and later, hungry from the walk, fish and chips
with bread and butter and a pot of tea in the café on the front.
I remember one holiday we stood outside the entrance of the
palatial Grand Hotel. We marvelled at the Gothic splendour:
cast-iron balconies, corner domes with porthole windows, the
red and orange terracotta and the great Corinthian columns.

'When I win the football pools,' I remember my father
saying, 'we will all stay here.' Sadly, that was never to be.

Most of the year I would be free of accidents and mishaps, save
for the odd scraped shin, cut finger and bruised knee, but when
it came to the holidays it was a different matter. I seemed to
attract accidents like a magnet. At the age of seven the family
had a rather cramped week in Auntie Nora's four-berth caravan, sited overlooking the sea near Flamborough Head. The
year before I had managed to get a piece of popcorn wedged
up my nose and had ended up with my father at the hospital.
The doctor had managed to extract the foreign body with a
long silver needle-like instrument with a tiny hook on the
end. My mother told me many years later that when I arrived
back from the Casualty Department she had asked me what
had happened to the popcorn.

'I ate it,' I announced.

Then I swallowed a marble, pretending it was a sweet, and made a return visit to the hospital. I had to take this pink, foul-tasting viscous medicine. Sitting on the toilet the next day there was a clunk and I announced loudly that I had got my marble back.

As she unpacked the bedding in the caravan at Flamborough, Mum warned me to stay out of trouble. 'And no accidents,' she said. Sadly I didn't oblige.

The holiday ended with another incident. I had been paddling at the sea edge at Filey, looking for crabs and shells and interesting pebbles. Suddenly I ran out of the sea screaming. My mother wrapped me in a towel but she couldn't see why I was so distressed. I was in agony and began rubbing my foot madly. Mum looked but could find no cut or bruise. I continued to writhe and scream and all those around on the beach began to gather around. I was carried to the first aid point and an ambulance was called. Mum went with me to Scarborough hospital while Dad looked after the other three children.

The conversation between Dad and the attendant at the first aid post was related in graphic detail later when I was home.

'I know what it is,' the individual who managed the first aid station had announced as Dad watched the ambulance disappear with siren sounding. 'He's gone and trodden on a weaver fish.'

'Whatever is one of those?' Dad asked.

'Horrible creature, the weaver fish,' he told my father. 'Ugly as sin, with three sharp spines in their backs. When it's cold, they bury themselves in the sand and when the sun comes out they come to the surface and put up these great sharp spines to catch their prey. Oh yes, I've seen quite a few in my time. I've seen six-foot policemen weep with one of these spines in his toe. Very painful.'

My father wanted reassurance, not a running commentary about the life and times of the weaver fish, and asked if I would be all right. The man sucked in his breath and shook his head. 'Could be . . . then again, they're very nasty poisonous fish.'

'Why doesn't someone warn people about these fish?' Dad asked him.

'If they did that,' replied the man, 'nobody would go in the sea.'

At the hospital my foot was plunged into a bowl of hot water and the spine was extracted.

Some years later I attended a talk at Broom Valley School. It was part of a lecture series intended to improve the minds of youngsters and a varied programme was presented through-out the year. The marine biologist who spoke about the wonderful world of the ocean showed some slides of the most unusual and dangerous creatures of the deep. I was fascinated.

'And this,' said the speaker, showing a slide of an incredibly ugly-looking fish with great fat lips, large protuberant eyes and three sharp spines on its back, 'is the Great Weaver. They are extremely shy and it is very unlikely you will ever see one.'

I raised my hand and announced proudly, 'I've trodden on one of those.'

The Punch and Judy show fascinated me when I was young. Punch, with his hunched back and gigantic curved nose, was naturally bad-tempered, argumentative, un-cooperative and no respecter of authority. He was the anarchist of the puppet world, laying into the policeman with his truncheon, hitting the baby, clunking his wife and sorting out the crocodile, and when he appeared he would be greeted by wild cheers from the children. I guess today he would be regarded as politically incorrect and far too violent for small children.

One day when we were spending a weekend in Scarborough, Alec took me, on the pretext that we going to see the Punch and Judy show, to see the beauty contest. We had asked Mum if we could go and she had refused, saying it was not seemly for young women to parade semi-clad in public. When we arrived at the outdoor bathing pool, long-legged girls in one-piece swimsuits and high heels carrying before them heart-shaped cards on which their competition number was displayed, were already promenading around the side, competing for the coveted sash. When Dad found us we were sitting between a group of ogling men, their Brylcreemed hair glistening in the sunshine, following the progress of the bathing beauties as they paraded before us.

'Come along, you two,' said Dad grinning, 'and don't let on to your mother where you've been.'

My mother was a bit strait-laced about these things and would never let us linger outside the shops to read the wonderfully rude postcards – we would have to sneak back when she was out of sight. The brightly coloured cards, many by Donald McGill, always seemed to feature vastly overweight women in tight striped bathing costumes, extremely shapely blondes and small harassed-looking men. One showed such a man poking at a shell and the woman commenting, 'He always has trouble getting his winkle out.'

The incident with the rock bun and the seagull still makes me smile. The family was having afternoon tea at the café on the seafront. Tea was served in heavy silver pots, and there was a matching heavy silver jug full of hot water for topping up and a heavy silver jug for the milk. The teapot was really hard to pick up because the handle got very hot. The cups, saucers and plates were equally large and heavy and were made of thick white pottery. Mum was in a bright summer dress, Dad (unlike many men, who were quite happy walking along the promenade or on the pier in vest and braces, some with knotted handkerchiefs over their heads) wore a linen jacket and flannel trousers. I have an old black and white picture of him strolling along the promenade with Mum on his arm and the four children and he looks very dapper. The sandwiches in the café were tasteless, the cakes sickly sweet and the tea weak and watery. Alec had a large rock bun which certainly lived up to its name. It was like a big lump of concrete with a few currants stuck in the top, and he kept picking at it and flicking bits at me.

'Look,' said Dad, 'if you're not going to eat it, throw it to the gulls.'

So my brother threw the rock bun as hard as he could and, amazingly, it hit a low-flying seagull. The bird plummeted and disappeared under the sea with a great splash.

'Good shot!' said a man at the next table, and a group of holidaymakers started to clap. 'They're a bloody nuisance them seagulls,' continued the man.

'They are the spirits of dead seamen,' said a woman at another table. 'It's bad luck to kill a seagull.' I immediately thought of *The Ancient Mariner* and the fate of the crew when the old seafarer killed the albatross.

Fortunately the gull reappeared, no worse for its ordeal, and started to attack the bun with a vengeance before flying off.

Quite a lot of the time my brother Alec and I made our own entertainment at the oily brown square of water fancifully called the boating lake. For a shilling my brother and I would, for half an hour, take it in turns to steer a noisy little boat round and round until the man in charge shouted out, 'Come in Number 4.' The boating lake was a really good place to go crabbing. We would beg a few bits of bacon rind from the butcher when Mum bought the pork pies for lunch, and spend hours with a length of string and a couple of buckets seeing which one of us could catch the most crabs. We sat on the edge of the pool dangling our string down into the murky brown water, waiting for the gentle tug that signified we had a catch. The trick in getting the crabs into the bucket was to pull on the string really slowly. The crab would dangle by one pincer and be pulled in slowly and carefully. They were usually only small catches, two or three inches across, but occasionally Alec would manage to land a big one. People would then crowd round. My brother was an expert at prising off the crab, which clung on tenaciously to the bacon rind. He would grasp the crab with thumb and forefinger behind the front pincers and pop it into the bucket.

When I took my sons crabbing years later, I demonstrated this technique and they became very adept at it. When the eldest, Richard, moved to Bermuda he took his small son crabbing on a little jetty and caught an impressively large crab. People gathered round and Richard decided to give a public demonstration of the way to hold the crustacean. Taking the crab with thumb and forefinger behind the front pincers he explained to little Harry that the crab was unable to pinch him and was quite harmless if held in this manner. Unfortunately for Richard the Bermudian crabs are somewhat different from the ones in the boating lake at Scarborough. They have a set of vicious claws at the side and Richard received a sharp nip before dropping the crab, which plopped back into the water.

A small observer, aged about six, shook his head and remarked, 'That was a very silly thing to do.'

30. A little tyke. Me at six.

29. The Phinn children outside Mrs Cadwalladar's boarding-house in Blackpool. Christine, Michael, Alec and me. We were, and still are, a close family.

31. I am the grumpy-looking one on the far right of the top row. What was my mother thinking of, sending me to the infants in a blazer with a rose in the buttonhole?

32. On the beach in Blackpool with Alec. He could swim like a fish and was rarely out of the sea.

33. Sitting on a sandcastle on Blackpool beach, aged eleven.

34. Christine, Alec, me and the neighbours' son, Sammy, at the house in Richard Road. We were the only people in the street with French windows.

35. I had just been made Deputy Head Boy. The smile says it all.

36. With my father and sister in Scotland. We had been looking for the grave of Margaret Macdonald.

37. The Class of 1956 at Broom Valley Junior School. I am in the second row, third from the left. There were forty-four children in the class.

38. Aged eleven. I am on the second row, far right. I was the only boy sent to school wearing a white shirt and a tie.

39. The photograph features three of my favourite teachers: Mr Willams, the headmaster (*centre*), Theo Firth (*second from the left*) and Alan Schofield (*far right*).

40. The staff of South Grove Secondary Modern School for Boys. Mr Pike, my inspirational English teacher, is fourth from the left in the middle row.

41. Posing as Oberon, King of the Fairies, in the frilly, balloon-sleeved shirt made of pink and blue chiffon, a costume I abandoned.

42. On the rocks in the Isle of Man with a friend.

43. 'Some are born great, some achieve greatness and some have greatness thrust upon them.' On stage as Malvolio, in cross-garters.

ere were the donkey rides and the Punch and Judy shows,
e trundling open-topped trams decked out with bright lights
nd, of course, the Tower, rising in a lattice of metal, and
Reginald Dixon playing 'Oh, I Do Like to be Beside the
Seaside' on the great organ. Part of the infinite charm of those
exhilarating days in Blackpool was the fact it was so wonderfully different and we were never bored.

The family stayed at Mrs Cadwalladar's boarding-house near
Gynn Square, which always seemed to be full of Scottish
people. It was a substantial three-storey terrace with, I guess,
five or six bedrooms. The front room downstairs was set out
with four dining tables for the guests. There were strict rules
about mealtimes, use of the bathroom, coming in 'after hours'
and 'keeping down the noise'. The food was plain and very
often inedible. Breakfast was always cornflakes, undercooked
fried eggs swimming in fat, greasy rashers of smoked bacon
and deep-fried bread, followed by cold toast. Salad was the
staple meal for tea: big weeping chunks of boiled ham or thin
slices of corned beef (which resembled Mrs Cadwalladar's legs
in colour and texture), hard-boiled eggs with blobs of salad
cream on top, over-ripe tomatoes and wilting lettuce. Her
offerings on Saturday and Sunday were sometimes more
substantial: tepid brown Windsor soup followed by a fleshy
boneless piece of steak with the consistency of shoe leather,
accompanied by vegetables which had been boiled tasteless,
or her famed Lancashire hot-pot: chunks of grey meat, swollen kidneys and chopped carrots swimming in a lake of thin
greasy gravy. This would be followed by apple pie: a glutinous
concoction of sour-tasting fruit beneath pale flaccid pastry.
Should we children betray the slightest dissatisfaction or leave
too much on the plate, the landlady's thin lips would purse in
displeasure. We took to emptying our mouths into our handkerchiefs when she was out of sight and disposing of the evidence
later down the toilet.

44. My first studio portrait
for the Youth Theatre.
I was attempting a
philosophical expression.

45. At a rehearsal for *Twelfth
Night* at the Rotherham
Civic Theatre.

44. My first studio portrait for the Youth Theatre. I was attempting a philosophical expression.

45. At a rehearsal for *Twelfth Night* at the Rotherham Civic Theatre.

46. Acting the part of Dr Diaforus in Molière's classic *The Imaginary Invalid*.

47-9. On the Isle of Man.

31

Most summers, when Steel, Peach & Tozer had its 'shut-down week' and the furnaces were cleaned, we had a fortnight in Blackpool. This was our family holiday; it was modest but the happiest of times. For my parents it must have been a break from routine and an opportunity to recharge their batteries and enjoy the simple pleasures of getting up later and having someone else do the cooking. Apart from Christmas, the fortnight in Blackpool held the greatest thrill. Most families like mine, on modest incomes and where the breadwinner had limited time off work, had neither the money nor the opportunity to travel and see the world and therefore spent the holidays at one of Britain's seaside resorts. Rotherham is about as far as you can get from the sea, so apart from the day trips to Scarborough, Filey and Bridlington and the school trips to the Isle of Man, I saw little of the coast. There was, therefore, an extraordinary feeling of excitement and anticipation when the summer holiday came around.

There was much to see and do in that bright, garish, noisy town so different from the place in which I lived. I recall the promenade illuminated by a million coloured lights, the huge piers stretching out into the battleship grey ocean, the packed beach with hardly a gap between the deckchairs, the pink and white sticky rock shot through with the name 'Blackpool'. I can still see the seafront shops selling fish and chips, whelks, candyfloss, breezy postcards, cheesy souvenirs and silly cowboy hats with suggestive slogans on the front. I can still taste the hot dogs with mustard that burnt my tongue and the greasy onions drizzled on the top; the blocks of Wall's ice cream supplied with the rectangular cone in which to put it. Then there were the donkey rides and the Punch and Judy shows, the trundling open-topped trams decked out with bright lights and, of course, the Tower, rising in a lattice of metal, and Reginald Dixon playing 'Oh, I Do Like to be Beside the Seaside' on the great organ. Part of the infinite charm of those exhilarating days in Blackpool was the fact it was so wonderfully different and we were never bored.

The family stayed at Mrs Cadwalladar's boarding-house near Gynn Square, which always seemed to be full of Scottish people. It was a substantial three-storey terrace with, I guess, five or six bedrooms. The front room downstairs was set out with four dining tables for the guests. There were strict rules about mealtimes, use of the bathroom, coming in 'after hours' and 'keeping down the noise'. The food was plain and very often inedible. Breakfast was always cornflakes, undercooked fried eggs swimming in fat, greasy rashers of smoked bacon and deep-fried bread, followed by cold toast. Salad was the staple meal for tea: big weeping chunks of boiled ham or thin slices of corned beef (which resembled Mrs Cadwalladar's legs in colour and texture), hard-boiled eggs with blobs of salad cream on top, over-ripe tomatoes and wilting lettuce. Her offerings on Saturday and Sunday were sometimes more substantial: tepid brown Windsor soup followed by a fleshy boneless piece of steak with the consistency of shoe leather, accompanied by vegetables which had been boiled tasteless, or her famed Lancashire hot-pot: chunks of grey meat, swollen kidneys and chopped carrots swimming in a lake of thin greasy gravy. This would be followed by apple pie: a glutinous concoction of sour-tasting fruit beneath pale flaccid pastry. Should we children betray the slightest dissatisfaction or leave too much on the plate, the landlady's thin lips would purse in displeasure. We took to emptying our mouths into our handkerchiefs when she was out of sight and disposing of the evidence later down the toilet.

For Friday's dinner, being Catholics, we were served fish – chunks of lukewarm cod smothered in a sticky white sauce with sprigs of parsley sprinkled on the top and accompanied by pallid boiled potatoes and bullet-hard peas. The fish served at the fish and chip shops was scrumptious: mouth-watering, sizzling, encased in tasty batter. Once Mrs Cadwalladar got her hands on a piece of fish she managed to kill it again. It was as if she meant it to be a penance. One year, on the second Friday of our stay, Mrs Cadwalladar apologized for not being able to get any fish.

'Oh dear,' sighed Dad. 'What a pity.' He winked in my direction. 'Don't you worry, Mrs Cadwalladar, we'll get some fish and chips from the shop on the front.'

Being a Roman Catholic had other advantages. I was allowed to go on the beach on Sunday, make sandcastles, play games, run about, eat ice creams and ride on the donkeys like any other day of the week. Some families staying at the boarding-house, however, were of the Nonconformist persuasion and the children were forbidden to set foot on the beach or play games on the Sabbath. Their buckets and spades, balls and bathing costumes were put away as if devices of the devil, and the children walked grave-faced to chapel in their Sunday best. When they returned they had to stay in and read or play instructive games.

Our first port of call when we arrived in Blackpool was W. H. Hills, the ice cream parlour on the front, and Dad would treat us to a 'knickerbocker glory': that tall, cone-shaped glass full of raspberry jelly, strawberries, chunks of tinned peach and different-flavoured ice creams, scattered liberally with crushed nuts and topped with a shiny glazed cherry. We would be given a long shiny metal spoon but, try as we might, we never did get to the last bit of peach at the bottom of the glass.

Every morning we children, dressed in khaki shorts, white cotton cap and sandals and wearing cheap plastic sunglasses, with our Brownie box cameras around our necks on a string, would walk with Dad along the promenade from the boarding-house to Gynn Square to get his paper. 'Smell the ozone,' Dad would say, breathing in deeply.

If the tide was out he would sit in a deckchair on the beach to read his *Daily Express,* keeping a wary eye on his three boys as we ran into the sea. I remember vividly the swimming trunks I wore: dark green, tight-fitting knitted affairs with a canvas belt and metal clasp which took some skill to keep on once sodden with water. There's a picture of me with my brothers, arms around each other, shivering near the sea's edge. We have just emerged from the water and are standing there in these heavy, sagging, uncomfortable outfits. After our swim we would build the most amazing sandcastles. We were equipped for the task with brightly coloured metal spades with long wooden handles. Mine was blue, Alec's red. We also had substantial metal buckets and a set each of little paper flags of all the nations to stick on our creations.

One morning we were keen to get started on our sandcastles but as we followed Dad along the promenade we saw, much to our disappointment, that the tide was in. This put brother Alec in a tetchy mood and he started complaining and drag-ging his spade behind him along the ground, making the most awful scraping noise. He was told several times by Dad to stop but he continued.

'If you do it again,' said Dad almost casually, 'I shall throw the spade in the sea.'

Alec desisted for a while but then started again to scrape the spade along the ground. True to his word, Dad took the spade from him and hurled it into the water.

'You just threw my spade in the sea,' gasped Alec.

'And if I hear any more from you,' said Dad, 'the bucket goes in as well.'

He did the same with the false teeth. I had bought a set of false teeth made out of pink and white rock with sugar pink gums and kept on clacking them like castanets as we walked along the prom one morning. I had been asked several times to desist but continued until they went the way of Alec's spade. I learnt from my father that when an adult warns a child he will do something he should carry it out. It was a good lesson to learn for a prospective teacher.

The Amusement Arcade drew children towards it like a magnet. We spent our pennies on the old slot machines or to manipulate a large metal claw in a glass case to try and grab a fluffy toy. I, being a Yorkshireman at heart, didn't waste my money on the 'Laughing Policeman' but would wait until somebody else spent a penny. In a glass case was a large puppet of a policeman who came to life when a coin was posted in the slot. He would rock from side to side, accompanied by a recording of someone laughing uproariously. It was infectious and a crowd would gather around and just start laughing. You couldn't help it.

Along the Golden Mile gypsy fortune tellers sat in small colourful sheds the size of wardrobes, with fancy red velvet curtains pulled back to reveal them like exhibits. They had exotic names like Gypsy Rose Smith and Romany Petronella and they all looked the same with their wizened brown faces and dark eyes, sitting behind small tables and dressed in typically gypsy fashion – coloured scarves wrapped around their heads, voluminous white blouses and long frilly skirts. They wore great golden rings in their ears and thick silver bangles on their skinny wrists. I longed to go inside and learn about my future but my mother pooh-poohed it.

'Gypsy Jasmine my foot,' she said. 'It's probably somebody called Enid Clamp from Cleckheaton. And if they are so good at seeing into the future,' she continued, 'what are they doing in a shed on the promenade at Blackpool?'

One of the highlights of our week in Blackpool was the evening out at the variety show in the theatre on the South

Pier. These were colourful lively affairs, with dancing girls, magicians, acrobats, jugglers, singing groups – the Beverley Sisters (Joy, Teddie and Babs), the Three Monarchs, Ruby Murray (later immortalized in rhyming slang for curry), the King Brothers, the Rocketeers; pianists – Rawicz and Landauer, Semprini, Winifred Atwell; soloists – Edmund Hockridge ('Canada's Favourite Baritone'), Kenneth McKellar ('The Voice of Bonny Scotland'), Ronnie Carroll ('The Irish Tenor'), Alma Cogan ('The Girl with the Giggle in Her Voice'), David Whitfield, Dorothy Squires and Ronnie Ronalde, the last billed as 'The World's Greatest Whistler'.

Speciality acts included Eddie Calvert ('The Man with the Golden Trumpet'), who would play popular favourites like 'O Mein Papa' and 'Apple Pink and Cherry Blossom White'. There was the man who swallowed live goldfish and then regurgitated them into a glass bowl (Dad later told us when we said it was cruel that they were fish-shaped pieces of carrot), a fire-eater who juggled flaming torches and who nearly set the front row on fire when he breathed out, an escapologist who writhed about the stage trussed up in chains, a small man in a red turban and a Hitler moustache with curly gold slippers who hurled a handful of vicious-looking daggers at a young woman positioned before a large wooden dartboard, and Bing Beales, this strange-looking, bald-headed, jug-eared performer with bad teeth who smacked himself noisily on the head with a tin tray as he sang the theme tune for a popular television series of the time – 'Head 'em up, move 'em out, move 'em out, head 'em up, Rawhide!' There were no warnings from the management for children 'not to try this at home'. A favourite was Syd Baker ('The Man of Bronze', brother of Hylda), who, covered from head to foot in yellowish-brown paint, contorted his muscles in time to the music.

At twelve I fell in love with Alma Cogan, the beautiful singer who appeared on stage in fabulous glittering voluminous dresses. She had a warmth and charm that captivated her audiences and when she sang she had a little sexy giggle in her voice. When I saw her beneath the lights looking down at me sitting in the stalls, I knew she was singing just to me:

> You dreamboat, you loveable dreamboat,
> The kisses you gave me set my dreams afloat.
> I would sail the seven seas with you
> Even if you told me to paddle my own canoe.

I looked forward most to the appearance of the comedians on stage and I laughed until my sides ached at the very best of the crop. Nearly all the stars at Blackpool came from the music hall tradition: Big-hearted Arthur Askey ('Hello, playmates'), Tommy Cooper ('Not like this, like that'), Richard (Dicky) Murdoch, Jimmy James with the huge glasses, trilby hat and loud tie and his gormless sidekick Eli, Dickie Henderson, Freddie Frinton, Beryl Reid, Arthur Haynes, Joan Whitfield, Norman Evans, Sandy Powell ('Can you hear me, mother?'), Professor Jimmy Edwards and Chic Murray. There was Frankie Howerd, who managed to have his audience doubled up with laughter though he said nothing inherently funny but just spluttered and 'Oooh-d' and 'Ahhh-d', jettisoning the script and departing into some wild fantasy of his own. 'No, don't titter,' he would spout, contorting his face. 'Pleeease, titter not,' he would continue in his strange throaty voice. 'Oh, pleeease yourselves.' These comedians knew only too well the comic power of accent and mannerism to create a character, and the catchphrases that were used helped the audience to bond.

I could never understand why my mother disliked the man with the silly laugh and the ukulele. She was easily shocked by anything that related to sex and the lyrics of George Formby's songs certainly had no appeal for her. Later when my brother Alec started to play the ukulele and bought a

booklet containing some of George Formby's more suggestive numbers, including 'When I'm Cleaning Windows' and
'My Little Stick of Blackpool Rock', it was promptly put in
the dustbin.

'You're not singing those songs in this house,' she said.

Later we retrieved the booklet from the bin, intrigued, as
children so often are when parents forbid something, and
examined the 'indecent' lyrics, which, by today's standards, are
pretty tame:

> Honeymooning couples do,
> You should see them bill and coo.
> You'd be surprised at what they do,
> When I'm cleaning windows.

> Pyjamas lying side-by-side,
> Ladies' nighties I have spied.
> I've often seen what goes inside,
> When I'm cleaning windows.

> The blushing bride, she looks divine,
> The bridegroom, he is doing fine.
> I'd rather have his job than mine,
> When I'm cleaning windows.

Top of the bill at the variety shows was often Al Read, Salford's
comic chronicler of working-class Lancashire life with his
meaningless catchphrases of 'Right Monkey', 'You'll be lucky,
I say you'll be lucky.' His weekly radio shows drew audiences
of 35 million and his humour still stands the test of time. It
was a humour that was observational and absurd rather than
vicious. Unlike some comedians of today, he was never malicious or spitefully critical of others. He steered clear of religion
and politics and his material had no edge to it. It was just

inoffensive and funny, and made funnier still by the deadpan delivery and the range of voices he employed. He was a brilliant observer of the domestic scene, with his vignettes highlighting the idiosyncrasies of everyday life. I learnt much about timing and use of voice from this master of repartee.

My favourite of all was the great Hylda Baker with her silent stooge, Cynthia, who managed to keep a face as rigid and serious as a death mask throughout the performance. Hylda Baker was a small woman (four foot, eleven inches) and characterized the fast-talking gossip. Her catchphrases, 'She knows, you know,' 'Be soon I said, be soon' and 'You big girl's blouse' became household words. It is reputed that when she appeared at the Stephen Joseph Theatre in Scarborough, Noel Coward observed, after the performance he had 'endured', that, 'I would wring that woman's neck — if I could find it.'

Hylda Baker was a direct descendant of Mistress Quickly and Mrs Malaprop and the precursor of Connie, the character who appears throughout my Dales books. She was one of those people who mangled and murdered the language with malapropisms and *non sequiturs* to great comic effect. In her moth-eaten fox fur, ill-fitting checked jacket, large handbag over the arm and misshapen hat, she had the audience rolling in the aisles with her facial contortions and her misuse of English. She would wriggle her body as if she suffered from chronic worms, crimp her hair, adjust her massive handbag and announce to the audience as she came on stage: 'I don't think you've had the pleasure of me.'

'I can say this without fear of contraception,' she would say. 'I went to the doctor and he was stood standing there, his horoscope round his neck. He said I had the body of a woman twice my age. You flatterer you, I said. I nearly had a coronary trombonist and fell prostitute on the floor.'

She would look up at her silent friend. 'Oooo,' she would mouth, 'Have you been with a fella? Have yooo? Have yooo been with a fella?' Cynthia would stare into the middle distance with a blank expression. 'She knows, you know,' Hylda told the audience. 'Oh yes, she knows, you know,' she would repeat and the whole audience shouted back the phrase. Simple, innocent, silly material but hilariously funny.

After one show I waited in the rain at the stage door to get her autograph. There was no one else waiting and my father doubted if she would appear. Perhaps the doorkeeper felt sorry for me and had persuaded her to come down, for after a while, still in her stage costume, the comic genius came out and signed my book.

'Have you been stood standing there, have you, you little man?' she asked of the wide-eyed little boy. I nodded. 'I bet you've been to the Blackpool illucinations, haven't you?' I nodded but was lost for words. 'Do I get a kiss?' she asked me.

'No,' I replied, colouring up. Then I caught sight of Alma Cogan making her way to the stage door. 'But I'll kiss her.'

Hylda Baker's last years were spent in a nursing home in Horton. She died at the age of eighty-one, alone in Horton Hospital in 1986. Britain's once most popular comedienne had been largely forgotten. When I met her niece at a literary luncheon in 2001, she was comforted to know that many years after her aunt's passing the unique talents of Hylda Baker were still appreciated and that her comedy lives on.

It was a nostalgic journey when I returned to Blackpool after half a century. I was there with my one-man show and performed on the same stage as my heroes of comedy. On the promenade the smell of donkey manure, candyfloss and seaweed had remained and took me back to my youth. I sat for a moment on a bench and recalled a little boy dressed in khaki shorts, white cotton cap and sandals, wearing cheap plastic sunglasses and with his Brownie box camera around his neck on a string, walking hand-in-hand with his father. Before leaving I bought myself a set of false teeth made out of pink and white rock with sugar pink gums.

32

At the end of my junior school career, all the children in the fourth year at Broom Valley Juniors sat the Eleven Plus. This examination, born out of the Butler Education Act of 1944, determined whether children would continue their education at the academically selective grammar and high schools, or, in the case of failure, at the technical or secondary modern schools. The whole structure of the Eleven Plus was based on the spurious premise that academic ability was based on a normal curve of distribution, that there are a few people at the top (the bright), a few at the bottom (the least able) and the vast majority in the middle (the average). The problem was that nobody had ever proved that academic ability was distributed in this way. Further problems levelled by the examination's critics were the relatively crude nature of the tests and the inherent unfairness. Which school a child went to in the 1950s depended not merely on academic ability or the performance in the examination, but on whereabouts in the country he or she lived. Nationally less than 20 per cent of the children sitting the Eleven Plus went on to grammar schools, but it could be as high as 40 per cent (as in Westmorland) and as low as 10 per cent (as in Sunderland).

Most of those in the fourth year at Broom Valley Juniors were resigned to the fact that they would not pass, but I, ever the optimist, thought I was in with a good chance. On the positive side I knew I was good at reading and writing and could cope easily with the questions about language. I could commit information to memory and my general knowledge wasn't too bad. I had a quick wit, a wry sense of humour and had the ability to tell a story. On the negative side I was not good at thinking on my feet, and arithmetic and problem-solving, major parts of the assessment, were not my strong points.

On the big day the forty-three top juniors of my class trooped silently into the hall as if we were to face an execution squad. We were all equipped with two sharp HB pencils, a clean eraser and a ruler. The desks had been moved out of our classrooms and arranged in serried rows facing the stage. The headmaster, Mr Morgan, clutching a thick wad of papers, explained how important the examination was, how we had to try our best and check through our paper carefully when we had finished. No one would be allowed to leave the hall until the end of the ninety minutes. He told us that there would be no talking, no sniffing and coughing, no getting out of our seats, no going to the toilet and anyone discovered copying would be in serious trouble. Those who had not done as we were told and brought a clean handkerchief were issued with paper tissues.

I had never seen an Eleven Plus paper before. I knew that some in my class had been practising on old papers in preparation for the test and that Harper's Bookshop in Rotherham sold such papers, but I was unfamiliar with the format when presented with the booklet. My parents were not into the business of cramming and practice papers, private tutors or any kind of hot-housing and there was no stress in the house in the build-up to the examination.

When I worked for Rotherham Education Authority I managed to acquire a copy of the paper I sat at the age of eleven. There were five sections: arithmetic, general English, comprehension, general knowledge and composition. In the general English section children had to identify parts of speech, punctuate, insert inverted commas, form plurals, change tense, provide synonyms and antonyms and answer a further range of other grammar and punctuation exercises. One wonders how youngsters today would cope with some of the questions in the composition section:

Write a short account on any four of the following: Everest, Westminster Abbey, The Gothic, William Shakespeare, Queen Salote, The Maoris.

Write an imaginary talk between an eagle and an owl.

Write a story ending with the words: '. . . and that is why the old sailor was allowed to keep his parrot.'

The adventures of a library book.

I imagine that I, like many, floundered in the arithmetic part of the test with questions like this:

A colony contains 30,000 people, made up of English, Dutch and natives, in equal numbers. Each year the English lose one tenth of their numbers and the natives add one tenth to their numbers. The Dutch remain unchanged. What will be the population of the colony at the end of two years?

It is interesting to note that the person who set the paper needed a few lessons in English grammar himself:

My best friend is tall and dark. I am nine and he is ten. Read the following sentences and write down my best friend's name.
    Harry is younger than me. He is short and dark. Dick is ten.
    He is a tall boy with fair hair. Tom has dark hair. He is older than me and is a tall boy. Frank is a tall boy with dark hair. He is nine.

I recall filling in the front page of the paper incorrectly and having to madly rub out my mistakes. Mr Morgan eyed me, shook his head, but said nothing. The test (apart from the arithmetic) was not too onerous and I went home reasonably confident that I would be among those wearing the grammar school blazer with its fancy badge with the Archbishop's mitre on it.

Towards the end of the term brown envelopes popped through letterboxes all over the country to tell parents if their son or daughter had been successful or not in passing the Eleven Plus. The night before the announcement of the results I couldn't sleep. I lay in bed, my body twitching and turning, measuring the passage of time by the alarm clock on the bedside table. A mood of doubt settled upon me and was made more intense by the silence. I was down for breakfast early that Saturday morning but couldn't eat a thing. I stood by the window in the front room waiting for the postman. When I saw him trundling up the hill, I ran to the end of the drive and waited at the gate to collect the envelope.

I recall my mother wiping her hands on the towel in the kitchen, taking the brown envelope into the living room, opening it and reading the contents slowly. 'I'm sorry, love,' she said, 'you didn't get through.'

Mum and Dad were very philosophical about it, and certainly didn't appear to show any great disappointment at my failure or start with recriminations. Having spent a lifetime in education I have met parents fixated on the educational performance of their children and who pressure them to achieve. Undue pressure, in my experience, very often stifles a child's creativity and undermines his or her confidence, and constant criticism and stress can develop into depression. As I write, there appears in the paper the story of a promising student who took his own life after gaining poor results in his A levels. It is a tragic case of a young man who felt he was a failure and a disappointment to his parents.

My father's attitude was that the test was but a piece of

paper and I should put it behind me. But I felt my lack of success deeply.

Unlike some other parents on our street, my mother and father had not promised their child anything if he passed. They merely told me to try my best – I could do no other. Some of my friends had been promised a bicycle if they passed, as if this would be a real incentive for them to work that bit harder – something to aim for. I wondered how they felt on failing and not getting the desired reward.

As I clutched the letter and started crying, my parents explained that all my friends in the street would be going to the secondary modern and that I could do as well there if I worked hard, but their words didn't soften the blow. I felt a failure and I felt indignant and angry too. I had so wanted to go to the grammar school, to walk proudly up Moorgate to the great castle-like edifice with the towers and turrets, attired in my black blazer, grey flannels and cap with the golden badge. At the time I expressed my annoyance and perceived unfairness by complaining and grumbling, until my parents told me to put it behind me and get on with things. It had happened and that was that. It was sensible advice.

I recall my sister, Christine, being particularly supportive of me at this time. She put her arm around me and comforted me, telling me it was not the end of the world. But it seemed so for me. Christine had passed her Eleven Plus with flying colours. She was bright and successful, loved school, was popular with her peers and was Deputy Head Girl at Notre Dame. Everyone was sure she would do well in life.

I learnt a great deal about Notre Dame, for Christine would tell things about the school to my parents over tea. I knew all about how relentlessly competitive and selective the convent high school was, how the girls were streamed into 'A' and 'B' classes, that they studied Latin, Spanish, geology, scripture and all these other strange and exotic-sounding subjects. There

was also something called 'deportment', in which they were
taught manners and etiquette and 'morals and ethics', the
main content of which seemed to be to warn the girls against
the dangers of predatory boys. At college I courted a convent
girl who informed me that the advice from one nun was:
'Never sit on a boy's knee, girls, unless you have a telephone
directory or some other thick book between you both.' I
wonder how many convent girls took such a tome to the
dance at the village hall. Another story, perhaps another urban
myth, was that the convent girls were not allowed to wear
patent leather shoes for the Christmas party in case they
reflected their knickers.

I had witnessed how each afternoon Christine would go
into the front room after tea and spend most of the evening
completing her homework. I looked forward to joining her.
My brothers, Michael and Alec, although clever and successful enough at school, were not as industrious as my sister and
polished off their homework in record time.

Christine liked to tell me about Notre Dame. I knew about
the long dark corridors at her school down which the nuns
glided slowly and silently, the no-talking rule when in school,
the many rules to be obeyed, the constant merits and deten-
tions and finally the ultimate terror – to receive a severe
talking-to from the headmistress, the formidable Sister Monica.
Physical chastisement was unnecessary; one look from Sister
Monica was all that was needed.

My sister had to wear a smart and stylish uniform, only
available from the authorized school outfitter: crisp white
blouse, green pleated skirt, white ankle socks, a boater in
summer and a green beret in winter and the regulation small
white gloves. Full uniform had to be worn at all times to and
from school and girls caught without it would be in trouble.
Each morning the girls would be inspected on their arrival at
the school, and should a skirt not be the regulation length or

the beret not on straight, the offender would get a demerit. The rules at the school were remorseless.

Young as I was, I knew there was a certain social cachet attached to the grammar school uniform. The caps and blazers showed the difference between success and failure. It was visible to all. People regarded these young women off to the convent high school on the bus to Sheffield, or boys on their way to the boys' grammar school, or the Rotherham high school girls walking through the town centre, rather differently from other students. Their uniforms, visible to all, showed which school they attended. They looked a cut above and sometimes acted so.

I imagined that I too would go to such a school as Notre Dame, so strikingly different from the Juniors, where everything was exact and ordered, so my disappointment was great when I discovered I would be attending the ugly red brick building near the town centre which I had passed many times. It was like a featureless factory, high and square, with its row of uniform windows.

In Rotherham, with its large population of 'baby-boomers', the number of children going on to the one boys' grammar and one girls' high school was relatively low. Those who are great champions of the selection of children at the age of eleven perhaps do not really appreciate that the secondary modern school never came close to achieving the parity of esteem with the grammar in any way. In many secondary modern schools the expectation of the students was low. I have met so many 'Eleven Plus failures' who believed themselves, on the strength of a test taken when they were eleven, to be on the educational scrapheap destined for the menial jobs in society, or at best going into apprenticeships. Certainly higher education was not considered an option for them.

The curriculum at the secondary modern was significantly different from that in the grammar schools. It was unashamedly non-academic. Of course there were exceptions, but in general there would be no academic rigour, the emphasis being on practical subjects like cookery, housecraft, metalwork, wood-work, rural studies and technical drawing. No modern language was on offer, and the students would not sit the school certifi-cate at the end of their school careers and would leave for work at the age of fifteen.

Secondary moderns had few of the facilities of the grammar schools. I used to walk up Moorgate to Boston Park, past Rotherham Grammar School, and marvel at the great ornate gothic-style building set in well-tended lawns, with its great curving drive leading to the impressive entrance. The cricket square was as smooth and green as a billiard table, the rugby and football pitches were free of mud patches and skid marks, the touchlines freshly marked, clean and straight. It looked to me like a stately home. How different it was from the school I would attend.

Looking back, I don't harbour any bitterness or indignation over failing the Eleven Plus. I don't wear my lack of success at eleven on my sleeve like some people I have met, who feel angry to have been labelled less able at such a young age. The fact is that at that time, under those circumstances, there were children who were cleverer and who performed better in the test than I. That is a fact of life. I was a perfectly average boy in possession of a perfectly average intelligence. Having brooded for a week after the results, moping about the house and looking miserable, I was taken aside by my father, who told me to put it behind me and get on with my life. He knew I was bright enough and had the potential to do well at the secondary modern and I should show everyone I could succeed. And so I learnt early on that failure is a part of growing up, and if, as I was encouraged to by my parents, a person has a healthy attitude towards failure and uncertainty, he or she can create, innovate and strive to achieve.

33

Thinking over what gave me the most pleasure in my childhood, I should place first and foremost reading. My mother,
a natural storyteller, taught me the nursery rhymes and read
to me from picture books. I knew all the old favourites –
Chicken Licken, *The Gingerbread Man*, *The Giant Turnip*,
Rumplestiltskin, *The Magic Porridge Pot* – and many more before
I started school. Most evenings, before I went to bed, she
would read aloud with me snuggled up next to her. I loved
listening to the story, following the words on the page as she
read and feeling that special physical closeness. Sometimes she
would change a word, take a bit out or add something, and I
could tell and told her so. I might not be able to read those
black marks on the page but I knew the stories so well. Later,
when the story was told and the light turned off, I would close
my eyes and dream of a world peopled with the magical characters I had encountered in the book.

One of my very first memories was hearing one of Enid
Blyton's *Bedtime Stories from the Bible*. I can still picture this
large red book with shiny pages and garish illustrations, and
clearly recall the images of a gentle-faced Jesus with his carefully trimmed beard, snow white cloak and sandals, telling his
stories to a group of avid listeners crowded around him. Then
came the Noddy books. Even now, sixty or so years later, I
still have my collection of Enid Blyton's stories on my bookshelf. I recall the very first Noddy book I read myself – *Hurrah
for Little Noddy*, the second volume in the twenty-four-book
canon. It was a crime story for little ones, in which innocent
little Noddy discovers a car heist at Mr Golly's garage and sets

off in hot pursuit of the thieves, only to end up in a head-on collision with a tree. Poor Noddy is blamed for the theft and P.C. Plod takes him to gaol. Predictably it all ends happily, with Noddy vindicated and the villains locked up. There has been much criticism of Enid Blyton, and many educationalists believe children deserve better reading material, but for me, as for many children, her stories had the power to keep me captivated throughout. Everything was there – characters, suspense, pace and action.

The Noddy books led inexorably on to my reading of Enid Blyton's other adventures, and I rattled through them at great speed and was quite happy to suspend my disbelief. Of course, the children in the Secret Seven and the Famous Five series were a world away from my own life. For a start they talked differently. You would never catch George and her friends dropping their aitches or speaking in anything other than sentences. They lived in the middle of the country in rambling old houses and thatched cottages, with babbling streams at the bottom of the garden and long lawns and perfectly tended flowerbeds. Their parents were happy, smiling, easy-going folk who never shouted or told them to finish their homework or do any chores. The children had spiffing adventures, discovered treasure, foiled villains and saved lives and then ran home for their lunch. They always seemed to be tucking in.

They were all very hungry at lunchtime. They went back up the cliff path hoping there would be lots to eat – and there was! Cold meat and salad, plum pie and custard, and cheese afterwards. How the children tucked in!

'What are you going to do this afternoon?' asked George's mother.

'George is taking us out in a boat to see the wreck on the other side of the island,' said Anne.

– Enid Blyton, *Five on a Treasure Island* (1942)

Thankfully George's mother did not live in this day and age or she would be prosecuted for child neglect, allowing the children (minus life-jackets) to take a leaky rowing boat out to a wreck. They can say what they like about Enid Blyton – that her stories are inane, simplistic and unrealistic – but she managed to get me hooked on books.

My father captured my imagination with his stories. He would bring back books from Rotherham Library or buy a couple of old tattered versions of the classics from the market, taking out his finds from the brown paper carrier bag where they had been hiding between the vegetables and fruit. Once he arrived from the market with a large hard-backed tome called *King of the Fighting Scouts*, which depicted on the front cover a garish illustration of a soldier on a rearing horse hacking his way through a horde of savages. For several nights my father read a couple of chapters, only to arrive at the denouement to discover that the last few pages of the book were missing. Undeterred, he made the end up.

My father took over from my mother this nightly ritual of reading to me when I was eight or nine. He would read a chapter or two at a time, ending on a high note and thus whetting my imagination for more. I would be keen for the next instalment the following night and be up those stairs in my pyjamas, face washed, teeth brushed, ready and waiting. It was a really clever way of making me go to bed at night. Boys who have had this sort of upbringing, where fathers tell them stories, read to them and associate reading with great pleasure and affection, learn to love books. A magical world is opened up to them.

Books and reading 'habituated me to the Vast', for as a youngster I would disappear up the garden and sit on the old bench behind the greenhouse or in the garden shed, or lie on my stomach on the lawn in the sunshine or hide in the branches of the cherry tree to read. I read even when I was supposed to be working, and in those childhood days I had my heroes and dreamed of how I could imitate their courage and prowess. At night, under the sheets with my torch, I would continue reading despite nudges and grunts from my brother Alec, with whom I shared the old double bed. I would disappear under the covers and enter a world of pirates and smugglers, adventurers and explorers, knights and war heroes. I would go to sleep dreaming of those wonderful adventures. I used to consume authors; when there was one book I really enjoyed, I would go all through his or her works (it was usually a 'he') one after the other. At first it would be Lewis Carroll's *Alice in Wonderland* or Charles Kingsley's *The Water Babies*, Edith Nesbitt, J. M. Barrie, A. A. Milne and Kenneth Grahame, and then, as I grew older, it would be *The Last of the Mohicans*, *The Children of the New Forest*, *Robinson Crusoe*, *Moonfleet*, *Journey to the Centre of the Earth*, *Tom Sawyer*, *Huckleberry Finn*, *Rob Roy*, *Black Beauty*, *Lorna Doone*, *Biggles*, *Kidnapped*, *The Red Badge of Courage*, *The Secret Garden*, *Uncle Tom's Cabin*, *The Count of Monte Cristo*, *Moby Dick*, *The Man in the Iron Mask*, *Around the World in Eighty Days*. I devoured Richmal Crompton, John Buchan, Stephen Crane, Conan Doyle, Georgette Heyer, Rider Haggard, J. Meade Faulkner and Alexandre Dumas.

The adventures of *The Three Musketeers* fired my imagination. What daring exploits and what colourful characters: the wicked Milady (with the tell-tale brand on her shoulder), poor Louise de Vallière, the beautiful and romantic Queen Anne, the Machiavellian goatee-bearded Cardinal Richelieu and, of course, the gallant band of musketeers.

Years later I still read the books of a vastly underrated novelist: H. G. Wells. Few authors can match his brilliance for narrative pacing and suspense, his command of gripping dialogue and his skill at creating that eerie, captivating atmosphere which keeps the reader glued to the page. I read *The War of the Worlds*, *The Time Machine*, *The Invisible Man* and *The*

Island of Dr Moreau, in quick succession. These great classics
should be on every English curriculum. It was *The War of the
Worlds* that for me towered above the rest. In 1938 Orson Welles
turned the novel into a radio show broadcast in the style of a
real news report, and so convincing was he that thousands of
panic-stricken Americans on the Eastern seaboard deserted
their homes in the belief that the Martians had actually landed.

But my very favourite author is the great R. L. Stevenson.
I read *Treasure Island* over and over again, until the spine fell
apart and the pages fell out. It was in my capacity as a school
inspector that I was asked to accompany a politician around
an infant school. He was a pompous, self-opinionated man
who bemoaned the decline in standards of reading. In the
lower junior classroom he asked the eight-year-olds if they had
read *Treasure Island* and was greeted with shakes of the head
from the children and incredulous stares from the teacher.

'It seems to me that it is a great pity,' he observed later, when
he bored us in the staffroom, 'that the children are not aware
of one of the greatest works of children's literature.'

I agreed that *Treasure Island* was indeed a classic but I did
point out that a story about treacherous cut-throat mutineers,
murderous pirates and a character who kills with a crutch is
not the most edifying diet for children aged eight. I guess he
was thinking of a simplified version. I well remember the fear
I felt inside when, at the age of eleven, I first heard my father
read those episodes in the novel and I came across Long John
Silver and felt something of Jim Hawkins's terror of 'the seafar-
ing man with one leg':

How that personage haunted my dreams, I need scarcely tell you.
On stormy nights, when the wind shook the four corners of the
house, and the surf roared along the cove and up the cliffs, I would
see him in a thousand forms, and with a thousand diabolical expressions. Now the leg would be cut off at the knee, now the hip: now

he was a monstrous kind of creature who had never had but the one
leg, and that in the middle of his body. To see him leap and run and
pursue me over the hedge and ditch was the worst of nightmares.

                    – R. L. Stevenson, *Treasure Island* (1883)

As I listened to my father I was there with Jim, hiding from
Long John Silver in the barrel of apples and overhearing his
murderous plans. I was with Jim in the sweet-smelling darkness, trembling with fear in case I was discovered. I was there
in the stockade, shoulder-to-shoulder with Squire Trelawney
fighting off the mutineers. Stevenson as a storyteller is unsur-
passed. It isn't only his powerful command of narrative,
description, character and dialogue, it is the way he creates
suspense, which is so vital to keep the reader entranced.

The children of my childhood were exclusively white and
working-class. All my friends, Terry, Jimmy, Michael, Peter,
Greg, Martin, Billy, were from homes similar to my own. Some
were a bit better off, others a bit worse off, but we all lived in
the same kind of house, ate the same sort of food, dressed the
same, had the same interests and went to the same school. Only
one boy on our street went to Rudston, the small private prepar-
atory school on Broom Lane, and he had his own friends and
never came out to play with us. I would sometimes see him
getting off the bus with his bright blazer and cap, loaded down
with heavy satchel and P.E. bag, but I never spoke to him.
   As a child I had no experience of people from other cultures
or races and, as far as I can recall, there were no black people
around in the Rotherham of the 1950s. My cherished book
as a small child, which my grandmother Mullarkey read to me,
was *Little Black Sambo*. It never occurred to anyone at home
or at school that this could be considered offensive. I loved the
eponymous hero who outwitted the tiger. My treasured books
when I became a 'free reader' were the Biggles series and the

Bulldog Drummond stories, and it would have been considered absurd at the time to call such British institutions racist. I loved the rip-roaring action in *Biggles Defies the Swastika*, and the exploits of his chums Algy, Ginger and Bertie. I still have those Biggles books lined up on a shelf in my study, all with little inscriptions from my parents. I cannot bear to part with them. How I loved my Biggles books, though when I re-read them now, I do feel some unease about parts of the writing.

So, as a child, books were as common in my life as knives and forks and I swam in an ocean of language.

34

There is a picture of me that my mother kept on the sideboard (which we called the 'buffet' for some odd reason), taken at the age of eleven, posing awkwardly in the back garden in my new black blazer (a good size too big) with a large shield-shaped badge on the breast pocket, long grey shorts (obligatory for first and second year pupils), held in place with a striped elastic belt with a snake clasp, knee-length grey socks pulled up tight to the bottom of the knees and anchored there with elastic garters, grey jumper, white shirt, striped tie and polished black shoes. My ears stick out like jug handles because I have had a particularly vicious 'short back and sides' haircut the Saturday before at 'Slasher' Simcox, the demon barber of Rotherham. A new satchel is over my shoulder. I don't look all that excited on my first day at secondary school. I was terrified, to be honest. I had heard all the rumours at my junior school about what happens to new boys and had spent a fitful night thinking about them. The older boys would wait at the gates shouting and jeering and getting ready to pull your hair, punch you in the stomach, clip you round the ear, steal your dinner money and flush your head down the toilet bowl – lambs to the slaughter. It was a tradition to get the 'first years'. My mother told me such stories were nonsense, and that if anyone did start to pick on me I should tell her and she would be up to school like lightning. I am afraid I was not altogether reassured.

On that first dread-filled morning I arrived nervously with my friends at the tall wrought-iron gates of a huge redbrick building with greasy grey slate roof and high square windows. To a small eleven-year-old it was a massive, towering, frightening edifice resembling a prison, or the workhouse I had seen in the film *Oliver Twist*. Of course, there were no gangs of vicious-looking youths lying in wait to pounce on us, just groups of boys dressed identically in black blazers with the red badge, some clearly new like myself and looking lost and anxious. The older pupils talked in groups and ignored the younger ones. In the midst of the crowd stood a teacher – a small, barrel-bodied, balding man with little fluffy outcrops around his ears. With hands on hips he stood in the middle of the playground, watching as we trooped through the gates. He was wearing plimsolls, and instead of a belt he had a piece of string fastened around the top of his trousers. He looked like a character from Dickens. I learnt later that this was the much-feared Mr Theodore Firth.

So here I was at South Grove Secondary Modern School for Boys, where 500 pupils and twenty-five staff occupied the top floor of the building. Below was the girls' secondary modern, which was, of course, out of bounds.

The headmaster was Mr Williams (T.W.), a silver-haired Welshman with a pronounced accent and that deep sonorous tone of voice deeper than a Welsh coalmine. Several of the other masters were from Wales: Mr Reece (Dai), Mr Davies (Cliff), Mr Griffith (Griff), Mr Price (Van) and Mr Jones (Bobbin' John). They were known as 'the Taffia', and, in common with the headmaster, they all had a genuine and bubbly enthusiasm for their subjects and for teaching. The Welsh call this passion 'hwyl', and it was not in short supply at South Grove. To this day I have a real affection for the Welsh people who sent their missionary teachers to educate the likes of me in Rotherham. I owe a great deal of any success I have had to those Welshmen. The other masters were equally good-humoured and supportive: Norman Hill, Les Wales, Eddie Dyeball, Alan Schofield, Ted Duffield, Wilf Badger, Ken Pike, Bert Gravill, Chipper Payne, Gerry Blowfield, Harry Cooper,

Nobby Clark and the one woman teacher I recall, the sylph-like Sybil Cartwright, who taught biology. I still remember them with affection.

Secondary school was very different from the Juniors. Not only were there more pupils and bigger buildings, no girls and a uniform, but we studied subjects rather than topics and had homework. All the boys were addressed by their surname and in the morning the form master would mark the register by shouting out our names, to which we would answer, 'Here, sir.' There was only one boy in the school who was referred to by his first name and that was John Balls.

Some writers, describing their schooldays, dwell on their unhappiness at the hands of bullies and the cruelty at the hands of teachers. They speak of board rubbers thrown across the classroom, trouser bottoms smoking after a vicious caning, sarcastic, incompetent and sometimes sadistic teachers. Well, my schooldays were very different.

Of course, being the only Roman Catholic in the entire school taught me what it felt like to be a member of a minority. My faith (and my name) certainly gave me a sense of being different. I found myself excluded from both R.E. lessons and daily morning prayers. Father Hammond was quite clear when speaking to my mother that I should not attend Protestant services. I laughed a little more heartily than other listeners when I heard a joke many years later, for there was a tad of truth in it.

SISTER MARIE-CLARE: Now, my child, what do you hope to become when you leave the convent?

SCHOOLGIRL: A prostitute, sister.

SISTER MARIE-CLARE (shocked): Good gracious, my child, you can't aspire to that.

SCHOOLGIRL: I've always wanted to be a prostitute, sister.

SISTER MARIE-CLARE (relieved): Thank the Lord. I thought for a moment you said Protestant.

It seems bizarre nowadays that such a restriction for Catholics, prohibiting them from attending non-Catholic services, was in place at that time. Was it thought by some priests that by attending a Protestant service Catholics might very well be lured away from Rome or that they would be somehow tainted? If this was the case, it was not in the spirit of the Vatican Council of 1959, which reshaped the face of Catholicism for the better. Pope John XXIII, who instigated this reformation, wished to break through the barriers that divided people, to strengthen the bonds of mutual love and help people to learn to understand one another. He was a remarkable and innovative Pope. Towards the end of my teenage years this began to bear fruit. Some years later, when Robert Runcie was enthroned in Canterbury Cathedral as the archbishop, Cardinal Hume took a formal part in the service and read the Epistle. No one could have envisaged such a thing when I was growing up: a Cardinal taking part in a Protestant service. Cardinal Hume, in his address, made reference to the unprecedented fellowship between the Church of England and the Roman Catholic Church and referred to one of the many tombs in the great abbey, the one shared by the Catholic Queen Mary I and her sister, the Protestant Queen Elizabeth I. 'Two sisters,' he said, 'estranged, not on speaking terms, misunderstanding each other.' He continued, 'Should we not learn from the inscription on their joint tomb, which bears the words: "Consorts both in throne and grave, here we rest, two sisters, Elizabeth and Mary, in hope of one resurrection"?' I guess Father Hammond was turning in his grave. Sadly, in the 1950s there were few such inter-Church relations.

Frequently I had to explain to the other boys why I was not allowed into assembly, and why I spent my time sitting in the English room reading or in the corridor when it was time for R.E. I found it difficult and at times embarrassing to do so, for at that age I wanted to be one of the group, the same as they were, not this boy with the funny name and the strange religion. When I was a school inspector, I felt a deep sympathy with the child whom I would discover in the school library sitting alone, not permitted by his or her religion to attend school services and assemblies.

There was, as in all secondary schools of the time, a rigid streaming system in operation. Boys were grouped according to their academic records sent from primary school, their Eleven Plus results and the battery of tests that the new boys were given in the first week. Top form boys had to be pretty good at every subject, good all-rounders. There were four streams, and at first I was placed in Form 1B. I settled in well and was quite happy there but my mother was not. Despite my protests, she made an appointment to see Mr Williams, told him I could cope in the top form and asked him to give me a chance. She must have been immensely persuasive, because give me a chance he did, and one Monday morning I arrived at school to be told by my form teacher to take my things into the next classroom and join Mr Schofield and 1A.

In the corridor later that morning Mr Williams stopped me. 'Now, lad,' he said, his eyes taking on an unmistakable intensity, 'don't you be letting your parents and me down. Endeavour, perseverance, industry, that's what's needed. You have to earn that place in the top class.'

At home that evening my mother explained that I had to prove her right, to work hard, apply myself, do my homework and not let her down. It is interesting to read my school report at the end of each year, which shows my mother's confidence in me was well-placed. I worked hard and flourished under the direction of talented and enthusiastic teachers, remaining in the 'A' stream right through my secondary school career. I invariably came top or near the top in my favourite subjects of English, mathematics, history and geography, and the teachers' comments informed my parents that I was making 'excellent progress', that I 'continued to give 100 per cent effort', and that I 'read widely and intelligently' and 'would do well'. My final school report from Mr Cooper, my form master, indicates how I thrived and was determined to succeed in my studies.

Gervaise (sic) has worked extremely hard in all the subjects that he takes and has achieved excellent results. He studies with intelligence and common sense and has the ambition necessary to succeed. His examination reports are most praiseworthy. He is a most painstaking and fastidious worker and is never satisfied with anything below his best. He takes a most lively and active part in all form and school activities, takes all his responsibilities as Deputy Head Boy most conscientiously and is a valued asset to the school. His cheerful co-operation is much appreciated.

I always felt at secondary school that the headmaster took a particular interest in me. On his daily walk around the building he would often stop to talk to the boys and would enquire of me how I was getting on with my work and what I was reading at the moment. He was a lover of poetry and would frequently declaim snatches of verse.

In the final year at the school the prefects were selected and I was told to report to the headmaster's room. To my surprise I was asked to be Deputy Head Boy.

'I can't, sir,' I told him.

Mr Williams looked perplexed.

'Why ever not, boy?' he asked.

'I'm a Catholic, sir,' I said, 'and I'm not allowed to attend Protestant services. The Deputy Head Boy has to read the lesson in assembly and take part in the Christmas carol concert at the parish church.'

'Is that the only reason?' he asked.

'Yes, sir,' I replied, sadly. I was on the point of tears.

He thought for a moment and then, reaching into the drawer of his desk, produced a small yellow enamelled shield which he pinned on my lapel. 'Let me deal with that,' he told me. Then he shook my hand and congratulated me. I walked back to the classroom on clouds.

One day, when I was in the fourth year, Mr Williams stopped me in the corridor. He looked at me with striking earnestness with those pale, all-seeing eyes before asking, 'Do you go to the theatre, young Phinn?'

'I've been to the Regent, sir,' I told him.

'To see what?'

'The pantomime and some of the variety shows.'

'Pah! Pantomime, variety shows,' he repeated dismissively. 'Have you seen plays, proper plays? Shakespeare, Ben Jonson? Marlowe? Ibsen?'

'No, sir,' I replied.

'Why not?'

'I don't know, sir.' I met his gaze steadily.

He drew in a slow breath. 'You ought to go to the theatre. Never mind the television and the cinema; it's the theatre – the window on to the world.'

'Yes, sir,' I said as he disappeared down the corridor, his black gown fluttering behind him.

I thought no more about it, but the following week Mr Williams stopped me again after assembly. 'Two tickets here,' he said, thrusting an envelope into my hand, 'for the Sheffield Lyceum. You'll enjoy it.'

Spruced up and with a rather reluctant friend in tow, I took the bus to Sheffield the following Saturday night to see a production of Sheridan's classic comedy, *The Rivals*. I had been in a theatre before, when I had been taken to the panto-mime as a small child and to the end-of-the-pier shows at Blackpool, but I had never been in a theatre as grand as the Lyceum. I was overwhelmed by the gaudy splendour of the great building with its ornate painted plaster ceiling, red-velvet-covered seats, great crimson curtains and highly decorated arch above the stage. The floodlit stage, the sparkle and glitter, the chattering audience that surrounded me, the actors in their colourful costumes and outrageous wigs, intoxicated me. I entered a different world.

Mr Williams sat several rows in front with the school secretary, Mrs Atkinson (whom he later married). He nodded when he saw me. At fifteen I had my first real experience of theatre and sat on the edge of my seat, fascinated by the scenery, the language and the characters. There was bluff Sir Anthony Absolute, and the poisonous Sir Lucius O'Trigger, who mistakenly believes he is conducting a romance by letter with the luscious and headstrong seventeen-year-old heiress Lydia Languish when in reality it is with her elderly aunt, Mrs Malaprop, a woman who is to the English language what a mincer is to meat. Lydia is destined to discover in Mrs Malaprop's immortal words that 'all men are Bulgarians'.

It was that small encounter and the intervention of Mr Williams that started my love affair with the theatre, and soon I was a regular theatre-goer. I would catch the bus to Sheffield to see the touring companies at the Playhouse and the Lyceum or watch the Rotherham Rep at the Civic Theatre. I saw classic dramas and farces, musicals and period pieces, and would often see Mr Williams in the expensive seats nodding at me approvingly.

I think it was round about the time I was fifteen that the Broom Valley Lectures began, and Mr Williams encouraged the older boys in the school to attend these improving activities. These lectures, organized by a scholarly and good-humoured man called Mr Chislett, were given by celebrities and distinguished local people and held in the hall at my former primary school. Some of the lectures were mind-numbingly boring, others were way over my head, but others, like the lecture given by a great bearded doctor who growled from the stage, I remember well. Illustrated with wonderfully gruesome slides, he took his audience through a whole pathological journey describing the various deadly diseases. Another memorable lecture was given by Sir Mortimer Wheeler, one of the best-known British archaeologists of his day. He was a great believer that archaeology needed public support, and was assiduous in appearing on television and radio to promote his passion as well as touring the county lecturing. He stayed after his lecture to talk to the young people in the audience. I had never met a knight before and he appeared every inch what I imagined one would look like. There was Lady Isobel Barnett, a stalwart of the popular television programme *What's My Line?*, the local Member of Parliament, whose name I forget, and George Cansdale, the television vet. The lecturer who made the most impact on my young mind was the larger-than-life commentator, journalist and television pundit Malcolm Muggeridge. I recall his strange way of speaking – like a member of the Royal Family being strangled – his remarkable facial contortions, his incredible self-assurance and the way he spoke extemporaneously. He was a great orator, and his speech, like all memorable speeches, depended for its impact on telling little comments and anecdotes that seized the listeners' attention. There are phrases which still stay in my mind and which I wrote down, like, 'All of us admire people we don't like and like people we don't admire,' and 'People do not believe lies because they have to, but because they want to.'

At about this time I started to write a weekly journal, a sort of writer's notebook, which I still have. If I am asked by children to give them some tips on how to become a writer I tell them: 'Read, read and read, for on the back of reading is writing, and keep a notebook to record things. And persevere.'

In the notebook I kept, most of the speakers at the Broom Valley Lectures merited a few cursory entries but I must have been fascinated by Malcolm Muggeridge, for I scribbled a good page. Everyone seemed to come in for his acerbic comments: politicians, the royal family, the Russians, the Americans, the Church of England – he savaged them all. When quizzed from the floor about his unconventional views, he leaned back, pulled an incredible face as if he was suffering from chronic constipation and replied that he had never been 'conventional', for 'only dead fish swim with the stream'.

Those lectures gave me such an insight into public speaking – how the presenter has to gain eye contact, pepper his or her talk with some humour, tell an anecdote to gain the listeners' attention, use timing and pace and vary the voice, be aware of the audience and, most importantly, if the audience starts to fidget and look bored, sit down. Public speaking, I learnt, is like drilling for black gold: if you don't discover oil pretty quickly, stop boring.

35

Mr Williams was what one might call 'a successful deviant'. I mean this in the kindest way. He was out-of-the-ordinary, a bit eccentric, certainly not your typical 1950s headmaster, severe and distant, whom you only saw when you were in trouble. T.W. was a teacher at heart and one who passionately believed in education, particularly for those pupils who happened to be ill-favoured or disadvantaged. He had a confirmed belief that all young people, whatever their circumstances, could be inspired by and deserve good-quality education, and he would constantly reiterate in assembly, 'Believe in yourselves, boys. Work hard and the world is yours. Anything is possible, if you really want to do it and you are prepared to strive for it.'

Tim Williams started life in a Welsh mining village and possessed that 'hwyl' in no short measure, along with an extraordinary air of authority. Every pupil recognized this and was in awe of him, because he rarely stayed in his room and could be seen all around the building and, impressively, he knew the name of every boy in the school. He would pass a boy on the corridor and comment loud enough for all to hear.

'Well done in the football yesterday afternoon, Kelly. I hear from Mr Davies that you played a corker.'

'How's the piano coming along then, Sinclair? Another grade under the belt yet?'

'Bit more effort I hear is needed in science, Braithwaite. Buck up, boy.'

'I would like a quiet word with you, Mortimer. Morning break, my room.'

In trying to recall my schooldays at South Grove I contacted my former geography master, Alan Schofield, who wrote back to me with a memory of Mr Williams:

For me he was the very best headteacher I ever worked for. He was excellent at delegation, trusted his members of staff and had a genuine passion for education. There are many instances of his generosity I could mention but one in particular sticks in my mind. He and I were going to an evening meeting and crossing the church square in Rotherham when we came across a fairly disreputable-looking character. As we passed, the man stood up straight and said, 'Hello, sir.' Tim immediately recognized him as a former pupil and stopped and chatted to him affably until I reminded him that we were to attend the meeting and were running late.

'Have you eaten?' he asked the man.

'No, sir,' came the reply.

'Then get yourself a good hot meal,' said Tim and pushed a ten bob note into his hand.

I have never forgotten that act of kindness and the episode, for to me it symbolized his attitude to all people.

Mr Williams was well ahead of his time in that he took bullying extremely seriously. The prevailing attitude in the 1950s was that if you were bullied you should 'hit him back and he'll leave you alone'. It never worked for me and I guess it didn't work for a whole lot of other children. Those who were bullied often kept quiet and endured the taunts and the violence in case they were thought of as being weak or cowardly. They avoided secluded parts of the school and stayed within sight of a teacher whenever they could, spent the lunch hour in the school library, arrived at school early, before the bullies, and delayed their walk home. I was lucky in that my bullying was only in primary school, was short-lived and I had an elder brother to defend me. At South Grove I can't recall any incidents of bullying. I'm sure there were some, but it just seemed to me to be a very happy place in which to learn.

Prefects and House Captains took their responsibilities seriously, and each would have a group of boys to watch over and be a point of contact for. This mentoring system was way ahead of its time. Most bullying, Mr Williams must have been aware, would take place out of the teacher's orbit, so he was a stickler for staff being on yard duty and for constant checking of the pupils' toilets. The Head Boy and his Deputy would patrol the school at breaktimes and lunchtimes and each prefect would have an assigned area to supervise.

When I worked as an OFSTED inspector, the toilets seemed out of bounds for teachers in some schools. I remember that in one large secondary school I visited the boys' toilets, which were disgraceful: there was no paper in the cubicles, no locks on the doors, no soap or paper towels and the place stank. On the back of one of the cubicle doors was a long list of names. 'Sign here,' it said at the top, 'if you think the head is a stupid or contemptible person.' It was, of course, the colloquial terminology that the graffiti writer had used for 'stupid or contemptible person', which I will not repeat, but I am sure you get my drift. I have to say that I was sorely tempted to add my name to the list.

If there is to be smoking, drug-taking and bullying it is most likely to occur in the boys' toilets and Mr Williams knew this. Many was the breaktime when the headmaster would stride in to ensure we were there for the purpose for which the facility was intended.

T. W. walked the school each morning after the registers had been taken, peering in through each classroom window to ensure that the scholars were working and the teachers teaching. He would repeat this practice just before lunch and near the end of the day. Sometimes he would stride through the classroom door and ask the teacher what we were doing and occasionally he would join in the lesson, to recite a poem, tell us an interesting fact related to the subject or ask a question. I suppose there must have been 'supply teachers' in those days but I cannot recall any. If a member of staff was away, Mr Williams invariably 'filled in'. I loved his quick wit, his wry sense of humour and I marvelled at his ability to tell a story. In those lessons he would take the opportunity to get to know about us and to discuss current affairs. Sometimes he would recite a poem, predictably by a Welsh poet – R. S. Thomas, Edward Thomas or Dylan Thomas – at other times he would relate a folk tale or tell a story.

In one lesson he related the story of the duck that waddled around the farmyard quite content. A bemused visitor enquired why the duck didn't fly away. It seemed in good health, with the wings to fly, but it made no attempt to take to the air. The farmer explained that as a duckling it had been tied to a post. At first it had tried to fly but the cord held it down. After many, many attempts the duck gave up. When it was free of its restraining cord the duck never tried to fly. You see it did not think it could. 'It's the same with you boys,' said Mr Williams. 'Never assume you are incapable of doing something. You must always try, have a go, chance your arm, try your wings. You might surprise yourself.'

I still see him now, with his pale face, dark smiling eyes and silver hair, and hear that deep resonant voice filling the classroom. Mr Williams was a generous, good-natured and dedicated man and will be remembered with great affection by the many pupils who attended South Grove.

There was not one subject I disliked at school. I loved art with the gently spoken Mr Cooper (Harry), in his old brown overall and polished black shoes. The art room was an Aladdin's cave of skulls, feathers, stuffed animals, old clocks, bits of driftwood, shells, pebbles, rocks, broken pottery, tins, boxes and all manner of objects and artefacts which Mr Cooper had collected over the years and which he thought might be useful when we came to sketching and painting. I recall that once two student teachers from the Rotherham College of Art took us for a week while Mr Cooper was away. With the best of intentions they decided to tidy up the art room and get rid of much of the clutter. Mr Cooper was not best pleased when he returned. It wasn't long before the room was back in its disorganized state. In the after-school art club, when a cleaner commented on the difficulty of cleaning such a messy room, Mr Cooper, tapping the ash from his cigarette (he would always light up after official school hours but constantly warned us of the dangers of 'the noxious weed'), observed that 'Genius is seldom tidy, my dear Mrs Sutton.' What a school inspector would make of that jumble of detritus in this day and age, I can make a shrewd guess, but we produced some excellent pieces, many of which won national competitions and were displayed in the local library.

It was not for Mr Cooper to have us copy out of books, trace figures, cut out shapes he had drawn, screw up tiny pieces of white tissue paper to stick on an outline of a sheep, or any of the other mindless activities I have sometimes witnessed in schools. We were shown how to mix paints, use a variety of pencils, mould clay, print fabrics and illuminate our calligraphy. We worked in inks, chalks, watercolours, poster paints, pencil, and always from first-hand experience, from the real thing, carefully observing, recreating in sharp detail, mixing the colours exactly.

Alec, my brother, was his star pupil and went on to art school and a very successful career in painting and music. I remember that once at the after-school art club, when I was in the first year, Mr Cooper looked at my pathetic effort – a clumsy drawing of a green wine bottle and bowl of fruit – with a critical eye, a cigarette dangling from his lips. 'I think the skill with the paintbrush stopped with your brother,' he remarked sadly.

When he had moved on to look at John Pacey's work, I screwed up my painting, threw it in the bin and left the room, angry tears stinging my eyes. The next morning a school prefect came to fetch me at registration. I was to report to Mr Cooper. I knew I would be in trouble for storming out of the room and not clearing up all the paints and brushes I had used. I waited outside the art room, rehearsing in my head what I would say to him. The door opened and the teacher emerged.

'I am sorry for what I said yesterday,' Mr Cooper said quietly and rather shame-facedly. 'I was in the wrong to compare you with your brother. I thought what a foolish thing it was to say as soon as I had said it and I meant to have a word with you at the end of the session but you went home. I can quite understand why you left. Anyway, I'm sorry. I hope you will accept my apology.'

'Yes sir,' I said. I could feel my heart thumping in my chest – a teacher apologizing to a pupil was unheard of.

'Thank you,' he said, and held out his hand for me to shake.

'It *was* pretty poor though, sir, wasn't it?' I asked him.

'I'm afraid it was,' he replied, smiling.

A teacher who admits to his mistakes and is prepared to apologize to a pupil gains infinitely more respect than one who is never in the wrong and sees the words 'I'm sorry' as a weakness. Mr Cooper went up greatly in my estimation that day.

Mr Payne (Chipper), who taught woodwork, never compared me unfavourably with Alec but he kept a constant reminder of how much better my brother was in that subject. Just inside the door of the workshop was a large square cabinet displaying all the masterpieces created by the most talented pupils over the years. There were perfectly executed examples of dovetail and mortise and tenon joints, polished wooden bowls, table lamps, veneered chessboards, ebony paperknives, carefully crafted serviette rings and carved figures. In the centre, in pride of place, was a beautiful inlaid box in different coloured woods with brass hinges and catch. A small label told everyone that this was the work of Alec Phinn. I suppose Mr Payne thought that I would be 'a chip off the old block', but he was soon disabused when he examined my first pathetic efforts in wood. Over that first year the only 'masterpiece' I managed to produce was a shoeshine box in pine. It was a strange-looking container, with a lid and a raised piece in the shape of a shoe and a space beneath for the various polishes, dusters and brushes. 'Unusual' was Mr Payne's assessment when I had completed this work of outstanding artistry. I took it home and proudly presented it to my father, who promptly tried it out by resting his foot on the raised piece. The construction collapsed under the weight, much to the amusement of my brothers and sister, who laughed heartily. I stormed upstairs, refusing Alec's offer to try and repair it for me. I later threw the remains on the fire in the living room, watching the bits of wood crackle and burn.

I was not a whole lot better at metalwork with Mr Blowfield (Gerry). He was a patient, good-natured man with fluffy outcrops of silver hair and a round rust-coloured face. He was never seen out of his steel grey overall. On playground duty or in assembly, on sports day and on parents' evenings, he always wore his overall. Mr Blowfield had a display cabinet too, and my brother Alec's bronze figure had pride of place within it, among all the masterpieces created by the most talented pupils over the years. After a year of cutting, filing, rasping and polishing I managed to produce a garden trowel (the handle later fell off) and a poker. The poker survived many years of constant use and proved an excellent implement when my father was making holes in the ground to plant his seeds.

I was a very indifferent scholar when it came to science. I recall little of Nobby Clark's lessons, but I do remember when one of the pupils (I shall save his embarrassment by not naming him) was sent to the Rotherham abattoir to collect some cows' eyes for dissection in the lesson. The boy kept a few of the eyeballs back and secreted them in a girl's pencil case. At the beginning of the lesson, reaching for her pen, the poor girl picked up a large, slimy, bloodshot eyeball and screamed blue murder. Unfortunately for the prankster, he was discovered and for his pains received three strokes on the backside. But he felt it was worth it.

It was at secondary school that I started to enjoy mathematics. This was because the teacher, Mr Duffield (Ted), made the lessons interesting and unthreatening. He was an even-tempered, immensely patient and good-natured man who used a very adroit and successful teaching technique. He would explain a mathematical concept clearly and slowly on the blackboard, twirling the chalk around in his fingers, and then ask, 'Put your hand up if you have understood what I have just said?' Of course most teachers would ask the opposite, 'Put your hand up if you do *not* understand,' and it would take a pretty confident pupil to raise a hand and display his ignorance to all the class. Mr Duffield's question was clever. One or two hands might be raised tentatively from the more confident among us. He would then ask a pupil to come out to the front of the class and teach the lesson again, stepping in on occasions to tweak or elaborate on the explanation. Then he would ask again. 'Put your hand up now if you understand.' It might take several re-runs of the lesson but in the end we had a firm grasp of the concept.

I started getting really good marks in maths. My mental arithmetic improved: 'Practice makes perfect,' Mr Duffield would say, 'so never miss an opportunity of working things out in your head at the shops, on the bus, before you go to sleep.' I soon mastered logarithms, sines and cosines, trigonometry and mensuration and found geometry fascinating.

But then, with O levels looming, I had to face my *bête noire*

– algebra. I just could not get my head around it. I would sit there at the table staring at the equations but not knowing where to start.

$$A = \underline{a + b} \cdot h.$$
$$2$$

Express b in terms of A, a and h

My brother Michael would try to help and sit with me going through the problem, but to little avail.

A few months before I sat my O levels I was on prefect duty in the yard when Mr Duffield approached. 'We have to do something about your Achilles' heel,' he said.

I glanced down at my feet, never having come across this expression before.

'Pardon, sir?'

'Your vulnerable part,' the teacher explained. 'Your weakness. Algebra.' The very word made me shudder. 'Once you have grasped the idea it's relatively easy, but we need to work at it. What about spending a few lunchtimes going through some problems with me?'

It was the last thing I wanted, but how could I refuse? 'Yes, sir,' I agreed, unenthusiastically.

'Tuesday suit?'

'I have chess club,' I explained.

'Wednesday?'

'I'm on prefect duty, sir.'

'Thursday?'

I could see I couldn't wriggle out of this one. He was nothing if not persistent.

'Thursday's fine, sir.'

The following Thursday I duly presented myself at Mr Duffield's classroom for my first experience of private tuition.

Mathematics was taught at the back of the hall. A partition

made of wood and glass would be slid across the middle of the hall after assembly and the desks and chairs rearranged to form a classroom. That first session was memorable not because I learnt much about algebra but because I was privy to an altercation between Mr Firth and a recalcitrant pupil who had been caught bullying a younger boy.

I had just started on a question with Mr Duffield – one of those deeply uninteresting and problematical kinds: 'A man goes into an ironmonger's shop and buys 4lb (four pounds) of rivets at 3/2 (three and tuppence) per pound; in a second shop he buys 2lbs (two pounds) of similar rivets at 3/6 (three and sixpence) per pound. What was the average price in shillings per pound paid for the rivets? How many pounds of rivets could be bought for one pound at this average price?'

Being of an imaginative disposition, my first observation was why would the man want to buy the same rivets from two different shops? Secondly, when he found that the second iron-monger charged more for the very same rivets why didn't he complain or return to the previous shop and buy his rivets there? These mathematical questions about dripping taps and fish swimming against the current always seemed to me to be silly.

This lesson to me was far from riveting until there was an almighty crash against the partition. The wood shuddered, the glass rattled and from the side of the structure came Mr Firth's booming voice.

'I'll teach you to bully people!' came his thunderous tones. Thump, bang, rattle, shudder. 'It's not nice to be bullied, is it?' Thump, bang, rattle, shudder. 'You touch him again and I'll have your guts for garters!' Thump, bang, rattle, shudder.

A moment later a round red head appeared around the door.

'I trust I didn't disturb you too much, Mr Duffield?' asked Mr Firth.

'No, not at all,' replied Mr Duffield calmly. 'Now, young Phinn, let's get back to the rivets.'

36

Cliff Davies, the P.E. and games teacher, was a muscular little individual with a real smoker's habit. His white moustache was edged with a brown nicotine stain, and many was the time I saw him with an untipped, harsh, ill-named Woodbine ('coffin stick') dangling from his lips. He was a remarkably agile man and in P.E. he would demonstrate handstands and flick–flacks, rope climbing and vaulting in his baggy blue tracksuit before we were encouraged to try. He took up golf when he was fifty and won every trophy at Sitwell Golf Club. I tried at P.E. but was pretty useless. I could just about manage a handstand, a forward roll, a clumsy leap over the vaulting horse and a slow climb up the ropes, but I could do little else. I could never emulate my friend Peter's feats of athleticism, but my incapacities never incurred criticism from Mr Davies.

South Grove had no playing fields, just a tarmacadam yard at the top of which were the old air raid shelters in which we changed for P.E., which took place in the all-purpose hall. There were no showers, so after our physical exertions there was quite a smell of sweaty bodies in the classroom.

For games we trekked through town and up to Herring-thorpe playing fields, come rain or shine, to use the pitches there. When we came to a road Mr Davies would march into the middle, hold up his hand and stop the traffic so we could cross. I enjoyed football but, as Mr Davies described me on my report, I was 'a boy who always tries his best but is a middling player'. His assessment was on the generous side. I was not a middling player, I was a poor player, a blundering liability in the team, always in the way of a pass or unintentionally blocking an open lane. Wearing my father's old football boots with the long laces and bulbous toe caps and leather studs, baggy black shorts and an old T-shirt, I galloped up and down the field on scraggy legs like a frightened rabbit, chasing a ball with which I never seemed to come into contact. The more I tried the more I was ignored. Many of the other players were really good, in fact several went on in later life to play for professional teams, but I always ended up in what they called 'the scrags', the last few to be picked by the team captains. I would stand there with the small, the fat, the clumsy and the apathetic and always be placed as a full back, out of the way, where I could do least harm. I still recall that heavy sodden leather ball arching its way through the air towards me and Mr Davies shouting from the touchline, 'Get stuck in, Phinn! Boot the ball, lad!' I was slow, clumsy and not over-keen on tackling the big lads wearing massive boots like Desperate Dan's in the comics. It was my distinction that after five years of playing football once a week, I never scored a goal.

It was quite a common occurrence when the match was in full play for a woman pushing a pram to take a short cut across the playing fields and walk straight across the pitch, weaving in and out of the players quite oblivious of the danger. We often had a stray dog join the game and run round the field after the players and ball, barking madly and causing mayhem until it was chased off.

Since I was so poor at sports and gymnastics, it came as a surprise in the fifth year when Mr Davies told me I was to be Captain of House. There were four houses at South Grove, named after four stately homes, Chatsworth, Welbeck, Sandbeck and Wentworth, and I was told I would be Captain of Chatsworth. Despite my protestations that I was unfit for such a position, being a pretty hopeless sportsman, I was given a little green metal shield to pin on my blazer lapel with 'House Captain' on it. Mr Davies explained that the position of house captain was more than just competing in the various sporting events. He wanted someone reliable, well-organized and popular with the other boys, who was able to 'rally the troops'. I felt very uncomfortable in this new role, particularly since the other house captains were extremely good at sport. What I found remarkable was that there was no resentment from boys much better suited than I to hold such a position. They were generous in their congratulations.

The only sporting contest I took part in was the swimming and I hardly distinguished myself, coming in second or third in most events. I did come first by sheer chance in the breast-stroke once when the swimmer streaking out in front (he literally did streak out in front) suddenly slowed down because his trunks slid down his legs and, much to the spectators' amusement and his embarrassment, he stopped to retrieve them.

I recall one boy at a swimming gala asking Mr Davies, who was dressed in a blue blazer and white flannels for the occasion, if it was allowed for the swimmers to breathe underwater. Mr Davies shook his head and sighed. 'And what do you think would happen, you silly boy, if you were to breathe underwater?' The youth thought for a moment. 'Would you be disqualified, sir?'

Cliff Davies was in charge of making sure everyone was in school uniform. I knew there were boys in the school worse off than myself and they had free school meals but I wasn't aware of any great differences – certainly not in the way we dressed. This was in part because Mr Davies made sure every boy in the school was well turned out, and he would frequently remind us that in the street we represented the school and needed to look smart. He would check the uniform religiously and, I learnt later when talking to one of my former teachers, would provide a black blazer with red badge, black and red striped tie, flannels and black shoes to any pupil whose parents couldn't afford them. This made sense, for I remember once taking a parcel wrapped in brown paper from home addressed to Mr Davies. When I enquired of my mother what was inside she didn't tell me. I guess it must have contained some of my school clothes that I had grown out of. In his room Mr Davies kept a box with shoe polish and brushes, and any boy wandering around the school with scuffed shoes was obliged to go and polish them.

Bert Gravill, a former army major, with a spine as straight as a gun barrel, was in charge of music. In assembly he would sit on the stage behind the old upright piano banging out a hymn tune. I would stand outside the hall hearing the stirring music and loud singing, wishing I could be a part of it. I would hum along with 'Onward, Christian Soldiers' and 'Fight the Good Fight' and wonder why Protestants had all the best hymns.

Mr Schofield was in charge of geography. He was a sensitive, tolerant man, always willing to listen but not a soft touch. He was never too preoccupied to talk informally to the pupils at breaktimes or too impatient to go over an explanation again if we were unsure. His classroom, decorated with great coloured maps, posters, newspaper cuttings, postcards and photographs, was kept neat and tidy. We would line up outside in silence, file in, stand behind our desks, wish him a 'Good morning, sir', and then be told to sit. Trained as a primary teacher, I guess he never possessed the letters after his name but he was a natural teacher who enjoyed teaching, handled dissenting voices with humour and always made us feel valued. Those of us who have been teachers know only too well how daunting it can be to stand in front of a group of large, volatile adolescents, not accustomed to sitting still and listening, and attempt to engage their attention and get them to do as they are told. It is important to appear strong and fearless, even if it is an act.

Many years later Mr Schofield, then in his eighties, came to hear me when I appeared on stage at the Strode Theatre in Street. I sat in the bar after my performance with his wife and family and we reminisced. He reminded me of the time he joined in with the laughter when a boy by the name of Paul Watson asked about a particular rock that his father had sent into school to be identified. It had traces of a coloured metal in it.

'Do you know what it is, sir?' asked the pupil.

The bright spark of the class, quick as a flash, shouted out, 'It's sedimentary, my dear Watson!'

Eventually the manager of the theatre had to ask us to leave. Before he left I held my former teacher in my arms and acknowledged him as the great teacher he was. I wanted to repay that fondness and respect that he had showered on me. Sadly, Alan Schofield died the following year.

Mr Jones was six foot three and a former Welsh Guards officer and only remained at the school for a short time. I guess he must have been filling in until he secured a more prestigious position in some public school, for he was certainly different from the other teachers. He was nicknamed 'Bobbin' John' from his habit of walking briskly down the corridor with a spring in his step, an unusually straight back and his head in the air. He seemed to bob along. He had an inordinately white complexion, bloodless as a bone dug out of a dusty pit, and a wonderfully clipped accent. Everyone said he was a hero and had rows of medals, but we could never get him to talk about the war. He invariably wore a blue blazer with brash gold buttons, carefully pressed flannel trousers, a crisp white shirt, striped military tie and highly polished black shoes. The boys would mimic his 'posh' voice and his straight-backed walk but he never, as he could have, resorted to the cane, the slipper or the metre rule. Mr Jones taught me to play chess, and each weekday lunchtime in the library (little more than a large bookcase at the rear of Mr Pike's English room) there would be pairs of serious-faced boys staring at each other across the tables with chessboards between them.

In 1961 the boys' and the girls' school amalgamated and women teachers, along with their pupils, made an appearance. Mrs Cartwright was already a teacher in the boys' school and I looked forward to being taught by other attractive and youthful women teachers. The new women staff, however, proved to be something of a disappointment to a youngster full of testosterone. They appeared old and plain. But then there was the consolation of having lessons with girls.

My favourite subjects at secondary school were English with Mr Dyeball and Mr Pike and history with Mr Firth. Although I passed my O levels (not all with flying colours, I should add), these were the only two subjects in which I showed any distinction. As Miss Greenhalgh had reminded me when I visited my former infant school, I wasn't 'top table' material. I was a plodder, a trier, one who had a reasonable memory for facts, a determination to succeed and a fear of getting into trouble. I guess for most of my teachers I was a very indifferent sort of scholar.

In the first two years at secondary school I had Mr Dyeball (Eddie) for English. He was a grammarian and a disciplinarian but he was fair, had no favourites and taught us the basics of grammar, punctuation and spelling with a real enthusiasm. He was a tall, slim man with jet black hair scraped back on his scalp and a neat parting to the side. He was always immaculately dressed, usually in dark suit, white shirt and college tie, and in the form picture taken at the end of my second year (when he was my form teacher) he sits in the middle of the rows of boys, knees together, arms folded tightly over his chest, smiling widely in his Prince of Wales check.

I used to enjoy parsing sentences – noun, finite verb, limitation of finite verb, etc. – and I was good at it. I can't see the point in mastering such a dry and esoteric practice now, but when you are good at something that others find difficult, you enjoy the success and feeling of superiority. It was the same with logarithms with Mr Duffield in maths. I have never ever in my life found occasion to use them, nor a slide rule, nor a simultaneous equation for that matter, but I enjoyed the challenge and the sense of achievement in getting things right. But I digress. Mr Dyeball gave me a solid grounding in the basics of the language which has been invaluable. He taught me the parts of speech, how to punctuate a sentence and how to spell. Every few weeks he would teach the class a spelling rule and give us a list of words to learn. I still have in my dusty old English book, rescued from the attic some years ago, the list of rules and the accompanying words to memorize, written in black ink and in carefully formed letters. He was a conscientious marker and corrector of work, and in red at the bottom of each of my essays he would write what he called his 'ideas for improvement', using phrases like 'Your work contains a superabundance of expressive adjectives,' or 'You have a good eye for description but don't overdo it.'

I still possess my English exercise books, all backed in brown paper as was the requirement. In them are letters, compositions, dictations, punctuation exercises, spelling lists, handwriting practice, grammar exercises, all surprisingly neat for a twelve-year-old and all carefully marked. There were also listed at the back of the books a set of 'Rules of Spelling':

> 'i' before 'e'
> Except after 'c'
> (Or when it's 'eigh',
> As in 'neighbour' or 'weigh').

Then there were what the teacher called his 'little wrinkles'. These were clever ways of remembering difficult spellings:

> The principal pal of the principal
> Is always polite on principle.

NECESSARY: one coffee and two sugars
ACCOMMODATION: two cottages and two mansions
ACCELERATE: two cars and one lorry
ACCEPT: two comics and one paper
DEFINITE: definitely no letter 'a'

There were also acronyms to help us remember:

BECAUSE: Big elephants can always understand small elephants.
RHYTHM: Rejoice heartily, your teacher has measles.
EMBARRASS: Every mother's boy acts rather rudely after some sausages.
WEIRD: When ever I run, disaster.
DIARRHOEA: Died in a Rolls Royce having over-eaten again.

Some years later in a school I came across another acronym, perhaps rather more memorable but more risqué, for helping older pupils in a biology A level class to remember how to spell one of the difficult words: 'Dash in a real rush, help, or exploding arse.' I don't think Mr Dyeball or Mrs Cartwright would have approved.

In the exercise books there were also 'Hints for Pronouncing "Ough"':

Though the tough cough and hiccough plough me through,
O'er life's dark lough, my course I still pursue.

Teachers like Mr Dyeball increased my fascination with this tricky, troublesome language. Should Mr Dyeball hear a boy using an expletive, however, the slipper would be produced. He had the remains of a plimsoll, just the thin rubber sole (nicknamed Sam) which he would use infrequently on any boy who misbehaved or used rude words. One day two boys felt it across their backsides for getting in a fight after school.

Mr Dyeball turned the corner of the red brick building to find the two young pugilists, red-faced and furious, facing up to one another.

'Don't you call me a bastard, ya bastard!' shouted one, holding his fist aloft just as the teacher appeared as if on cue, like the villain in a pantomime.

'My room!' ordered Mr Dyeball. Sam was produced from the bottom drawer of the desk and put to good use.

Another time a pupil brought to school a small, multi-coloured ball called 'Superball'; they were the rage at the time. When thrown down, this amazing ball bounced off the floor incredibly high and shot off in every direction. The boy was telling us about the amazing qualities of his 'Superball' when another pupil snatched it from his hand and threw it at the floor. To great cheers it bounced up high and ricocheted off the ceiling, bounced again and smashed the light fitting just as Mr Dyeball entered. He always seemed to appear at the opportune moment. The culprits owned up and received their punishment bravely, returning to their desks rubbing their rears and trying to stem the tears.

On another occasion a boy stuffed a blackjack in his mouth just when the bell sounded for the end of break. Blackjacks were liquorice chews and could be bought for a penny each, and they turned the inside of your mouth a really ghastly black colour for several hours. Eddie's pet hate was boys chewing in class.

On this particular day it was unfortunate for the blackjack chewer that he was the one at whom Mr Dyeball directed his first question. Despite his heroic efforts, the boy was unable to disguise the fact that he had a mouthful of sticky black chew and when he began to speak he sounded like Charles Laughton playing Quasimodo in the film version of *The Hunchback of Notre Dame*.

'Whatever is wrong with you this morning?' demanded the teacher. 'Spit it out, lad!'

And the boy did just that – right across the desk. This was accompanied by loud 'Uuuuurrrrghs' and 'Arrgggghhhs' from the other pupils. Mr Dyeball opened his bottom drawer and we knew what was in store for the miscreant.

Sam didn't last much longer after this incident. One boy, I forget who it was now, but I guess it was one who had felt the stinging pain of the slipper across his backside in the past, crept into the classroom and posted Sam down the grille at the back of the classroom. Behind the grille there was a pipe leading down into the boiler room and the heating system. One cold afternoon, when the heating was full on, the most awful smell of burning rubber emanated from the grille. We all knew it was Sam slowly smouldering beneath us. Mr Dyeball never did find out.

Ken Pike, who later went on to become the distinguished headteacher of Spurley Hey High School in Rotherham, taught me for my O levels in English Language and English Literature. He was an inspirational teacher who spoke with wonderful conviction and developed in me a love of language and a passion for literature.

As an inspector I often used to think that if the material were to be appropriate to the age and maturity of the students, and if the teacher managed to interest and challenge them, if they possessed some sensitivity, understanding and had a sense of humour, there would be far fewer discipline problems in schools. It is often when the lessons are dull and the teacher lacklustre that poor discipline emerges. Mr Pike had a great sense of humour. It is of inestimable importance that teachers do have a sense of humour, indeed a sense of fun.

37

For O level English Literature we studied *Macbeth*, *A History of Mr Polly*, an anthology of poems called *Fresh Fields* and a collection of extracts entitled *The Comic World of Dickens*. I had never read Dickens before but devoured the O level text from cover to cover the day it was given to me, staying up late to do so. Charles Dickens had an immediate and deep resonance for me. He was unlike any novelist I had read before, creating wonderfully descriptive and unusual characters whose names have become embedded in the national consciousness: Betsy Trotwood, Mr Murdstone, Fagin, Little Dorrit, Lord Deadlock, Sarah Gamp, Mr Pickwick.

When, as an inspector of schools, I observed some tedious, ill-prepared lesson where the pupils trawled through Shakespeare or Seamus Heaney in maximum, pleasure-destroying detail, I would remember Mr Pike and think how lucky I was to have been taught by him. I could have listened to him for hours as he paced the front of the classroom declaiming Shakespeare or when he sat on the end of his desk reading the poetry or explaining some technicality in the English grammar system. His lessons were meticulously prepared, well taught and supported by invaluable notes, which I have to this day. Homework was set regularly and our books were marked rigorously (in pencil, not in red). On school inspections I used to dislike intensely the sight of children's work covered in red pen, as if the teacher had bled over it. No editor to my knowledge 'marks' a writer's work in red ink. My coveted distinction in English at O level was much to do with Mr Pike's excellent teaching.

Like all great teachers he did not stick slavishly to a script but would deviate and tell stories to arouse our interest. What I learnt from Ken Pike was the importance of young people having high expectations and self-belief.

When he and his wife Margaret bought a new house on Herringthorpe Valley Road with a large square plot of land at the back resembling a bomb site, Mr Pike asked if I would like to earn some extra pocket money and help him dig it over. I spent many a Saturday, with my friend Raymond Sadler, forking out the couch grass and the stones, uncovering bones and bits of clay pipe, the occasional corroded coin and rusty shard of metal, all the while watched by Mr Pike's three young sons. We talked as we dug, and I learned a great deal about books and literature. On those Saturday morning digs, my ongoing fascination with words and writing developed apace.

Mr Pike started a book club when I was in the second year. Each week pupils could, if they wished, bring in sixpence or a shilling and receive a coloured stamp with a picture on the front of some famous writer. Of course, Shakespeare commanded the two-shilling stamp, then came Chaucer, then Dickens, and for sixpence (the least we could pay) we got poor old Emily Brontë. We would buy a stamp at the end of the lesson and stick it into a small square book. At the end of the month an order was placed and a week or two later a box arrived containing all the purchases. It sounds pretty tame these days, but back then there was a deal of excitement when the brown box was delivered to the classroom and Mr Pike took out the contents and passed them around. He would handle each book almost lovingly, talk about it for a while and then dispense it to the boy who had bought it. I loved the smell of a new book and still do.

My very first purchase was *The Diary of Anne Frank*. The description in the catalogue had said it was a powerful and poignant account in diary form set during the Second World

War and was a story of great personal heroism and amazing courage. I didn't take a great deal of notice of the title, which, with hindsight, wasn't an altogether bad thing. I thought the book would be a rattling good action-packed war story, with lots of battles – a bit like D-Day Dawson, whose daring exploits I read each week in my comic. D-Day Dawson had a bullet lodged near his heart and could die at any moment, but, being the devil-may-care hero, he was totally fearless and carried on with winning the war, lobbing grenades at the Krauts, rattling his machine gun, creeping behind enemy lines, saving his pals and being bedecked with yet more medals for his outstanding bravery. D-Day Dawson was like all good British soldiers – he never did anything underhand or dishonourable. I was greatly disappointed when I started on the first page of *The Diary of Anne Frank* to discover it was a seemingly very ordinary account written by a girl who lived in an attic in Amsterdam. But I persevered and soon became intrigued by the details of every-day life, the petty squabbles, inconsequential conversations, small incidents and touches of humour, described by a bright, rather precocious girl spending her teenage years in a cramped apartment, while outside was the horror of the Occupation and the dreaded Gestapo. One entry I remember to this day: 'Whoever is happy,' wrote Anne, 'makes others happy.'

When I was invited to Amsterdam in 2001 to deliver a lecture there, I visited the house of Anne Frank and found it an immensely moving experience. Visitors walked around in silence, clearly very much affected by the photographs, diary extracts, letters, horrific facts and historical details shown on the displays. We walked through the small entrance to the upper floor, originally hidden by the bookcase. How could several families manage to survive in this space for so long? I asked myself. Still on the wall were the little cut-out pictures, one of Princess Elizabeth, which Anne had stuck up.

In 2002 I took my daughter Elizabeth to see the stage version of *The Diary of Anne Frank* at the Lyceum Theatre in Sheffield. I remembered sitting in that vast theatre, now beautifully restored to its former glory, all those years ago to see a very different production: *The Rivals*. Lizzie and I were now in the posh seats in the circle, but I glanced back to see the very top of the balcony where I had sat in the seats Mr Williams bought for me nearly forty years before.

At the end of the last act of the play, Anne runs down the stairs on stage chattering excitedly. She is now a young woman and tells her parents how good it is to be alive on such a bright sunny day. She is full of optimism and hope. Her mother and father, clasping each other, stand frozen centre stage. Beneath the stairs in the half-light, unseen by Anne, are two sinister figures in dark trench coats. The Gestapo have found them. When the curtain fell there was no applause. The huge theatre was completely silent. Then people left the theatre quietly, unhurriedly. Lizzie cried on the way home. The following day she read my old dog-eared copy, bought from the book club, of *The Diary of Anne Frank,* from cover to cover.

A Christmas treat at the school was the showing of a film to the whole school, crammed into the hall. It was a black and white film flashed on to a large white sheet pinned to the back of the stage, and the projector invariably broke down at various intervals, usually at the most exciting parts, to loud catcalls and whistles of disapproval. Being Christmas and near the end of term, the teacher operating the projector was tolerant of the noise. The film always seemed to be a Second World War drama like *The Cockleshell Heroes* or *The Cruel Sea*. In *Ill Met by Moonlight*, the youthful Dirk Bogarde was on stirring form as the British army officer given the task of working with the partisans in occupied Crete to kidnap a local Nazi commander. We booed when the Germans came on screen and cheered the British. We were all very patriotic in those days.

★

I guess I must have had a very pronounced Yorkshire accent when I was at school, but my teachers made no attempt to teach me to 'speak properly' as the poor woman in the primary school had attempted to do. Of course, Mr Dyeball and Mr Pike would correct us if we were slovenly in the way we spoke; they were quick to point out jargon, colloquialisms and slang and certainly would not tolerate swearing, but we were never criticized for the way we spoke. We were encouraged to answer questions, express our views, perform choral readings, read plays aloud in class, debate and make presentations. I am grateful for that, for to attack a child's way of speaking is to attack something which is so much a part of him, which he brings from his home and which he has learnt from his parents. I have met so many people with regional accents who had teachers who tried, by one means or another, to 'knock it out of them'. They have been corrected, held up to ridicule, given lines and sometimes punished for supposedly mispronouncing words.

So – I have been massively fortunate in my schooling. Much of what I hold dear was first shown to me by teachers like Miss Greenhalgh, Mr Williams, Mr Firth, Mr Schofield and Mr Pike. They inspired me, encouraged me, took an interest in me, and convinced me that, despite my humble background and my average abilities, I could achieve anything.

It was Mr Williams who decided that some of the Eleven Plus failures were bright enough to be entered for GCE O level and persuaded his staff and the local education authority to go along with him. It was unheard of at the time for a secondary modern school to enter students for external examinations, and it was thought by many that if these youngsters hadn't come up to scratch at eleven they wouldn't achieve much five years later. It is a fact that there are some of us in life who are 'late developers', and I have met many people who performed poorly at school but flourished in later life.

The prevailing view at the time was that the secondary

modern pupils would be best occupied studying practical subjects like woodwork, metalwork, technical drawing, rural studies, housecraft and cookery – to equip them for apprenticeships and the more menial jobs in society. Leave the academic stuff to the teachers at the grammar school.

The pupils at South Grove were the product of a working-class generation which clearly knew its place in the pecking order. At the time there was little in the way of aspiration for boys at the secondary modern beyond going down the pit, working in the steelworks or maybe getting an apprenticeship. They were raised in a close-knit, homogenous community and learnt not to have too many expectations, because this would only lead to disappointment later on. Young people, very largely, accepted this and knew their place in the world, their only ambition being to secure a job locally that they could keep for the rest of their lives.

Mr Williams, the product of a working-class Welsh mining family himself, thought otherwise. He believed that many of his pupils had real potential to succeed academically and he was determined to give them a chance. So the staff at South Grove embarked on an exciting initiative to teach the older pupils the O level syllabuses. It was a brave enterprise when I look back, for many of the teachers, I guess, were inexperienced in teaching for external examinations, unlike their colleagues up the road at the grammar school. My teachers were being tested themselves, and perhaps this was an added incentive for them to work with greater enthusiasm, drive and determination. In the event the cynics were proved wrong, for many of us left South Grove with a string of O levels, many with distinctions in the different subjects. For example, twenty-seven in Mr Pike's class passed O level English Language and twenty-two passed O level English Literature, with some, like myself, achieving the very highest grades.

It was impressed on us by the headmaster when we embarked

on the courses that we had to work very hard, spend a deal of time on our studies and be prepared to stay in at night to complete the large amount of homework that inevitably would be set. He also told us that the school was, in a sense, being tested and we should prove wrong those who didn't think we were capable.

Listening to Mr Williams telling us that we were the first in this new initiative, the guinea pigs, and that we shouldn't let him and the school down, I was determined to succeed and applied myself seriously to my studies. After school I would walk down Moorgate Road into town and straight to the public library, where I would spend a couple of hours in the peace and quiet of the reading room. It was an enormous, silent place with wall-to-wall shelving, large square tables and hard-backed chairs. It smelt reassuringly of floor polish and old books. I would sit at one of the large tables below a leaded window, which was set ten feet above the floor so that no one could peer in and those in the library would not be distracted by the bustling world outside.

The public library tended to attract a certain clientele. The regulars included the industrious mousy girl with round glasses poring over a textbook, the unshaven individual in the flat cap reading the *Rotherham Advertiser*, the intense-faced woman researching her family history, whose table was piled high with books, the elderly man come in out of the cold who gently snored in the corner and the sad-faced misfit, in the National Health glasses and wearing a ridiculous coloured bobble hat, who spent his time flicking aimlessly through a tome the size of a doorstep on some esoteric subject like *The Illustrated Encyclopaedia of Medieval Woodcuts*.

Behind the curved wooden counter sat Miss Tissiman, the librarian, scanning the room, ever alert and watching in case anyone should raise a voice or be seen eating.

I got to know Miss Tissiman well during the two years I

studied for my O levels. At first I was daunted by the prim little figure in the white blouse and grey pencil skirt, with silver hair scraped back savagely over her scalp and into a tight little bun. When I asked for a particular book she would emerge from behind her counter and lead the way to the appropriate shelf where the tome was to be found. On one occasion she came over to my desk, both hands clasped in front of her, and told me she had observed me using the books. I felt suddenly guilty of something. She then explained that when turning a page one should do so by sliding an index finger beneath the top of the page and turning it. 'To do as you are doing, turning the page from the bottom, damages the paper and leaves a thumb mark.' I apologized. She gave a small smile. 'Most people turn the page from the bottom. You are not alone in doing so.' Since then I have always turned the pages of a book the way the librarian taught me and passed the instruction on to those I have taught.

On another occasion, after she had rung her small bell to signify that the library was about to close, she stopped me and commended me on my diligence.

'Perhaps when you have completed your studies,' she told me, 'you might consider a career in a library. You clearly like books.' Then she gave a little smile before adding, 'And know how to handle them.'

The following week she presented me with a collection of pens, some paper and a pencil case, explaining that these had been left unclaimed in the library and perhaps I could make use of them.

Miss Tissiman was another person in my life who opened a door for me. As the O levels approached she suggested that I study some past papers, to give me an idea of the kind of questions which might come up, and on one occasion she sat with me, dictionary in hand, stressing that I should become very familiar with the words used by the examiners, words like 'consider', 'evaluate', 'assess', 'describe', 'estimate', 'calculate', 'justify' and 'summarize', because many a student has failed through not answering the question.

The week before the start of the three-week examination period I told the librarian that I wouldn't be coming into the library again for some time. She shook my hand and wished me well.

'Remember to read the questions carefully,' she said, 'check through your work and never leave the examination room early.' She gave a little smile. 'I'll be thinking of you.'

38

Mr Theodore Firth (Theo) was a very different sort of teacher from the other members of staff at South Grove. He was a stout, red-cheeked man with tufts of sandy-coloured hair at the side of an otherwise bald head and had a roar like a lion and a stare like the sweep of a scythe. He was the archetypal Yorkshireman: bullish, plain-speaking, lacking in sophistication, a no-nonsense sort of man who could put the very fear of God into his pupils. There was no pacing up and down the classroom for him, no sitting on the end of the desk and, above all, no noise. He would stand like some great Eastern statue, legs apart, arms folded over his barrel chest, jaw jutting out, surveying the neat lines of desks that faced the front of his classroom.

Many pupils lived in fear of this larger-than-life character, and when we entered his room we did so in complete silence and with great trepidation.

Mr Firth rarely addressed any pupil by his or her name. Boys were invariably called 'Johnny' and girls 'Mary', but in my last year at South Grove he started to call me Phinny or Phineas.

Mr Schofield recalls Theo thus:

When I first joined the staff at South Grove, I was greatly impressed by the number of strong characters, some of whom were very forceful. The most memorable was Theo Firth who specialized in history. He had a fearful countenance and his classroom was meticulously clean and ordered. Strangely enough he often came to school in an old sports jacket with leather patches on the arms, no tie, baggy corduroy trousers, plimsolls in the summer and Wellington boots in the winter, which made him look a somewhat bizarre, unkempt character. I often wondered what happened to his teeth, for his gums were bereft save for one large tooth, what he called his 'pickle-chaser'. When container dinners were served at the church hall near the swimming baths, Theo was always in charge of taking a contingent of dinner boys down Alma Road in perfect order. People often commented how well-behaved the pupils were. Of course, no boy would have been so foolhardy as to misbehave when Theo was in charge.

Young people these days clearly know a great deal more than I did at school on a whole range of subjects; they seem more adventurous, outspoken and sophisticated, but many I have met on my visits to schools sadly don't have the grasp of English history and knowledge of important historical dates that I had at their age. One reason for this is that history, when I was a lad, had a much higher status in the curriculum and was compulsory for all, but another, more important, is that I had a teacher who brought the subject to life.

At primary school I undertook projects about the Anglo-Saxons and the Celts, the Romans, the Egyptians, the Vikings and the Normans as children do today, and then at secondary school I started on the fascinating journey of discovery through the history of England and then Great Britain, learning about significant events and famous characters, important treaties and world-changing wars, great battles and life-changing inventions in chronological order. Now pupils choose their options and after the age of fourteen it may be the case that they never study history again.

Some would say that there is no room in education for teachers such as Mr Firth, those unusual individuals who are out of the ordinary, idiosyncratic, who don't always follow the various directives. In my view they are wrong. Such teachers frequently have a greater impact than the more conventional teachers and are often remembered years later when the 'ordinary' teachers have been long forgotten. Mr Firth was strict but he was scrupulously fair, totally committed but rather unpredictable and, provided you worked hard and were well-behaved, he posed no problem. He insisted on every pupil's undivided attention, neat and accurate writing and work to be completed on time. In answer to his questions he expected the right hand of the pupil to be raised straight as a die and for the pupil to answer clearly and confidently. He could, so I was told, be a violent man and rumours were rife about him. The only occasion when he lived up to this fearsome reputation was when I was in my last year at South Grove and witnessed him dealing with the bully while I was trying to get my head around algebra with Mr Duffield on the other side of the hall partition. I had never seen him hit a boy in any of the history classes I attended.

Even before I met the man, my brother Alec had related gruesome accounts about how Mr Firth had hurled an insolent pupil through a partition in the school hall and there was blood and broken glass everywhere. Another time he was reputed to have thrown a board rubber at an inattentive pupil and the unfortunate boy was been taken comatose to Doncaster Gate Hospital. Then there was the occasion when Theo had supposedly hit a boy so hard with his slipper that he had set the unfortunate miscreant's trousers on fire. Another time, it was said, he flicked, with unnerving dexterity, a piece of chalk which ended up lodged in a boy's nostril. Stories about Theo, largely invented I guess, were legion, and such a reputation did wonders for his discipline.

I recall my first history lesson with Mr Firth. We nervous first years queued up outside the history room as he walked up and down the line scrutinizing us as a sergeant-major might inspect his new recruits. We filed into the history room and were assigned seats (hard wooden desks with fold-up seats, lids and holes for inkwells, entirely unsuitable for growing adolescent boys with long legs), and, much to my chagrin, I was placed on the very front desk. Portraits of English monarchs lined the walls, with a timeline stretching above them, and at the front, dominating the room, was an impressive teacher's desk on a dais. At the side, under the window, was a substantial bookcase containing neatly stacked books and folders, a set of dictionaries and some reference texts. Directly outside the window, in full view of all the class, was a flagpole, which Mr Firth seemed to regard as his very own. On St George's Day the white flag with the red cross would be hoisted, and the Union Jack was flown on Trafalgar Day and the Queen's birthday. The Friday before Remembrance Sunday and on Armistice Day the Union flag flew at half-mast.

I began to really like history. I would sit silently, listening wide-eyed as Mr Firth related in his deep gruff voice stories which would later be written as notes on the blackboard for us to copy into our exercise books. We learnt of the tragic death of the noble Richard III ('maligned by Shakespeare and betrayed by his supposed friends'), the murder of the seventeen-year-old Duke of York in the Wars of the Roses ('beheaded by the perfidious Lancastrians and his head placed on a spike on the gates of York'), the ill-fated Queen Katherine of Aragon ('poor betrayed Spanish princess'), the embittered Mary Tudor and mad King George III. I learnt about Mary, Queen of Scots ('put to an untimely death by her jealous cousin, mishandled, traduced, a political pawn in the hands of the cold-hearted, treacherous Scottish lords'), the mighty Spanish Armada ('defeated by the plucky English sea-dogs'), the Gunpowder Plot ('which was all a put-up job by Queen Elizabeth's scheming adviser, the Lord Cecil'), the foolish and fanatical James II ('who threw his throne away') and poor, weak misguided Bonnie Prince Charlie ('the rightful King of England'). Of course he would tell us that there was the other side of the story; it depended on what accounts you read, but it was rare that the other side of the story was ever revealed to us. I still possess my history notebooks, which contain some memorable if suspect assertions: 'Henry VIII was a bloody tyrant who, when he could not get his own way or when anyone challenged his authority, resorted to murder. He had his chancellors beheaded, left his opponents to die lingering deaths in the Tower of London, killed off two of his wives and, because the Pope wouldn't give him his own way, broke from Rome and started his own church.'

We were given our exercise books and textbooks and instructed to back them in brown paper for the following lesson. We were told we must write neatly in fountain pen and warned that there would be serious repercussions for any foolhardy boy who failed to hand in his homework on time. He then reached for a stick of chalk and twirled it around in his fingers. We all covered our noses.

It sounds extremely daunting at first, but I soon learned that 'his bark was worse than his bite', that Mr Firth was a bit of a showman with unflinching opinions about the events of history. He was above all a performer, always master of his audience, always in command of the stage. Theo, like many impressive teachers, was something of an actor. I am sure he knew we were mimicking him when we were out of his sight, copying his rituals, his gestures, his way of speaking, his mannerisms, and I guessed he played up to his caricature.

I well recall his description of the Battle of Culloden. The ill-equipped and bedraggled clansmen were dragged from their homes in feudal observance to their chieftains to follow Bonnie Prince Charlie. Armed with only claymores and farming implements, they met the long ranks of heavily armed and disciplined English redcoats, who knocked them over like ninepins. Several pupils were asked to come out to the front of the class with rulers to represent the bayonets of the English troops and the claymores of the Scottish. Theo demonstrated that each English soldier had been instructed to bayonet the opponent to his right, who would be lifting his sword arm and thus exposing his body. In my mind I saw and heard the vivid picture of the English army in crimson jackets marching in strict order, bayonets fixed, the periwigged officers on white horses, the skirling of the Highland pipes and the wild rush of the tartan-clad clansmen.

Three incidents relating to Mr Firth remain in my mind. The first was when I was in the fourth year. A new boy arrived. We never found out exactly why he had suddenly appeared halfway through the O level course, but it was rumoured that he had been expelled from the grammar school for pinning a large bed sheet to the front of the school with 'FOR SALE' written in large letters on it. I shall call the new boy Desmond Smith, to save his embarrassment if he ever gets to read this. I guess now he is a highly successful businessman, entrepreneur or captain of industry, or some very upright judge or distinguished doctor. He was obviously very clever and the work he was set and the questions asked were no problem for him. But Desmond was a real handful, and I guess he had what these days a psychologist might diagnose as Attention Deficit Hyperactive Disorder. He just couldn't sit still for a moment or keep his mouth shut. From the start the new boy didn't seem at all in awe of Mr Firth. He would shout out, make comments and offer his unsolicited views, much to the teacher's irritation. The quiet calm and orderly routine of his classroom was disturbed and the teacher did not like it. In fact Theo looked somewhat unnerved on occasions and grimaced angrily. When he was in trouble with Mr Firth, which was most of the time, Desmond would be made to stand at the front where he would shuffle, fidget and pull faces. Amazingly, Mr Firth never hit him.

On one occasion Desmond returned to school after a few days' absence. He sauntered into the classroom, the last in the line, and took his place next to me at the front.

'And why were you off school, Smithy?' enquired Mr Firth.

'I was ill, sir,' came back the reply.

'Nothing trivial, I hope,' said Mr Firth, reaching for a stick of chalk.

On another occasion Mr Firth remarked rather caustically after he handed back our essays, 'You know, Smithy, keep up this standard of work and you have a promising future behind you.'

'Thank you, sir,' replied Desmond, smiling widely as if he had been given a rare compliment.

On one occasion the teacher asked the class why it was decided that Admiral Lord Nelson should be buried in Westminster Abbey. Desmond raised a hand. 'Because he was dead, sir?' Even Theo had to smile.

Desmond seemed unperturbed by the sometimes scathing wit of the teacher, but he must have been waiting for the moment to strike. We were all to discover that Desmond had this amazing skill. He could throw his voice. On one memorable morning, when Mr Firth turned to write his copious notes on the board, there was a clucking noise. The teacher swung around and glared.

'Who was that?' he demanded. There was an eerie silence as the teacher surveyed the blank faces staring back at him. 'I said who was that?' he repeated, raising his voice. He scanned the room. 'Who made that silly noise?' There was still no answer. 'Was it you?' he asked Desmond, who had been placed next to me at the front where the teacher could keep an eye on him.

'Oh no, sir,' replied Desmond in the most outraged voice. 'I don't even like chickens, sir.'

'Humph,' grunted the teacher. Then he addressed the class. 'I shall ask again, who made that silly clucking noise, and if the boy responsible does not own up, you will all remain in during break.' Of course, we all knew who the culprit was but we kept quiet. No one likes a sneak in a school. So that morning break we were all made to stay in. The following lesson,

each time Mr Firth turned his back on the class, there came
the clucking noise. No one dared laugh but inside we were
weeping with laughter. We remained in the classroom again at
morning break. After he had kept us in for the fourth consec-
utive break, Mr Firth had to concede that this was not the best
means of flushing out the phantom clucker because as soon as
the bell sounded for the end of break we would all rush out to
the toilets and then arrive late for the next lesson. Clearly Mr
Firth's colleagues had convinced him that there was a more
effective method of discovering the mischief-maker.

The next lesson and the one after that Mr Firth, much to
our surprise, ignored the clucking. I guess he knew it was
Desmond but the noise seemed to come from the back of the
room, which must have confused him. Mr Firth made certain
that there were few occasions when he had to turn his back
on the class, for when we arrived at the history room for the
last lesson of the week we found the notes already written on
the blackboard. As we copied them into our exercise books,
Mr Firth glowered at the front, legs apart, arms folded over
his chest. Desmond was obviously getting to him. But sometimes during that lesson the teacher forgot, and as soon as his
back was turned the phantom clucker struck again. The very
next lesson was on the Monday morning and, through sharp
observation, Mr Firth discovered the culprit. He was patrolling
the room, clutching a large textbook and ostensibly looking
over our shoulders to ensure we were writing neatly, when
there was a faint 'Cluuuuckkkk, cluuuuckkkk, cluuuuckkkk.'
Mr Firth ignored it and continued to stroll from desk to desk.
'Cluuuuckkkk, cluuuuckkkk, cluuuuckkkk,' came the noise
again. By now, after several lessons of clucking, we pupils had
all got quite used to the noise, so we carried on writing.
'Cluuuuckkkk, cluuuuckkkk, cluuuuckkkk,' came the noise
again just as Mr Firth arrived at Desmond's desk. The teacher
raised the great tome and brought it down with a resounding

thud on the boy's head with the words 'Cock-a-doodle-do!'
That was the last we saw of Desmond. The next lesson Mr
Firth warned us, I think with a twinkle in his dark eyes, 'And
anyone else who has the mistaken belief he is a chicken or any
other farmyard creature, I suggest he thinks on.'

The second memorable moment was when a parent came
up to school to 'get him'. I was in the fifth year and a prefect
on duty after school, standing at the top of the stairs by the
science labs making sure the pupils kept to the left, didn't run
and left the school quickly and quietly. Most of the pupils by
this time had gone home and I was about to go to the art club
when the excited voice of another prefect came up the stairs.

'Oi, Phinny, tha'd berrer come and see this!'

I ran down the stairs, three at a time, to see a teacher blocking the door as a very large and angry man, furiously red-faced,
attempted to enter the school. Mr Price, Head of Religious
Education and a very inoffensive and quiet-natured man, was
attempting to reason with the aggressive visitor.

'I'll cut 'is throat!' the man was shouting. 'So 'elp me, I'll
cut 'is throat! I'll murder t'bastard!' Then, catching sight of
me, he ordered, 'Thee theer, thee wi' bloody badge on thi
blazer, go and tell that theer Mester Firth to get down 'ere
now. I wants to see 'im! When I gets 'old of that bastard, I'll
cut 'is bleedin' throat, I swear I will.'

'You will do no such thing!' snapped Mr Price in my direction. 'Go and fetch Mr Williams, and be quick about it.'

I rushed up the stairs, three at a time, down the top corridor
and into the school office where I managed to gabble out to
Mrs Atkinson, the school secretary, what was happening. Mr
Williams, who had clearly heard my account, emerged from
his office which was the adjoining room, putting on his black
academic gown in the process. He told Mrs Atkinson to call
the police and to gather any other male members of staff who
might still be on the premises and tell them to report to him

at the school entrance. The headmaster then strode along the corridor and down the stairs, his gown billowing out behind him, to confront the aggressive visitor, with me at his heels trying to keep up. I wasn't going to miss this for the world.

I remember the headmaster was incredibly calm as he informed the furious parent that Mr Firth had gone home and that the matter about which he was so upset could be discussed and resolved when he had calmed down. The man was not placated and told Mr Williams, stabbing the air with a finger, to 'move out o' mi way or I'll move thee!' The headmaster informed the man calmly that he would have to get past him to get into the school and he stood his ground. I could see Mr Price tensing up for a fight. Disappointingly, no fight ensued. After more shouting and cursing, fist-shaking and spitting, the man departed.

It was the last history lesson before we went on study leave to revise for our O levels. We lined up as usual, filed into the room, sat at our desks, took out our books for the last time, and then there was a sudden eruption of laughter from the boys nearest the window. There, flying merrily in the wind at the very top of the flagpole, was a large pink bra.

'Quiet!' boomed Mr Firth, striding to the window. He turned to face us and we all went quiet. We expected him to explode with anger but he didn't. He pointed to the smallest boy in the class. 'Johnny, go down to that flagpole and remove that offending piece of lingerie.'

No one, in my experience, argued with Mr Firth and the boy dutifully ran out of the classroom.

A minute or two later Mr Firth opened the window, stuck his head out and shouted, 'Lower it down!'

'Can't, sir,' came back the reply from the boy, 't'rope's bust.'

'What?' roared the teacher.

'Rope's been yanked off, sir. I can't gerrit down.'

'Well, climb up the flagpole and remove that brassiere!'

The idea today of a pupil shinning up a flagpole is unthinkable, but in those days no one gave it a second thought.

We had to remain in our seats but eventually the boy's head could be seen appearing at the window as he shinned up the pole. We were itching to get out of our seats to get a closer look. The boy fastened himself like a limpet to the top of the flagpole and reached up to get the bra. In one great yank he pulled it loose and held it up in triumph. This was accompanied by loud cheers.

'Quiet!' ordered the teacher.

The bra was brought back to the classroom and placed on Mr Firth's desk. It was a substantial garment of a bright salmon pink, and as it lay before the pile of books it looked like two mountains. The boy who had retrieved the garment was smirking fit to burst but Mr Firth ignored him. 'Does this belong to anyone?' he asked, holding up the bra. There was a strange quaver in his voice.

Trying desperately to stifle our laughter we all shook our heads and replied in unison, 'No sir.' Then there was a splutter from the back, a stifled giggle and a snuffling as we all tried to stem our mirth.

Then something quite amazing happened. Mr Firth blinked, his jaw tightened, he bit his lips momentarily and he forced a small smile. Then he tipped his head back and laughed. It was a loud, deep-throated belly laugh and we all joined in. How we laughed that morning. It was so loud and spontaneous that Mr Williams, on his ritual tour of the school, appeared at the door. We stopped laughing immediately and sat up at the sight of the headmaster. Mr Williams entered the room. We all stood. He caught sight of the large pink bra and looked baffled.

'Is everything all right, Mr Firth?' he asked.

'Perfectly, headmaster,' came the reply. 'Perfectly.'

39

I considered myself very lucky as a boy because, unlike some of my friends, I had two holidays in summer. There was my week in Blackpool, and then I went with the school on summer camp to the Isle of Man for a full fortnight. A hundred boys aged eleven to fifteen, ten members of staff, some with their wives and families, the school cooks and Vic Globe, the school caretaker, with his wife Dorothy and children Ray and Jane, would set off in three coaches from the top of Alma Road and journey to Liverpool, where we would take the ferry to Douglas, then another coach to Port Erin, and spend two memorable weeks on the small island. There were no seat belts on the coaches and the smaller boys sat three to a seat. Teachers would be locked up these days for such supposed irresponsibility, but this was in the 1950s and there was little said about health and safety.

If you were on Mr Dyeball's coach or Mr Clark's you had a full three-hour journey to chatter, play games or sleep (we had to set off at the crack of dawn to miss all the traffic). We only sang ('Ilkley Moor Baht 'at', 'She'll Be Coming Round the Mountain' (the clean version), 'Ten Green Bottles' and 'Old MacDonald Had a Farm'), on the way home. Eddie and Nobby sat in the front seats with their wives, and provided we didn't get out of our seats, block the driver's rear view mirror, wander up and down the aisle or make too much noise we were left alone. It was a different matter in Mr Firth's coach. He would commandeer the microphone from the driver and give a running commentary all the way, pointing out places and buildings of historical interest.

'We are now passing from the White Rose County to the Red. Some of you will recall what I taught you about the Wars of the Roses. The bloodiest battle of the war took place at Towton near here where the river ran red with blood'; 'It is said that Cardinal Wolsey, on his journey south to meet Henry VIII after his unsuccessful attempt to arrange a divorce for the King, stopped at Caywood Castle which is a stone's throw from here.' Much as I liked history, this was too much like school. On one journey to Liverpool the bus driver must have been equally irritated by this constant stream of historical information and surreptitiously flicked the switch, turning the teacher off. Mr Firth, oblivious of the fact that no one could hear him, rattled on regardless while behind the seats we all played our games and whispered to each other.

I have never found it at all surprising that many people have a nostalgic feeling about islands. In their minds these bits of land set in vast empty oceans have a mystique all of their own. The Isle of Man was as different from Rotherham as any place could be, with its clear azure seas, great towering cliffs, quaint stone cottages, great castles, long promenades, miniature steam trains and cats without tails.

On the ferry from Liverpool to Douglas we sometimes faced high seas. While most of us were leaning over the side or in the toilets heaving and splashing, with the sea heaving and splashing outside, Theo would be in the bar with a bacon sandwich and a pint of Guinness. On route from Douglas to Port Erin we passed over the Fairy Bridge. We all had to shout, 'Moghrey mie, Vooinjer Veggey – Good morning little people,' or we would have rotten weather. On our way back, after two gloriously sunny weeks, we would have to chant, 'Fastyr mie, Vooinjer Veggey' – 'good afternoon little people' and then, 'Gura mie – Thank you.'

We stayed at Castle Rushen Primary School, a squat, grim, grey building at the crossroads to Port Erin and Port St Mary, sleeping in the classrooms. The teachers' rooms, down one end of the corridor, and the cooks' rooms, down the other, had iron bedsteads, squares of carpet and curtains at the windows. We had none of these luxuries. Our accommodation was basic to say the least. The classrooms had been cleared of the heavy lidded desks, hard-backed chairs and cupboards and we set up our canvas camp beds in rows on the hard wooden floor. There was no place for modesty and no chance of privacy, and any peeping Tom so inclined could peer through a classroom window at any time of day or night to see twenty boys in different stages of undress.

We had roll call at 8.30 a.m. and by that time had to have made our beds, tidied our rooms and be washed and dressed and in the school hall for a hearty cooked breakfast. Then the day was ours to do whatever we wanted, provided we arrived back at the school for roll call at 5.00 p.m. During the day there would be a member of staff on duty at the school and he would organize football, tennis, cricket and various other games for those boys who preferred to stay. I was always keen to be out and about with my friends. There was so much to do: travel around the island on the miniature steam trains, sunbathe on the beach, ride on the Laxey Wheel, visit the castle at Douglas, swim in the sea, take a fishing trip out in the harbour, explore caves, climb up the cliffs to Bradda Head, hire a bicycle and cycle (without a helmet) along the narrow country roads. Such a holiday these days would be unthinkable. Every school trip organizer now has to be qualified, have first aid training and carry out a rigorous risk assessment prior to any school trip taking place. The idea of letting 100 unsupervised adolescent boys loose on a small island for two weeks in this day and age is frankly laughable. And yet nothing happened in all the five years I went on summer camp. No one got into trouble with the police, there was no vandalism, bad behaviour, serious accidents or drunkenness. No one scrawled graffiti on walls, stole from the shops or caused a nuisance. It was expected that we would behave. The very thought of having to face Mr Firth, now in his holiday gear of knee-length shorts, thick leather belt with silver buckle, khaki shirt and jungle hat (it was rumoured he had been a commando in the war and had seen off a whole troop of Japanese soldiers single-handedly with the knife he used for sharpening pencils in class), with his round weathered face and piercing eyes, was enough to keep us out of bother. Of course, Mr Firth's graphic description of what happened to miscreants on the island should they come before the Manx courts and be sentenced for punishment – a severe thrashing with a thin cane called a birch – might have had something to do with our exemplary behaviour.

At 6.30 p.m. we ate a substantial meal and spent the evening playing board games, watching black and white films on the old projector, reading, writing letters and postcards home, drawing, playing Bingo (it was then called Housey-Housey) or just talking. There were no television, computer games or mobile phones.

My parents warned me before I set off for the Isle of Man to be careful and try not to have an accident – as was my wont. I did try, but one year I was swimming in the clear blue waters of Port Erin Bay when pumping its way towards me I saw this huge mass of translucent jelly, purple in the centre and with long stringy tentacles. I had never swum as fast in my life, and thrashed towards the shore closely followed by the other swimmers. One of the tentacles, however, attached itself to my arm and later my hand and wrist swelled up, turned a strange blue colour and started to hurt. My friends were fascinated but entirely unsympathetic, predicting that it would not be very long before my arm withered and fell off. Mr Firth took me to the doctor, who prescribed the appropriate medicine. After a couple of days the swelling went down and the colour faded.

Rather than warn us all of the dangers of swimming in a sea inhabited by such dangerous creatures, Mr Firth informed those on his dinner table that evening that life was full of risks and then gave a very informative lecture on the life cycle of the Portuguese man-of-war jellyfish.

When three boys arrived back at the school after the first day looking like cooked lobsters and complaining of sunburn, Mrs Clark smeared them liberally with calamine lotion and that was the end of the matter.

Another year my brother Alec came into the school after a day's fishing off the pier carrying a huge conger eel that he had caught. Another feared creature with its razor-sharp needle teeth, like a huge black and slimy snake, this predatory creature lived in the shallow coastal waters of the island. One snap of its massive jaws and you could lose your fingers. Rather than telling my brother off and warning others not to fish off the pier in case such a monster of the deep might be caught and could maim them for life, Mr Firth and the teachers dined off conger eel that evening, cooked to perfection by the cook. Alec was given a taste and half a crown for his efforts.

It was with a great sense of excitement that I visited the Isle of Man nearly forty years later. In 2001 Pat Corrin invited me to speak at a charity luncheon in Douglas and I jumped at the chance to revisit the island. Jack, her husband, a true-blue Manxman and former Deemster (high court judge), took me on a nostalgic tour. I was made to feel so welcome. A year later I was back, this time at the invitation of the Senior Primary Education Adviser, to run a course for teachers, and I was able to visit Castle Rushen Primary School. It was very different now. Although the squat, square, grey stone exterior had changed very little in the intervening years, inside, the building was unrecognizable. Gone were the hard wooden floors, the metal-framed windows, the long cold green-tiled corridors, the wooden desks and the small, rather smelly toilets.

I stood with the headteacher in this bright, welcoming and cheerful entrance, the walls covered in children's writing and paintings, and was taken back forty years, to when I stood on that spot, an eleven-year-old with his little case and an apprehensive expression. It seemed a world away.

40

I was susceptible to girls since reaching double figures, but it was only when I was fourteen that I first started seriously thinking about them. I found out all too soon that I had a habit of falling for those who showed little interest in me, unlike my best friend Peter, who had his pick. Even when the girl had never met me the relationship seemed to flounder.

I was fixed up with a pen-friend by a colleague of my mother's and began corresponding with Katie, who lived in Milwaukee. Her photograph showed a bright-eyed, blonde-haired, all-American girl with a massive smile. She looked stunning. The photograph I sent her was of a dark, brooding, rather plain-looking boy. My letters must have seemed dreadfully pedestrian compared to hers, despite the fact that I embroidered and exaggerated and sometimes invented stories to make my life seem less drab and where I lived more exciting. Katie lived in a place as far removed in my mind from Rotherham as I could imagine. The photographs of the town in which she lived exuded affluence. It looked a clean, safe, wholesome place with long, straight, leafy streets, huge wooden houses with verandas and beautifully tended gardens, a stately white town hall and an imposing hospital. There was a diner with a huge neon sign above it, a grand picture palace, gas stations, a plaza and a high school as big as a castle.

Katie's letters would tell me about the wonderful facilities at her school, the sports stadium, baseball games, swimming pool, ice hockey rink, running track, the high school band, the cheerleaders, the drama productions, the wonderful student social areas and her academic success. In one letter was a picture of her in a ballgown before setting off for the high school prom. She was on the arm of a tuxedoed boy with a tanned face, a cheesy smile, a huge bow tie, his hair slicked back. Of course, I knew his name just had to be Chuck. What could compare – that I had just summoned up the courage to dive from the first block at the swimming baths? That I had been to see the stuffed animals at Clifton Park Museum? That I had learnt three chords on the ukulele? That I had reached Grade 4 on the piano? Despite my efforts to try and make my life of some interest, it must have sounded to her a pretty dreary existence, and the letters stopped.

After the disastrous date with Brenda, I was very apprehensive when my best friend Peter suggested that I make up a foursome. He was 'walking out' with a strikingly pretty, dark-haired girl and she had this friend, Jocelyn (I have changed the name to save her blushes), a thin, shy girl with thick straw-coloured hair and as long-legged and languid as a heron. Like many boys my age, I had become very fastidious about my personal appearance and spent a deal of time examining my face in the mirror for spots, brilliantining my hair, dousing my body with my brother's after-shave, scrubbing my teeth and making sure my fingernails were clean. I am sad to admit that it did not have the desired effect.

For a few weeks the four of us went to the cinema, played tennis, took bus rides to Sheffield, drank strawberry milk shakes at the Ring o'Bells Café in All Saints' Square, listened to Beatles' records and went for walks around Clifton Park – all very innocent. There was no 'hanky panky' as my Aunt Nora would say.

I had a sneaking feeling from the very first that Jocelyn only went out with me because she liked Peter and this was a way she could see a lot of him. I noticed the way she looked at him when he was talking and it was pretty obvious after a few weeks that she had a crush on him. Well, what girl wouldn't? He had curly, straw-coloured hair, the looks of the male model and a physique to match, and he was clever, confident and good company. Peter's father was a distinguished alderman of the town, a justice of the peace and a school governor and the family lived in a house overlooking the playing fields. Peter's elder brother was an actor. When my friend tired of Lynne and found another girlfriend, Jocelyn gave me my marching orders, but I can't say I was that bothered and certainly didn't lose any sleep over it. We had little in common – I liked books and reading and she liked dancing and clothes. I did once persuade her to go with me to the Lyceum Theatre in Sheffield to see a production of *Julius Caesar*, but I guess she only agreed because Peter's elder brother was in the cast.

In 2005, at the time of writing this account, I was appearing at the Broadway Theatre in Catford as part of my tour, *An Evening with Gervase Phinn*. I had not thought of Peter for many years, so it was a surprise when at the book signing after the show I looked up to find him there with a great grin on his face. I had not seen him for forty years. Much to his embarrassment and to the amusement of his wife, Andrea, I reminded him of our innocent exploits with the girls of Rotherham in the 1960s and of the string of girls who would queue up to go out with him. With Peter was his young son. Things got even stranger when he told me that the young man's name was Finn.

The next girlfriend was Judy and she was very different from Jocelyn. She had thick curly blonde hair like a doll's, which stuck out at the sides like giant earmuffs, and she had small breasts like the knobs on my grandmother's dresser. I met her in Rotherham Library, where she was poring over a thick tome in the corner of the reference section. I was revising for my O levels and sat down at the large oak table opposite her. She kept on glancing up when I had my head down and I kept on glancing up when she had her head down. When we glanced up at the same time, we started laughing and got talking. Then there was a coffee at the Ring o'Bells Café and I asked her out to the cinema.

I guessed that Judy would prefer to see a romantic film where all the people seemed to do was talk in posh accents, give deeply meaningful looks and snatch the odd kiss, but I loved the films with excitement, films which in their sheer inventiveness had my eyes glued to the screen, films like *Invasion of the Body Snatchers* or *The Blob*. They were badly acted and the special effects were sometimes laughable, but I was hooked on them. I didn't mind if you could see the zip down the back of the costume of *The Man from Planet X*, or that Godzilla was a magnified puppet and about as frightening as Noddy. However, after the last unforgettable experience with Brenda, when we'd seen *The Amazing Colossal Man*, I decided to give *Zombies of the Stratosphere* a miss and take Judy to see a historical adventure.

We went to the Tivoli (the 'flea pit') to see *The Black Rose,* a romantic, action-packed tale starring Tyrone Power (what a name!). The bastard son of a Saxon nobleman flees medieval England for the Far East, where he falls for a beautiful Eurasian woman on her way to the court of Kublai Khan. He rescues the beautiful slave girl and confronts the Mongolian warlord, wonderfully overacted by Orson Welles behind heavy Oriental make-up. Judy sat through the film with her hands clasped tightly on her lap, totally impassive. When I tried to slide my arm around the back of her seat, she winced as if I had flicked water in her face and shuffled her body forward. And out of reach. There was no way I was going to chance kissing her. I thought it was a brilliant film, Judy thought it was stupid. It soon became apparent that when I made a comment or an observation she would take an opposing point of view.

The big showdown came on our next date. It was over blood sports. I couldn't get excited either way about fox-hunting but I did enjoy going out to Wentworth Woodhouse to see the hunt setting off from Lord Fitzwilliam's stately home, all resplendent in red coats (I was told by Judy that they were actually called 'pinks'), white breeches and highly polished black boots. Judy was a vehement opponent.

As a child I was always kind to animals (and still am), and never so much as pulled a leg off a crane-fly or stamped on a cockroach, but I couldn't get all upset about fox-hunting. I had seen what a fox could do when I went up to Archer's Farm. When the fox had broken into the hen coop and had bitten the heads off every one of the chickens, it had left the magnificent feathers of the rooster scattered all around the farmyard. Mr Archer had shaken his head angrily. 'I know the bloody creature has to live,' he said, 'but why doesn't it just take one of the chickens instead of killing the whole bloody lot!' This, of course, cut no ice with Judy.

Then there was the fact that my brother Alec went with his falcon to Boston Park. This to Judy was barbaric. I disagreed. It was an amazing sight to see the bird of prey fly high up in the sky, wheeling around gracefully before plummeting on its unsuspecting prey. To see my brother swirl the lure around his head and see the falcon winging its way back to land on his gloved fist was astonishing.

Although I could see things were deteriorating, I agreed to accompany Judy to the girls' high school Christmas dance. This was held in the school hall – a dark, cold place that smelt of floor polish and cabbage. It had been decorated with sprigs of holly and trimmings, pictures of snowy landscapes and other festive scenes to brighten the place up, but it still looked and smelt like a school hall. There was, of course, no mistletoe. It was a decorous affair and girls had been warned by the headmistress in a special assembly to wear appropriate outfits: three-quarter-length dresses, low heels and no plunging necklines. Boys should wear ties and sober jackets and come with a formal invitation, otherwise they would be refused entry. Some teachers observed proceedings with eagle eyes from the vantage point of the hall balcony, while others stalked the floor ensuring that nothing untoward happened. The dancing was of the ballroom variety and included the Gay Gordons, the Military

Two-Step, the progressive barn dance and the waltz. It must have looked comical, big strapping lads with slicked-back hair and acne galloping, spinning, twirling their partners and then, for the waltz, shuffling around the floor treading on feet. The waltz was an opportunity for us to make contact with our partners. We were told by the teachers prior to the music starting that the boy was allowed to encircle a girl's waist but must keep his partner at arm's length, a full yard apart. Inevitably, as soon as the music started, we pulled the girl in close so our bodies touched, until we were spotted by a hawk-faced teacher who soon put a stop to any of that.

During the evening I got the chance of dancing with Barbara, a big-bosomed, athletic girl who pulled me to her and then clung on like a limpet until we were separated by a tut-tutting teacher. Barbara had soft brown eyes and smelt of flowers and made my heart flutter.

'You're not a very good dancer,' Judy told me waspishly as I walked her home. 'And I saw the way you were smooching with Barbara. She's a man-eater, you know.' Was Judy jealous, I wondered? I didn't say anything but savoured the memory.

Things were not going well, and they went further downhill when I was invited round to her house for tea. It was a large detached villa with spacious rooms with high ceilings, heavy velvet curtains and a ticking grandfather clock in the hall. The front room (which Judy called the 'lounge') was meticulously tidy, with a marble fireplace, two great armchairs and a sofa covered in cushions, a thick plain brown carpet, an antique sideboard and a heavy oak bookcase full of books. Clusters of porcelain figures and fancy plates were displayed in alcoves. It was the sort of room I imagined Sherlock Holmes would have in Baker Street.

Judy's mother, a stern-looking, pinched-faced woman with close-set, unsmiling eyes, observed me with a sort of amused tolerance, but her jowly, thick-lipped father, the very image of a military martinet, treated me with barely suppressed animosity. I sat nervously on the edge of the sofa as if at an interview for a job, fielding a whole lot of questions about my family, my background, my father's occupation, where I lived, what were my hobbies and which school I attended.

'So you don't attend the grammar school then?' asked Judy's mother, her voice dripping with condescension.

'No,' I replied, 'I failed my Eleven Plus.'

'Really?' She cocked her head in an arrogant fashion. There was clear surprise in her voice when she observed, 'And Judy tells me you are sitting your O levels?'

'Yes, that's right.'

'I wasn't aware that students at a secondary modern sat O levels,' said her father.

'Well, at South Grove we do,' I told him.

'And do you think you will pass them, young man?' he asked.

'Yes,' I said simply.

He gave a dismissive grunt. Judy's mother gave a dry little cough and looked chillier than ever.

'And do you attend church, Gerald?'

'Yes,' I said. 'And my name's Gervase.'

She arched an eyebrow and made a little moue with her mouth.

'I go to St Bede's at Masborough,' I told her.

'The Roman Catholic church?' She gave an unconvincing smile but there was no mistaking the disapproval in her voice.

The interrogation was endless and Judy made no effort to help me out. There remained a polite and meticulous coldness, and I knew for certain that I was an unsatisfactory suitor for their precious daughter. I could well do without this, I thought. I declined a drink of lemonade and said I had to go. How I wish I had had the gumption to tell them, 'I have to dash, I have an appointment at the VD clinic this afternoon.'

I saw Judy at the library the following week. 'Mummy and

Daddy don't think it's a good idea that I should see you any more,' she told me.

'I couldn't agree with them more,' I replied, and returned to my books.

When I was fixed up with a blind date by David, another friend, I was glad to wave goodbye to Judy. David's new girlfriend had an exotic sounding name – Ophelia or Giselle or something of the sort – and each Saturday morning she attended ballet classes. The owner of the dance school, an extremely regal-looking woman with a wonderful coiffure, had given her premises – a small dark annexe adjoining a looming black stone Methodist chapel – a grandiose name, something like the Marcia Mann Academy of Dance and Dramatic Arts. One Saturday, David, keen to show off his new conquest, took me down to the annexe. We placed three house bricks on top of each other to enable us to peer through the window at the girls, who were going through their balletic motions. There were about twenty or so girls of amazingly different shapes and sizes, in pink or white tights and short frilly skirts, cavorting, bending, stretching, jumping, leaping about and kicking their legs in the air. An old woman sat at an upright piano hammering away while another woman, in black, with silver-white hair and a hooked nose, put them through their paces. We were so engrossed in watching the budding ballerinas that we were unaware of the small window opening. Miss Mann's assistant, another witch of a woman, with a face that if looks could maim would have had us on crutches, bellowed out at us. 'Depart, you adolescent voyeurs, or I shall be compelled to call the constabulary!' I had no idea what a voyeur was, but I liked the sound of it and used it the following week in an essay for Mr Pike.

Giselle or Ophelia's cousin was called Sandra and very different from the long, lithe and ethereal beauty David was courting. Sandra was a homely sort who wore her frizzy red hair in bunches. She wore large spectacles which hid her rather beautiful jade green eyes. She was one of life's innocents and collected miniature porcelain jugs and plates with the names and crests of seaside towns displayed on them. I remember how elated she was one Sunday when we went for a walk in Whiston Meadows. (When we 'walked out' we never held hands. Sandra preferred to link her arm through mine. We must have looked like an old married couple.)

'My Uncle Cyril brought me back Filey and Bridlington last week,' she said, hardly able to contain her excitement. 'All I need now is Sandsend and Whitby and I've got the complete set of Yorkshire seaside resorts.'

'Wow!' I said, trying to muster up some enthusiasm.

Sandra started knitting me things. What was it about me that seemed to attract adolescent knitters? First Brenda and now Sandra. The first item she produced was a pair of massive grey and blue gloves with two fingers shorter than the rest, and then it was a sherbet yellow scarf, which hung around my neck like some hideously bright anaconda. She had knitted herself a matching one, and was upset when I failed to wear it when I took her to see a Rotherham United match and wore my red and white football supporters' scarf. I could just imagine what the fans would have thought, and done, had I walked through the gates at Millmoor wearing the coloured monstrosity around my neck. Sandra was a nice enough girl but had the personality of petrified wood. There would be little or no conversation and anything I said would be greeted with, 'Yes, I know.' After three weeks I was not only exceedingly hot in all the woollen outfits but also exceedingly bored with nice homely Sandra and told her on the Doncaster bus that there was no future in our relationship.

'But I'm halfway through a jumper for you,' she told me, pouting and pulling away her arm, which had been linked through mine. 'And it matches mine.'

After Sandra I gave girls a bit of a rest for a while and concentrated on my studies. The opposite sex was too much like hard work.

41

Since I was small the circus has held a great fascination for me. In this day and age it is pretty tame by comparison to the shows that were staged in the 1950s. Most modern circuses are equally colourful but not as lively, diverse and exciting as those of the past. Gone are the more unusual and exotic acts, the risky displays, the outrageous characters and most of the animals. There was great excitement in the Phinn household when the circus came to town. Gandey's Circus set up on a piece of waste ground outside Rotherham. The huge tent, the 'Big Top', was erected, surrounded with brightly painted caravans and large cages, and an open-topped van with a loudspeaker blaring out martial music toured the town advertising the show. For the first performance the road to the circus was chock-a-block with excited children and their parents.

The circus was a wildly colourful, noisy and varied affair, with tumblers, acrobats, knife-throwers, fire-eaters, jugglers, trapeze artists, tightrope walkers, bareback riders, lion tamers and clowns. I never found the clowns that funny. In fact, the figure with the fixed smile, tufts of red hair, great black-lined eyes and crimson nose was a frightening character, as was his companion – a sad, pasty-faced pierrot dressed in a white costume and a strange pointed hat. I loved the animal acts: the lion tamer in his red frock coat, close-fitting white trousers and shiny black boots, who cracked his whip to make the creatures snarl and spit and paw the air menacingly, the black bear that danced, the chimpanzees, dressed in garish clothes, the lumbering elephants and camels and the prancing horses.

There was one highly unusual act, featuring an abnormally

small man. It was called 'Chuck the Midget'. A large beefy individual picked up this little man and hurled him along a greasy mat, much to the amusement of the audience. Even as a youngster I thought this an incredibly cruel thing to do, and I was even more appalled when the same little man reappeared later in the show to be shot out of a cannon as 'The Human Cannonball'.

It was the drama of the circus that appealed. My experience of the theatre as a child was restricted to the end of the pier shows in summer at Blackpool, the occasional stage show at the Regent Theatre in town and the pantomimes at Christmas.

I had never seen classic plays until Mr Williams got me hooked on the theatre, and then I became a regular member of the audience at Rotherham Civic, Sheffield Playhouse, Doncaster Civic and the Sheffield Lyceum, but I had been in a theatre before. Occasionally my parents took me to a variety show at the Regent. The Regent was the only theatre in Rotherham and when I was a child it was opulence itself, with its velvet seats and high ceiling. I liked the excited chatter, the heady atmosphere and the colourful 'turns'. The variety evenings featured a mixture of musical and comedy performances by such entertainers as Ernie Page, 'England's leading impersonator', Sybil May, 'the famous Welsh Contralto' and Neville Roe, 'the boy soprano, with the voice of an angel'. Sometimes the shows included speciality acts like Patsy Silver, 'the Tomboy of the Air', Les Calantas, 'daring acrobats on the high wire', a juggler who threw flaming torches high in the air, and a rather aged magician in a shabby black tailcoat, with an assistant who was past her best (as my mother remarked), and whose tricks didn't quite work out. I was enthralled by 'Pianotoes Jacobson', the man with no arms, who played the piano with his toes. I waited at the stage door starry-eyed for the performers to autograph my programmes and thought they were so wonderfully exotic. Sadly 'Pianotoes' didn't make an appearance. I should have liked to have him sign my autograph book with his toes.

Also at the Regent risqué shows were staged that were certainly not deemed suitable by my parents for a young boy. When I appeared on stage at the Rotherham Civic Theatre in 2005 I was fascinated by the framed posters that covered the walls, advertising shows at the Regent Theatre in the 1950s. There was *Goodbye to Striptease*, featuring 'the ravishing and adorable Linzi, the Body Beautiful', and Daubney and Fay ('pert, pleasing and tasty'). There was Paul Raymond's 'fabulous Jane (saucy, spicy and sexy)' in 'the greatest of all sex shows, even more daring than ever before', 'the lovely Annette, Britain's loveliest model and her MUFF in nude studies' and featuring the 'Dance of the Fans, hotter than Harlem'. What amused me most about the posters were the details at the bottom about the clientele and the prices: 'OAPs – one shilling, Friday only, children – one shilling and one and six, Monday to Friday.' What parent would take a child to see Annette, who posed naked for the entire world to see – save for her muff?

I loved the pantomimes with their simple plots where good always triumphed, the outrageous cross-dressing characters, the doggerel, the ridiculously silly jokes and play on words, the foolish antics, the bright colours, the spectacularly gaudy costumes, the lively music and the audience participation, where you were encouraged to shout out as loud as you could. It is a remarkable fact that the pantomime has survived to the present day and is as popular as ever, despite competition from television, videos, DVDs, block-buster movies and sophisticated computer games. Everything about this over-the-top theatrical genre appeals to children and when things go wrong, which they frequently do, this is an added bonus.

I was never frightened by the wicked witch or the cruel stepmother, the villainous King Rat or the scheming Sheriff of Nottingham, because I had met these characters in the stories my parents had read to me and I knew in my heart that they would eventually get their come-uppance. It was great fun, however, watching screaming children terrified by the 'baddie' being hauled from their seats and taken out by their embarrassed parents.

It is an old theatrical chestnut: 'Never act with animals or children.' Both are, of course, entirely unpredictable. Once, so my father reminded me (although I have to admit I cannot remember, so it might be one of his tall tales), the Shetland pony harnessed to Cinderella's crystal coach (a large, round pumpkin-shaped cardboard cut-out) made an appearance on stage amidst delighted 'Oooohs' and 'Aaaahs' from the audience. Just as Cinderella emerged from her magical carriage in her shimmering silver dress and sparkling glass slippers, the pony decided it was a good time to relieve itself. The contents of the creature's bladder splashed on to the floor and trickled across the stage, into the orchestra pit and on to the piano, much to the alarm of the pianist and the amusement of the audience and the actors. Buttons, with great presence of mind, disappeared and returned a moment later with a mop and the lines:

> Goodness gracious, dearie me,
> Cinders' pony's done a wee.

I do remember, however, the time when Buttons tried his hardest to get a little boy who sat in the middle of the front row to respond. We were at the end of the row so we had a bird's-eye view. The six-year-old stared at the action on stage with a deadpan expression, refusing to join in when everyone else was cheering and booing, shouting and singing. Every actor tried to get the child to react – Cinderella, the Fairy Godmother, the Wicked Stepmother, the Ugly Sisters, Baron Hardup – all to no avail. Buttons saw this as a personal challenge. He would run on to the stage with 'Hi Kids!' and all the children would shout back. 'Hi Buttons!' All, that is, except the child sitting in the middle of the front row with the impassive expression. Buttons began to look pointedly at the child.

'I get really upset if children don't say "Hi Buttons",' he said sadly.

'Aaaaah,' commiserated the audience.

'And there's a little boy on the front row who hasn't said it yet.'

'Aaaaah,' chorused the audience again.

Still there was no response from the child, so Buttons left the stage, skipped down the steps leading to the auditorium and, taking the child's hand, managed to prevail upon him to join him on stage with a promise of a present.

'Now, little boy,' he asked, 'what's your name?' The child stared at him in silence.

Buttons tried another tack. 'Are you having a good time?' Still there was no response. Buttons persevered. 'Have you anything to say to Buttons?' The little boy looked up and replied in a deadpan voice, 'Does tha know summat, tha bloody daft thee,' and returned to his seat.

On another occasion Simple Simon asked for some children to join him on stage. From the sea of waving hands he selected an angelic-looking little boy of about six. The child duly joined the actor on stage and was given the microphone.

'You entertain the audience while I am gone,' Simple Simon told the child.

The idea was that the child, standing in the centre of the stage nervous and alone and not knowing what to do, would generate a deal of laughter from the audience as he looked around apprehensively. Simple Simon had picked the wrong child. The little boy, not at all disconcerted by the full theatre, suddenly went into a stage act to rival the best stand-up comedian and much to the delight of a very appreciative audience.

'I say, I say, I say,' began the child, and proceeded to tell a rather risqué joke. There was a great round of applause. The boy continued. 'Have you heard the one about the Englishman, the Irishman and the Scotsman?' Simple Simon reappeared on the stage in quick time and grabbed the microphone from the budding comedian.

'Thank you very much, little boy,' he said, laughing half-heartedly.

'I've not finished,' protested the child, attempting to get back possession of the microphone.

'Oh yes, you have,' said Simple Simon, escorting him off the stage.

'Oh no, he hasn't!' chorused the audience.

My father told me of another occasion, when the actor playing the pantomime Dame collapsed in the interval and had to be taken to Moorgate Hospital. The theatre manager appeared before the curtain prior to the commencement of the second act to announce: 'The actor playing the part of Dame Trot will not be appearing in the second half. He's been taken ill.'

The audience in one great chorus shouted: 'Oh no, he hasn't!'

'Yes, he has,' replied the manager in all seriousness.

'Oh no, he hasn't!' the audience shouted back.

'Oh yes, he has!' shouted the manager angrily.

One afternoon just before Christmas, when I was ten, my father took me to see the pantomime at the Leeds City Varieties. We caught the train from Masborough station and walked through the city crowded with shoppers. It was one of the few very special occasions when it was just me and my Dad, no brothers or sister. The City Varieties is the oldest extant music hall in the country, an intimate, colourful and atmospheric little theatre, hidden between two arcades. All the greats of variety theatre have performed here: Charlie Chaplin and Houdini, Tommy Cooper and Hylda Baker,

Marie Lloyd and Les Dawson and, of course, the legendary Ken Dodd, who takes some persuading to leave the stage once he's started. I appeared on stage there myself in 2006 in my one-man show and spent the intermission leafing through the visitors' book, fascinated by the many entries. Before my performance I stood on the empty stage looking down at the empty stalls and recalled a small boy sitting on a plush red velvet seat with his father, his eyes wide, entering a magical world of the pantomime.

It was at Leeds City Varieties that I first saw the great Sandy Powell, who hailed from my home town of Rotherham, and heard his famous catchphrase, 'Can you hear me, Mother?' For a few weeks afterwards I would imitate this catchphrase at home, much to the irritation of my family, until my father put his foot down and said, 'That'll be enough!'

Sandy Powell's comedy was clever, clean, inoffensive and hilariously funny. Part of his act was when he appeared on stage dressed in a soldier's scarlet tunic with pillbox hat askew on his head and holding a particularly ugly dummy, which was dressed identically. He was a hopeless ventriloquist and his dummy would often fall apart in his hands. His act was interrupted by a posh-sounding member of the audience, in real life his wife Kay.

'Tell me sonny,' he asked the dummy in a deep throaty voice, 'where do you live and where were you born?'

'I vass born in Volchergrankon,' replied the dummy.

'Where was he born?' asked the woman.

'Wolverhampton. Oh, I wish I'd have said Leeds. I'm glad it wasn't Czechoslovakia.'

My first sortie on to the stage was when I was thirteen and at a school concert I performed a song which Sandy Powell made famous. I was accompanied on the piano by Mr Gravill, the music master. At Christmas I insist on singing this ditty at family gatherings, much to my children's embarrassment.

When I was a right young lad
My father said to me:
'Seems to me tha's growin' up,
Now what's tha goin' to be?
It all depends upon thyself,
It's only up to thee,
I won't say much to thee ageean,
But tek a tip from me.
'Ear all, see all, say nowt,
Ate all, sup all, pay nowt,
It's a long time, remember
From January to December,
So 'ear all, see all, say nowt,
Ate all, sup all, pay nowt,
And if ever thy does summat for nowt,
Always do it for theeself.'

Until Mr Williams, my headmaster at secondary school, stopped me in the corridor and gave me the two tickets to see Sheridan's comic masterpiece, therefore, my experience of theatre was limited. After that I became hooked and would try to see as many productions as I could. I paid for the tickets by supplementing my pocket money by getting a paper round and digging Mr Pike's garden.

My interest in the theatre flourished when I joined the South Yorkshire Theatre for Youth. This was an amateur dramatic society for young people, formed by the Head of the English Department at Wath Grammar School. Bill Hammond was a charismatic, larger-than-life figure – one of the world's enthusiasts, a brilliant teacher with a passion for theatre. Over the summer holidays, for two intensive weeks, he would give up a fortnight of his time to rehearse young actors from all over the south of the county for a production which would be staged the following September in Rotherham and Doncaster. Auditions and rehearsals took place at South Grove School, and many young hopefuls turned up one Saturday in July with prepared extracts to perform before Bill and his assistant producer, George Manchester, who was another Wath Grammar School English teacher. Although Mr Pike suggested to me that I might like to try my hand at acting and audition for a part, I was at that time far too under-confident. The caretaker at South Grove, Vic Globe, was the stage manager for the productions and he asked me if I would like to help him backstage. I readily agreed. I loved the cinema and the theatre, and any chance to be involved first hand, albeit with an amateur production by a group of adolescents and only in a minor capacity, working behind the scenes, really appealed to me.

I agreed to work backstage, looking after the props, helping with the lighting and the sound and generally assisting with anything that the stage manager asked me to do. I longed to join the young actors on the stage but was far too shy and reticent. They seemed so clever, self-assured and talented.

On the first day of rehearsals – for the *The Imaginary Invalid*, a translation of Molière's classic drama *Le Malade Imaginaire* – I watched fascinated from the wings as supremely confident young people demonstrated how adept they were at acting. Of course, being a menial backstage helper, I was not a part of the lively discussions which took place at breaks and lunchtimes between the budding actors. I would sit on the sidelines watching and listening. Everyone seemed to know everyone else and they were so bubbly and amusing, assertive and self-assured.

On that first day the young actors entered into the drama with great gusto. They all seemed to know the theatrical terms I had never come across before: SM, ASM, Lampy, down stage right, up stage left, backdrop, wings, apron, flats, spots, gels, gobos, prompt corner, silvers, blacks – it was a whole new language to me. Most of the cast knew their lines pretty well word-perfect and were so much at ease on the stage.

On the third day an extremely suave, rather pompous boy – I cannot recall his name, but I had observed him the previous day telling a group of adoring girls about being accepted at one of Oxford's oldest colleges to study Greek or something incredibly impressive – never turned up. Mr Hammond asked if I would oblige by reading the part of Dr Diaforus. This was a very meaty part. Dr Diaforus was a patronizing, arrogant and ambitious man who wanted his son, the dim-witted Thomas, to marry the rich daughter of his friend. I had a real stab at it, and after my rendition the producer took me aside and asked why I had not auditioned. 'You are very good,' he said, 'natural timing, a good ear for language and an excellent stage presence. Next year we'll find a part for you.' It was as if I had been awarded the 'Free Reader' badge again. I walked on clouds. I was even more ecstatic the following day when the producer told me Mr High-and-Mighty wasn't coming back and the part of Dr Diaforus was mine if I wanted it.

I loved the rehearsals, the camaraderie backstage, the sharing of jokes and anecdotes, the assignations and the attention-seeking exhibitionism that surrounded me. I loved watching my fellow actors going through their paces, listening to the producer shouting out directions, the smell of the theatre, the bright lights, the mugs of hot sweet tea, the bacon sandwiches and fizzy lemonade in the dressing rooms. I had never before in my life felt so much a part of a group of entertaining people.

We were all understandably nervous on the first night but it was thrilling: the rushing about, the hustle and bustle, the excited voices, the nervous conversations, the last-minute alterations to the costumes and, of course, the make-up. My face was transformed from a spotty youth's to an aged man's by the liberal use of Leichner theatrical make-up. The effect was startling. My face was darkened with Numbers 5 and 9, then wrinkles were painted on my forehead and an ugly mole added to my cheek, shadows appeared under my eyes and a thin black line was traced across my lower eyelashes. The final touch was the grey straggly beard. A long pigtail of grey crêpe hair was teased out under the steam of the kettle, and the facial hair was stuck on with some evil-smelling sticky brown glue which made my face sting. A stick of carmine completed the effect and my lips changed to the colour of dried blood.

'You look absolutely revolting,' said a fellow actor.

'Thanks,' I replied, getting into my costume.

The play was performed at the Rotherham Civic Theatre. In addition to the role of Dr Diaforus I was given the part of the Prologue. 'You do a very good patronizing look,' Bill told me, 'excellent at looking down your nose, and I like the way you strut. You will start the play off.' Dressed in dark blue pleated silk frock-coat, embroidered waistcoat with silver buttons, silk knee breeches, high-heeled black shoes with buckles, frilly cravat and ridiculously curly, shoulder-length wig, I was the first on stage, appearing before the curtain to introduce the drama.

'Break a leg,' said the stage manager as I took a deep breath, ready to make my appearance. I had no idea what he meant. That first night it wasn't butterflies in my stomach but great kangaroos leaping up and down. I was terrified.

To open the play on the very first night is daunting for any actor, however experienced and confident. I appeared under the spotlight to see the producer in the centre of the front row nervously rubbing his chin, eager parents, friends, the theatre critics from various newspapers (the *Rotherham Advertiser*, the *South Yorkshire Times*, the *Sheffield Star*, the *Yorkshire Post*), and row upon row of people watching and ready to judge. Off stage I knew that all the cast would be watching intently too, nervously preparing themselves for their own entrances. It was now up to me to set the scene.

The single most enjoyable experience in appearing in that first play was the sense of elation before and after the perform-ance. Every night my heart would race with expectation and be high with happiness. There is something very special and exhilarating about being a part of a company of actors backstage, listening to their exaggerated stories, how they try to outdo each other with anecdotes and jokes, listening to the accents they put on, and above all feeling the warmth of their compan-ionship and of being part of a group of like-minded people.

For the end-of-show party we young thespians donned a bewildering array of clothes. Let's face it, we were show-offs and this was the night when we were going to show off. I was sartorially ready and willing and arrived in a corduroy jacket with wide lapels and leather elbow patches (which had once belonged to my Uncle Alec), a mustard-coloured waistcoat with silver watch chain (minus the watch), a bright green bow tie (borrowed surreptitiously from my brother Michael) and green socks. I must have looked laughable, dressed like a young Oscar Wilde, but then everyone in the cast had dressed over the top. After all, we were actors.

It was such a thrill to be part of that production of *The Imaginary Invalid*. Everything was so new, so different, so excit-ing, and my confidence blossomed. As a member of the cast I was no longer on the sidelines watching and listening – I was part of a group of lively, interesting and amusing young people. They readily included me in their conversations and sought out my opinions, laughing at my jokes and making me feel interesting and important.

A girl called Jeanette had a minor part in *The Imaginary Invalid*, and after one show she told me she thought I was the best actor. Flattered, I asked her out. I decided that the cordu-roy jacket and bow tie were not the most appropriate garb for a night out at the 'flea pit', so reverted to tight black trousers, white open-necked shirt and lapel-less jacket (all the rage at the time). I Brylcreemed my hair, splashed on Michael's after-shave and polished my shoes.

We sat on the back row at the Tivoli (where they had those double seats especially designed for courting couples) and watched *The Beast from Twenty Thousand Fathoms*. Freed from their Arctic home, where they had been in a state of suspended animation, great prehistoric creatures were brought to life by an atomic blast. One giant beast lumbered down the coast of North America, devastating everything in its path and causing widespread panic. It went out in a blaze of glory at Coney Island. From what my brother tells me about Coney Island today, it appears it still hasn't recovered from the devastation of the *Beast of Twenty Thousand Fathoms*. Today such films, with their wooden acting, amateur sequences, patently unrealistic dialogue, ludicrous sound effects and plastic models trundling across the screen, would make us laugh out loud, but at the time they were truly frightening. Jeanette clung to me the whole time like a Whitby limpet and we kissed, just before the lights came on and the National Anthem was played. Girls were now back in my life.

42

The following year I was given the part of Venturewell in *The Knight of the Burning Pestle*. This period piece by Beaumont and Fletcher, written in 1607, is a parody of plays about the romantic adventures of air-headed knights and of the theatre itself. Throughout the play, a well-to-do citizen and his garrulous wife keep interrupting with dim-witted comments and advice and insist on their apprentice playing the lead. The citizen was played by Peter Smith, who was able to perform an unnerving impersonation of Frankie Howerd. He peppered his lines with the outrageous comedian's catchphrases, 'Oo, no don't,' and 'No missis, titter not,' and 'Perleese madam, don't mock. Have some respect.' Peter was a natural comic but prone to excessive improvisation on and off stage.

I was cast as another mean-minded, avaricious and thoroughly nasty old man who had great plans for his effete son to marry the rich and innocent daughter of a family friend. My son was portrayed by Bernard, a tall, long-haired and pale-faced boy who acted his part to perfection. He would stare vacantly into the middle distance sighing, wipe his brow dramatically, walk in an affected manner with short quick steps and swinging hips and deliver his lines in a high lisping voice.

In one scene Peter had to evict the son from his master's house and did so rather too energetically. He poked him hard in the shoulder, pushed him roughly through the door and kicked him so hard on the backside that the poor boy was propelled a good distance across the stage. This performance was well received by the audience, which roared with laughter.

'You really don't need to be so heavy-handed,' Bernard told

him after the first night, as he removed his make-up in the dressing room. He rubbed his arm dramatically and pulled a pained face. 'I've got bruises.'

'I'm only getting into the part, Bernie,' Peter told him.

'Well, don't be so rough, and don't call me Bernie,' replied Bernard.

The following night Peter, much to Bernard's alarm, appeared on stage armed with a length of rope, which he used to very good effect. He banged it so loudly on the table the whole set shivered, swung it around his head and finally brought it down on Bernard's shoulders. There was a desperate high-pitched wail from the victim.

'If you do that tomorrow,' Bernard told him off stage as he rubbed his shoulder, 'I shall walk off.'

The next night, true to his warning, when Peter appeared with the rope, Bernard stamped his foot, ballooned with anger, shook furiously and, to great applause, stomped off stage, leaving Peter alone to deliver an impromptu soliloquy. A moment later, to everyone's surprise, Bernard reappeared armed with a rope, only his was bigger, heavier and thicker than Peter's. Bernard, still smarting from the previous night's onslaught, belted Peter over the top of the head and, to great laughter and applause, exited stage right.

The producer was not best pleased and gave both actors a thorough dressing down, warning them that this kind of unrehearsed activity on stage should cease immediately. The following day the *South Yorkshire Times*, which carried a review of the production, was read with great interest. The young actor who came in for the greatest praise for his outstanding portrayal of a most difficult and demanding role was Bernard.

Many years later a Performing Arts inspector reminded me of this episode when she related a similar incident where an actor settled a score on stage. I guess this is an apocryphal account (my colleague was a great storyteller and consummate actor), but it is well worth repeating. My colleague chaired a panel which awarded grants for sixth-form students to attend music and drama colleges. One particular young man was very talented and also extremely arrogant, and had applied to RADA, the Royal Academy of Dramatic Art, arguably the very best and most prestigious drama college in the country. After a bravura performance as Hamlet for his audition, the young man won his award and the inspector was asked by the boy's headmaster if she would like to see the young man in action playing the lead in the school's production of *Macbeth*. The future star of the London stage was indeed very convincing as the Scottish tyrant and dominated the scenes, dwarfing all the other actors with his outstanding performance. On the first night the eleven-year-old boy playing the part of Seyton, an officer attending Macbeth, a rather insignificant part compared to others in the play, made his final entrance to inform Macbeth of the Queen's demise. With bowed head and in a faltering voice the boy delivered his one final line: 'The Queen, my Lord, is dead,' and exited stage left. Macbeth then launched into his memorable soliloquy:

> She should have died hereafter;
> There would have been a time for such a word:
> Tomorrow and tomorrow and tomorrow
> Creeps in this petty pace from day to day,
> To the last syllable of recorded time . . .

At the second night's performance Seyton's relatives were in the audience, in fact the first two rows were crammed with parents, siblings, uncles, aunts, cousins and neighbours. They waited patiently for the entrance of the boy. When the young actor came on stage to deliver his one line there was an audible in-drawing of breath from the assorted relations and friends, and the whispered voice of a proud mother from the front row could be heard announcing, 'That's our Wayne.' Seeing his adoring fans, the boy decided to embellish his part a little and, throwing his arms in the air, he wailed, 'The Queen, my Lord, is dead! She's dead! She's dead! She's dead!' In one final harrowing shout he announced as he beat his breast, 'She's deeeeaaaaad!' He then left the stage to thunderous applause from the front two rows.

The future star of RADA was not at all pleased when he found the boy in the dressing room later. There were histrionics on a grand scale. 'Just say your line and get off the stage!' he ordered before strutting off to remove his make-up.

On the last night of the production young Seyton, still smarting from the reprimand, came on stage to deliver his line. Macbeth prepared himself for his powerful soliloquy but was rather lost for words when the boy announced, 'The Queen, my Lord, is making a remarkable recovery.'

The following year, when I auditioned for a part in *A Midsummer Night's Dream*, I asked the producer, Howard Tucker, if I might have a stab at a part other than an avaricious, mean-minded, bad-tempered old man. I suppose by this time I was getting a bit above myself. I remember using a newly discovered phrase. 'I'm being typecast,' I told him. Howard smiled and told me he would consider my request when he came to casting the play. The letter arrived a week later, informing the aspiring actors which parts had been assigned to them. I was certainly not an avaricious, mean-minded, bad-tempered old man in this play – I had been cast as Oberon, King of the Fairies. I had really wanted the part of Bottom or Pinch or another of the Mechanicals, so I felt deflated. Howard, however, explained at the first read-through that this was a main role and I had some of Shakespeare's most beautiful verse to declaim. I felt a little mollified.

A Midsummer Night's Dream was the set O level text that year. This was good news and bad news. The good news was that we were guaranteed full houses but the bad news was that the theatre would be full of students studying the play. I cannot say I was entirely enthusiastic about appearing as a fairy before a theatre full of students about my age, but there was one real benefit. I got to kiss Titania, the Queen of the Fairies, who was played by the delectable Shirley Ramsey. Shirley was a most attractive girl – shapely, elegant and very desirable as well as being an outstanding actress, and I was very much looking forward to the scene when she lay prone on her bed of flowers and I awaken her from her dream with a kiss.

My apprehension at playing the part of a fairy was, however, heightened greatly at the costume fitting. Shirley emerged from the girls' dressing room looking stunning in a pale blue and pink chiffon dress, white tights, pale silk shoes and sporting a tiara of dried red roses. She gave me a knowing smile. She knew something which I clearly did not. I soon found out. My costume was colour coordinated with hers. I had a sort of frilly, balloon-sleeved shirt made of the same pink and blue chiffon, but mine stopped just above the waist, a pair of white tights displaying something I would have preferred covered up, and large white pumps. The whole ensemble was completed with an enormous wreath of brightly coloured dried leaves, acorns and pine cones, to be worn on the head. As I stared at myself in the full-length mirror in the dressing room I shook my head. 'No way,' I murmured. 'No way am I wearing this.' The costume mistress, who thought I really looked the part in her creation, told me in no uncertain terms that I *would* be wearing the costume.

'I can't be doing with primadonnas,' she snapped.

'I look like a prima ballerina,' I replied, 'and I am not wearing this.'

'Well, if you don't like it,' she said, 'you can make it yourself.'

My sister Christine came to the rescue. She created for me a magnificent black silk shirt (which extended below the waist to cover my embarrassment), decorated with elaborate motifs of stars and moons in gold sequins, a flowing cape and a crown of shiny golden laurel leaves. The producer had stressed that Oberon was a strong, dark and brooding character and he took little persuasion to let me wear the costume. In fact, he was extremely reasonable. 'Unless you feel comfortable in your costume,' he said, 'you won't feel comfortable acting the part.' Everyone, except the wardrobe mistress, agreed that I looked really impressive when we came to the dress rehearsal. Bill Crouch, in charge of make-up, transformed my face. With the help of 5 and 9 make-up he concealed the angry acne in my cheeks and gave me a dark and swarthy tan, highlighted my eyes and reddened my lips. For the first time I began to feel comfortable in the part and I threw myself into the role.

The play was well received, and with each performance my amorous scene with Shirley became more adventurous and exploratory. On the first night it was a peck on the cheek, but by the time of the final performance I had really got into my stride and gave her a great smacker full on the lips. Her eyes shot open. 'Stop that off!' she hissed. 'You're a sex maniac!' Shirley never did go out with me, but I had a number of offers from girls who had seen the performance and waited for an autograph outside the stage door. Letters were delivered to the dressing room telling me how good I was on stage and inviting me to parties. One letter I still keep. It tells me, 'You have lovely legs.' This acting business made me feel pretty good.

In my final year at the South Yorkshire Theatre for Youth I had a gem of a part – Malvolio in *Twelfth Night*. Malvolio is the vain, narrow-minded, humourless steward of the Countess Olivia and the part is challenging and great fun to act. The joke that Maria, Lady Olivia's maid, plays on Malvolio, the kill-joy and spoilsport, is perhaps the funniest scene in Shakespeare, no matter how often it is performed.

On the second night of the production the cast was

somewhat disconcerted when, peering through the curtains in the wings, they saw the first two rows full of students all clutching books. After the success of the last Shakespeare play, when the seats had sold out in record time because of the play's popularity with schools, the producer had decided to pick another play which was on the O level set text list. It was clear that many in the audience that evening had brought along copies of the play, intent on following us as we spoke our lines. Despite the producer's reassurance that no one would shout out if we fluffed a word, we were all nervous. The boy playing Duke Theseus came off stage after the first scene and frightened us all by relating how the students ran their fingers along the lines in their texts as he recited them.

In my scenes my eyes were increasingly drawn to the students in the first two rows, with their books on their knees. All I saw was the top of their heads. The scene where Malvolio is awakened by the carousing of the outrageous drunken Sir Toby Belch and his friends is one of the play's highlights. That evening I entered in a long nightgown and cap with my chain of office around my neck and I railed at the revellers:

My masters, are you mad? Or what are you? Have you no wit, manners, nor honesty, but to make an alehouse of my lady's house . . . ?

The student playing Sir Toby was a seasoned and very talented actor. He spluttered and spat and staggered drunkenly across the stage. Finally he thrust his face into mine and swung the heavy metal chain around my neck with the words:

Go, sir, rub your chain with crumbs.

The sharp points on the chain cut into my flesh and I exclaimed, 'Bloody hell.' There was a deal of consternation on the front two rows when, try as they might, the students following in the text tried to locate the words. This was followed by frantic whispering.

On the next night, with three strips of Elastoplast around my neck, I was not chancing another cut throat, so I divested myself of the chain just before my entrance. When it came to the famous line there was, of course, no chain for me to rub with crumbs. With remarkable aplomb Sir Toby told me:

Prithee good sir, go taketh a running jump!

It was fortunate that there were no students in the audience that night, following his lines in their books.

Those productions with the South Yorkshire Theatre for Youth were memorable and were the start of a long career in amateur theatre. I went on to act at college, at the schools in which I taught and with various local drama groups. I was Duncan in *Macbeth,* Chitterlow in *Half a Sixpence*, Mr Brownlow in *Oliver!*, Hobson in *Hobson's Choice*, the SS Lieutenant in *The Sound of Music*, Glorybee in *The Beeple*, the Reverend Lupin in *Sweeney Todd* and Wackford Squeers in *Smike*, as well as many other parts.

One memorable thespian experience was when I was in the Lower Sixth and was persuaded by the producer of a local amateur dramatics group to take a minor part in a murder-mystery drama. Norman, a small balding man who invariably wore a pair of extremely tight jeans and a multicoloured T-shirt, was a very different kind of producer from Bill Hammond. He had tantrums if the actors failed to follow his precise instructions, and sometimes went off in a sulk. I was cast as the police sergeant who accompanied the investigating officer and only appeared briefly in the second and the final acts. I had but a few lines and most of these consisted of, 'Yes, sir,' but Norman insisted I assume a Cockney accent to give the character 'depth'.

I looked far too young for the part of a police sergeant, so to affect maturity the man in make-up, having slapped a thick coating of grease paint on my face and drawn a series of carmine lines across my forehead, stuck a small square black moustache beneath my nose, applied with a thick brown sticky adhesive. I had just started shaving and the application of the glutinous gum to my upper lip caused unbearable stinging. Then the itching started.

On the first night, I appeared on stage dressed in a grey gabardine raincoat and large black trilby hat bound round with a shiny black ribbon. Catching sight of this incongruous figure with the silly black moustache, upper lip twitching, someone in the audience called out, 'Bloody hell, it's Charlie Chaplin.' Things tended to go downhill after that, for the next time I appeared on stage the joker in the audience shouted, 'Ey up, Charlie's back!' When I did open my mouth this was greeted with titters from the audience.

When I exited stage right Norman was waiting for me in the wings, red and flustered. He ripped the moustache off my face and without a word stormed off. At the curtain call I bowed (minus the moustache) with my fellow actors and heard the joker in the audience call out, 'Ey up, Charlie's had a shave!'

At the beginning of the final act the murderer appears on stage and shoots a second victim. At the second performance the starting pistol failed to go off. Thinking on his feet, the murderer rushed across the stage and throttled his man as the curtain descended.

Not wishing a repetition of this in the next performance, the following night Norman produced two short planks of wood held together by a hinge. When brought together they made a cracking sound resembling a gunshot. Vernon, the stage manager, was positioned off stage with the device in case the starting pistol failed to fire at the performance. This amateur dramatic production was getting increasingly amateur.

Norman, checking that everything was ready for the murder scene, asked Vernon, 'Have you got the clap?'

'No, Norman,' replied Vernon, 'it's just the way I'm standing.'

The review of the play in the local paper made mention of 'the young man playing the part of the police sergeant'. It was said that 'he added a touch of levity to an otherwise dreary plot'. One of the lead players, who did not merit a mention, was not at all pleased with this acknowledgement and glared at me when I entered the dressing room for the final performance.

'Who does he think he is, Laurence bloody Olivier?' I heard him asking another aggrieved member of the cast who had not been mentioned in the paper either.

I decided that this would be my last excursion on the amateur stage.

43

For the two years of the O level course I had worked hard and got a good set of GCE passes. The door on to the wide world was now open for me. Walking through town a week after the results, a great booming voice echoed across All Saints' Square: 'Phinny! Phinny!' It was Mr Firth. Unusually for a sunny summer's day, he was dressed in an old tweed jacket with leather patches on the elbows and lining the cuffs, heavy brogues, shirt, cardigan and tie. 'Phinny!' he shouted, 'over here!' Taking a deep breath I walked over to meet him.

'Now then, Phinny!'

'Morning, sir,' I said, standing to attention.

He thrust out a hand the size of a small spade. 'Well done,' he said. 'I'm very pleased with your history result but I think you could have done better.'

'Yes sir,' I replied. I almost felt like apologizing.

'If Cardinal Wolsey and William of Orange had come up, I reckon you would have got the top marks, but that's the luck of the draw with exams. It's a lottery. Always has been and always will be. Anyhow, you didn't do all that badly.'

'Thank you, sir.'

'And now it's the sixth form, is it?'

'No sir.'

'No?' he snapped.

'No, sir,' I told him. 'I'm leaving. I'm going to be a trainee accountant.'

'A trainee bloody accountant?' It was the first time I think I had heard any teacher swear. 'A trainee bloody accountant?' he repeated.

'Yes sir,' I said. 'I had an interview at Hart, Moss & Copley on Moorgate Street just before my results came out and Mr Copley said that if I get five good O levels, including maths and English, he would take me on.'

Mrs Gill, Mum's best friend, was Company Secretary at Thomas Wilde & Son in Sheffield and she had arranged for me to have a preliminary talk with a senior partner at Hart, Moss & Copley, Chartered Accountants. I had presented myself at the plush offices on Moorgate Street, in a new suit, hair short and slicked back, with highly polished black shoes, and sat before one of the senior partners. He appeared every inch what I imagined an accountant would look like, in his dark suit and with a pair of half-moon spectacles perched on the end of his nose.

'Well, young man,' said the senior partner, tapping my letter of application before him on his desk, 'you've done adequately enough in your school exams though not spectacularly well, you seem a biddable young man and are smartly turned out.' He looked over the rims of his spectacles and scrutinized me. 'Do you reckon you have the makings of a trainee accountant?'

'Yes, sir,' I replied.

'Well, if your references from school are in order, I'm minded to give you a chance.'

'Thank you, sir,' I mumbled, feeling myself swell with pride. He looked at me expectantly and began rotating his thumbs slowly around one another. He was clearly waiting for something further from me.

'Well, young man,' he continued, after a long pause. 'Go ahead. Sell yourself.'

I must have acquitted myself reasonably well because he nodded approvingly after each answer. 'Now, I see you have the required O levels but you will have to take a lot more exams to become a qualified accountant. It will not be easy. You're prepared for that, are you?'

'Yes, sir.'

'Can you can start in September?'

'Yes, sir.'

He leaned across the desk and held out a hand. 'Welcome to Hart, Moss & Copley,' he said, smiling.

'And that's what you want to do, is it?' asked Mr Firth, when I told him about the interview. 'Add figures up all day in a dark and dusty office? Deal with tax forms and tiresome financial audits? Be a trainee accountant?' He stressed the words 'trainee accountant' as if they were an insult. 'Whatever do you want to be a trainee accountant for?'

'It's a good job, sir.'

'You want to teach, lad, teach. That's your future – teaching – inspiring young people. It's the best job in the world. You think on, Phinny, teaching's for you.'

Three days later I received a letter from the Rotherham Education Office inviting me to attend an interview with Mr Bloomer, the Director of Education. I had never met Mr Bloomer but had been at primary school with his daughter and knew that he was a very important man, in charge of all the schools in the town. I reported to the reception at the Education Office on the appointed day and at the appointed time and waited in the outer office. I couldn't understand why he would wish to see me. The secretary occasionally looked up from her papers but said nothing until the buzzer on her desk sounded.

'You may go in, young man,' she told me, 'and remember to call the Director "sir".'

The room I entered was large and dark-panelled. Great glass-fronted bookcases full of leather-bound tomes lined one wall, and framed pictures and prints, no doubt drawn and painted by the town's children and students, were displayed on the other. Opposite the bookcases a window gave an uninterrupted view over the town. Many years later, when I was appointed as General Adviser for Language Development with Rotherham, I was shown into the very same room. The desk, bookcases and prints were still there and the smell had lingered too.

Mr Bloomer sat behind his large mahogany desk and invited me to take a seat in front of him.

'Now then, young man,' he said, 'what is this that I hear about you leaving school before your A levels?'

I explained that I had been offered a junior position at an accountant's in the town.

'Your headmaster has had a word with me and he is of the opinion that you ought to stay on.' He looked down at a piece of paper before him on the desk. 'You've done pretty well in your O levels and have a bright future ahead of you. Your teachers think highly of you, as indeed does Mr Williams, who feels you should continue your studies.'

'Yes, sir,' I replied, not really knowing what to say.

'If you *were* to stay on at school, what A levels would you take?' he asked.

'I've not really thought about it, sir,' I replied.

'Well, give it a little thought now.'

'I suppose I would take the subjects I like best,' I replied eventually. 'Probably English literature, history and geography.'

'Arts subjects,' said Mr Bloomer. 'Not really the sort of subjects suitable for accountancy, I should have thought. It seems to me mathematics would be more appropriate.'

'Yes, sir.'

'Now look, young man,' he said looking across the desk, 'I agree with Mr Williams. I think you should stay on and do your A levels. If, after that, you still feel accountancy is the profession for you, then you can become a trainee, but get a few A levels under your belt first. I feel certain Mr Copley will take you on if you still feel inclined to become an accountant.' It seemed to me that everyone knew about my intentions and had a vested interest in my future. I suppose Mr Firth had related our conversation in All Saints' Square to Mr Williams, who, in turn, had contacted the Director of Education to use his influence.

'You know,' he said, 'Mr Williams and I are very proud of the fact that some young people like you, who didn't get the chance to go to the grammar school, have done so well. You have achieved results much better than some who did pass their Eleven Plus and you have done that through hard work and determination. My advice, young man, is to stay on at school and keep your options open. Have a word with your parents and see what they say. You might consider training for the teaching profession. We need people like you in our schools.'

At the time I didn't think it was particularly unusual for the Director of Education to summon a pupil to his office and give him the benefit of his advice, but now I know that it was. It seems amazing to me when I think about it now that someone as important and as busy as Mr Bloomer should take a personal interest in just one student. It had never occurred to me until Mr Firth raised the matter that I should train to become a teacher, but after that encounter with him in All Saints' Square and subsequently with Mr Bloomer, a seed was planted and things in my life began to change. Had I not met Mr Firth on that day my life might have taken a very different course.

In September 1964 I joined the sixth form at Oakwood Technical High School for Boys. I thought perhaps that the headmaster might meet me, introduce himself and welcome me to the school, but he left that to the school secretary, a bright and cheerful woman who said that should I want to know anything I should come and ask her. I found that Mrs Ranby was true to her word, and I often called into the office for her help and advice. On that first day she took me down the cold tiled corridor to the sixth form classroom, chattering inconsequentially and pointing things out.

'You'll be very happy here,' she told me. I can't say that I felt reassured.

On that first morning, like any new boy, I felt apprehensive and under-confident as I stood in my smart new black blazer and badge in front of the Lower Sixth class, to be introduced by the form master. I recall that he got my name wrong – something I have had to put up with for most of my life. Indeed, on all the reports from Oakwood both my names are spelt incorrectly. All eyes stared at me as if I were some strange exhibit in a museum case. Perhaps these superior-looking boys were wondering just how an Eleven Plus failure would cope with the academic rigour of advanced study. They had gone through the school together, sat and passed their examinations together and made close friendships. These boys I now had to mix with were well-established. I knew nothing of their backgrounds, what they discussed, their academic achievements, and I had no experience of their world. I knew no one at the school on that first morning, and although I felt nervous and lonely as I glanced at the staring faces before me, I was determined to stay the course. I remember thinking to myself that I was as good as they were, and even if I didn't settle in here, make friends or even enjoy the courses, studying at the high school would be a means to an end. I had a good string of O levels, some with distinction, and had a firmness of purpose. I would persevere, keep my head down and work hard.

As it turned out, some of the boys were friendly and I was soon disabused of the idea that they were all stuck up and stand-offish. Mathematics, history, economics, music, geography, the sciences could be offered at A level in the boys' school but not English literature or French, so I, along with five other boys, had to study for part of the time in the girls' high school.

It was a strange and not altogether unpleasant experience striding down the corridor at the all girls' school to be eyed by gaggles of giggling girls in brown uniforms and observed by sharp-eyed women teachers in black gowns and with severe expressions. We must have looked gauche and gangly as we entered the room of the Head of the English Department.

Miss Mary Wainwright was a diminutive, softly-spoken woman dressed in a pristine white blouse with a lace collar, done up at the neck with small pearl buttons. She was swathed in a long, pleated tweed skirt, dark brown stockings and small leather brogues. The delicate embroidered handkerchief that she secreted up her sleeve would be occasionally plucked out to dab her mouth. Save for the large cameo brooch placed at her throat, she wore no jewellery and there was no vestige of make-up. She lined up her new students, a motley group of spotty, lanky boys, and peered up at us. 'I've never taught boys,' she said, and then, after a long pause and with a twinkle in her dark eyes, she added, 'But I've heard of them.'

We studied two of Shakespeare's greatest plays – *Richard II* and *Hamlet*, the longest and most tedious of Chaucer's *Canterbury Tales* – *The Knight's Tale* and *The Prologue* – *The Grapes of Wrath* by John Steinbeck, *Joseph Andrews* by the eighteenth-century novelist Henry Fielding and the poetry of John Keats. I was pleased to see that Thomas Hardy's tragic tale *The Mayor of Casterbridge* was on the syllabus, but disappointed that D. H. Lawrence and Charles Dickens were not.

In the first week I kept a very low profile, saying little but watching the other students, who did not appear as clever and self-assured as I'd imagined they would be. I was pleased that the first text we studied was *The Mayor of Casterbridge*. I had read several of Thomas Hardy's novels and really enjoyed them, and I was familiar with some of the literary devices he was prone to using.

As soon as Miss Wainwright opened the book and started to read I was in a world I loved and in which I felt familiar. Occasionally she would stop, make a comment and smile with a curious wistfulness, as if there was something she recalled fondly from a distant past.

The first essay I handed in to Miss Wainwright concerned our initial impressions of Henchard, the main character in the novel, and I spent long hours in the central library in town writing, rewriting and referring to various reference books. When the essays were handed back my heart leapt. Following a long and detailed assessment of my effort written at the bottom of the page in small neat handwriting, I had been awarded a B+.

Miss Wainwright took me aside after the lesson. 'That was extremely promising,' she told me, smiling. 'It's a very good start. I am sure you will do well.' From then onwards I gained in confidence, contributed in the lessons and achieved good marks.

What incredible good fortune it was for me to have had this remarkable woman for my teacher. Miss Wainwright, a woman of great learning and infinite patience, was passionate about her subject and had the ability to bring the works of Shake-speare to life.

'Shakespeare is not a novelist,' she once told us. 'He is a poet and a dramatist and the greatest writer that has ever lived.' What was so memorable about this remarkable teacher were her eyes. They shone with intensity, especially when she was discussing her favourite subject, the bard himself.

Miss Wainwright regularly organized coach trips to the neighbouring theatres to see performances. In one production of *Richard II* in Sheffield, the actor playing the lead of 'the sun king' was a small man with an enormous yellow codpiece in the shape of a risen sun. In the opening scene, when all the nobles assembled in their finery on stage, the King entered sporting this remarkable appendage, which caused a great deal of mirth in the audience of largely schoolchildren and students. Even greater amusement was caused when the king sat down, for the codpiece would rise up in an extremely vulgar manner. It soon became too much for the audience to bear and great guffaws emanated from different parts of the theatre. When the King arrived in successive scenes he was greeted by loud

cheers and comments such as, 'Ey up, it's thundercrutch again.'
The production was temporarily halted and the manager, over
the microphone, informed the audience that if it did not
remain quiet and cease interrupting then the production would
cease. When the King made his next entrance it was notice-
able that he was wearing a rather tasteful and considerably
smaller codpiece in a discreet black.

Miss Wainwright took us to see a production of *King Lear*
at the Rotherham Civic Theatre. The acting was wooden and
the costumes bizarre, but the beauty and poignancy of the
language came through. King Lear, confused and deranged,
entered with his dead daughter draped in his arms and crying
to the heavens:

> Howl, howl, howl, howl! O, you are men of stones:
> Had I your tongues and eyes, I'd use them
> That heaven's vault should crack. She's gone for ever.
> I know when one is dead and when one lives:
> She is dead as earth.

Miss Wainwright — sitting one away from me in the row,
began to dab her eyes with the lace handkerchief.

44

My geography master at A level was another inspirational teacher called J. A. Taylor (JAT). I very nearly gave the subject up after the first couple of weeks but was persuaded otherwise by Mr Taylor. JAT taught the regional geography part of the course and supervised the local study, the other teacher taught the meteorology and physical geography components. When I arrived for the first lesson of physical geography, copies of the textbook we would be using, this maroon-covered tome called *Physical Geography* by Horrocks, were distributed but there was one textbook short.

'I wasn't aware that you were joining this group,' the teacher announced, and I was told to share with another student. The boy next to me, understandably, was not that pleased, for it meant we had to take it in turns to take the book home to do our homework. Looking back I feel it would have been more considerate of the teacher to have asked two other boys who knew each other to share, not the new addition to his class, who didn't know anyone and felt nervous enough. I cannot say I felt that comfortable in this teacher's lessons. He never welcomed me when I first arrived or asked about me or took any real interest in me as the course progressed. When I did on occasions see him about something he would reply stiffly and hurriedly, like a man who had more important things to do.

The first assignment was on a topic that I just could not get my head around – 'Isostatic Equilibrium'. The grade I received was poor and the comment indifferent. So, one breaktime, I saw Mr Taylor, who was the head of the department, and told him I was thinking of giving up the course, that I really didn't feel up to it. He persuaded me to continue, telling me my grade at O level, a few marks off a distinction and better than many in the group, was a good indication that I could cope with the course.

The following week he discovered that I did not have a physical geography textbook and was sharing. He sighed and shook his head and asked why the other teacher had not provided one for me. I explained that I had been told to share and that's what I had been doing. The following lesson Mr Taylor presented me with a brand new and updated edition of Horrocks.

JAT clearly loved his subject and taught us with such enthusiasm and rigour, believing that geography was best studied in the field – 'first-hand experience' was his favourite catchphrase. I remember once, on one of his trips, we scanned the landscape looking for drumlins, described in our textbook as 'basket of eggs scenery'. I imagined them to be small hummocks, but when I enquired of Mr Taylor where these 'drumlins' were he threw back his head and laughed and then informed me that I was standing on one – this huge rounded hill. 'First-hand experience,' he said. I learnt then that fact can sometimes be as fanciful as fiction, for the descriptions in Horrocks seemed to me to bear little relation to the real world.

JAT organized many a field trip at weekends, during the school holidays and for a week out of school at the end of each term. These were eagerly anticipated, especially since we joined up with the girls from the girls' high school, under the watchful eye of JAT's wife, the formidable Mrs Taylor, who was head of the geography department there.

One memorable field trip was to Malham Cove. We had read about 'clints' and 'grykes', limestone pavements and caverns, potholes and subterranean rivers in our physical geography textbook. I was not prepared, however, for what I was to see. We approached by a footpath from the south, and this immense bow-shaped cove came into view like some great walled cathedral. It was breathtaking. I had never seen anything quite as bleak and rugged. Mr Taylor had us stand beneath the towering cove and not say anything at all – just take it in for a moment. Then he explained that it had been formed millions of years ago when the earth's crust had cracked, fracturing the rock so that it dropped vertically. 'It's over two hundred feet high,' he told us, 'a thousand feet wide and once a crashing waterfall cascaded over the vertical cliff, creating a fall higher than the Niagara Falls. Now can your small minds take that in?'

We spent that week at the youth hostel in the ancient village of Malham and saw bubbling springs and crashing cataracts, crags and scars, ravines and overhanging cliffs, and the spectacular Malham Tarn, one of the two natural lakes in the Yorkshire Dales.

Mr Taylor asked if anyone had come across the novel *The Water Babies* by Charles Kingsley. I was the only one who had read the story of Tom, the little chimney-sweep who meets the babies in the cool clear water. Mr Taylor related the story of how Charles Kingsley, having passed through Bradford and witnessed the squalor and filth, visited Tarn House in Malham in 1858 as a guest of the millionaire philanthropist Walter Morris. Kingsley was struck by the stark contrast of the dark industrial city and the stunning limestone scenery, as I was on that first visit. He was a skilled botanist and was asked by the children of the house to explain the streaks of black on the face of the cove. He explained that they were made by a little chimney sweep called Tom slipping over the clifftop and sliding down into the stream. Here was his inspiration for the classic fantasy story.

I discovered the North York Moors in the sixth form on another of Mr Taylor's expeditions. This silent and bleak world

with its great tracts of heather and bracken fascinated me. We
stayed in youth hostels and explored the incredible landscape,
visited great abbeys like Byland and Rievaulx, ate our sandwiches in the shadow of lofty castles at Helmsley and
Pickering, and sat in the sunshine outside local inns in villages
untouched by modern life. One weekend Mr Taylor led us
deep within the North York Moors towards the coast at
Ravenscar. The journey followed the old Viking route known
as the 'Lyke Wake'. Legend has it that the Vikings carried the
'lyke' or corpse across the forty boggy miles to the sea, where
the body was given up to the waves. With the coming of
Christianity the practice was continued but it took on a deeper
meaning, and the walk came to symbolize the journey of the
soul towards heaven. I had never seen such magnificent scenery in my life. Beneath a shining blue sky there stretched a
landscape of every conceivable colour: brilliant greens, swaths
of red and yellow gorse that blazed like a bonfire, dark hedge-
rows speckled in pinks and whites, twisted black stumps,
striding walls and the grey snake of the road curling upwards
to the hills in the far distance. Light the colour of melted butter
danced among the new leaves of early summer.

On one expedition in the heat of midsummer the party of
sixth-formers, led by Mr Taylor and his wife, trekked up a
lonely moorland hill on the North York Moors, through the
soft couch grass and sweet-smelling heather. Arriving at the
brow, we peered down at the panorama before us and there
on a soft grassy bed was a pair of lovers in a passionate embrace,
the sun beating down on their naked limbs.

As we were ushered away from the summit by a red-faced
Mrs Taylor, one cheeky student asked her husband, 'Is that
what is meant by first-hand experience, sir?'

For my local study I chose the relatively affluent area of
Sheffield called Broomhill. As the date for the deadline for
handing in the project approached, I spent most Saturday

mornings in the Sheffield public library researching, poring over old maps and newspapers and making notes. In the afternoon I would take a bus up to Broomhill and walk around the area taking photographs, visiting factories, parks and shops, undertaking residential and industrial surveys and interviewing people who lived and worked in the area. This was the part of the course that I really enjoyed.

I remember interviewing the manager of the Snuff Mill, a large prepossessing figure in a tweed suit who punctuated his answers by taking a pinch of the toxic powder between finger and thumb from a small silver box and sniffing it up his nose, below which was a small brown stain where the snuff had lingered. He then produced a large coloured handkerchief and sneezed into it loudly.

'You seem like a likely lad,' he told me when I had finished asking my questions. Then after a heavy clearing of his throat he asked me, 'Do you fancy a career in snuff?'

I replied that it had never occurred to me. 'You could do worse,' he told me. And I thought, yes, and I could do better.

On another occasion I was taking a photograph of a large imposing villa when the owner, an elderly man in a threadbare cardigan and old trousers, approached me and asked me what I was doing. When I said I was working on a geography project for school, he insisted on explaining to me the geological features of the area before disappearing into his house and returning with a booklet about Sheffield and its environs.

'You can have this,' he told me. 'It might be useful.' Then he added, 'I wrote it.'

I discovered later that the man in question was a former lecturer in geography at Sheffield University.

Mr Taylor was waiting outside the examination room to see how we had all found the A level paper when the big day arrived. I had revised pretty thoroughly and felt I had performed reasonably well, but I was disappointed that the one question Mr Taylor had predicted was very likely to come up – to 'discuss the reasons for the decline in the cotton industry in the southern states of the USA' – had not appeared in the paper.

'But it did,' he told me when I mentioned this to him later.

He opened the paper. The question read: '*King Cotton is dead!* Discuss.' I learnt then just how tricky language can be in examinations and how the wording of a question can cause problems for the candidate in a totally unexpected way. I had never come across the expression before. I remember thinking it must be a famous American industrialist I had never heard of and went on to the next question.

It has been my unquestionable good fortune to have been taught by Miss Wainwright and Mr Taylor, to have had my mind stretched, my aspirations raised and my love of literature and the world around me developed. Whenever, as a schools inspector, I observed an outstanding sixth-form lesson, I often thought of those two teachers; I shall be forever grateful and remember their warmth, encouragement and commitment.

I returned to my past through an unexpected door. When my first Penguin book had been published and appeared in the best-seller list, I was invited back to present prizes and speak at my alma mater. It was strange walking down the echoing corridor at Oakwood with the headteacher, the familiar school smell of floor polish and disinfectant still lingering on the air, and up on to the stage. It was even stranger to be introduced as one of the school's most distinguished and successful former pupils.

The day I left the sixth form I accompanied my mother for the Stations of the Cross followed by Mass at St Bede's. Father Hammond, moving from one plaster tablet to another, each depicting Christ's journey to the Cross, genuflected and intoned:

Jesus who for love of me
Didst bear Thy cross to Calvary,
In Thy sweet mercy grant to me
To suffer and to die with thee.

It was a weekday and there was a sparse congregation largely composed of elderly women telling their rosary beads and muttering. Mum strode purposefully down the central aisle and sat in the very front pew, just as Mr Ryves had done years before. Her presence was unmistakable to Father Hammond, when he emerged from the presbytery and ascended the altar steps and began Mass. At each response my mother answered loudly and clearly. We went to communion together as the organist played the hymn, 'O, Bread of Heaven'. Father Hammond held up the host, paused, and placed it gently on my mother's tongue. She said later it was like coming home.

At the end of Mass we went together to the small Lady Chapel at the side of the altar and lit a penny candle. We lit it together and fixed it on a spike on the brass candleholder and made our silent prayer – for me it was to be successful in my exams. I guess my mother knew that the priest would send for her and he did. An altar boy approached us and told her that Father Hammond would like to speak to her. My mother walked with a determined step into the presbytery, and before the priest could utter a word she told him that I had now left school and she would be receiving communion once again. He could no longer forbid her to take the Eucharist.

The priest looked nonplussed.

'I was just going to ask you, Mrs Phinn,' he said quietly, 'if I might prevail upon you to play the piano at a Union of Catholic Mothers meeting next week.'

My mother and I laughed all the way home.

The following week there was another chance encounter with Mr Firth in All Saints' Square.

'Fancy coming to the Isle of Man again?' he asked. 'You could help supervise the lads and get a bit of practice in at being a teacher.'

I jumped at the chance. So, along with two friends from the sixth form, I joined the South Grove School party. I shared a small room with the other two sixth-formers and we were allowed infinitely more freedom, treated very differently by the teachers and given more responsibility. By this time, pending the necessary A level results, I was about to study for my degree and certificate in education and make teaching my career. Mr Firth was right. The experience of supervising the younger boys, checking the rooms, lending a sympathetic ear to the homesick, reading stories to the first years, refereeing the football and rugby matches, organizing board games and running the tuck shop was invaluable.

One meeting I shall never forget. I was on my way back from Port St Mary one early evening and passing the Station Hotel, when I saw Mr Firth, sitting by himself, his arms comfortably crossed on his chest, his head tilted towards the sun and with a pint of Guinness before him.

'Gervase!' he called out. 'Come and join me.'

I was no longer Phinny. I felt very grown-up.

I sat next to this incongruous figure in his baggy brown shorts, old walking boots, shapeless shirt and jungle hat. 'Ah,' he said, 'the unadmitted pleasure of solitary contemplation.' He took a gulp of beer. 'Results out soon then,' he said.

'Yes, sir.'

'Nervous?'

'Yes, sir.'

'You'll be all right,' he said, then asked, 'Are you eighteen?'

'Yes, sir.'

'Then I'll treat you to a drop of the black stuff – an early celebration.'

It was my first half pint of Guinness and I didn't like it at all. It tasted bitter and unpleasant, but I sipped slowly and we sat there in silence for while. I wanted to say something but the words got caught in my throat.

'So,' he said, 'you are going to be a teacher?'

'Yes, sir, if I get the grades.'

'You'll get the grades.'

'Hope so.'

He took another huge gulp of his Guinness and leaned back in the chair, the sun on his face.

'I'm glad you decided against becoming a bloody account-ant. There's too many of those buggers about.'

I smiled. 'I think I maybe have something to offer as a teacher,' I said.

'I'm sure you have. You're good with the young ones. I think you'll make a fine teacher. You have the personality for it. You study for your degree and your teaching certificate, be deter-mined, single-minded, don't let anything or anyone distract you from that course. At college you'll find many temptations and people a lot cleverer than you are and maybe sometimes you will feel like giving up, Well, don't.' He looked at me for a moment. 'And what do you think makes a good teacher?'

'Someone who believes that all children matter, whatever their background and ability,' I told him. 'Someone who builds up their self-esteem and expectation. I guess someone who likes the company of children and tries his best to make the lessons interesting. And someone who keeps an orderly class-room. A teacher like you, sir.'

Theo nodded but said nothing.

'Well, I had better be getting back,' I said. 'I'll not finish the Guinness if you don't mind. It's not really my cup of tea.'

Theo nodded.

'And thank you, sir,' I said.

'My pleasure.' He smiled. 'It's your round next time.'

'I meant thank you, sir, for all you have done for me. I always enjoyed your lessons and wouldn't have done as well in my exams without you. You know, I should never have gone in for teaching had you not persuaded me to stay on – ordered me to stay on, rather. I owe you a lot.'

He rubbed his chin. I could see he was moved by what I had said. This tough, frightening, eccentric figure was on the verge of tears. 'Well, you had better get back,' he said. 'Good luck with your results.'

That was the last time I saw Theodore Firth, sitting alone in the sunshine with a glass of Guinness in his hand.

I couldn't go into school to get my A level results and I had arranged that my friend Philip would send them on to me. I had never really felt a part of Oakwood. I was glad to leave and really didn't wish to return. I guess I always felt something of an outsider in the school, and saw my studying there as a stepping-stone to college to get a degree and train as a teacher. If I stayed the course in higher education, and I knew I had the determination and the perseverance to succeed, I would model myself on teachers like those at South Grove who worked tirelessly to restore self-esteem in those who considered themselves failures. They were men and women of vision and humanity dedicated to learning, ones who had made such a powerful impact in my life.

In the sixth form I had taken no part in the sports, attended none of the social activities, nor had I made much of an effort to mix with the other students. I had kept my head down and worked hard. I must have appeared a retiring, uninteresting and rather lonely figure. I was, of course, immensely fortunate to have had outstanding teachers like Mary Wainwright and Alan Taylor and shall be forever in their debt.

The A level results came as a great surprise. I got the highest grade in the group for English (a coveted grade A) and was awarded the English prize, and I achieved a grade B in geography, with a distinction in the project. Many years later I received a letter from my former geography teacher. In it Alan Taylor wrote:

I only allowed the most talented pupils to attempt historical geography pieces of work since having studied the reconstruction of place in time at university I knew the techniques and knew how difficult the study was. You succeeded beyond all expectations and set a standard that I expected other students to follow in any project that they attempted. Suffice it to say that I ultimately became the Chief Examiner in Geography for the JMB. You taught me, and set me standards for which I am eternally grateful.

It is difficult to describe my elation on hearing what I had achieved, and I felt that Mr Williams and the staff at South Grove Secondary Modern had been fully vindicated in having faith in youngsters like me who at eleven had been considered to be non-academic.

Once back from the Isle of Man, there followed a week of gentle teasing at home. I just could not take the smile off my face. Michael started referring to me as 'the prof' or 'brainbox' and Alec, on a visit home from Ireland, talked to me in a mock affected accent, telling me I was now far too important to share the time of day with him. My father said little, but I could see in his eyes and expression how very pleased and proud he was of me. He had saved a cutting from a national paper which I still have today. It was written by the journalist Peter Laurie, who wrote in 1965 that 'to have been consigned to the limbo of the secondary modern is to have failed disastrously and very early on in life'. I, like many other youngsters who failed the Eleven Plus, some of whom I have met over the forty years I have been involved in education, proved him wrong.

My mother baked a date and walnut cake to celebrate and invited Mrs Rogers to join us for tea.

'I always knew he was artificated,' she said, raising the cup of tea to her lips.

45

Like many students wanting to earn some extra money, I worked on the post during the Christmas holidays. This was my first experience of the world of work. The Post Office employed casual labour at this time of year to help deliver the vast quantity of cards, posters, calendars and parcels and, along with many other students, I arrived early at the Central Post Office in Rotherham to be assigned a patch.

On the first day I accompanied the postman, a small, red-haired, jolly little Irishman with a pale moon face, around the area I was to take over from him for a couple of weeks. Paddy had an untipped cigarette almost permanently lodged between his lips, so when he spoke he hardly opened his mouth. He was good company, although I sometimes found it difficult to decipher what he said what with the Irish accent and the limited movement of the lips. Paddy showed me how to carry the heaving postbag without 'putting my back out', what buses to catch, the short cuts to take, about the difficult residents I would encounter and the dogs of which I should be wary. I was fortunate with my 'postman'. Other students were not so lucky with their mentors; some were very grumpy and unpredictable individuals and one, a 'joker' who liked to play tricks on the green students, was reputed to have put a couple of house bricks in the bottom of the postbag of his student replacement and the poor lad carried them all around the area until he discovered them underneath all the letters. Rumour had it that the boy in question had, the following day, after the prank and in a fit of pique, posted all the letters down a grate and spent the morning in the Ring o' Bells café in Rotherham.

My area was Brinsworth, a part of Rotherham I came to know very well, as four years later I was to secure my first teaching position when I qualified as an Assistant Teacher of English at the purpose-built Brinsworth High School. Brinsworth was one of the most desirable rounds, a short bus ride away from the town centre and blessedly free of hills and isolated dwellings. It was a densely populated area of well-kept semi-detached houses, older more modest terraces and council-owned prefabricated structures, so I didn't have a long trek. There was a small arcade of shops and the one public house: the Three Magpies.

On the second morning delivering letters I suffered my first injury. While posting a card through a letterbox the dog, no doubt crouching in wait, grabbed the envelope as I fed it through, pulling my hand with it. The sharp spring on the letterbox snapped on my fingers like the teeth of a shark. The following day I had a cunning plan. I selected the biggest and most impressive card, slowly fed it through the letterbox, waited until the dog got a grip, then yanked it back, smacking the beast's head on the door. Inside I could hear the creature going wild and ripping up the cards, followed by the shouts of the irate owner.

At one house where I was to deliver a calendar, the door was answered by a small boy in vest and underpants.

'Is your mummy in?' I asked him. He shook his head.

'Is your daddy in?' There was another shake of the head.

'Is there anyone else in beside you?' I asked.

'There's our Joan,' he told me.

'Could you go and get her?'

'No.'

'Why?'

'I can't lift her out of the cot.'

There was a crescent of sheltered bungalows on my round. Each morning an elderly woman (I can't recall her name after so many years so I shall call her Mrs Smith) would be waiting at the door of her house to ask if there was anything for her. There never was. She was a friendly old lady, clearly very lonely, who just wanted to pass the time of day and have contact with another human being. I would be offered a drink but would politely refuse, explaining that I had a lot of cards to deliver. One very cold morning I had a smaller postbag than usual, had made good progress and could have just done with a warm drink, so I accepted Mrs Smith's offer. I was shown into a cluttered room with a stale and mouldy smell. There was a small artificial Christmas tree in the corner and on the mantelpiece was a line of Christmas cards. I knew, of course, that none of these had been sent that year.

Listening to this elderly lady talk, and hearing about her memories of the war, I realized that it is a truism that every one of us has a story to tell. They might not be massively exciting stories, dramatic, full of incident and intrigue, but nevertheless they give fascinating insights into the lives of ordinary people and should be preserved. Sadly many are not.

Mrs Smith had lived in that part of Sheffield which had suffered the greatest at the time of the Blitz of 1940 and 1941. She had vivid memories of when the Luftwaffe bombed the steelworks in Sheffield. Her street had been largely demolished and her house and all her possessions with it. She was able to describe accurately the scene of destruction, the terrible loss of life, the panic and terrible sense of loss, but there were moments of rare humour. For example, in a hurried effort to get dressed and into the air-raid shelter at the sound of the sirens she had put both legs through one opening in her bloomers and fell helplessly on the floor, totally incapacitated, until her calls for help attracted a neighbour who came to her rescue.

'I couldn't go in the shelter without my bloomers on,' she told her rescuer. 'What would people think?'

'I should think those in the shelter have enough to think

about, Doris,' said the neighbour, 'without being interested or bothered whether you're wearing your knickers or not.' Another neighbour arrived at the air-raid shelter to discover that she had forgotten something. Hurrying back to her house, she was stopped by the ARP warden.

'And where are you going, Maggie?' he asked. 'Don't you know there's an air raid on?'

'I've left my teeth on the kitchen table,' she told him.

'Get back in the shelter,' he said. 'Germans are dropping bombs, not bloody sandwiches.'

During the war, she told me, bananas were in very short supply. Only pregnant women were able to get them. Mrs Smith's sailor boyfriend at the time knew she had a real liking for this particular fruit and managed to get her one. On a date to the local cinema, as they sat cuddled up together in the darkness on the back row, he told her he had a little surprise for her and thrust a banana into her hand. 'My father's warned me about sailors,' she told him, and slapped the poor man's face before promptly leaving the building. The following day he called at the house to explain, bringing the said banana as proof.

On the very last day I delivered a card to Mrs Smith. It was from the post boy.

Just after the sixth form and during the weeks before departing for college, I secured a part-time job in a large bread factory on Greasborough Street, on the outskirts of Rotherham. On the first morning, the other three students and I met the foreman, a loud, bald-headed, rotund little man called Chuck.

'What's thy name?' he fired at the first student.

'Edward,' came the faint reply.

'Reight, Ted, get thee sen down theer, thar on t'Farmhouse Crusties.' He turned to the next. 'And what's thy name?' he snapped again.

'Robert,' the nervous student replied.

'Reight, Bob, get thee sen down theer,' he said, pointing in the opposite direction, 'tha'r on t'slicers. And watch weer tha' put thee hands. We don't want fingers in t'bread.' He held up a hand, showing two missing fingers. Poor Bob gulped. Then he turned his attention to the third student, a tall, blond-haired nervous-looking youth with a face erupting with acne. 'And what's thy name?'

'Julian,' came the reply.

Chuck looked as if he had been smacked in the face. 'Julian?' he exclaimed. 'Thy name's Julian?'

'Yes,' the student whispered.

Chuck's voice roared the full length of the factory. 'Hey lads, we have a Julian in!' This was followed by wild guffaws from the twenty or so men, and by Chuck mincing along with his hand on his hip. Then he turned to me. 'And thee at t'back, what's thy name, pal?' he asked, wiping the tears of laughter from his eyes.

'Dick!' I shouted.

I learnt a great deal about life, work and human nature in that bread factory.

Chuck, aided and abetted by some old hands, took delight in playing tricks on the students. I guess it was because a life baking bread, after the initial fascination, became incredibly boring and predictable and these clever ruses lightened the monotony. But there may have been more to it than that. It may have been born out of resentment – the fact that these bright young things would earn a bit of pocket money over the holidays and then swan off to university and end up with fat salaries and company cars. If they ever did return to the bread factory it would be as pen-pushing managers and company accountants, engineers or directors. They needed bringing down a peg or two, showing everyone they were not that clever.

Some of the tricks played were funny, harmless pranks, others were cruel and humiliating. One student discovered a dead mouse underneath his sandwiches in his snap box and spent most of the shift retching in the lavatory. Another had his bike loaded on to a van with the bread and had to walk all the way home. One poor lad, Ray, with his pale eyes and wispy attempt at a beard, was told by Chuck to report to the stores.

'Tha can't go into factory wi' that bloody excuse for a beard sproutin' on tha chin,' he told the student. 'There's such a thing as 'ealth and 'ygiene, tha knaas. All 'air has to be covered. That's why we all wear net caps and overalls and special shoes. Thy 'as to either shave off that beard o' yourn or get it covered up. In t'meantime, go down to the stores and ask for a beard cap.'

'A what?' asked the student.

'A beard cap,' repeated Chuck. 'To cover up that bum-fluff.'

The student duly reported to the stores, where the man in charge enquired of him, without a trace of a smile, what size beard he had.

'I'm not sure,' stuttered the student.

'Is it a four and seven-eighths or a five and one-eighth?'

'I've no idea,' the student replied.

The storeman sighed wearily. 'I reckon it's a four and seven-eighths.' He ducked underneath the counter, emerging a moment later shaking his head. 'We're clean out of four and seven-eighths.'

'Should I try a five and one-eighth?' asked the student.

'None of them in either,' replied the man. 'There's been a rush on them.' Then, producing a large white cloth, the store-man told the perplexed and credulous student, 'You shall have to wear this round your face for the time being.'

The poor lad, now probably an eminent doctor or a university professor, spent the whole of the morning with a white cloth wrapped around his head. He only discarded the 'beard cap' when the manager, on his daily walk around the factory, asked him if he had a sore tooth.

I was not immune from the tricks. My first job was to wheel

the bread from the factory to the vans for loading. The loaves
would be stacked on sliding metal shelves on a tall trolley with
heavy rubber wheels. At the very bottom was a locking device,
triggered by a push of the foot. Of course, Chuck never
mentioned the lock and on my first trip down the long ramp,
observed by the foreman with arms folded over his chest, the
trolley gathered speed, then careered out of control, collided
with a van and spilt its load. I was devastated and began frantically picking up the bread.

'Bloody marvellous, that!' shouted Chuck, drawing everyone's attention to my distress and embarrassment. 'Bloody
students don't know their arses from their elbows. All that
bloody learnin' and he can't push a bloody trolley wi'out dropping all t'bread. Comes out of tha wages that, tha knaas.'

On the next occasion I was let loose with the trolley, Chuck
sidled over, surreptitiously activated the locking device with a
secretive flick of his foot and then sauntered off with the words,
'And watch what tha're doin' this time.' I spent the next five
minutes pushing and pulling to get the trolley moving.

It was Francis who helped me out. He was a quietly spoken
and thoughtful Polish man who spent most of his breaks reading in the staff canteen. He never swore, never complained
and helped me and other students out on many an occasion.
He showed me the lock and how best to manoeuvre the
unwieldy trolley. He then warned me never, under any circumstances, to go down to where the confectionery was prepared
by the women under the supervision of the forewoman, Dora.
I would, in due course, be told by Chuck to go and fetch some
imaginary tool but I should always make some excuse. He kept
this trick back for a couple of weeks later, when the students
had dropped their guard. Many an unsuspecting student, Francis told me, had entered the confectionery department, been
grabbed and had fruit flans, doughnuts, Eccles cakes and mince
pies pushed down his pants. It was rumoured that one poor

victim had been stripped by the women and had fresh cream daubed all over his privates.

One morning Chuck sidled up. 'Go down the confectionery and ask Dora for a triple screwtop flange extractor,' he instructed me.

I set off but spent the next five minutes hiding in a cubicle in the lavatory. I then returned. 'Dora told me to tell you that she needs a note from you,' I informed Chuck seriously. 'She said that the last triple screwtop flange extractor she sent up here has gone missing.'

'Clever bugger,' mouthed Chuck, ambling off down the factory. After that he left me alone.

Postscript

In October 1966 Uncle Ted, in his white van, took me, my case and books, electric kettle, toaster and my portable Olivetti typewriter to Leeds, where I spent the next four years studying for my degree and certificate in education. Apart from the school trips to the Isle of Man, the annual fortnight in Blackpool and the brief encounter with camping in Derbyshire, I had never been away from home. My enthusiasm and eagerness the evening before setting off to train as a teacher was palpable. The great wide world awaited me, a world of new friends and greater challenges, and I embraced it with open arms. It was the start of an exciting adventure.

I remember my first few weeks at college in Leeds thinking just how fortunate I had been with my teachers. Many of the students, the great majority of whom had been to grammar or independent schools and with whom I shared accounts of my own schooldays, described with little pleasure their own experiences in education. They spoke of their schools with little affection, as 'exam-factories', rigid authoritarian structures where they spent their time ingesting and regurgitating facts. They described sarcastic and sometimes violent teachers, tedious lessons and the obsession with examination results and Oxbridge entries. South Grove was different. The teachers were not scholarly or highly qualified, they didn't walk the corridors in academic gowns, but they were first-rate educationalists. They created an atmosphere where the pupils' curiosity could flourish, where we were allowed to think and question, where classrooms were cooperative, good-humoured places, where learning was not derived by the acquisition of a few arid facts but from an understanding and appreciation of the material. It was a child-centred environment well before the term was widely used by the progressive commentators of the late 1960s.

Over the subsequent years more doors were opened for me by people who played an influential part in any future success I might have had. There was my tutor at Leeds, Dr Raymond Cowell, who developed further my love of books and reading; the first headteacher I worked for, the visionary, ever-supportive Dennis Morgan, who picked me to join the staff at Brinsworth High School soon after I had qualified as a teacher; and Brian Lee, the kindly and erudite Chief Education Adviser for Rotherham, who appointed me as the General Adviser for Language Development some years later. Then in 1998 Esther Rantzen came into my life. Following a talk I gave in support of Childline (the organization she founded) and which she attended, I was asked to appear on her prime-time television show and was brought to the public's attention. This led to the legendary Jenny Dereham of Michael Joseph publishers, editor of James Herriot and Miss Read, inviting me to write an account about my life as a school inspector in the Yorkshire Dales, a book which became (more to my surprise than anyone else's) a best-seller. By chance, the theatre promoter Nigel McIntyre heard me speak on stage at Derby and opened another door, signing me up for a nationwide tour with my one-man show.

Finally there is my long-suffering wife, Christine. She has given me four wonderful children and has for thirty-six years put up with this mercurial, moody, demanding, garrulous character with the funny name. Recently she came to hear me on stage at the magnificent Royal Hall in Harrogate.

'Did you ever imagine, Christine,' I asked her as she sat in the middle of the front row, 'in your wildest dreams, when you married me, that I would be doing this for a living?'

She smiled. 'Darling,' she said, with all the blunt honesty of someone born in Yorkshire, 'you are never in my wildest dreams!'

Good Parents

(Parody in answer to Philip Larkin)

They tuck you in, good parents do,
They kiss your cheek and hold you tight,
They fill your world with gentle dreams
And pray you'll have a peaceful night.

For they were tucked in, in their turn
By mums and dads who loved them so,
And by such loving quickly learnt
To love their children as they grow.

Good parents hand such happiness on,
It's endless like the sky above,
So learn this lesson parents do,
And teach your children how to love.